Converting Conflicts in Preschool

Converting Conflicts in Preschool

Janice J. Beaty

Professor Emerita
Elmira College

Harcourt Brace College Publishers

Fort Worth   Philadelphia   San Diego   New York   Orlando   Austin   San Antonio
Toronto   Montreal   London   Sydney   Tokyo

Publisher	Ted Buchholz
Senior Acquisitions Editor	Jo-Anne Weaver
Developmental Editor	Tracy Napper
Project Editor	Sarah E. Hughbanks
Production Manager	Thomas Urquhart IV
Art Director	Jim Dodson
Electronic Publishing Coordinator	Cathy Spitzenberger
Photographs	Janice J. Beaty

ISBN: 0–15–501223-1

Library of Congress Catalog Card Number: 94-75160

Copyright © 1995 by Harcourt Brace & Company

Tables from *Picture Book Storytelling: Literature Activities for Young Children* by Janice J. Beaty, copyright © 1994 by Harcourt Brace & Company, reproduced by permission of the publisher.

Address Orders to:
Harcourt Brace & Company
6277 Sea Harbor Drive
Orlando, Florida 32887-6777
1-800-782-4479 or 1-800-433-0001 (in Florida)

Address Editorial Correspondence to:
Harcourt Brace College Publishers
301 Commerce Street, Suite 3700
Fort Worth, TX 76102

Printed in the United States of America
4 5 6 7 8 9 0 1 2 3   0 5 4   9 8 7 6 5 4 3 2 1

To M. Ann Gilchrist
whose creative ideas helped develop this book

Preface

Conflict between children is the most frequently mentioned concern facing preschool teachers today. More children than ever before are engaging in aggressive classroom behavior. Yet traditional methods of discipline no longer work for many of these youngsters. The time has come for a new approach.

Converting Conflicts in Preschool offers such a solution. It describes a simple technique that converts children's conflicts to positive feelings rather than having them result in blame and shame. It helps teachers become transformers of classroom disputes, rather than referees or disciplinarians. And it assists young children in developing "other-esteem" (empathy) toward one another, rather than ill will.

The chapters that follow demonstrate how this approach can convert such conflicts as possession disputes over toys and materials, attention-getting conflicts where children act out, power struggles over who goes first, personality clashes where jealousy arises, group-entry disputes when an outsider is refused admission, superhero play that gets out of hand, name-calling conflicts that are more than teasing, and blaming conflicts where no one takes the blame.

A chapter on each of these interpersonal encounters includes recent child development research that sets the stage for the new conversion technique. Two observational checklists help teachers assess their own classroom situation. But it is the nine case studies that illustrate most vividly how "other-esteem conflict conversion" really works. Read "The Case of the Crowded Rocking Boat" or "The Case of the Tricycle Takeover" to see for yourself.

Early childhood classroom personnel have spent a great deal of worthwhile effort promoting the self-esteem of young children, helping children feel good about themselves. Now it is time to take the next step: helping children develop other-esteem, learning to feel how the other child feels when something goes wrong. In the meantime, teachers will learn that conflict is not wrong, but a necessary learning opportunity for young children; that children in conflict are not wrong, but may need to learn a different response; and that it is not up to the teacher to set things right by him- or herself, but to be a transformer, helping children themselves convert conflicts to positive feelings.

Acknowledgments

Many thanks to the people whose careful reading of the manuscript helped shape the final results, including my partner Ann Gilchrist, colleagues Bonny Helm from Corning, New York, and Sandra Novick from Charlotte, North Carolina, as well as the reviewers:

Joanne Bernstein, Brooklyn College;
Rhoda Chalker, Florida Atlantic University;
Diane Cromwell, American River College;
Richard Elardo, University of Iowa;
Susan Hepler; and
David Kuschner, University of Cincinnati.

My sincere appreciation also goes to the teachers who participated in trying out this new conflict conversion approach, including Gussie Worstell, Teacher/Director of Columbia Head Start in Columbia, Missouri, and her teaching staff of Jo Lubbering, Deanna Turner, Lori Taylor, and Maria Lacy; to Sandra Novick who worked with Jewel D. Funderburk, Kimberly D. Burgess, and Debra Lynne Deatherage, day care and nursery school teachers in Charlotte, North Carolina; to the parents of the Helm Nursery School, Gingerbread House Day Care, and Columbia Head Start, whose children's photos illustrate this book; to Jack Allison, manager of Day's Inn, Columbia, Missouri, and David Thayer, director of Central Missouri Counties' Human Development Corporation; to libraries at the University of Missouri, Columbia, and Elmira College, Elmira, New York; to Debbie Hagler, owner of My Bookstore in Pensacola, Florida; and finally to my editors Jo-Anne Weaver and Tracy Napper for their helpful encouragement and support.

Contents

Chapter 4   *Who's in Charge? (Power Struggles)*   **65**

Chapter 5   *I Don't Like You! (Personality Clashes)*   **83**

Chapter 6   *Why Won't You Let Me? (Access Struggles)*   **107**

Chapter 7   *Bang, Bang, You're Dead!*
(Aggressive Dramatic Play)   **125**

Chapter 8   *Don't Call Me Stupid!*
(Name-Calling Conflicts)   **143**

Figures and Tables

Cases

It's High Time!

Conflict is a natural part of living and working together in groups. It is good that conflicts arise in the early childhood classroom because it is only through facing conflicts that children can learn the skills necessary to resolve real-life problems. (Crosser, 1992, p. 28.)

CONFLICTS IN THE CLASSROOM

As every teacher of preschool children knows, conflicts in the classroom occur every day. Children playing together become involved in conflicts. Teachers working with children experience them. Students training to become teachers must face them. Most people tend to view such conflicts as negative, because they find them difficult to handle. Many teachers, teacher assistants, and student teachers wish they would just go away.

This textbook presents conflict in a different light. First of all, it defines conflict in a positive way: *A conflict is an interpersonal encounter needing a positive emotional resolution.* As this text will clearly point out, such an encounter need not be negative at all, because, in truth, most conflicts can be learning opportunities for both children and adults. The Chinese must have recognized this truth long ago, since their word for "crisis" (or conflict) is the same as their word for "opportunity." Conflicts today give young children an opportunity to learn:

1. empathy or "other-esteem"—feeling how the other person feels when something happens to him or her
2. conversion techniques—how to convert their conflicts to positive feelings

Because conflicts involve powerful feelings, the way teachers deal with conflicts helps children learn about themselves and other people in a dramatic way. Teachers should be thankful for such opportunities for children and themselves to learn these crucial lessons in life. Children who learn how to convert conflicts to positive feelings in early childhood have the tools to convert adulthood conflicts as well. Adults armed with such tools will then be able to convert and defuse interpersonal, intercommunity, and even international conflicts.

CONFLICT IN THE WORLD

Sound utopian? Yes, indeed, but the time is upon us to make such a difference in the lives of youngsters—of people—and of the world. If we do not, who will? Crime, violence, poverty, drugs, pollution, toxic poisoning, disintegrating cities, a deteriorating environment, and the quality of global life make it imperative for the inhabitants of Earth to change the way they do things. It is high time, and the way to begin such change is with our children.

Start by learning to deal positively with conflict. But like the ever-widening ripples of a pebble dropped into a pond, the conversion of conflict to positive feelings in one person, or in one classroom of little persons, can develop into a tidal wave of "getting along" with families, friends, neighbors, and, yes, even nations.

KINDS OF CONFLICTS

Just what kinds of "interpersonal encounters" make up conflicts in the early childhood classroom? This text deals with eight kinds of conflicts found in most early childhood programs. The first and most common type is *possession disputes* (Shantz, 1987, p. 287). Preschool children ages three, four, and five are self-centered beings who may not be used to operating within a group. They are often the center of attention at home. They are said to be at an *egocentric* stage of development because they perceive themselves to be at the center of their world. They think everything revolves around them. If they want to play with a toy that another child is using, many preschool youngsters simply will take the toy, causing a "possession dispute" with the other child. If they have a plaything they themselves are using, many preschool children will refuse to give it up to someone else.

Young children's egocentric natures also create a second kind of conflict when they call attention to themselves in inappropriate ways. *Attention getting* can result in conflict when youngsters use aggressive or inappropriate behavior—for instance, to demand attention. A third common type of conflict in the preschool classroom is the *power struggle*. Certain children want to be in charge of everything that happens around them. They want to be first. They want the biggest ball, the first turn on the tricycle, the principal role in dramatic play. In the block center they may force others to build the kind of building they want. On the playground they often compel others to play their way. If other children resist, a "power struggle" ensues.

A fourth type of conflict involves children who clash with one another because of personality differences or jealousy. Such *personality clashes* may not occur as frequently among the youngest children, but these clashes may be even more important to convert to positive feelings in the long run because they teach children how to get along with all kinds of people.

A fifth type of common classroom conflict, the *group-entry dispute*, occurs when individual youngsters try to enter a group of children already at play. The players often reject these individuals unless they use appropriate techniques to gain entry. Play access struggles often occur with such activities as dramatic play and block building.

Aggressive behavior, such as fighting, may result from any of the previously mentioned conflicts that get out of control. On the other hand, *aggressive dramatic play* itself can bring on a sixth type of conflict. Children taking the roles of "superheroes" as shown on television sometimes take part in more than rough-and- tumble play. Out-of-control behavior and even physical violence has entered many classroom dramatic play areas in the guise of "Ninja Turtles," "Power Rangers," or other television characters.

A seventh type of conflict often results from unpleasant *name calling*, sometimes done by a child in teasing or fun, but often hurtful or embarrassing to the recipient. Finally, an eighth kind of dispute, the *blaming conflict*, occurs when children deny responsibility for their actions and try to shift the blame onto somebody else. Such blaming disputes often occur in combination with the other types of conflict. The following chapters discuss these eight areas of conflict, concluding in Chapter 10.

ESCALATION OF VIOLENCE IN THE PRESCHOOL CLASSROOM

Surely, classroom conflicts like those described have occurred since time immemorial. Conflicts between young children have been the bane of many a preschool teacher's existence, but in recent years something new has appeared. The levels of violence and aggression in children's encounters have increased dramatically. What used to involve an exchange of words now involves an exchange of fists. What used to end in disagreement now causes an explosion of temper. Hitting and biting for no apparent reason have increased (Carlsson-Paige & Levin, 1992, p. 34). How did this happen? Where did it all come from?

Researchers studying children's reactions to war and violence believe that young children merely reflect the violence that surrounds them in their daily life. Television especially presents them with hours of manufactured brutality, as well as the real, everyday violence featured on news programs. This media barrage tends to desensitize children (and the rest of us) to violence. When we see a person being kicked, beaten, or killed, our consciousness registers this the first time as: "Isn't that awful! Someone needs to do something about it!" But when we see the same kicking, beating, and killing over and over again, it enters our consciousness as: "This seems to happen more and more these days." Thus, we become desensitized to violence.

Researchers report that "children, ages three to six years, spend an average of four hours a day watching television. By the age of 18, they will have spent the equivalent of seven years watching (more time than spent in school) and will have seen over 26,000 killings" (Carlsson-Paige & Levin, 1992, p. 35).

In addition, children's cartoons and TV entertainment programs feature superheroes that seem to resolve all their problems through violence. Superheroes such as the Teenage Mutant Ninja Turtles, Masters of the Universe, Power Rangers, and GI Joe especially appeal to boys. The guns and war toys marketed by such programs put toy weapons into the hands of young children so that they practice the kind of violence they see on the television screen. What an effective method for teaching that the best way to resolve conflicts is through violence! These superheroes also appear on cereal boxes, lunch pails, T-shirts, and even children's pajamas. How can young children learn that fighting to resolve conflicts is wrong?

If children live in poverty, they may see violence in the streets. If children live in homes where adults are out of control, they may experience violence close up. Young children learn by imitating the role models around them. It is no wonder that the use of violence as a way to solve problems has entered the preschool classroom.

Past Experience with Classroom Conflicts

Yet the conflicts themselves do not necessarily need to be changed. The way we deal with them however, does. In the past, most preschool-classroom conflicts have not been treated as this text treats conflicts, as "interpersonal encounters needing a positive emotional resolution." The focus, instead, has been on either *preventing* conflicts from happening or *disciplining the instigator* of the conflict after it occurs.

The assumptions have been: conflicts are negative, conflicts are wrong, the teacher must stop all conflicts, she must discipline the children who started them. Unfortunately, this approach has not stopped conflicts from occurring. On the contrary, incidents of aggression have continued and the violence has increased, as previously mentioned. More hitting, biting, and throwing seems to go on in preschool classrooms than ever before (Carlsson-Paige & Levin, 1992, p. 34). Experienced teachers in preschool programs such as Head Start report:

> *aggression has increased and has become the primary first choice in a child's attempt to settle a dispute or resolve a conflict. For example, a child will lash out and hit immediately if someone threatens him, rather than using a less aggressive response. (Worstell, 1993)*

Even the commonly-used "basic behavior limits" guidelines, followed by most preschools, which state that children are not allowed to:

1. Hurt themselves
2. Hurt others
3. Damage materials

have not been enough to limit aggression. Teachers and their coworkers who enforce these limits with firmness and consistency report that out-of-control behavior on the part of certain children continues to increase. This textbook supports the use of these basic child behavior limits as the cornerstone of a rational classroom behavior system, but takes them one step further: how to deal with children who get out of control despite the behavior limits.

In the past teachers have dealt with conflict in a number of ways. In "possession disputes," for instance, when one child takes another child's toy and the other child hits back, the teacher often has done one of the following:

1. Removed the toy and put it away, thereby removing the source of the conflict.
2. Removed the disruptive child and given the child something else to play with, or, in the case of a violent interaction, forced the instigator to remain in the "time-out chair" until he apologized.
3. Set up a turn-taking arrangement, and used a timer or other device for the children to take turns.
4. Told the victimized child to use words and not fists with the aggressor.

All of these time-honored solutions may stop the conflict. One may be more effective than another, depending upon the child and the conflict. None of these solutions, however, really *converts the conflict to positive feelings.* The same thing may happen with the same child again and again. In fact, all of these solutions take a Band-Aid approach to all, assuming either that the conflict is wrong or that the child is wrong, and that it is up to the teacher to set things right.

CONFLICT AS A LEARNING OPPORTUNITY

This text takes a different point of view. It believes: 1) conflict is not wrong, but creates an important learning opportunity; 2) the child is not wrong, but he or she needs to learn a different method of handling conflict; and 3) it is not the teacher's sole responsibility to set things right; instead, the teacher must act as a *transformer* who helps children learn to convert conflicts to positive feelings.

Finally, we must realize that "converting conflicts to positive feelings" can and should be *taught directly to children as a planned part of the classroom curriculum.* We work in a crisis situation regarding conflict in the preschool classroom. We must take decisive measures to help young children learn better ways to deal with conflict than those they see in the media, on the street, or at home.

CHANGING THE ADULT MIND-SET

Before we can help the children in our classrooms to convert their conflicts to positive feelings, we must do some transforming of our own. We must change our own minds and hearts about how we view conflicts and their resolution, how we view disruptive behavior and discipline, and how we view our role and the child's role in conflict conversion. We must come to understand that:

1. Conflict in the preschool classroom provides a learning opportunity. Learning opportunities are necessary for us and our children. We need to have opportunities to grow and develop as people. The more dramatic the opportunity, the more effective the learning can be. We should feel encouraged that we recognize classroom violence as our children's call for help. We might not have heard the message if it had not been so loud.

Furthermore, we need to recognize that the preschool classroom itself functions as a human relationships laboratory. The entire center is thus full of human beings who must understand and accept their feelings and those of others. (Read et al., 1993, p. 19) Preschool is often the place where a child confronts a large number of peers for the first time. Thus it becomes a particularly critical place for youngsters to learn to convert their inevitable conflicts to positive feelings. The opportunities for learning conflict conversion may never again be quite so powerful, nor the results so potentially long-lasting.

2. Both we and our children need to learn new and positive ways to deal with conflict.

We have heard the message. We must respond to these calls for help in new and positive ways, remembering that the old ways of treating classroom conflicts were not effective. Blaming, shaming, scolding, and punishment treated the child as wrong. The child is not; he or she has simply become involved in an interpersonal encounter that may be out of control. Removing the child or removing the disputed object did not convert the conflict to positive feelings.

Therefore, we need to start afresh in our thinking and feeling. The child is not wrong. He or she does not require discipline. Conflict is not wrong, but provides an opportunity to learn. The violence needs to be stopped and children need to be taught new and better ways to convert their conflicts to positive feelings. This text demonstrates ways to do so.

3. The teacher must intervene calmly in violent conflicts in order to help children convert disputes to positive feelings.

Young children's conflicts operate outside themselves. They hit someone, they take something from someone, or they disrupt the play of someone. In contrast, converting these conflicts must come from inside themselves. When teachers intervene to stop conflicts, they must remember that the only ones who can truly resolve the problems are the participants themselves, not the person intervening. The teacher can stop the conflict but must not take control of the conversion of the conflict.

This textbook intends to help teachers and teachers-in-training learn a new role in conflict resolution, that of the *transformer*, a person who changes the situation by intervening to help children convert conflicts to positive feelings, and to help teachers learn to act calmly, so that children can learn effective ways to convert conflicts on their own.

4. The teacher must set up situations in which children can learn how to convert conflicts to positive feelings and practice these methods outside of conflict situations.

It's up to the teacher to set up situations where children can practice conflict conversion methods outside of conflict.

We set up our classrooms with materials and activities for children to develop large and small motor coordination, to develop cognitive problem-solving and thinking abilities, to develop communication skills, and to develop creativity. Yet how many of us have given any time in the curriculum to teach children the skills of dealing with conflicts? Such skills should be taught directly by teachers and practiced regularly by the children themselves in order to be properly learned.

This text offers creative ideas and activities for teaching conflict conversion, and shows that resolving conflicts is not a subject that should be approached with reluctance or dread. Conflict resolution is an exciting new addition to the preschool curriculum that should be welcomed. A new day in interpersonal relationships is finally about to begin in our preschool programs!

CAN YOU CHANGE YOUR MIND-SET?

You must change your own mind-set in order to accomplish the successful conversion of conflicts into positive feelings. You must believe that *children who create conflicts are not bad*, but just need help, and that *conflicts are not bad*, but provide important learning opportunities for us all. Can you bring yourself to believe that the young children who do these inappropriate acts are really good children? In addition, will you also allow yourself to consider that the inappropriate acts themselves provide a necessary learning experience?

Mark Twain said it all when he told us: "Troubles are only mental; it is the mind that manufactures them, and the mind can forget them, banish them, abolish them." (Twain, 1990) Can your mind do this?

CONVERTING CONFLICTS TO POSITIVE FEELINGS

The teacher, teacher assistant, and student teacher must take the first step in converting conflicts to positive feelings, by changing their own mind-sets about children's disruptive encounters with one another. With a new mind-set, the teacher can act appropriately when things get out of hand.

When to Intervene

Teachers need not intervene in every interpersonal encounter that occurs. Frequently, children can resolve their own conflicts, and they should be given every chance to do so. However, some children definitely need help in converting conflict situations. Teachers soon recognize these children by their repeated aggressive behaviors. Some other children need occasional help when conflict situations get out of hand, because they seem unable to convert them themselves. In addition, some situations seem to cause conflict in and of themselves, no matter who is involved. Case in point, the single tricycle on the playground that frequently causes a turn-taking conflict. The computer that everyone wants to use at the same time generates a similar situation.

Before deciding to intervene in a conflict, *the teacher should give the children every chance to settle it on their own.* In situations where things seem to get worse instead of better, where children reach an impasse with neither side giving in, or where the conflict has degenerated into aggressive behavior such as hitting or throwing things, the teacher should step in, knowing exactly what to do.

Teachers need to use their common sense about intervention. They should not let children hurt one another or damage equipment as the basic behavior limits guidelines point out. Violent behavior or out-of-control emotions signal that intervention has become necessary. Shouting and crying also can be indicators. In these situations, teachers know that a real conflict-conversion learning situation has arrived.

FIGURE 1.1

When to Intervene in Children's Conflicts

1. When children hurt one another or damage materials.
2. When the conflict degenerates into aggressive behavior such as hitting, biting, or throwing things.
3. When children shout or cry.
4. When the conflict reaches an impasse and neither side will give in.

How to Intervene

First of all, the teacher must remain calm, cool, and composed. No matter how loud or violent the conflict, the teacher remains the quiet place in the center of the storm. When tempers flare or children strike out, teachers need to stay calm and unruffled no matter how upset the children become. Such calmness helps to put a damper on out-of-control emotions.

How do you keep yourself calm? First of all, you should *take charge of your own emotions.* Center yourself. Do not let negative emotions rise up in you that will erupt into harsh or scolding words, an irritated tone of voice, an angry expression on your face, or strong movements of your arms or legs. Lift your head and take a deep breath. Do not let thoughts like "Oh, no! Not again!" or "That terrible Jeremy is hitting people again!" come to your mind.

If you feel yourself getting angry, treat the feeling objectively. Remember that you have no reason to get angry. Say to yourself, "Oh, I can feel myself getting angry. Well, I'll just let it go through me and be rid of it." Stop for a minute and let the anger evaporate. It will if you will let it.

The success of the conflict-conversion technique that you and the children will be applying, uses *emotions* and their application as its basis. Be careful not to let your own negative emotions take the lead, which can easily happen. You must first be in control yourself before you can act. Remember that both you and the children face an important learning opportunity. If you feel yourself getting out of sorts, stop and take a few breaths until you are calm. Smile to yourself at this important chance for learning, then take action.

Teachers must use their own judgment in the next step. Depending on the type of conflict, some teachers prefer to say both children's names calmly, and direct them out of the situation. Others prefer to step in by separating the adversaries, either by putting an arm around each child (lovingly, not harshly), or linking arms with the children, or taking hold of each child's hand and leading them to a quiet place. You must decide.

Although many teachers focus on the aggressor in order to stop aggressive behavior, often more effective action focuses on the "victim" at first, especially if a child is using aggression to gain the teacher's attention. The aggressor soon comes to recognize that the teacher gives attention to the other child. Your response in itself may eventually change an aggressive child's actions. Again, you must decide.

To gain the attention of both children, you should speak their names quietly, calmly, and repeatedly until they acknowledge you by stopping the conflict and calming down. Give them a chance to calm down. *The conflict conversion technique will not work if the children are still arguing, fighting, crying, or resisting all attempts to calm them.* You may need to hold one or both children for a while, saying their names quietly, over and over again. Often, making eye contact with a child can be enough to defuse her anger or allay her fears. If the child can see you smiling, for instance, then she knows you are not upset with her. (And you should not be, remember?) You are a transformer and a conflict converter, not an angry teacher. Take all the time you need.

Once the children have calmed down enough to respond to you, you will need to decide *where* to talk with them. If two children are in conflict by themselves, draw up a small chair so you can sit next to them at eye level, and talk with them and listen. If the conflict is with a group of children, gently draw them away from the others to a place where you can talk with them alone. Be sure you stay at eye level and do not loom over them during the next stage of conflict conversion.

Try to limit your intervention to two children even if others are involved. Usually one child conflicts with one other child, sometimes two others. If a child experiences problems within a larger group, try to talk with that child and with one other from the group who seems most involved. The conflict-conversion technique you will follow works best with two children. Their conversion can spread later to the other children involved.

Next, in a calm voice ask each child in turn the first of the three conflict-conversion questions listed below, and listen carefully to their answers. Which child you ask first depends upon each child's degree of calmness. Start with the child who seems most at ease. Or, just ask the question generally and let either child answer.

Conflict-Conversion Questions

1. What's happening, _____ (child's name)?
2. How does _____ (other child) feel?
3. What will make him (or her) feel better?

These three questions have been carefully designed to lead each child from where he is over to the other child, not only defusing the difficult situation, but also allowing each child to become a part of the outcome. These deceptively simple questions engage the child's mind and emotions in a way that they may not have been engaged before, and encourage them *to try to feel the way the other child feels*; to *empathize* with the other child.

Question #1: What's happening, _____ (child's name)?

Once she has intervened, the teacher as transformer calmly asks each child in turn what happened, and listens carefully to their reply. This gives each child a chance to justify his position. The replies may be entirely different. Jessica says: "He took my play dough." Luther says, "She hit me." Both children may be correct and feel justified in their actions, and believe that the other child is wrong. You, as the teacher, listen nonjudgmentally to each. After both children have spoken, you should then reflect aloud in unbiased words what seems to have happened. Take it slowly and easily so that both children hear and understand what you say. They can correct you if you did not get it right.

Jessica, you say that Luther took your play dough. And Luther, you say that Jessica hit you.

This process gives children not only the chance to feel justified in their actions, but also to feel that the teacher acknowledges what happened. The calmness in the teacher's voice lets the children know that the teacher is not upset. She does not pronounce judgment. She does not blame either child. Neither does she let one child blame the other. The teacher, in fact, treats the situation as an important learning opportunity for the children rather than a win-or-lose contest.

When teachers become involved in "whose-fault-is-it?" or "who-started-it?" questions, they themselves end up as losers. No one is at fault. It is life. *Fault finding should never be a part of the conflict-conversion method described in this text. Assign no blame to either child and thus project no shame.* The teacher here merely repeats the facts as the children themselves have stated them. She should not let herself get drawn by the children into "whose fault is it?" questioning, which is not the point. The text poses the question, which the children answer next: *How does the other person feel?* Through "feeling as the other person feels" (other-awareness or other-esteem) children learn to come to terms with conflict.

Question #2: Luther, how did Jessica feel when you took her play dough? or Jessica, how did Luther feel when you hit him?

This question presents a quite different point of view for most children, catching many of them off guard. They are used to teachers asking them how they feel about themselves. To ask a child how he thinks the other child feels suddenly switches the focus away from himself. "How did Jessica feel when you took her play dough, Luther?" He may be so surprised that he cannot answer, or he may say "I don't know." If the child cannot answer, the teacher can say, "Look at her face. Does her face tell you what she felt like?" If the child still cannot answer, you can say, "Ask her how she felt."

Once she has intervened, the teacher as transformer calmly asks each child what's going on.

Jessica may very well answer quite accurately because she has another chance to state her case. She may say, "I was mad." The teacher should then reflect aloud this statement: "Jessica says she felt mad when you took her clay, Luther."

The teacher should then ask Jessica: "How did Luther feel when you hit him, Jessica?" It may surprise Jessica that there are two sides to this conflict, but the so-called victimized child also can learn to feel things from the other person's point of view. She may answer: "I guess he didn't like it, but he took my play dough!" The teacher should reflect aloud *only the answer to her question:* "Jessica says that you didn't like it when she hit you, Luther. Is that how you felt?" Luther then gets his turn to vent his hurt feelings. Even after the heat of an emotional conflict, children can focus their attention in this way and may even become intrigued with the proceedings because both receive an equal chance from an adult to express their point of view and contribute to the outcome.

Some teachers think that this approach about feelings will take too long when they are busy with the rest of the class. However, in a classroom with two adults, one of them always has time enough to intervene in an out-of-control situation. If you have time enough to talk to the child (even just to send him to a time-out chair), then you certainly have time enough to ask about feelings. In fact, time-out chairs are more often used for the teachers' convenience, not for the children's benefit, whereas questions about feelings actually help children learn empathy.

Question #3: What will make Luther feel better, Jessica? or What will make Jessica feel better, Luther?

Once again, the children must focus on the other child. And, once again, this process is something new for the children. Usually, they are asked what will make them feel better. In this case, they soon come to realize that they can influence the outcome of the dispute. Jessica may reply: "Maybe if I give him some of my play dough." The teacher then asks Luther if he would feel better if Jessica gave him some play dough. He agrees that he would.

Then she asks Luther what would make Jessica feel better. Luther may still be surprised to consider the fact that Jessica has bad feelings, too, even though he was the one who got hit. If he answers that he does not know, the teacher should press him gently to think about it some more. Maybe he could consider how he feels when someone takes something of his. What would make Jessica feel better? Maybe he should give Jessica something in return, he might decide. How about a cookie cutter to cut her play dough into animal shapes? She agrees.

When both children have finally agreed to a solution, the teacher needs to state it aloud, and then tell the children how she feels: "Jessica agrees to give you some of her play dough, Luther. And, Luther, you agree to give Jessica a cookie cutter. I'm really proud of both of you for thinking about each other's feelings the way you did. When we think about the other person's feelings, then we try not to hurt them. Would you like to shake on that?" Children often want to shake hands or give a "high five" to seal their agreement.

This solution sounds so simple, but think about it for a moment. Do you really believe that a child recognizes how another child feels when he is punched or bitten or yelled at? Classrooms that have tried this approach agree that children really can feel empathy. Most young children have not been asked to consider the way another person feels. Nor have many adults. In fact, some people believe that all the troubles in the world can be blamed on people's lack of empathy.

> *People commit negative acts because they cannot*
> *feel the pain they cause others. (Clow, 1989, p. 67)*

Can people be taught to "feel the pain," to empathize? It is the premise of this text that *preschool children can be taught and can learn to feel what the other person is feeling*, to empathize with an adversary in a conflict situation. Until now most mediation attempts by adults have asked children to focus on *themselves* (for example, "How do you feel?") rather than on *how the other child feels*.

Children know about feelings. They live openly through their emotions at this age more than at any other time of their lives. In fact, young children communicate more naturally through emotions than they do through words. However, to be asked to feel the emotions of the other person is something new for most children in conflict situations to consider.

The *conflict-conversion questions* mentioned above provide the key to helping young children develop the ability to feel the way another person feels, setting the stage to resolve the conflict in a positive manner. We call this feeling of empathy "other-esteem" and believe that many children lack this element in their development. The chapters to follow will help teachers restore this missing element, thus helping classrooms to eliminate much violent behavior.

 FIGURE 1.2

How to Intervene in Children's Conflicts

a. Decide if you should intervene or if children can resolve the conflict on their own.
b. Calm yourself. (Breathe deeply.)
c. Calm the children. (Say their names; make eye contact.)
d. Use the following conflict-conversion questions with each child.

Conflict-Conversion Questions

1. What's happening, _____ (child's name)?
2. How does _____ (other child) feel?
3. What will help him feel better?

e. Engage these children and others in a learning activity later in the day based on this type of conflict.

A "POSITIVE-FEELINGS ACTIVITY"

Sometime later in the day the teacher should bring the two children together again with a small group or with the total group at a circle time, to share with the others how they settled the conflict peacefully. Some teachers call this activity a "positive-feelings activity." First, the teacher tells the group briefly about the conflict between Jessica and Luther. Then she asks Jessica and Luther to describe what they decided to do to make the other person feel better. Finally, the teacher may read a book, use hand puppets, or tell a brief story about a similar conflict. She then can ask the children how the characters or puppets may have felt about their problem, and what the characters did about each other's feelings.

Many children's books do not focus on how the characters feel. Your job as a transformer must focus your children's awareness on such feelings. They can have the fun of making up a new ending to the stories you read if they wish. Such activities will open up for your children many possibilities for new and positive endings to their own interpersonal struggles. A bibliography of children's books on the topics discussed appears at the end of each chapter. If you do not have an appropriate children's book to use during the positive-feelings activity, make up a story about children in a similar conflict, or use one of the many activities described in each chapter. A list of these activities appears at the end of each chapter under IDEAS +.

When children come to understand that the teacher takes their problems seriously and will help them work out their own solutions to conflicts without resorting to blaming or punishment, even three-, four-, and five-year-old children can learn to practice such strategies on their own.

IDENTIFYING FEELINGS

Before youngsters can begin to state how another child feels, however, they must first learn to identify their own feelings with words. Such words as "angry," "happy," "sad," "proud," may be only empty terms to the youngest of the children who have not yet put words to the feelings that they experience. Thus you can assist them in learning the words that go with the feelings. Children can truly learn to empathize, to feel as another feels, once they can identify within themselves what these feelings are called and what the words really mean. Not until then will they be ready to convert their conflicts with peers into positive feelings.

How can you help? You can incorporate "feelings activities" into all aspects of your curriculum. First, think about what *to feel* really means. Think of some feelings your children might want to express and make a list of them. Does your list include: bold, shy, happy, sad, brave, scared, calm, excited, glad, mad, proud, or ashamed? Then think of ways that these feelings can be communicated to children.

For example, you can use pictures or photos of people or children showing facial expressions that illustrate each feeling. Draw your own smiling or frowning faces. Mount a picture on the wall at the children's eye level for discussion at group time. Then, add a second picture and discuss both. Have children volunteer to make a face like the picture on the wall. Keep adding other pictures when you are sure the children understand the feelings already displayed.

Play various feeling games with the pictures. Give each child in the group a mirror and let him practice making a face for the feeling that you point to on the wall. A child volunteer can demonstrate one feeling at a time for the others to guess. Have the guessers go up to the pictures and point to their choice. Have another child walk around the group demonstrating one of the feelings for the others to guess. Pass a beanbag around the group while music is playing. When the music stops, the child holding the beanbag gets to demonstrate a feeling.

Make duplicate photocopies of your feeling pictures and use them in all sorts of games. For example, laminate smaller pictures onto the front of a deck of playing cards and let children play matching games with them. Be sure to have at least four cards for each feeling. Paste an enlarged face of each feeling picture onto the bottom of a small paper bag to be used as a paper-bag puppet. Preschool children can do this by themselves, making their own feelings puppets. Then have pairs of children role play, demonstrating the way their different puppets feel. Laminate tiny faces of the feeling pictures onto small wooden blocks with clear vinyl plastic. Have at least four blocks showing the same face, so that children can match the blocks or stack them.

By now the children should know what feelings look like and act like, but how do they sound? Have children experiment with a tape recorder about the sounds of certain feelings. They can say, "My name is Cindy. Can you guess what feeling this is?" (Make a crying sound.) Then let the others try to guess. The person who made the sounds can tell them if they are right. Are they surprised to hear different sounds for the same feeling? The same sounds for different feelings? What kind of sound do they make for "shy"? Some children record silence.

Make beanbag games for some of the most popular feelings, for example, *happy, scared, excited, mad,* or *brave.* Take a cardboard carton, paste and label a feeling picture on the outside, and cut a hole underneath it large enough for a beanbag to be thrown through it; or draw smiling and frowning faces. Then let the children try tossing the beanbag through the hole, which can be the mouth of the face. They can stand as close as they want. If they score a hit, they get to make the sound of the feeling.

Also, make cardboard "sandwich boards" for children to wear over their fronts and backs with an enlarged labeled picture to advertise a particular feeling. In like manner, make masks with a face showing an emotion for children to wear. Play the feeling games at circle time, within the circle, and then put them away so that the children will not get out of control. Children love to run around the classroom demonstrating "angry" or "mad," but this is not the point of the activity, and, if it happens, the only one who will really be angry or mad is you!

Reading books about feelings and then discussing them works best with individuals or in small groups where children can be close to the reader and really see the illustrations. *Sometimes I Feel Like a Mouse: A Book About Feelings* (Modesitt, 1992) has large-print words on one page and a chalk drawing of a child showing how she feels like a particular animal on the opposite page. If this becomes a favorite, have each child in the small group demonstrate one of the feelings. Obtain animal pictures like the twelve shown in the book, or make photocopies, and label and mount them on the wall of the story center for use in other feeling games. Be sure to read the last page of the book, which assures the children about feelings.

> *There is no such thing as a right or wrong feeling.*
> *All feelings are okay. Your feelings are your friends.*
> *It's important to listen to them. (Modesitt, 1992)*

Titles of other books about feelings appear at the end of this chapter. When children actually start to identify feelings, the conflict-conversion technique used throughout this text can begin to make a difference in the way they treat one another.

The chapters that follow describe in detail how teachers and children can learn to deal with conflicts such as possession disputes, attention getting, power struggles, personality clashes, group-entry disputes, aggressive dramatic play, name-calling, and blaming. They demonstrate how children can learn to transform conflict to positive feelings by using the conflict-conversion strategies we have been discussing.

Such strategies really do work with children. Once you try them, you will be pleased to find that they can be learned without difficulty, are easily applied, and benefit the children. Then the ripples of "getting along" will begin to spread outward from your children, to you, to your associates, to the world!

IDEAS + IN CHAPTER 1

Feelings Activities

1. Find pictures of people that illustrate a feeling.
2. Make a face to show feelings.
3. Make a feelings face in a mirror.
4. Have a feelings guessing game.
5. Pass around a feelings beanbag.
6. Play a "match-the-feelings" card game.
7. Make feelings puppets out of paper-bags.
8. Make feelings matching blocks.
9. Tape-record sounds of feelings.
10. Play feelings beanbag toss.
11. Make "sandwich boards" advertising feelings.
12. Make feelings masks.
13. Read books about feelings.
14. Obtain animal pictures of feelings.

TRY IT YOURSELF

1. Think about your own personal experiences with conflicts as a child. How did the adults in your life handle them? Give several examples. How did this handling of conflict affect you?
2. What kinds of conflicts have occurred in your preschool classroom? How were they handled? How did the children respond?
3. Give several examples of classroom conflict situations in which a caregiver or teacher should not become involved.

4. What conflict-conversion questions might you ask as a transformer? What kinds of questions would be inappropriate?
5. Develop a positive feelings activity that would be appropriate to teach young children about anger and use it with them. How do they respond?

REFERENCES CITED

Carlsson-Paige, N. & Levin, D. (1992). When push comes to shove—Reconsidering children's conflicts. *Child Care Information Exchange, 84,* 34–37.

Clow, B. H. (1989). *Heart of the Christos.* Santa Fe, NM: Bear & Co.

Crosser, S. (1992). Managing the early childhood classroom. *Young Children, 47*(2), 23–29.

Modesitt, J. & Spowart, R. (Ill.). (1992). *Sometimes I feel like a mouse: A book about feelings.* New York: Scholastic.

Read, K., Gardner, P. & Mahler, B. C. (1993). *Early childhood programs: Human relationships and learning* (9th ed.). Fort Worth, TX: Harcourt Brace Jovanovich.

Shantz, C. U. (1987). Conflicts between children. *Child Development, 58:* 283–305.

Twain, M. (1990). *The wit and wisdom of Mark Twain.* Philadelphia, PA: Running Press.

Worstell, G. (1993). Unpublished Interview. Columbia, MO.

OTHER SOURCES

Carlsson-Paige, N. & Levin, D. (1985). *Helping young children understand peace, war, and the nuclear threat.* Washington, DC: National Association for the Education of Young Children.

Carlsson-Paige, N. & Levin, D. (1992). Making peace in violent times: A constructivist approach to conflict resolution. *Young Children, 48*(1) 4–13.

Carlsson-Paige, N. & Levin, D. (1992). Moving children from time-out to win/win. *Child Care Information Exchange, 84,* 34–37.

Carlsson-Paige, N. & Levin, D. (1987). *The war play dilemma: Balancing needs and values in the early childhood classroom.* New York: Teachers College Press.

Carter, M. (1992). Disciplinarians or transformers? Training teachers for conflict resolution. *Child Care Information Exchange, 84,* 46–51.

Damon, W. (1988). *The moral child: Nurturing children's natural moral growth.* New York: The Free Press (Macmillan).

Deutsch, M. (1973). *The resolution of conflict.* New Haven: Yale University Press.

Eisenberg, N. (1992). *The caring child.* Cambridge: Harvard University Press.

Fisher, R. & Ury, W. (1981). *Getting to yes: Negotiating agreement without giving in.* New York: Penguin Books.

Levine, L. E. & Hoffman, M. L. (1975). Empathy and cooperation in 4-year-olds. *Developmental Psychology, 11*(4), 533–534.

NAEYC. (1993). Position statement on violence in the lives of children. *Young Children, 48*(6), 80–85.

Parry, A. (1993). Children surviving in a violent world—Choosing non-violence. *Young Children, 48*(6), 13–15.

Yarrow, M. R., Scott, P. M., & Zahn-Waxler, C. (1973). Learning concern for others. *Developmental Psychology, 8* (2), 240–260.

CHILDREN'S PICTURE BOOKS ABOUT FEELINGS

Aliki. (1984). *Feelings.* New York: Mulberry Books.

Boynton, S. (1987). *A is for angry: An animal and adjective alphabet.* New York: Workman Publishing.

Cain, B. S. & Patterson, A. (Ill.). (1990). *Double-dip feelings: Stories to help children understand emotions.* New York: Magination Press.

Curtis, C. M. & Aldrich, C. (Ill.). (1992). *Fun is a feeling.* Bellevue, WA: Illumination Arts Publishing.

Duncan, R. (1989). *When Emily woke up angry.* Hauppauge, NY: Barron's Educational Series.

Greenfield, E. & Cooper, F. (Ill.). (1988). *Grandpa's face.* New York: Philomel Books.

Grifalconi, A. (1993). *Kinda blue.* Boston: Little Brown.

Ichikawa, S. & Gauch, P. L. (Ill.). (1992). *Bravo, Tanya.* New York: Philomel Books.

Kraus, R., Aruego, J. & Dewey, A. (Ill.). (1977). *Noel the coward.* New York: Simon & Schuster.

Modesitt, J. & Spowart, R. (Ill.). (1992). *Sometimes I feel like a mouse.* New York: Scholastic.

Murphy, J. B. & Collins, H. (Ill.). (1985). *Feelings.* Windsor, Ontario, Canada: Black Moss Press.

Preston, E. M. & Bennett, R. (Ill.). (1969). *The temper tantrum book.* New York: Viking.

Richter, B. & Jacobsen, A. (Ill.). (1978). *Something SPECIAL within.* Marina del Rey, CA: DeVorss.

Simon, N. & Lasker, J. (Ill.). (1970). *How do I feel?* Chicago: Albert Whitman.

Simon, N. & Leder, D. (Ill.). (1974). *I was so mad!* Chicago: Albert Whitman.

Stanton, E. & Stanton, H. (1978). *Sometimes I like to cry.* Chicago: Albert Whitman.

Tompert, A. & Kramer, R. (Ill.). (1988). *Will you come back for me?* Morton Grove, IL: Albert Whitman.

Vertreace, M. M. & Speidel, S. (Ill.). (1993). *Kelly in the mirror.* Morton Grove, IL: Albert Whitman.

Zolotow, C. & Lobel, A. (Ill.). (1963). *The quarreling book.* New York: Harper & Row.

Zolotow, C. & Shector, B. (Ill.). (1969). *The hating book.* New York: Harper & Row.

It's Mine!
(Possession Disputes)

It is evident that one common source of conflict in early childhood, as in adult society, is struggle for the possession of tangible resources; in children's groups, these usually consist of toys and other play materials. (Hay, 1984, p. 14)

POSSESSION DISPUTES IN THE EARLY CHILDHOOD CLASSROOM

As young children make the transition from home to an early childhood center, they often become overwhelmed with this strange new environment filled with all kinds of toys and activities. Shelves packed with blocks, books, and puzzles greet their eyes. Child-sized furniture welcomes them to dramatic play areas. Easels with paints, brushes, and paper wait for them in art areas. There are riding trucks, rocking boats, and climbing equipment. Water tables with squeeze bottles or sand tables with shovels and sifters may beckon them. Saws, hammers, and safety goggles hang from pegboards in woodworking areas. Guinea pigs in cages whistle for their attention. All of this is arranged for them. Unbelievable!

Young three-, four-, or five-year-old children may believe that all of these wonders really wait there for them *alone*. Their self-centered natures allow little room for other children and their wishes. "I'm going to play with the biggest truck," they declare, and set about to do so, but somebody else has the same idea. When that somebody gets to the biggest truck first, then what?

Thus begins the first and most common type of conflict in all early childhood classrooms: the possession dispute over a toy. From the earliest formal observations of preschool children's conflicts (Dawe, 1934) to the most recent findings from laboratory preschools, all researchers have come to the same conclusion: property struggles over toys and materials make up the most frequent disputes in early childhood classrooms. (More than half of Dawe's 200 quarrels involved property struggles.)

Hay (1984) reports that "the vast majority of conflicts reported for children in the second year of life are object struggles." This trend continues with three- and four-year-olds. In some programs 90 to 100 percent of the conflicts involve objects, but as children grow older the number of disputes over toys seems to decrease (although it is still the most common kind of conflict). Perhaps this decrease occurs because children eventually learn that the toys are there for everyone or that they can gain control of a favorite toy without a confrontation.

We can understand how children coming together for the first time may each want the same toy at the same time. A child's own desire for a particular toy takes precedence over the wants of another child at first. She wants the doll with the blue dress so she takes it, even if another child has it. "First come, first served" has little meaning for a child in the beginning because she does not see things from any perspective but her own. She has to learn that other children may have the same desire as she does and the same claim on the object. She has to learn "other-esteem."

What about your classroom? Before you can begin to convert conflicts with young children, survey your own environment. Do you find that conflicts among your children follow the same pattern as those reported by others? Some teachers say that conflicts among preschoolers have increased over the years or that conflicts have become more violent. Is this true for you as well? Take a day or so to find out about your own class. The observational tally form, *Types of Classroom Conflicts* (Fig. 2.1), given on pages 24–25, can help you survey your own children's behavior. Run off several copies of the form, use one for each day you and your coworkers observe, and then tally the results. Compare your results with the research findings:

1. Materials/space–possession conflicts occur most frequently.
2. Conflicts do not occur frequently every day.
3. Children settle most conflicts without adult intervention.
4. The same few children are involved repeatedly.

OCCASIONAL CONFLICTS AND FREQUENT CONFLICTEES

If conflicts occur infrequently in most preschool classrooms, and if the children settle most disputes themselves, why should we be concerned? The teacher has good reason for concern; however, our major focus should be the occasional conflict that gets out of control. Strong emotions engendered by out-of-control children affect everyone in the classroom. Children look to the adults in charge to help them overcome such predicaments. Emotionally-charged incidents make the best learning opportunities. The stronger the emotions, the greater the lesson that will be learned by everyone.

Furthermore, the few children who repeatedly become involved in conflicts desperately need our help. *While most children learn to resolve most conflicts on their own, some children need our help in learning the necessary interpersonal skills.* All the children in the class can benefit from this.

Children's own conflict resolution strategies may need changing. Also, the conflict resolutions themselves may have faults. Perhaps there are better ways of resolving possession disputes than those currently being used. For example, some children resolve toy disputes by dominating others. Other children simply give up or give in. If children have not learned how to convert conflicts to positive results, then you can contribute greatly to their ability to get along in the world by teaching them how.

DECREASING POSSESSION DISPUTES

If conflicts provide learning situations for children, should we even make an attempt to decrease them? Most preschool teachers strive for a smoothly running classroom. If interpersonal conflicts constantly interrupt children's activities, we owe the children changes so that they can resolve their own problem situations. We can do this without constant adult intervention. Of course, several

FIGURE 2.1

Types of Classroom Conflicts

Center _____ Class _____ Children's Ages _____

Date _____ Time _____ Observers _____

(Directions: Use one form for entire class; use initial of child's first name for each conflict observed; for example: J/B, J/B, S/W.)

Materials Conflicts

    With blocks   _____

    With manipulatives   _____

    With role-play props   _____

    With art materials   _____

    Uses aggression   _____

    Teacher must intervene _____

Attention Getting

    Aggressive gestures   _____

    Aggressive words   _____

    Aggressive actions   _____

    Teacher must intervene _____

Power Struggles

    Tries to control materials _____

    Tries to control actions   _____

    Insists on being first   _____

    Uses aggression   _____

    Teacher must intervene   _____

Personality Clashes

    Uses aggressive gestures   _____

    Uses aggressive words   _____

    Uses aggressive actions   _____

    Teacher must intervene   _____

Group-Entry Disputes

    Tries verbal force   _____

    Tries physical force   _____

    Aggression against materials   _____

    Teacher must intervene   _____

Aggressive Role Play

    Loud, aggressive words   _____

    Hits or pushes others   _____

    Hits or throws materials   _____

    Disrupts others' play   _____

    Teacher must intervene   _____

Other:_____

_____

_____

_____

adults could spend much of their time standing over the youngsters and preventing squabbles. While such action may stop the conflicts, it does little to help children in the long run. They become dependent upon adults to control their behavior and fail to develop their own skills for resolving interpersonal problems. Furthermore, many adults use inappropriate blaming and punishing methods to prevent conflicts, which may interfere with children's development of self-esteem and other-esteem, important qualities necessary for their future success.

What about in your classroom? If you assert that you have no conflicts among the preschoolers in your program, then you may need to consider why? Do the adults totally control the children's behavior? It is unusual to have no conflict among a group of egocentric young preschoolers. No conflict means no opportunity for children to learn interpersonal skills. You may need to ease up on adult supervision, and give children the opportunity to make their own choices and develop their own control.

There are several effective ways to decrease the number of children's possession disputes which directly involve the children. These successful approaches have evolved over the years as preschool teachers have struggled to help children manage their own out-of-control behavior. What other methods have you tried?

 ### FIGURE 2.2

Ways to Decrease Possession Conflicts in the Classroom

1. Provide adequate and appropriate space in learning centers.
2. Provide turn-taking and self-regulating arrangements for space and materials.
3. Provide enough materials for several children to use at once in each learning center.
4. Provide more than one of each favorite toy, tool, or dramatic play prop.
5. Introduce new toys or materials to the total group at the outset, establishing a turn-taking arrangement.

The physical environment of the classroom can have a direct bearing on the number of possession conflicts that occur. You can actually decrease the number of possession conflicts by the way you arrange your classroom, its materials, and its activities. You will find that the type of materials available, their distribution in the classroom, and the accessibility of space have a direct relationship to the number of possession quarrels that take place (Ramsey, 1986, p. 174). A look at the physical arrangement of the typical preschool classroom shows how this can happen.

PROVIDING ADEQUATE AND APPROPRIATE SPACE IN LEARNING CENTERS

Most classrooms for young children are organized into a number of learning centers, sometimes called activity areas or learning stations. These centers may be sectioned off by low room dividers, shelves, or groupings of child-size furniture. They typically include such areas as:

Block Center
Dramatic Play Center
Manipulative/Math Center
Story/Library Center
Writing Center
Sound/Listening Center
Art Center
Music Center
Science Center
Computer Center
Large Motor Center

Other areas might include cooking, woodworking, and sand or water tables. In addition, there may be a large space for whole group activities such as circle time, although this space may be included in one of the centers.

The way these centers are set up helps to control what happens in them. If the center is too large for the activity, more children may come into it than the materials can accommodate, or the children may mill around instead of playing with the materials. This especially is likely in Block Centers with a lot of floor space and many shelves, but few blocks or accessories. A Small Block center with an adequate number of blocks but too little space can cause similar problems. Children who cannot use areas properly often end up squabbling, fighting, or misusing materials.

If you have a small room and your children experience overcrowding in certain areas, you can try several approaches to ensure enough space for everyone. If you have too many learning centers in one room, eliminate some and alternate them with the remaining centers from time to time during the year. Another effective method uses masking tape on the floor or carpets to section off building space in small block areas. You can use masking tape on table tops to regulate space for block building, although some find it too confining.

What would make a space inappropriate? If the learning center is sectioned off in such a way that children cannot tell how to use it, then it has been arranged inappropriately. For instance, the Block Center should have shelves pulled away from the walls and used as room dividers to set off the area and make it clear to everyone that this space is reserved for building with unit blocks. Otherwise, you may have children running through the open area, visitors stepping over blocks, or children riding on vehicles that crash into block structures.

On the other hand, a center may be sectioned off too snugly. Room dividers that surround an area and leave an opening only large enough for one child at a time to enter invite space-possession trouble. The children within may try to exclude others or to defend limited-access spaces as their own private property. Lofts, ready-built playhouses, and cardboard carton huts with one entrance present similar problems. Ramsey (1986) noted that such spaces tend to be the sites for territorial disputes, possibly because

> *the enclosed areas are more easily defended and*
> *physically allow children to attempt to exclude*
> *others. The second possibility is that, when chil-*
> *dren are in an enclosed area, they have a sense of*
> *privacy and/or a feeling of intimacy which may*
> *be violated when others approach. (Ramsey,*
> *1986, p. 175)*

Your youngsters are reacting naturally. They need to have a feeling of property ownership even within the group, and they certainly have a need for privacy from time to time, just as you do. You should be aware of such needs and such possibilities for conflict. Lofts and private spaces are important classroom areas. As a conflict transformer, you must help children learn to regulate turns and space on their own.

If you run out of space, use your own creativity and that of the children. You will be surprised at the ideas they may suggest, which may in turn trigger your own creative flow! If you would like to teach children to prevent squabbles in the current space before they get started, try one of the turn-taking or self-regulating arrangements discussed next.

PROVIDING TURN-TAKING AND SELF-REGULATING ARRANGEMENTS FOR SPACE AND MATERIALS

How many children do you expect to accommodate in each center, especially the most popular ones? Your reply will depend on the space available and the size of the class. With a typical group of twenty three- and four-year-olds in an average-size classroom, you might set up the centers as follows:

Block Center: six children
Dramatic Play Center: six children
Manipulative/Math Center: eight children (two tables)
Story Center: six children

Writing Center: four children (one table)
Sound Center: two children
Art Center: six children (four at table; two at easel)
Music Center: unlimited (under loft)
Science Center: unlimited (on window shelf)
Computer Center: two children seated
Large Motor Center: unlimited (loft with ladder and slide)

If any of these areas becomes overcrowded during free choice time, some teachers post signs showing the number of children an area can accommodate. Others set up a self-regulating method for children to use on their own. The Block Area might have six necklaces or six color coded tags hanging on hooks at the entrance to the area for children to wear when they play with blocks, for instance. When all six necklaces are in use, other children must play elsewhere while waiting for a turn.

Children choose activity areas in other classrooms by hooking their name cards or photos on one of several numbered hooks at the entrance to the center they want. Other teachers establish turn-taking procedures through a sign-up sheet, with a pencil attached to a small clipboard at the entrance to each center. Children love to scribble or print their names in one of the spaces on the sheet and then cross them off when they leave the area. Writing your own name for a turn seems so grown-up, even if it is a scribble that only you can read.

Children love to scribble or print their names on a sign-up sheet.

Having an established turn-taking method for use of popular materials or equipment also helps children prevent squabbles. If children know ahead of time what to do when several of them want the same piece of equipment, they can work out an equitable solution among themselves. Some teachers have children use a kitchen timer, a three-minute egg hourglass, or a stopwatch to alternate short turns for playing with an Etch-a-Sketch, a new doll, or a riding vehicle. For equipment that needs longer time, such as a computer, a sign-up sheet may be better.

Each of these turn-taking and self-regulating methods gives the children control over their own use of materials without resorting to possession disputes or relying on adults to tell them what to do.

PROVIDING ENOUGH MATERIALS FOR SEVERAL CHILDREN TO USE AT ONCE IN EACH LEARNING CENTER

Common sense seems to dictate that preschool classrooms should have enough materials for the number of children served, but often teachers or center directors think of classrooms as a whole rather than as learning centers. There may be plenty of toys and games for a whole room, but not enough in individual centers. Check your own classroom. If you have sectioned off the Block Center to accommodate six children, check whether you have enough blocks for each child to build a large building. If not, you can either order more blocks or reduce the number of children allowed in the center at one time.

Block kits for preschools tend to include many categories of unit blocks but less of each kind of block than in kits for kindergartens. Many teachers prefer to purchase the blocks separately in order to have enough units, doubles, and quadruples, the most useful and popular kinds. Ramsey found that 78 percent of the classroom materials involved in children's possession disputes were blocks (1986, p. 177):

> Some specific functions of the blocks that were
> most often associated with conflict were the use
> of blocks to create boundaries, the accumulation
> of blocks in individual building projects, and the
> creation of structures with small openings such
> as garages.

Every possession conflict cannot be prevented by room arrangement or increasing the amount of materials, but, where research data gives us this kind of information about children's quarrels, we should act on it. Providing more blocks for each of the builders helps prevent them from infringing on their neighbors' structures.

The same holds true for manipulatives. "Manipulatives were most frequently the objects of conflict when two or more children were trying to use the same small space and objects (e.g., doing a puzzle together) or when the activity depended on accumulation (e.g., stringing of beads)" (Ramsey, 1986, p. 179). Check your shelves of manipulatives to ensure the quantities of each material will accommodate the number of children. Otherwise, either reduce the number of children or add to the manipulatives. A Manipulative/Math center with two tables set up for eight children should include a great many of the materials from the following table (Beaty, 1992, p. 104):

TABLE 2.1 MANIPULATIVE/MATH MATERIALS

Toy cars	Keys and locks	Picture dominoes
Seashells	Golf tees	Lotto cards
Buttons	Uncooked pasta	Color bingo
Bottle tops	Slotted wheels	Tic-tac-toe
Pebbles	Giant dice	Stacking blocks
Seeds	Shape blocks	Nesting cubes
Nuts	Color bricks	Snap blocks
Toy planes	Geoboards	Parquetry blocks
Toy animals	Pegboards	Bristle blocks
Abacus	Game boards	Cylinder boards
Lacing dolls	Computer games	Cuisenaire rods
Play money	Colored chips	Toy cash register
Boxes	Sectioned boxes	Egg cartons
Cards	Paper punches	Markers and caps
Rulers	Yardstick	Carpenter's rule
Balance	Stopwatch	Kitchen timer
Hourglass	Postage meter	Balance
Puzzles	Zipping/buttoning frames	

If you lack table space, section each tabletop into four spaces with masking tape, but only if the children also agree that this will help them stay within their own space.

PROVIDING MORE THAN ONE OF A FAVORITE TOY, TOOL, OR DRAMATIC PLAY PROP

Although individual children have particular interests, most children do seem attracted to certain toys and materials in the center. A single tricycle on the playground often becomes the focus of loud arguments. An eggbeater or a baster in the water table may incite a conflict, as will one riding truck, a single hammer, or one pair of safety goggles. In the Manipulative/Math Center, one toy cash register or one toy pounding set sometimes starts a flurry of disputes. Dramatic play props may do the same if there is only one of the favorites: a firefighter's helmet, a steering wheel, a telescope, or a stethoscope. If you have such highly desirable single toys in your classroom, you may want to purchase duplicates.

Some teachers remove the object of a dispute rather than provide more than one. Before taking such action, however, classroom staff should stop and reconsider. Removing a disputed object deprives the children of two things: the use of the toy and also an opportunity to resolve any conflict about it. As the children begin to resolve their own disputes, they should be the ones to remove a toy temporarily, because they should be in control of the conflict conversion, not the teacher.

Introducing New Toys or Materials to the Total Group at the Outset, and Establishing a Turn-Taking Arrangement

When you bring new toys and materials into the classroom, take time to introduce them to the total group, perhaps at the morning circle. If appropriate, pass the item around to let the children hold it and see how it works. Show the class where it will be kept (perhaps on a shelf with its name clearly labeled), and put the item there. Then discuss with the children how they can take turns using the new toy. Let them make their own suggestions.

Maybe they will want to use one of the turn-taking methods already in place. A sign-up sheet, kitchen timer, egg timer, or stopwatch may work fine. Or, to start off, children may want to draw their names out of a hat, just as adults do. The children who want to play with the item need to print or scribble their names or initials on squares of paper that you provide. They may want to draw names every time for turns with a particularly popular new object. That might be a magnet set, a toy camcorder, or a battery-operated keyboard.

Such total group discussions about attractive toys help children to understand that when you have only one highly desirable item for a class of twenty children and many children want to play with it, an arrangement needs to be made. Some children may even decide that two can play with the object at once. If this is agreeable with the others, then two names can be drawn.

Besides preventing disputes over favorite toys, such turn-taking practices can also help children when real conflicts occur. They may be able to resolve such conflicts on their own by suggesting a turn-taking solution. But if things get out of control and the teacher has to intervene, then the children can answer Conflict-Conversion Question #3, "What would make the other person feel better?" with a real knowledge of the strategies that help.

THE TYPICAL POSSESSION CONFLICT IN THE PRESCHOOL CLASSROOM

Remember that conflicts are not all bad and neither are the children involved in them. Conflict is, rather, "an interpersonal encounter needing a positive emotional resolution." It is a social occurrence, not a child's negative personality trait. According to researcher Hay, conflict is "a form of social exchange between at least two people. Thus any single conflict is a developmental phenomenon in its own right; it extends over time, and has a beginning, middle, and end" (Hay, 1984, p. 2).

With young children the time involved is brief, indeed. Dawe (1934) found that only three of her two hundred quarrels lasted over one minute. Modern researchers agree. The conflicts of Hay's two-year-olds averaged only twenty-three seconds each (Hay, 1984, p. 11). Laursen and Hartup (1989) found that of the 154 quarrels they observed among nursery-school-children (aged three to five years), 63 percent lasted ten seconds or less.

The typical possession conflict lasts about twenty-three seconds.

What happens during that ten to twenty-three seconds? In the typical property struggle Child A, the instigator of the conflict tries to gain possession of an object being used by Child B. He may try to grab the object, make an assertive statement ("It's mine!" or "I had it first!"), give a command ("Give it to me!"), try negotiation ("If you let me have it, I'll let you play with my car,"), use a verbal threat ("Let me have it, or I'll knock down your building!"), make a threatening gesture (raise a fist), or actually carry out physical aggression (push or hit Child B or knock down Child's B's building). Child A may use several of the above strategies in the course of the conflict, or only one, depending on Child B's response.

Still, within the same ten to twenty-three-second time frame, Child B responds. He may give up the desired object if he finds Child A's strategies convincing or his threat too overpowering. More typically, though, he continues the conflict by resisting. He may ignore the request, continue playing without recognizing Child A's intrusion, refuse verbally ("No, you can't have it, because I got it first"), make a counterproposal ("If you get the blocks off the shelf for me, then you can play with the car when the road is finished"), or postpone the settlement ("You can have it after I'm finished"). (See Figure 2.3.)

The conflict may end there, continue in the same mode with the two children exchanging assertions, or it may escalate into pushing, fighting, yelling, or crying on the part of one or both. If the conflict gets out of hand, an adult may intervene. More typically, however, the conflict comes to a conclusion within the ten to twenty-three second time frame with one or other of the children giving up or giving in.

 FIGURE 2.3

Children's Strategies During Possession Disputes

Child A	Child B
Tries to take object	Gives up object, or
Makes assertive statement	Ignores request
Gives command	Refuses verbally
Tries to negotiate	Makes counterproprosal
Uses verbal threat	Postpones settlement
Uses physical aggression	Resists physically
	Calls for help

The Teacher's Response

How should you respond to a typical possession dispute? Most teachers prefer to let children settle such conflicts on their own. They feel that children learn best from one another about how to resolve a possession dispute. Unless the conflict becomes violent, this method may be the best tactic. Only you know your children and their typical behavior. Your survey of the *Types of Classroom Conflicts* also gives you data of this sort. You may agree that most possession disputes, unless violent, should be resolved by the children themselves. If you find, however, that one child always seems to be dominating the others, even nonviolently, you may decide to intervene with the conflict-conversion strategies discussed in Chapter 1. The following cases take a look at typical possession disputes. As you read them, think about how you would respond as a classroom staff member in the same situation. For review purposes, the three conflict-conversion questions a teacher will use appear prior to each of the case studies in the text.

Conflict-Conversion Questions

1. What's happening, (child's name) _____?
2. How does _____ (other child) feel?
3. What will make him (or her) feel better?

#1 The Case of the Purple Cape

Setting: Talia's mother has sent in a box of dress-up clothes for the children to play with during dramatic play. A group of children takes them out of the box and scatters them around on the floor of the Dramatic Play Center. Talia picks out a hat and a lace shawl to wear. Heather puts on high-heeled shoes and struts around. Luis and Sam both discover a purple table cloth at the same time and decide that they want it for a cape. They both grab an end of the "cape."

Luis: *Give it to me! I got it first!* (pulls hard)

Sam: *It's mine! Let go! I saw it before you did!* (hangs on)

Luis: *No, you didn't. You let go! It's my Superman cape.* (gives a very hard pull)

Sam loses his grip, and Luis falls over backwards with the cape and cries. Teacher comes over to see what happened. Sam walks away.

Teacher: *What happened, Luis? Are you okay?* (helps Luis up)

Luis: *Sam made me fall!* (sniffles) *He was trying to get my Superman cape!*

Teacher: *Sam, come here a minute. Let's find out what happened.*

Sam: *I didn't make him fall. He fell by himself. He was pulling too hard.*

Teacher: *Sam, Luis says that you made him fall when you were trying to get the Superman cape. And, Luis, Sam says you fell by yourself when you were pulling too hard. So, Sam, how do you think Luis feels about all this?*

Sam: *He shouldn't have pulled so hard.*

Teacher: *That's probably true. But tell me, how do you think Luis feels?*

Sam: *I don't know. He probably hurt himself. But it wasn't my fault.*

Teacher: *Well, we're not trying to find out whose fault it was. We're just talking about feelings. And you say that Luis probably hurt himself. So maybe he feels bad, right?* (Sam shrugs. Luis nods his head, yes.)

Teacher: *And, Luis, how does Sam feel about this?*

Luis: *He was trying to get my Superman cape!*

Teacher: *Yes. That's what you said. But how does Sam feel, Luis?*

Luis: *He feels like he wants my cape.*

Teacher: *You say he feels like he wants the cape. Does he feel good about it, Luis?*

Luis: (Shakes head) *He feels bad because he doesn't have it.*

Teacher: *So, maybe, Luis, you both feel bad. You feel bad because you hurt yourself, and, Sam, you feel bad because you don't have the cape. What would make Sam feel better, Luis? What do you think?*

Sam: *I'd feel better if I had the cape.*

Luis: *You can't have it!*

Teacher: *Well, Luis, I'm asking you to think about what would make Sam feel better?*

Luis: *If he had the cape. But I'm still using it!*

Teacher: *You say that Sam might feel better if he had the cape, Luis. Will you let him use it when you're finished?* (Luis nods.) *Is that okay with you, Sam?* (Sam nods.) *Good. So, Sam, what do you think would make Luis feel better?*

Sam: *I don't know. He's got the cape.*

Teacher: *Well, think about it. He hurt himself when he fell. What would make him feel better? We want you both to feel better.*

Sam: *Maybe if I played with him while he was Superman. And then he could play with me when I'm Superman.*

Teacher: *That sounds like fun. Would that make you feel better, Luis?* (Luis nods vigorously.) *Okay. So, Luis, you're going to have the Superman cape first and Sam is going to play with you. Then Sam is going to have the Superman cape and you are going to play with him. Can you take turns with the cape by yourselves?* (They agree to use the kitchen timer.) *Okay. Good. Thanks for talking about this, boys. I see that you really can think about how someone else feels, Luis and Sam, and that makes me feel good. Want to shake on that?* (Boys shake hands.)

Positive-Feelings Activity: Later that day the teacher calls the class together for a positive-feelings activity. She tells them that positive feelings came from Luis and Sam when they had some trouble over a purple cape. She asks the boys to tell what they did to make the other person feel good. Then she reads the class the book *Just Not the Same* about sisters who will not share anything. Afterwards, the children talk about how they think the sisters in the book felt. When a book like this is not available, the teacher can put a puppet on each of her hands and do a brief puppet play illustrating a similar conflict.

TEACHER'S ACTIONS, CASE #1

In Case #1 the teacher carefully kept the focus on *the other child's feelings*, not allowing herself to be swayed by the boys into discussing whose fault it was. Her calmness and matter-of-fact approach helped the two boys become calm. Although Luis blamed Sam for his fall and Sam blamed Luis, both boys allowed their thoughts to be refocused on feelings, on how the other boy felt. The teacher remained nonjudgmental, restating what the boys had said about one another's feelings until the boys themselves truly focused on feelings and not on blame. The follow-up activity later in the day reinforced their learning by having the boys repeat not what had happened, but what they each did to make the other boy feel better. They ended the conflict with a handshake, an important positive-feelings way to conclude the conflict conversion.

This approach differs greatly from the way children's conflicts have been handled in the past. This teacher helps the children to develop "other-esteem," to feel the way the other person feels. She helps them convert their negative emotions to positive feelings and leaves them in control of the solution. Such an approach, repeated again and again in a classroom, has a persuasive effect on children's behavior. They truly begin to see things from the other person's perspective. Conflicts may not cease after using this approach; for they are a built-in part of human nature, but the feelings engendered by conflicts may change from negative emotions to empathy and even to understanding the other person's point of view.

Case #2 describes a space-possession dispute where the teacher intervenes because the conflict escalates to hair pulling and crying. The children involved are the girls that had been playing with clothes in the dramatic play area in Case #1, plus one other girl, Becky.

Conflict–Conversion Questions

1. What's happening, (child's name) _____?
2. How does _____ (other child) feel?
3. What will make him (or her) feel better?

#2 The Case of the Crowded Rocking Boat

Setting: Two children, Talia and Heather, sit opposite each other in a wooden rocking boat in the gross motor area. They are talking and not rocking. They have room for two more children, one on each seat. Becky comes over and tries to climb into the rocking boat. Talia prevents her by pushing her away and then rocking the boat as hard as she can. Becky tries to stop the rocking, but she cannot. She grabs Talia's long hair, making her cry. The teacher intervenes.

Talia: *Becky, you can't get in with us!*

Becky: *I can sit here if I want to!*

Talia: *No you can't* (pushes Becky away). *Rock the boat, Heather, don't let her get in!* (rocks boat hard)

Becky: *Stop rocking! I can get in if I want to!* (grabs Talia's hair and pulls; Talia cries)

Teacher: *What's happening here, Talia?*

Talia: (stops crying) *Becky pulled my hair!*

Becky: *They won't let me get in the rocking boat.*

Talia: *We don't want her to play with us.*

Teacher: *Becky, Talia says that you pulled her hair; and, Talia, Becky says she wants to get in the boat. And I can't let you hurt each other, so let's see how we feel about this for a minute. Becky, how does Talia feel about this?*

Becky: *She won't let me in the boat!*

Teacher: *I know. That's what you said. But how does she feel about having her hair pulled? Try to feel how she feels.*

Becky: *I guess it hurt her.*

Teacher: *Does it feel painful because it hurt her?* (Becky nods yes.) *And what about you, Talia? How does Becky feel because she can't get in the boat?*

Talia: (silence at first) *We were here first!*

Teacher: *Yes, you were there first. But how does Becky feel because she can't get in the boat?*

Talia: *We don't want her to play with us.*

Teacher: *Think about how Becky feels. How would you feel if you couldn't get in the boat?*

Talia: *I wouldn't like it.*

Teacher: *Becky, Talia says she wouldn't like it if she couldn't get in the boat. Is that how you feel?* (Becky nods yes.)

Teacher: *So now we know how you both feel. Talia feels pain because you pulled her hair, Becky. And Becky feels that she doesn't like it because she can't get in the boat. Becky, what do you think would make Talia feel better?*

Becky: *If I said "I'm sorry I pulled your hair."*

Teacher: *Talia, Becky says you might feel better if she told you she's sorry she pulled your hair. Is that right?* (Talia nods yes.) *And, Talia, what do you think would make Becky feel better?*

Talia: *If we let her in our boat. But we don't want her to play with us.*

Teacher: *So what could you do to make Becky feel better?*

Talia: (tentatively) *We could let her rock the boat.*

Teacher: *Would that make you feel better, Becky?*

Becky: (Becky nods yes.) *But they should let me in and rock me when they're finished.*

Teacher: *Okay. So Talia will feel better if you say you're sorry, Becky.* (Becky mumbles "I'm sorry.") *And Becky will feel better if you let her rock the boat, and then you'll rock it for her when you're finished, Talia. Do you agree?* (Talia nods.) *How will you know when it's Becky's turn?*

Talia: *After Becky rocks us ten times. No, twenty times.*

Teacher: *Okay. So, after you rock them twenty times, Becky, it's your turn in the boat to be rocked, okay?* (Becky nods yes). *Well, girls, I really appreciate the way you worked this out. You can really feel how each other feels when things go wrong. And you can find good ways to make each other feel better. Want to shake on that?* (Becky and Talia shake, and then, Becky and Heather.) *And how about a silly poem to make us all laugh:*

"It's time, I believe,
For us to leave;
But the rocking boat says: It isn't.

(Teacher quickly points to each girl, and they each respond as fast as they can with a phrase from the end of a verse they all know, and soon all burst into laughter.)

It is! It isn't!
It is! It isn't!
It is! It isn't! It is!

(Paraphrased from Opie, 1992, p. 53)

Positive-Feelings Activity: Just before lunch the teacher calls the class together to talk about this positive action. She describes what happened and asks the girls to relate what they did to help the other one feel better and then does a puppet-play conflict or reads a book such as *Move Over, Twerp*, which tells about the clever thing little Jeffrey does to get back his seat from the big kids on the school bus. Becky, Talia, and Heather want the verse they said repeated, so they all say it in unison, and then go around the class saying "It is," or "It isn't," when the teacher points to them.

TEACHER'S ACTIONS, CASE #2

This teacher really has caught the essence of the conflict–conversion "feelings strategy." She intervenes because something has happened to make Talia cry. She asks what happened and then repeats only enough of what the two girls say to answer her question. The adult intervener needs to be careful not to repeat fault-finding statements that the children may make. If she stresses only *what happened* in its briefest form, she still will be allowing each child to justify her actions without dragging down the argument to *whose fault it was.*

Next she asks Becky how Talia *feels* about having her hair pulled. Becky would rather talk about *why* she pulled Talia's hair, her justification. The teacher acknowledges that she has heard this already, but that now she wants to know from Becky how Talia *feels* about the hair-pulling behavior. This part settled, the teacher now turns to Talia with the same query, how does Becky *feel* because she cannot get in the boat. Notice that the teacher does not use the words "because *you won't let her* get in the boat," which lay blame, something the teacher needs to avoid if she wants conflict conversion to center around *feelings.* Then the teacher restates the comments each girl made about the other's feelings. She concludes the conflict conversion by asking each girl what would make the other one feel better. Children often are surprised by this turn of events. They expect to be asked what would make *them* feel better, but because the teacher continues her focus on empathy (that is, feeling like the other person), she accomplishes *three things:* (1) she diffuses the negative feelings generated by the actions of both girls; (2) she allows each upset party to determine the action to be taken by the other (if the other accepts, then conflict is resolved; if the other rejects it, then the teacher pursues conflict-conversion question #3 until the child finally accepts something); and (3) the teacher does not impose her own ideas on the children.

This last accomplishment ranks as the most important. Had this teacher imposed her own solution, she would have short-circuited the conflict-conversion strategy by taking the solution out of the hands of the children involved. In addition, it would probably never have entered the teacher's head to have Becky rock the boat for Talia as a solution to this conflict! Children have such creative ideas. The fact that both parties quickly agreed to this solution further indicates how brief children's disagreements are and how easily two adversaries can come together again in play. Talia may have thought that she was punishing Becky by having her rock the boat twenty times, but Becky's instant acceptance of this solution probably meant that she saw it as a good way to gain access to space in the boat. The girls' own solutions worked out far better than a teacher-imposed resolution could have, as it would probably have left behind hard feelings and a sense of being blamed and punished. What would you have done?

POSITIVE-FEELINGS ACTIVITIES TO USE
AFTER POSSESSION DISPUTES

Each time a teacher or staff member intervenes in a children's conflict as described above, a positive-feelings activity should be scheduled later in the day. Such an activity instructs the other children on how they, too, can resolve such conflicts. If more than one conflict occurs in which the teacher has to intervene, she can decide which one to focus on for this activity or she can refer to more than one. Many children enjoy relating how they converted their conflict.

The adult involved should be the one to describe the conflict very briefly, afterward turning it over to the children to tell *how they helped the other child feel better.* The children involved should be congratulated again by the adult and applauded by their peers. This activity not only will reinforce their learning, but will also help everyone understand that a *positive emotional resolution* provides the only appropriate solution for conflicts in the classroom. Children who resolve conflicts in this manner receive congratulations from their teachers and their peers. Everyone ends up feeling good.

Some teachers also like to end the brief session by reading a book, reciting a verse, using hand puppets, or doing an art project directly related to the theme of the conflict. Some suggested children's books to read that involve possession conflicts can be found at the end of this chapter. If you do not have an appropriate book to read, make up a story of your own about a similar conflict and ask the children how the story characters felt. Or, use two hand puppets (one on each hand) and have them enact a similar conflict over a toy they both want to play with.

Conflict-conversion strategies of this sort do not take as much classroom time as it seems. For one thing, the teacher only intervenes in children's conflicts when one child cries or when things get out of hand. Many teachers believe that any time spent teaching children how to resolve conflicts peacefully is well spent, especially when the children themselves achieve the resolution.

One teacher remarked that whenever no serious conflicts occur in her classroom for several days at a time, she still spends a few minutes having a positive-feelings activity, because she wants the children to be reminded of how to convert conflicts to positive feelings when conflicts do occur. She reminds us that these "possession disputes" belong to the children, not the teacher. They own the conflict and they should own the resolution. Does this happen in your classroom?

IDEAS + IN CHAPTER 2

Possession-Dispute Activities

1. If there are too many learning centers in one room, eliminate some and alternate their use.
2. Use masking tape on floors and carpets to section off block building space.

3. Pull block shelves away from walls and use as room dividers.
4. Post signs in learning centers indicating the number of children the center can accommodate.
5. Have necklaces or color-coded tags for taking turns.
6. Hook name cards or photos on numbered hooks for taking turns.
7. Have sign-up sheet with pencil attached to small clipboards in learning centers.
8. Use kitchen timer, egg hourglass, or stopwatch to regulate turns.
9. Order more materials or reduce the number of children in each center if there are squabbles over materials.
10. Provide enough blocks for each builder.
11. Reduce the number of children or add to manipulative materials.
12. Section each manipulative table into four spaces with masking tape.
13. Purchase duplicates of highly desirable toys.
14. Introduce new toys to the entire group.
15. Draw names out of hat for turns with toys.
16. Read class a turn-taking story.
17. Later in the day, have children repeat what they did to make other children feel better.
18. End conflict conversion with a handshake and a smile.
19. Repeat conflict-conversion verse with all the children.
20. Avoid using blaming words during conflict conversions.
21. Give congratulations to children involved in disputes and have class applaud their actions.
22. Read a book, recite a verse, use hand puppets, or do an art project related to the theme of the conflict.
23. Have a positive-feelings activity to give children practice when there are no conflicts.

TRY IT YOURSELF

1. After completing the *Types of Classroom Conflicts* tally sheet, determine whether the situations always occur separately or as several combined. From your experience with preschool children, give an example of a possession dispute that combines more than one type of conflict.
2. Name a common error made in the setup of learning centers that could contribute to an ongoing materials dispute?
3. How would you determine the appropriate materials for three of your learning centers, and how would you arrange them to reduce conflicts?
4. In "The Case of the Purple Cape" how would you approach the children and lead them into a conflict-conversion setting?
5. List three sharing games that you might use in the positive feelings activity? Try one of them and report the results.

REFERENCES CITED

Beaty, J. J. (1992). *Preschool appropriate practices,* Fort Worth: Harcourt Brace.

Dawe, H. C. (1934). An analysis of two hundred quarrels of preschool children. *Child Development,* 5, 139–157.

Hay, D. F. (1984). Social conflict in early childhood. *Annals of Child Development,* 1, 1–44.

Laursen, B. & Hartup, W. W. (1989). The dynamics of preschool children's conflicts. *Merrill-Palmer Quarterly,* 35,(3), 281–297.

Opie, I., Opie, P., and Sendak, M. (Ill.). (1992). *I saw Esau: The schoolchild's pocket book.* Cambridge, MA: Candlewick Press.

Ramsey, P. G. (1986). Possession disputes in preschool classrooms. *Child Study Journal,* 16(3), 173–181.

OTHER SOURCES

Beaty, J. J. (1994). *Picture book storytelling: Literature activities for young children.* Fort Worth: Harcourt Brace.

Crary, E. (1984). *Kids can cooperate: A practical guide to teaching problem solving.* Seattle: Parenting Press.

Krogh, S. L. & Lamme, L. L. (1986). But what about sharing? Children's literature and moral development. In J. B. McCracken (Ed.), *Reducing Stress in Young Children's Lives.* Washington, DC: National Association for the Education of Young Children.

Ramsey, P. G. (1991). *Making friends in school: Promoting peer relationships in early childhood.* New York: Teachers College Press.

CHILDREN'S BOOKS ABOUT POSSESSION CONFLICTS

Alexander, M. (1981). *Move over, Twerp.* New York: Dial Press.

Glen, M. (1992). *Ruby to the rescue.* New York: G. P. Putnam.

Havill, J. & O'Brien, A. S. (Ill.). (1986). *Jamaica's find.* Boston: Houghton Mifflin.

Havill, J. & O'Brien, A. S. (Ill.). (1993). *Jamaica and Brianna.* Boston: Houghton Mifflin.

Keats, E. J. (1975). *Louie.* New York: Greenwillow Books.

Lacoe, A. & Estrada, P. (Ill.). (1992). *Just not the same.* Boston: Houghton Mifflin.

Pfister, M. (1992). *The rainbow fish* (J. Alison, Trans.). New York: North-South Books.

Look at Me!
(Attention Getting)

Deeds of violence in our society are performed largely by those who are trying to establish their self-esteem, to defend their self-image, and to demonstrate that they, too, are significant. (May, 1972, p. 23)

ATTENTION-GETTING STRUGGLES
IN THE PRESCHOOL CLASSROOM

Children aged three to five are still in an egocentric stage of development. Many of them believe that the world revolves around them and that people and things exist to serve them first of all. Then, as their preschool experiences broaden to include many others like themselves, most youngsters come to realize that they must share this new-found wonder world with others. They no longer can expect to be the first every time, to get the best toy, or to play in the learning center of their choice when it is already filled with others. They learn to wait for a turn or to negotiate for a toy. They gradually become socialized.

Other children, however, do not seem to learn these lessons. They demand to be first. They push others aside. They hit, throw things, and raise a fuss when they cannot have their own way. Such children seem to choose conflict and confrontation over peaceful negotiation. These youngsters may spend the entire day going around disrupting other children's play. They seem almost pleased with the negative attention they attract and appear to relish being punished. Children like this do not seem to know how to make friends. They often push their way into play groups but find few of their peers who will play with them. The harder they try to "crash the party," the more they are rejected by the other children.

Do you know any children like this? Your ears as well as your eyes may alert you to their presence in your classroom. Listen to the names being called out by upset staff members or indignant children during the day. Do you hear the same one or two names over and over? Do these same children repeat their inappropriate actions again and again no matter how heavy the consequences they experience? This chapter will address these attention-seeking children.

Why is it that most children can adjust to playing with others in harmony, whereas some cannot? Many psychologists and sociologists who have studied human behavior suggest that: "Children who feel incompetent or incapable of influencing others will resort to extremes in control behavior" (Smith, 1982, p. 160). Children with a poor self-image may take out their negative feelings about themselves on others in the classroom.

The actions they engage in to compensate for their own negative feelings tend to be disruptive attention-getting ploys. Hitting or shoving other children, disrupting activities, or destroying materials for no apparent reason certainly call attention to themselves. Even if these children receive reprimands or punishment, they must feel that such actions serve their purpose or they would not keep repeating them. "Look at me!" they seem to be saying, "I am somebody! My actions will make you all look at me!" And they do.

THE PURSUIT OF INTERPERSONAL INFLUENCE

Psychologist Rollo May believes that all people strive throughout their lives for influence (that is, making a difference) in human relationships. From early childhood to old age, human beings try to influence others around them simply by their presence. If this fails, they begin making stronger and stronger attempts at interpersonal influence. This use of personal power has been measured by May along a continuum gradually increasing in force:

1. Power to be
Infants reflect this life force by crying for attention, and young children do so by trying out objects and materials around them.

2. Self-affirmation
The belief in the self as worthy constitutes self-affirmation. Young children who feel good about themselves affirm their worth by standing up for themselves and showing pride in what they do. "Mom, look at me!" they shout when they accomplish something.

3. Self-assertion
If self-affirmation does not gain a child influence or attention, then self-assertion emerges and demands notice. Children with a poor self-image often begin interpersonal relationships by demanding attention in the negative manner previously noted.

4. Aggression
Aggression comes out as confrontations with others either physically or verbally. If children find that self-affirmation and self-assertiveness do not succeed in their attempts to influence others, then they may resort to aggression.

5. Violence
Severe physical aggression or violence results when none of the above levels of power makes a difference in a person's ability to gain influence. (Adapted from May, 1972, pp. 137–179)

This chapter deals with levels two and three of May's continuum, the attention-getting levels of self-affirmation and self-assertion. Chapter Four continues the discussion with children's power struggles that can result in aggression and violence.

When children feel good about themselves as worthy individuals, they have no need to resort to inappropriate attention getting. They express self-affirmation and self-assertion positively. They stand up for themselves with pride, not anger. They interact with others with dignity, not disruption. The preschool teaching staff, then, should place special emphasis on helping children improve the way they feel about themselves, especially children who try to impress others by inappropriate attention-getting methods. At the same time the staff will want to help such children learn to feel how others feel when negative things happen to them, to empathize with others, in order to convert their conflicts to positive feelings.

Children with a poor self-image may have developed negative feelings about themselves long before they entered your program. Often, they may come from families who neglect them, abuse them, or overindulge them. They may be children who receive such constant scolding, severe punishment, or complete neglect, that they come to feel that they have no value and nobody wants them around. Since their presence does not seem to make a difference to others in any positive way, they begin using negative methods of assertion. If this gains them the attention they so desperately desire (and it usually does), then they continue using such inappropriate strategies as their chief mode of interacting with others.

IMPROVING A CHILD'S SELF-ESTEEM IN THE CLASSROOM

You and your coworkers must try to bring about a change in these children's view of themselves. You may not be able to influence the way they are treated at home, but you can make a difference in the classroom. How do you go about it?

Acceptance

First of all, *you must accept the child unconditionally just as he or she is now.* This child is not bad. Her actions may not be appropriate, but you can help her to change her actions once she knows that you and your coworkers accept her unconditionally. How can you let her know how you feel?

To begin with, you must truly accept the child deep within your own heart, not simply with lip service. If you do not truly accept the child, she will soon pick up your feelings. Children read nonverbal cues better than most adults. You may admit that you truthfully cannot like this child as she is. She may be poorly dressed, mean-looking, behave badly, and have a negative attitude that sets you on edge. You just cannot like her, you think to yourself. Every time she makes another child cry, she reinforces your negative opinion of her. Liking this child is not what is being asked of you, but you are being asked to accept her unconditionally *whether you like her or not.* Accepting is different from liking. Accepting gives a positive feeling within yourself, not a judgment.

As a professional early childhood staff member, you must make this the first part of a two-part commitment if you plan to continue in this profession: to accept the children in your class the way they are. They may not all look nice or act nicely. They may come from a different social status or culture than your own. Some may have physical or emotional impairments. Some may not like you. No matter. Your first professional duty is to accept all of the children unconditionally. The second part of your commitment is of equal importance: to work with each child, helping each to grow and learn to the best of his or her ability. Once you have made this commitment to accept the attention-provoking child, you can take the next step to help her improve self-esteem.

Nonverbal Cues

Next, you must *show the child that you accept him or her through nonverbal cues.* Nonverbal cues may be facial expressions, such as eye contact, smiles, laughs, twinkling eyes, looks of delight, or winks; head position, such as cocking, jutting the chin forward, or lifting the chin; and other body language, such as coming close, bending over, squatting, nodding, touching, hugging, clapping, shaking hands, blowing kisses, or making victory signs. Even your tone of voice is a nonverbal cue:

> *Children understand how you feel about them by the*
> *way you act toward them rather than by what you*
> *say. Your tone of voice, for instance, conveys as*
> *much or more meaning than your words. How do*
> *you sound to the child you seem to have trouble*
> *accepting totally? Switch on your tape recorder*
> *when you are in an activity area with the child.*
> *After class, play back the tape and listen to yourself.*
> *(Beaty, 1992, p. 173)*

If you do not like the way you sound, practice sounding differently until you get it right.

Being close to the child and touching him give especially important nonverbal cues of acceptance to preschool children. How do you express affection? A hug, a hand on the shoulder, or an arm around the waist say more to a child than any words can express. Perhaps no one has shown love and affection to this attention-grabbing child before. No wonder he does not feel good about himself. No wonder he uses inappropriate means to get your attention. Love and affection are as important as food to a growing child. Be sure you include a rich diet of each for all of the children in your class.

> *Do not allow the current exaggerated concern*
> *about "good touches and bad touches" to alter your*
> *display of affection toward your children. Your*
> *"good touches" are necessary for the growth of a*
> *positive self-concept in your children. (Beaty,*
> *1992, p. 173)*

Camras (1980, p. 884) reports in *Children's Understanding of Facial Expressions Used During Conflict Encounters* that "children can accurately decode facial expressions which are used during conflict encounters." Young children can interpret accurately such emotions as happiness, sadness, anger, and fear when they see them expressed on the face of another child. This ability helps them to feel what the other child is feeling during conflict, in other words, to empathize or to feel "other-esteem" for another child.

Children, unlike many adults, do not hide their emotions. Happiness or sadness spreads across their faces for all the world to see. What about you? You need to remove your expressions of frustration or anger toward a child, and let your positive feelings shine through. Is your face really in tune with your words? It is your expression that children read best of all. Mark Twain (1990) knew what he was talking about when he said: "Words are only painted fire; a look is the fire itself."

Smiles

How does your face look to an out-of-control child? Before you intervene in a conflict situation, take a moment to look in the full-length mirror that should be in the Dramatic Play Center. Does your face show tension? Are your eyes glaring? Are your eyebrows knitted? Are your teeth clenched? Is this really how you feel? Take another moment to calm down and center yourself. Take a deep breath and let it out slowly. Smile at yourself in the mirror. Be prepared to smile at the children in conflict. Now you are ready to be a conflict transformer!

Nonverbal cues such as smiles are *so* important in the early childhood classroom. All of the staff members should smile because they enjoy themselves and the children. All of the children should smile because their teachers are smiling and because they feel happy. Smiles are so easy to produce and so powerful in their positive impact. Check out your own children and your coworkers. Do you see as many smiles as you should? If not, do not go around criticizing anyone, which will not create smiles. Instead, do some creative, fun, outlandish things to produce smiles in others.

For instance, make a funny face. Put on a funny hat and go waltzing around the classroom until someone notices. Then put the hat on that person and get another one for yourself. You should have a whole collection of funny party hats for just such occasions. If you do not, bring in some paper bags to fit on top of heads like a hat and paint funny, smiling faces on them with the children. Create a "tunnel of smiles" with a large cardboard carton. Cut out an entrance and exit to this "tunnel" and draw frowning faces at the entrance and smiling faces at the exit. Have the children crawl through and come out smiling. Wear a hand puppet and regulate its mouth by turning the corners down and up. Show children that the puppet feels sad with its mouth turned down. Ask them to make the puppet smile. What can they do? Tell a joke. Sing a song. What about smiling at the puppet?

No matter what happens, young children are wonderfully exhilarating to be with, even those in conflict. If you do not have fun teaching preschool children and you cannot seem to change this feeling, perhaps you should consider changing your career. Not everyone is suited to teaching. Young children deserve to have happy, smiling teachers around them as behavior models, so that they, too, can develop this positive feeling about themselves.

Young children deserve happy, smiling teachers around them as behavior models.

Success

The third thing necessary to support a child's development of self-esteem is *setting up the classroom and its activities so that the child can experience success.* Children need to experience success many times over in order to feel good about themselves. Look around your classroom. Have you arranged the learning centers so that children can use them effectively? Have you put toys and materials on low shelves for easy access by children? Do you have enough materials for everyone? Are they appropriate for the children's developmental levels? For instance, do you have a range of children's puzzles from simple to complex?

Watch and see how the attention-grabbing child plays with materials. If he does not stay with one activity long enough to complete it, he will never experience success. Sit with him at a table and have fun making a puzzle with him. See if he can remake it on his own when you are finished. Congratulate him if he does. How do you congratulate your children? Do something different. Make a fuss, clap your hands, stand up and twirl around, do a "high five" with the child or blow kisses. Children should enjoy themselves in your classroom, and you should enjoy yourself. Make it a fun place to be!

There are many other ways to encourage success among children with poor self-esteem. Invite them to tape-record their names, addresses, and something they like to do. Then play it back. Congratulate them for making the tape. Arrange for them to do some of the activities they like. What other ways can you think of for children to experience success in your classroom? Be sure to congratulate them when they can finally convert their conflicts with other children into positive feelings. That is a success worth crowing about! Thank them when their number of attention-getting conflicts has diminished. That will truly tell you their self-images have improved.

 FIGURE 3.1

Improving a Child's Self-Esteem in the Classroom

1. Accept the child unconditionally.
2. Show your acceptance through nonverbal cues such as smiles.
3. Set up the classroom activities for the child to experience success.

DEVELOPING EMPATHY AND "OTHER-ESTEEM" IN EARLY CHILDHOOD

In addition to feeling good about herself, the attention-grabbing child also needs to learn how others feel when they are the victims of her inappropriate actions. We call this feeling "other-esteem," an important but often neglected balance to the emphasis in our society towards promoting "self-esteem" in individuals. (Gilchrist, 1993)

Many caregivers have done an exceptional job of promoting self-esteem in their children. Children with a poor self-image have improved dramatically through early intervention programs such as Head Start. But few early childhood programs give the same kind of attention to the other side of the coin, that is, the development of an awareness in children of how other people feel when someone does something negative to them. In our concern to help children feel good about themselves, we seem to have neglected the development of this equally important sensitivity. Thus, many children do not seem aware that their aggressive or disruptive acts have caused bad feelings in another child until the other child or the teacher points this out. This book bases its conflict-conversion technique on the development of this "other-esteem" in preschool children.

The attention-seeking children discussed in this and following chapters can actually learn such empathy. In order to convert their conflicts to positive feelings, these children need to be able to feel the way the other child feels, to experience *other-esteem*. Both *other-esteem* and *self-esteem* must be equally developed to achieve balance in a human being. Not all humans express other-esteem. Perhaps they were never encouraged to develop and practice it in their early years.

Our society must change its priorities. Its one-sided focus on promoting the self-esteem of individuals must be broadened to include the development of other-esteem. The place to start is with our children.

To understand the development of such empathy in early childhood, we need to look at a youngster's ability to see and feel things from another child's perspective. We know that even toddlers can take another person's point of view when they dress up and play the roles of a mother, a father, or a doctor in the classroom dramatic play area. But what does this really mean as far as their understanding of another's feelings? A great deal of child development research has, in fact, looked at such perspective-taking, (that is, the *cognitive* ability to understand how other people think and feel). Researcher Hoffman (1982, p. 23) found:

> with the beginning of a role-taking capability, at
> about 2 or 3 years, children become aware that
> other people's feelings may sometimes differ from
> theirs, and their perspectives are based on their
> own needs and interpretations of events. More
> important, because children now know that the
> real world and their perceptions of it are not the
> same thing, and that the feelings of others are
> independent of their own, they become more
> responsive to cues about what the other is feeling.

Many studies of children's perspective-taking abilities have been done through interviews with classroom youngsters who are presented with stories or pictures of interpersonal dilemmas, and then asked to answer questions about the conflicts from different points of view. From such studies Selman (1980, 1981) identified five levels of social perspectives. The three that pertain to young children are:

<u>Level 0: Egocentric or Undifferentiated Perspective (3–7 years)</u> Children can recognize thoughts and feelings within themselves and others, but can't distinguish between theirs and the others.

<u>Level 1: Differentiated Perspectives (4–9 years)</u> Children recognize that others' thoughts and feelings might be different from theirs; that two people might react differently to the same situation.

<u>Level 2: Reciprocal Perspectives (6–12 years)</u> Children learn that they can be the object of others' thoughts and they become concerned as to whether they are liked by others.

Although Selman believes that most preschool and early elementary children function at Level 0, we realize that children's actions are different from their words. Researchers who look at children in natural settings thus report that preschoolers in real classroom situations actually seem to "tune in" to others' perspectives more than they do to questions about hypothetical situations (Lee, 1989).

Actually, a high functioning level for children aged three to five years does not consist of their cognitive reasoning about feelings, but their actual use of feelings. They live at more of an emotional level during these years than at any other time of their lives. They know how they feel and how the other child feels, although they cannot always put the feelings into words because of their limited verbal skills. As Ramsey (1991, p. 18) notes:

> *Because even very young children resonate to others' emotions, children can empathize and communicate on an emotional plane before they are consciously aware of others' perspectives.*

This is what we ask children to do in our conflict-conversion activities: *resonate to the other child's emotions.* Thus, the teacher who asks children in conflict to respond to Question #2, "How does the other child feel?" can expect to get an answer that is quite accurate. Even children who are unable to respond to this question know how they themselves feel about the situation. The other child may very well feel as bad as they do. As they begin to understand that the other child has feelings, too, then the idea of empathy, that is, other-esteem, can start to grow within them.

As they listen to the other child in the conflict also respond to the same feelings question, these instigators of conflicts will hear how the other child describes their (that is, the instigator's) feelings. "Yes, that's how I felt." If the child got it wrong, the instigator can set him straight. Thus, each child learns more and more about tuning in to empathy, and so does the teacher.

You can help children tune in to the other's feelings by directing them to *feel* the way the other child feels, rather than to *think* about how she feels. Emotions are not a cognitive function. A child learns how another child feels by observing her reactions to the situation, by interpreting what her facial expression says, and by actually feeling within herself how the other child feels.

We talk about gut-level feelings, which refers to the fact that we do not have our feeling center in our head, but in our mid-section, in our solar plexus. Just as adults do, children can feel "a knot in the stomach" when they get angry. Children need us as conflict transformers to help them focus on feelings rather than on thoughts. To do so, we can use Conflict-Conversion Question #2 to ask how the other child feels. When children understand that other-esteem interests the teacher most, they will begin to tune in to the other child's emotions.

FIGURE 3.2

Improving a Child's Other-Esteem in the Classroom

1. Ask the child how the other child in the conflict feels.
2. Ask the child to look at the expression on the other child's face and listen to her words.
3. Ask the child to try to feel the way the other child feels.

TYPICAL ATTENTION-GETTING CONFLICT

Children who crave attention often try to get it in negative ways, as has been previously mentioned. They are not necessarily upset with another child in particular, but just have this strong need to make their presence felt. Some children ignore them, but if they try hard enough or long enough, they will usually find someone who will resist, and thus give them what they want, the teacher's attention or, more likely, her displeasure. Keep in mind the conflict-conversion questions the teacher will be using as you read the next case.

Conflict-Conversion Questions

1. What's happening, _____ (child's name)?
2. How does _____ (other child) feel?
3. What will make him (or her) feel better?

#3 The Case of the Bothersome Child

Setting: During the Free Choice period most of the children are occupied, but four-year-old Frankie cruises around as usual bothering everyone. He puts his hand right in the middle of Tracy's finger painting, but quickly moves away before she can respond. He bumps into Daniel (on purpose?), who is painting at an easel, making him splotch his painting. He takes one of Corey's miniature cars and quickly puts it in his pocket, but Corey doesn't see this, so he drops it on the floor. Then he gives one of the riding trucks a hard shove across the floor so that it crashes into Alex's block structure, knocking it down. Feisty little Alex hops up, rushes over to Frankie and tackles him to the floor before he can get away. Frankie screams, and the adult volunteer worker comes over. Everyone has gone through this scene with Frankie before. The volunteer who has learned how to be a "conflict transformer," first shoos away the onlookers who have gathered so that she can talk to the boys without interference. Then she knows enough to address Alex, the original victim, first.

Volunteer: *What's happening here, Alex?*

Alex: *Frankie knocked my building down, so I mashed him.*

Frankie: *He didn't mash me! He couldn't mash me!*

Volunteer: *What's happening here, Frankie?*

Frankie: *His building was in the way of my truck. So it got knocked down.*

Alex: *He did it on purpose. He's always doing things like that!*

Frankie: *I am not!*

Volunteer: *All right. Never mind that. What I asked you was: what's going on? And, Alex, you said that Frankie knocked your building down and you mashed him. And Frankie, you said Alex's building got knocked down by your truck. Now, Frankie, tell me this. How does Alex feel about his building getting knocked down?*

Frankie: *I don't know.*

Volunteer: *Look at his face, Frankie. Does his face tell you how he feels?*

Frankie: *I guess he feels mad.* (Alex nods yes.)

Volunteer: *Okay. You say you guess he feels mad. And what about you, Alex…* (Alex interrupts.)

Alex: *I did feel mad. And I still feel mad.*

Volunteer: *I hear what you say, Alex. But what I also want to know is, how Frankie felt when you mashed him?*

Alex: (shrugs) *I guess it hurt him, 'cause he screamed. But it served him right.*

Volunteer: *Well, we're talking about feelings right now, and Frankie says you felt mad, Alex, because his truck knocked down your building. You say Frankie felt hurt because you mashed him and knocked him down. So it seems to me that you both don't feel very good about all this. Frankie, what do you think would make Alex feel better?*

Frankie: *If his building was back up?*

Volunteer: *Alex, Frankie says you might feel better if your building was back up. Would you?* (Alex nods yes) *And, Alex, what do you think would make Frankie feel better?*

Alex: *He never feels better!*

Volunteer: *Well, think of how he could feel better. You might be surprised.*

Alex: *Well, if he would help me build up the building again.*

Volunteer: *Is that right, Frankie? Would you feel better if you helped Alex build up his building again?* (Frankie nods yes.) *Okay, so you're both going to help each other feel better by building up that building again, okay? Good, then let's shake on it. Boys, I'm really glad we talked about this. It's good that you know how other people feel when things happen to them. Then, maybe they won't happen again. I want to see that building when it's done. Maybe we can get a picture of it. Okay?*

Positive-Feelings Activity: Before the end of the class, the teacher calls everyone together for this activity. She wants the whole class to hear this because they have all had run-ins with Frankie. She turns the meeting over to the volunteer, who asks Alex and Frankie to explain how they helped each other feel better after the building got knocked down. Then the teacher reads the book *The Grouchy Ladybug* about a ladybug that goes around trying to pick a fight with everyone for no apparent reason. Afterward, the children join in trying to figure out why the ladybug wanted to fight in the first place. Someone says maybe it got spanked at home. The teacher agrees that sometimes people do things that other people don't like because they feel bad inside from something that happened to them. If the teacher had not had a story to read about negative attention getting, she could have used two animal hand puppets to demonstrate the concept.

HELPING ATTENTION SEEKERS BECOME OCCUPIED

The teacher who had been observing what was happening with Frankie, and later saw how easily he played with Alex in rebuilding the block structure, decided after this latest incident to have a group meeting just before Free Choice every day. She would go around to each of the children, asking them to choose an activity and go directly to the activity they had chosen. She would call attention to Frankie in a positive way by saying how well he had played with Alex in the block area yesterday. Then she would ask Frankie to choose an activity (after a number of children had chosen their areas but none of the areas was full), letting Frankie look over what everyone else had chosen and go with someone he really wanted to play with.

By getting Frankie occupied at the outset, she could avert his usual attention-getting destruction. Then she would be sure to praise him for whatever activity he engaged in during that Free Choice period. She shared these ideas with her staff during their weekly planning session. They quickly decided to try warding off Frankie's destructive forays rather than dealing with them afterward. They also decided to use more nonverbal cues, such as smiles, around Frankie to show him they really accepted him.

The volunteer pointed out that Frankie did seem to be able to "read" Alex's mad feelings by looking at his angry face, and that he also showed empathy because he knew immediately what would make Alex feel better. She passed around the instant-print photo she had taken of Frankie and Alex standing next to their rebuilt block building, both with big smiles on their faces. Afterward the other staff resolved to try the conflict-conversion strategy themselves the next time Frankie called attention to himself in an inappropriate manner. The assistant teacher later said she finally realized that Frankie was not being a bad child when he disrupted the play of others—he just needed loving.

After this planning session discussion the head teacher realized that she could only convince the staff to use conflict-conversion techniques by reminding them when children were actually in the midst of conflict. Talking about using these new conflict-conversion ideas made a good start, but putting the new and different ideas into practice in the classroom took courage.

The volunteer had tried first. She and the teacher had talked about Frankie, and the volunteer had offered to try out the new conflict-conversion strategy the next time Frankie caused trouble. When Alex tackled Frankie, the teacher reminded her to try it. They both were delighted over how well conflict conversion worked. The teacher thanked the volunteer for showing all of them that it could be done. Actual children's conflicts could really be converted to positive feelings! She also thanked the assistant teacher for revealing her insight about Frankie—that he just needed loving. You and your coworkers can use some of these strategies to help decrease attention-getting struggles in your classroom: first, by improving the self-esteem of the attention-seeking child through acceptance, positive nonverbal cues, and promotion of his or her success; then, by helping the child to develop other-esteem by calling his or her attention to the feelings of others; and, finally, by helping the child to become occupied in the activities of the classroom.

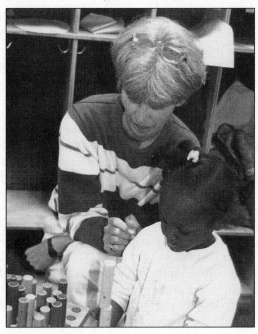

By getting children occupied at the outset, teachers can avert attention-getting conflicts.

 FIGURE 3.3

Decreasing Attention-Getting Struggles in the Classroom

1. Improve the self-esteem of the attention seeker through acceptance, nonverbal cues, and success.
2. Develop the child's other-esteem by calling attention to the feelings of others.
3. Help the attention seeker to become occupied.

IDEAS + IN CHAPTER 3

Attention-Getting Activities

1. Accept the attention-provoking child whether you like him or her or not.
2. Work with each individual child, helping all to grow and learn to the best of their abilities and yours.
3. Show the child you accept him or her through nonverbal cues.
4. Tape your voice and listen to how you sound.
5. Practice sounding different until you get it right.

6.   Express affection to the child by being close, and touching and hugging.
7.   The expression on your face should be in tune with your words.
8.   Look at your face in a mirror before intervening in a conflict.
9.   Do some creative, fun, outlandish things to induce smiles in others.
10. Use funny party hats to make smiles.
11. Create a "tunnel of smiles" with a cardboard carton.
12. Have the child make your hand puppet smile.
13. Set up the classroom so children can experience success.
14. Sit with the attention-grabbing child to help him finish a puzzle successfully.
15. Congratulate successful children with clapping, twirling, "high fives," or blowing kisses.
16. Have children tape record names, addresses, and something they like to do.
17. Help children tune in to feelings of others by directing them to feel the way the other child feels.
18. Have children observe the other child's reactions to the situation and interpret what their facial expression says.
19. Have a group meeting before the Free Choice period so that each child can select and go directly to the activity and person of his or her choice.

TRY IT YOURSELF

1.   What are some clues you have observed in a child's behavior that can mean he or she is struggling with self-esteem?
2.   What can you do about your attitude if you find a child to be repulsive to you? How can you accept her as she is? Try it and see how it works.
3.   Describe three activities that would help a child develop other- esteem in your classroom. Try one and discuss results.
4.   In "The Case of the Bothersome Child" why did the volunteer ask each child to describe the conflict? What would you have done?
5.   Do you agree with the teacher's decision to call attention to Frankie in a positive way? How would you do it?

REFERENCES CITED

Beaty, J. J. (1992). *Skills for preschool teachers.* New York: Merrill/Macmillan.

Camras, L. A. (1980). Children's understanding of facial expressions used during conflict encounters. *Child Development, 51,* 879–885.

Gilchrist, M. A. (1993). Other-esteem, society's missing link, (unpublished manuscript).

Hoffman, M. L. (1982). Development of prosocial motivation: Empathy and guilt. In N. Eisenberg, (Ed.), *The Development of Prosocial Behavior.* New York: Academic Press.

Lee, P. (1989). Is the young child egocentric or sociocentric? *Teachers College Record, 90,* 375–391.

May, R. (1972). *Power and influence.* New York: W. W. Norton.

Ramsey, P. G. (1991). *Making friends in school: Promoting peer relationships in early childhood.* New York: Teachers College Press.

Selman, R. (1980). *The growth of interpersonal understanding.* New York: Academic Press.

Selman, R. (1981). The child as a friendship philosopher. In S. R. Asher & J. M. Gottman (Eds.), *The Development of Children's Friendships.* New York: Cambridge University Press.

Smith, C. A. (1982). *Promoting the social development of young children: Strategies and activities.* Palo Alto, CA: Mayfield Publishing Co.

Twain, Mark (1990). *The wit and wisdom of Mark Twain.* Philadelphia, PA: Running Press.

OTHER SOURCES

Camras, L. A. (1977). Facial expressions used by children in a conflict situation. *Child Development, 48,* 1431–1435.

Eisenberg, N. (1992). *The caring child.* Cambridge: Harvard University Press.

Eisenberg, N. & Miller, P. A. (1987). The relation of empathy to prosocial and related behaviors, *Psychological Bulletin, 101*(1) 91–119.

Iannotti, R. J. (1985). Naturalistic and structured assessments of prosocial behavior in preschool children: The influence of empathy and perspective taking, *Developmental Psychology, 21* (1) 46–55.

CHILDREN'S BOOKS ABOUT ATTENTION GETTING

Alexander, M. (1988). *Even that moose won't listen to me.* New York: Dial Books.

Arnold, T. (1992). *The signmaker's assistant.* New York: Dial Books.

Carle, E. (1977). *The grouchy ladybug.* New York: Crowell.

Guilfoile, E. & Stevens, M. (Ill.) (1973). *Nobody listens to Andrew.* New York: Scholastic.

Keats, E. J. (1979). *Maggie and the pirate.* New York: Macmillan.

Lester, H. & Munsinger, L. (Ill.). (1992). *Me first.* Boston: Houghton Mifflin.

Schreier, J. (1993). *Hank's work.* New York: Dutton.

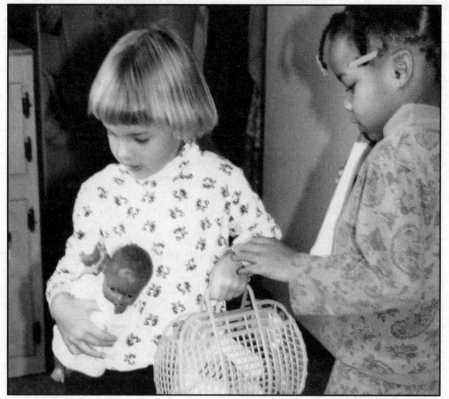

Who's in Charge?
(Power Struggles)

Analysis of the themes of young children's conflicts suggest that they fight over a number of the same things that adults do. They quarrel over space and resources and over more social issues, including the degree of control they have over their peers' activities. (Hay, 1984, p. 18)

POWER STRUGGLES IN THE EARLY CHILDHOOD CLASSROOM

As young children become accustomed to the early childhood classroom, their types of conflicts change somewhat. Instead of quarreling over the possession of objects, they shift to issues of control. Certain children want to be in charge of everything. They want the first turn, the biggest piece, and the best toy. They also may want to be in control of others. Other children should play the way they demand, should take the dramatic play roles they assign, or should stop doing what they are doing.

When their peers resist, these children find themselves involved in a power struggle. Shantz (1987, p. 287) finds that whereas the largest percentage of preschoolers' conflicts involves object possession, "the second largest category appears to be conflict over another child's actions or lack of action." Toddlers and young preschoolers argue mostly over objects, but Shantz (1987, p. 287) notes that a change takes place:

> *As children get older, an increasingly smaller pro-*
> *portion of the conflicts are about the physical envi-*
> *ronment (e.g., objects and space) and an*
> *increasingly larger proportion concern control of the*
> *"social environment."*

How is it in your classroom? If you take time to observe your children and tally their conflicts using the *Types of Classroom Conflicts* form (see Figure 2.1), you will have a better understanding of how your children interact with one another. Use the form at the beginning of the year and then later on. Do you also find a difference in the types of conflicts present later on? If you find that power struggles are indeed on the increase, then you will want to learn more about their causes and their prevention.

POWER AND POWERLESSNESS

Rollo May (1972, p. 20), in his discussion of the role of power in human relationships, views power quite differently than most people:

> *A great deal of human life can be seen as the conflict*
> *between power on one side (i.e., effective ways of*
> *influencing others, achieving the sense in interper-*
> *sonal relations of the significance of one's self) and*
> *powerlessness on the other.*

Power should not be considered negative, he claims, because it differs from force or negative aggression. Power is the ability to make a difference, which is essential for all living things. The word *power* itself comes from the Latin *posse*, "to be able." All human beings, including little children, strive "to be able," to be significant as a person and to be able to make a difference. The struggle for self-esteem is the struggle for this type of positive power in a person's life.

Preschool children are caught up in the early stages of this development which starts at home. They are born as self-centered beings intent on surviving. They let everyone around them know their desires, with their cries for food, for attention, and for affection. If they can make a difference at home with their sounds and actions, then they begin to develop a feeling of their self-worth, of their importance as a person. Their expressions of *power to be* and *self-affirmation* as discussed in Chapter Three have been successful, and they feel good about themselves.

In a preschool classroom, they have a completely different environment from their homes. Do they have power here? Can they make a difference? Those children who have used their power at home to develop a positive self-image should have no trouble in the classroom. They will stand up for themselves and show pride in what they do in a manner acceptable to others. They may be assertive, but in a positive way.

Children who have been thwarted in their expressions of self-affirmation, however, develop in a different way. These children who may have been neglected, abused, or overindulged may not have developed a feeling of their power, their ability to make a difference. In fact, they may feel *powerless*. Some powerless children seem to withdraw into apathy. Others try to regain their sense of power by striking out against the world.

> *If his need for love and care is unmet, he may well become destructively aggressive and spend his life wreaking revenge upon the world.... Or if he has no boundaries, nothing against which to test his strength, no opposition in the firmness of parents, he may turn his aggression against himself in nail-biting and self-recrimination or senseless anger against anyone who happens to come along. (May, 1972, p. 124)*

A sense of powerlessness on the part of an individual creates power struggles in the preschool classroom, as well as in life itself. If children feel they have the power to make a difference, they no longer need to argue or fight for control over their peers. Preschool staff members can make a difference in the lives of children struggling for power and help them to regain a sense of control over something in the classroom.

REGAINING A SENSE OF POWER

Regaining a sense of power has to do with the ability to make a difference. What can a power-seeking child do in the preschool classroom to make a difference? Being in charge of something the child can feel joyful about can give a child this sense of power. Make a list of the activities in the classroom that a child can be placed in

*Putting a child in charge of something he can feel joyful
about gives him a sense of power.*

charge of. Start from the beginning of the day and go through the entire schedule.
Your list may include items such as those in Figure 4.1:

 FIGURE 4.1

Regaining Power by Being in Charge of a Classroom Task

Be in charge of taking attendance
Be in charge of the guinea pig
Be in charge of setting up easels and paints
Be in charge of giving out Learning Center tags
Be in charge of getting mail from the office
Make paper bag puppets for book characters
Prepare egg carton display boxes for the Science Center
Make rhythm instruments for the Music Center

Be in charge of helping others tape record stories
Be in charge of signing out books to take home
Be in charge of name tags for snack, lunch, or activities
Be in charge of sign-up clipboards for the riding vehicle
Be in charge of the kitchen timer for turn taking

First, you must accept the power-seeking children and show your acceptance with nonverbal cues as discussed in Chapter Three. Then get to know them well enough to recognize their likes and dislikes. In order to have the youngsters in charge of something, you need to know what they will feel good about doing. A child who talks about animals or seems to enjoy animal stories, for example, can be in charge of the guinea pig for a week or so at a time. Talk with her about the task. If she agrees to take it on, make a badge for her to wear with a guinea pig symbol on it. She will need to put clean newspapers in the animal's cage every morning, and to fill its water and food containers. She can get lettuce from the refrigerator from time to time. She may want to carry the animal over to the Block Center, build an enclosure for it, and take a picture with the instant-print camera. If her interest in the guinea pig continues, she may want to read the book *Guinea Pigs Far and Near* (Duke, 1984), or tape record her own story about guinea pigs on the cassette recorder.

Be sure that these tasks are not merely routines but real services for the classroom. They should also be fun for the child and satisfy his craving to be in charge. A child who shows an interest in science may like to be in charge of preparing egg carton display boxes for the Science Center. Have him choose one or two other children to help him. He will need to collect the empty egg cartons from his classmates when they bring them from home. Then he and his "crew" can cut the tops off the cartons and paint the divided sections. Peel-off stickers can be put on the different sections when the paint is dry, and transparent food wrapping can be prepared for covering their tops when children's collections of nuts, pine cones, seashells, stones, seeds, or little plastic dinosaurs are ready for display.

As long as a power-hungry child shows interest in his task, try to find ways to help him continue it. Ask what other kinds of containers he and his crew would like to prepare. They could collect margarine cups and color code them to make sorting games for miniature plastic items. Then, they also could decorate empty shoe boxes to store the games.

Watch and see how the child in charge works with his partners. If he tries to take control in a harsh or dictatorial manner, you can talk with him about how he thinks the other children feel when he orders them around like that. Can he say the same thing in a way that will make them feel good about doing it? What about his tone of voice and his facial features? Put a stand-up mirror in the area where he is working and have him glance at it when he is giving orders. Make it fun for him, not a punishment. Would he like to take an instant print of himself in the mirror, making a gruff face and a smiling face?

Can putting children in charge like this really make them feel more powerful? The answer is yes. One reason is that you, a powerful adult, have turned over some of your power to them. You easily could have stayed in charge of any of the tasks mentioned. However, you turned control over to them. They may not be able to articulate their feelings of power, but deep inside they know. Be sure, then, that they truly are in charge, and that you do not have them perform the task your way. Then observe what happens with these children at other times. If their sense of being able to make a difference is strong enough, they should stop doing unkind things to others. As Stubbs remarks:

> *Every unkind or harmful act committed on the*
> *planet has been done by someone who felt power-*
> *less in some way, and the stronger the feeling of*
> *powerlessness, the greater the unkindness or harm*
> *in the act. (Stubbs, 1992, p. 74)*

RESISTING POWER SEEKERS

Children who give in too easily to their power-seeking peers only encourage them to keep using their assertive tactics. If the strategy works, power seekers will continue using it. If threat, aggression, or even violence gets them their own way, then they often adopt it as their principal method of operation. They may have learned it inadvertently at home. Children who cry, scream, or make threats against their parents or adult caregivers sometimes end up getting their own way. If this happens often enough, these children may adopt such a strategy against others, especially peers.

Screaming for power or seizing it by force from someone else does not make a person powerful. Only a powerless person uses such tactics, and in the end, he remains powerless. A person cannot gain real power by taking it forcefully from someone else, only by receiving it naturally because he is worthy of it. All your children are worthy, whether they know it or not. You should help them all to *feel* worthy. Then they will feel powerful and will no longer need to struggle for power.

However, if certain children in your class always yield to the "bullies" without any resistance, they are encouraging them to continue using such tactics. Thus, a second way you can reduce power struggles in the classroom is to help these nonresistant children stand up to their oppressors. Observe what kinds of behavior such pliant children demonstrate when aggressive children impose on them. Many victims of overbearing peers simply give in or give up without a word. Some merely mutter "No," without much conviction. Had they said "No" firmly and given a reason for saying it, the results might have been entirely different, according to current research. Ramsey (1991, p. 35) mentions several different kinds of opposition that children make to the demands of a control-seeking child:

1. A simple "no"
2. A reason for opposing ("I'm using it now.")
3. A counterproposal (offers a substitute)
4. A temporizing move ("You can have it in five minutes.")
5. An evasion (directs the opponent to another activity)

A simple "no" on the part of the child being challenged does not usually work. However, several researchers have found that *giving a reason for opposing the challenge* seems to work best in preventing the antagonist from getting his way. As Ramsey points out: "The second type was most frequently used by children in both preschool and early elementary school, suggesting that these children have learned that refusals must be bolstered by reasons in order to be effective" (Ramsey, 1991, p. 35).

Listen to the children who are being imposed upon. How do they respond to the antagonist? If they simply give in or say only "No" without giving a reason, you can help them become better resisters of their power-seeking peers. Talk with them about what you have observed. Say to Cindy that you noticed Greta always takes Cindy's toys or pushes ahead of her when they are in line. Ask Cindy if she would like to learn a simple way to stop Greta.

Some children just do not know how to control their assertive peers. They have not picked up the strategies that others use successfully. You may have to coach

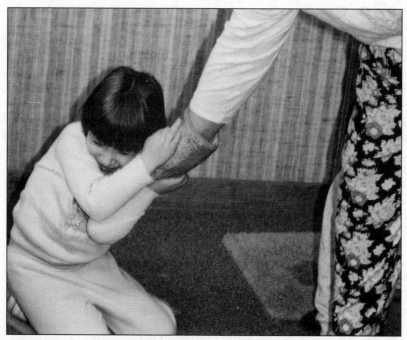

You may have to coach a child directly on how to resist assertive peers by using hand puppets.

such children. Do a little role play with Cindy and two hand puppets. Have Cindy pretend to be Greta and you take Cindy's role. Show Cindy that Greta will back off if Cindy *gives a reason for saying no.* Then switch puppets and let Cindy try this herself. Play the roles several times. The next time the real conflict happens, support Cindy when she gives Greta a reason for her refusal. When you note that Cindy can finally stand up for herself on her own, congratulate her with a hug or handshake and be sure to give her a big smile.

Cindy may also be a child who feels powerless. Rather than trying to gain power in the classroom by controlling others, she may be the type of powerless youngster who withdraws into herself and allows herself to be pushed around by more assertive peers. Try helping her regain a feeling of power and self-worth by putting her in charge of an activity that sparks her interest.

OVERCOMING THE FEAR OF BULLIES

On the other hand, some children allow others to dominate them because they are afraid to resist. Fear can be a very powerful emotion. Many fears of young children (and of all of us) have no rational basis. Nevertheless, they feel very real. Children who bully readily tune in to the fears of timid youngsters. Such aggressors seem to know instinctively whom to pick on and which ones will not resist their strong-arm tactics. Such encounters may never develop into overt conflicts because the fearful child gives in immediately. Nevertheless, timid children also need help in learning to convert their fears into positive feelings. How can you help such children stand up to a bully?

If you have noticed such vulnerable children in your class, you can help them by working with them one-on-one before another strong-arm encounter occurs. For example, read a story to the child one-on-one and then discuss how the main character overcame a powerful bully. Stock your library with some of the picture books that feature the overcoming of fear listed at the end of the chapter, and read one to the timid child at an appropriate time before a conflict ensues. In these books the characters overcome their fear of bullies in the ways listed below.

 FIGURE 4.2

Book Characters' Methods for Overcoming Fear of Bullies

1. Playing the banza (banjo) with a heart on it because there is no stronger protection than the heart (*The Banza*).
2. Playing a trick on the big boys. (*Goggles*).
3. Tricking the Skog monster with a kite (*The Island of the Skog*).
4. Revealing fear about a bully to a friend (*Loudmouth George and the Sixth-Grade Bully*).

5. Roaring to scare the bullies (*Monster Mama*).
6. Playing a trick on the Big Bad Wolf by making stone soup (*Stone Soup*).
7. Playing a trick on the hunters by pretending to be tacky, not neat (*Tacky the Penguin*).
8. Playing a trick by relying on a brother (*The Three Billy Goats Gruff; The Seven Chinese Brothers*).
9. Building up his body to scare the urban gorillas (*Willy the Wimp*).
10. Pretending to be a spitting cobra to scare the terrible "Long One" who is actually a little green caterpillar (*Who's in Rabbit's House?*).
11. Snatching the fire from the crocodile (*Rainbow Bird*).

Most of these weaker characters ward off their stronger opponents by trickery, getting help, making a sound, playing an instrument, or pretending. Can your timid children do the same? Preschool children pretend very well. Have them pretend to be brave. Can they close their eyes and imagine they are strong and fearless? Perhaps they can picture themselves as a powerful animal. Do a role play with them in which you pretend to be a bully trying to control them. Ask them how they feel when they pretend to be brave. Then have them respond to your commands by saying "no" firmly and giving a reason.

Ask timid children what they do to overcome other fears, such as being afraid of the dark. Do they sing or whistle? Anna, the main character in the film *The King and I*, whistles a happy tune so no one will suspect she is afraid. She whistles to fool the people she fears, and at the same time fool herself. She tells the children in the film that you can be as brave as you make believe you are. Can your timid children make believe they are brave by whistling, singing, or humming a happy tune? Have them try it.

An older child in one class tried making the boy that always picked on her feel good himself. She said that she felt good when the sun was shining on her, so she tried to imagine that the sun shone on him whenever he came around. She also smiled at him, no matter how inappropriately he acted. Her mother taught her this trick, which usually brought good results. Young children who love to make believe should have no trouble pretending about the warm rays of the sun shining on someone. If they use smiles as well, they may soon trick themselves into feeling powerful rather than like a victim. This can defuse the actions of their antagonist, too. What strategies have you used to make yourself feel invincible?

SERVING AS A POSITIVE ROLE MODEL IN THE USE OF POWER

How do you and your own use of power come across to the children in the classroom? Obviously, as an adult you have more power than they do. How do you use it? Or, as psychologist Rollo May might ask, what kind of power do you use? He specifies five different kinds of power that most people use at one time or another:

1. Exploitive
2. Manipulative
3. Competitive
4. Nutrient
5. Integrative

(May, 1972, pp. 105–109)

Exploitive Power

Power in its simplest and yet most destructive form forces another person into subjugation: this is exploitive power. Some of your powerless children use this type of power to control their peers. Exploitive power has been used by dictators and ruthless companies to exploit their subjects or their employees. As a role model for your children, you must avoid using this type of power yourself.

Certainly I am not exploiting the children in my class, you may loudly protest! For most teachers of preschool children that is undeniably true. Nevertheless, teachers who order children around, or who make children obey simply because they are little, are using exploitive power. This type of control yields little pleasure either for the teacher or the children. Young children usually resist direct orders, which upsets teachers and makes them even more insistent. Instead, both teachers and children should interact with willingness and joy. Preschoolers will do almost anything for the teacher who treats them with respect and good humor. Instead of ordering Jeff to pick up the blocks because he took them off the shelf, the wise teacher makes pickup a game. "I'm putting on your favorite tape, Jeff. Let's see if you can get the blocks back on the shelf before it finishes playing. Can you do it? Here goes!"

Children imitate the behavior of the adults around them. If you want to see what behavior model you present to your children, watch them closely and listen to how they talk. Can you hear and see yourself in their words and gestures? Do not give power-hungry children the model of an adult bully for them to copy. There are better ways to gain the children's cooperation.

Manipulative Power

This second type of power also involves power over another person, but it is subtle. Persons use manipulation sometimes without realizing what is happening. Adults can easily manipulate children, especially young children. However, it is just as destructive as exploitive power. Adults who choose to work in early childhood classrooms because of the affection they receive from the children may be involved in a manipulative power game.

Young children are exciting to be around. They are so alive, exuberant, and delightful to work with. Most teachers enjoy being showered with the affection the youngsters show them. In return they give themselves to the children just as generously with warmth, devotion, and the strenuous work of managing a class of lively youngsters. These teachers do not use manipulative power.

However, some adult classroom workers take more than they give to children, possibly without even realizing it. Their own chaotic, often loveless lives may have only one bright spot: their work with the children and the affection the children give them. As a result they may lavish affection on one special child just to flatter him and bring him closer. Actually, such teachers are using a subtle form of manipulation.

Creating such a teacher's pet always involves the danger of delivering unspoken messages to the other children: 1) they are not as good as the chosen one because they were not chosen, and 2) if they act toward the teacher like the chosen one does, maybe she will choose them, too. Children should not give you their affection for this reason. Working with preschool children takes a tremendous amount of stamina and dedication. If you are not prepared to give children much more than you will ever receive from them, then the field of early childhood education may not be for you. You may first need to get your own life in order so that you will be able to give more of yourself to the children, and not just take affection from them through manipulation.

Competitive Power

The third power category, competitive power, uses power *against* another person, rather than *over* another. Although older children and adults often enjoy competitive games and activities, this type of power is inappropriate in preschools. You realize that a lighthearted rivalry among friends sometimes creates the best motivating force for stimulating people, but not with little people. Beware of using competition in your activities for preschoolers. Competition means that one person goes up because another person goes down.

Young children have not yet reached the cognitive understanding of such actions. They understand that people win games. They see it on television and hear about it in their families. They themselves expect to win. What they do not understand is losing. For preschoolers, to lose is a crushing blow. Games are more than just a diversion for preschoolers, they are life itself. Young children's work is play. They learn everything through playful exploration.

They are not yet old enough to learn appropriate lessons through losing. Losing makes a preschool child feel bad, unworthy, and totally powerless. Teachers who realize this do not use competitive games where someone wins and someone loses. Nor do they model competitive behavior themselves or even use the terminology of winning or losing. You will not hear such teachers asking "Who did the best?" or "Who's going to be first?" They understand, just as their children do, that these questions also mean someone is not the best and that someone may be last.

Nutrient Power

The fourth power category involves power *for* the other person, rather than power *over* or *against* another. Parents use this positive aspect of power to nurture their children, and teachers of preschool children exert it because they care for the welfare of their group. As a behavior model for the children in your class, you should be an expert in using nutrient power. The strategies you employ for managing individuals and groups of children should reflect your competence with this positive aspect of power.

Instead of sounding off across the entire room with: "Tammy, how many times have I told you not to take the baby dolls out of the housekeeping corner! You always scatter everything around!" (exploitive power), you can walk across the room and say quietly: "Oh, Tammy, I see you have the baby dolls out for a walk again. Where are they going? Don't forget how tired they get. They will want to be back in their bed in the housekeeping corner when they're finished" (nutrient power).

In this way you have affirmed that Tammy knows how to play with the dolls, that you enjoy pretending with her, too, and that she has a role in deciding how to carry out this play. She also understands what you expect her to do when she finishes playing. Using nutrient power like this works so much more effectively than using the exploitive power of ordering or scolding.

Listen to the adult voices in the classroom to hear how many of them express nutrient power. Tape record these positive voices. At the next planning session talk about expressing this kind of power and play the tape. Ask a pair of staff members to choose one of the power types and tape record a role play of themselves *pretending* to use such power. Then they can share the results at a planning session.

Integrative Power

The fifth and final power category involves power *with* another person. This power supplements and strengthens another person's power and leads to her growth. In using this power with children, the teacher looks for aspects of their development that need strengthening, rather than areas of weakness. Then she lends her support to their personal power in order to stimulate growth or change.

For example, the teacher might say to Vicente, who has scribbled all over the tabletop as well as on his paper, "Oh, Vicente, look how hard you worked on your drawing this morning! You really like to draw with crayons, don't you? You get so carried away that the crayons keep right on drawing even on the tabletop. Do you want to clean it up by yourself or shall I help you?" Such a comment is much more effective than a scolding and an order: "Vicente, look what you did again! You really messed up the table! Now clean it up!"

By using your nutrient power to help Vicente grow and change, you are complimenting his work, but also pointing out in a constructive manner that if crayon markings don't stay on the paper, then they need to be cleaned up, which you will help him to do. Children learn in this way. All Vicente would have learned from a scolding is that he doesn't know how to use crayons. Scribbling on the tabletop, whether done accidentally or deliberately, does not have the same meaning for children as it does for adults.

Preschoolers are in an experimenting, exploring, *processing* stage of development. That is what you should expect them to be doing in your program. Cleanup is not important to them, although it may be to you. If you understand that youngsters are not being *bad* when they scribble on the table, only experimental, then you will provide them with art materials that can be cleaned up easily and use your nutrient power to make cleanup fun.

Children can be reminded of the behavior limits you established at the outset, which include not harming themselves, other children, or materials. Tell Vicente matter-of-factly: "Remember how we talked about taking care of our desks and tables? Let's put down newspaper so your scribbles will not get on the tabletop."

A few of the methods for decreasing power struggles in your classroom are listed below.

 FIGURE 4.3

Decreasing Power Struggles in the Classroom

1. Help children regain a sense of power by being in charge of a meaningful classroom task.
2. Help vulnerable children to resist power-seeking peers by having them give a reason for opposing them.
3. Help vulnerable children overcome the fear of bullies by pretending to be brave.
4. Serve as a positive role model yourself in the use of power with children and adults.

TYPICAL POWER CONFLICT

Although you may reduce the number of power struggles in the classroom, you probably will not eliminate them. Remember that conflicts are not bad but simply are learning opportunities for you and the children. You would not want such opportunities eliminated completely. Otherwise, how would your children learn how to behave when power struggles occur in the outside world? They have come to your classroom to learn positive strategies for dealing with the problems that life may bring them. Power struggles are important learning occasions. Case #4 looks at a typical control conflict that occurs among preschool children. The questions you will be using include:

Conflict-Conversion Questions

1. What's happening _____ (child's name)?
2. How does _____ (other child) feel?
3. What will make him (or her) feel better?

#4. The Case of the Tricycle Takeover

Setting: Every day on the playground certain children fight over the center's one and only tricycle. The staff has tried a number of strategies to eliminate these conflicts, such as having a sign-up clipboard for taking turns or using a kitchen timer. That works for most of the children, but not always for Adam. Adam likes to throw his weight around by bossing certain children. When he sees George having fun or doing something different, he often interferes. In this case the teacher did not notice what was happening until he had knocked over the trike with George on it, and George was letting the world know about it by screaming. This was not a typical possession conflict but a true power struggle between Adam and George. The teacher hurried over to intervene, helping George get up. He did not seem to be hurt.

Teacher: *What's happening here, boys?*

George: (gasping for breath) *Adam... Adam... He pushed me over!*

Adam: *I did not. He fell over himself. I just gave the trike a push. He was trying to make it go, wasn't he?*

Teacher: *Okay. George, you say you got pushed over. And, Adam, you say you gave the trike a push and George fell over. We know George ended up on the ground. Adam, how does George feel about that?*

Adam: *It's not my fault that the trike fell over.*

Teacher: *Okay. I hear what you say. But what I am asking you is how does George feel about it? Look at his face. How does he feel, Adam?*

Adam: *He looks like he feels bad.* (George scrunches up his face as if to cry again.)

Teacher: *Okay. You say he looks like he feels bad.* (George relaxes his face a little.) *Do you feel bad, George?* (George nods yes.) *And, George, how does Adam feel about it?* (no answer from George) *George, look at Adam's face. How does he feel about it?*

George: *Nothing happened to him. He did it!*

Teacher: *I hear what you say, George. But how does Adam feel about it? Look at his face. How does he feel?*

George: (looks at ground and mumbles) *I bet he feels glad.*

Teacher: *Look at his face, George. Does he look glad?* (George looks up and shakes his head no.) *How does he feel?*

George: *Maybe he feels ... bad.*

Teacher: *George says maybe you feel bad, Adam. Do you?* (Adam nods his head yes.) *Well, okay. So George feels bad and Adam feels bad. I can understand why. It doesn't feel nice to fall on the ground or to push somebody and have them fall. Well, Adam, what do you think would make George feel better?*

Adam: *I don't know. Maybe if I pushed him around slowly.*

Teacher: *Is that right, George. Would it make you feel better if Adam pushed you around slowly on the trike?* (George looks puzzled. Then he nods his head yes.) *Are you sure, George? Do you want Adam to push you?* (George nods yes) *Okay. Well, George, what do you think would make Adam feel better?*

George: *If I push him?*

Teacher: *If you push him? Would that make you feel better, Adam? If George pushes you on the trike?* (Adam nods.) *Okay. So, George, you're first on the trike and Adam is going to push you slowly. Once around the playground? Okay. Then it's Adam's turn, and you're going to push him once around the playground, George. Does that sound okay? Are you both feeling good? Okay, take it easy. No more spills. Thanks for working that one out, boys. You really can tell what makes someone feel better. How about a "high five" all around! Okay. Have a good time on the trike. Then it's going to be Nancy's turn.*

Positive-Feelings Activity: After the children come in from the playground, the teacher calls them all over to the library corner where she reads them the book *Andy (That's My Name)* about the little boy with his name standing up in big letters in his wagon. The big boys take over his wagon and his letters, and he gets pushed down. She asks the children how they feel Andy felt and how the big boys felt. Then she asks George and Adam to tell how they made each other feel better on the playground after George got pushed down. Finally, she scatters a large set of wooden alphabet letters on the rug and asks the children to see if they can find any of the letters in their names, like Andy did.

TEACHER'S ACTIONS, CASE #4

As is so often the case, the teacher did not really see what happened out on the playground: whether Adam deliberately pushed George over or whether he was pushing him on the trike and it fell over by accident. The teacher got involved when she heard George scream. In the end whose fault it is really does not make a difference because converting conflicts does not find fault or take blame, but teaches children how to empathize, how to feel the way the other person feels. We remember that:

> *People commit negative acts because they cannot*
> *feel the pain they cause others. (Clow, 1989, p. 67)*

As children learn other-esteem through conflicts like this, they really are able to convert them to positive feelings. This outcome surprised all three of the people involved in "The Case of the Tricycle Takeover." George felt good because the teacher recognized what happened to him. Adam felt good because he was not blamed as usual for his actions. And the teacher felt *super* because the two boys resolved a power struggle peacefully. As a result, she decided to leave the single trike on the playground in case other "golden opportunities" of conflict were waiting to happen!

If she had not possessed a book about conflict to read to the children, this teacher could have done a puppet play with two hand puppets, one on either hand, acting out a similar power struggle.

IDEAS + IN CHAPTER 4

Power Struggle Activities

1. Give the child a sense of power by being in charge of something he can feel joyful about.
2. Accept power-seeking children and show your acceptance with nonverbal cues.
3. Recognize the likes and dislikes of power-seeking children.
4. A child who enjoys animals can be in charge of the guinea pig.
5. Make a guinea pig badge for her to wear.
6. Be sure tasks are fun and not drudgery.
7. A child who enjoys science can prepare egg cartons for display boxes and margarine cups for sorting games.
8. Ask the child in charge to glance at himself in a mirror when he is giving orders.
9. Have the child take an instant photo of himself making gruff and smiling faces in a mirror.
10. Do not intervene in the child's task and have him do it your way.
11. Help nonresistant children stand up to their oppressors.

12.   Have them give a reason for opposing the challenge of an antagonist.
13.   Coach them on how to behave with a bully through a puppet role play.
14.   Congratulate the child when she finally stands up for herself.
15.   Read a story with a similar theme to a child who is being bullied.
16.   Have a child pretend to be brave in a role play with you.
17.   Have timid children whistle, sing, or hum a happy tune.
18.   Have children imagine the sun is shining on themselves and a bullying child.
19.   Have them use smiles to trick themselves into feeling powerful.
20.   Make pickup a game rather than a scolding time.
21.   Watch and listen to see if you can see and hear yourself reflected in the children.
22.   Do not use competitive games or the terminology of winning or losing.
23.   Listen and tape record adult classroom voices of examples of nutrient power.
24.   Tape record a pair of staff members role-playing one of the power types.
26.   Look for aspects of children's development that need strengthening, rather than areas of weakness.
27.   Provide art materials that can be cleaned up easily, and make cleanup fun.
28.   Create a puppet play about conflict using two hand puppets.

TRY IT YOURSELF

1.   Are there ways to empower a child that you have used or plan to use that are not mentioned in the text? Try one and describe the results.
2.   With the increasing problem with authority in our country today, how can you as a teacher or caregiver make a difference as an authority figure? Try it and report the results.
3.   Tape record an adult (teacher, caregiver or yourself) pretending to talk to a child in a way that illustrates exploitive power, competitive power, and nutrient power. Play the tape and see who can identify each power mode.
4.   Do you agree with the text that it did not make a difference who was at fault in "The Case of the Tricycle Takeover"? Why or why not? What would you do as a teacher? Try it in a power conflict and see how it works.
5.   What are three types of positive feelings activities dealing with aggression that you can use? Try one of them and discuss the results.

REFERENCES CITED

Clow, B. H. (1989). *Heart of the Christos.* Santa Fe, NM: Bear & Co.

Duke, K. (1984). *Guinea pigs far and near.* New York: E. P. Dutton.

Hay, D. F. (1984). Social conflict in early childhood. *Annals of Child Development, 1,* 1–44.

May, R. (1972). *Power and influence.* New York: W. W. Norton.

Ramsey, P. G. (1991). *Making friends in school: Promoting peer relationships in early child-hood.* New York: Teachers College Press.

Shantz, C. U. (1987). Conflicts between children. *Child Development, 58,* 283–305.

Stubbs, T. (1992). *An ascension handbook.* Livermore, CA: Oughten House Publications.

OTHER SOURCES

Jones, E. & Reynolds, G. (1992). *The play's the thing: Teachers' roles in children's play.* New York: Teachers College Press.

CHILDREN'S PICTURE BOOKS FEATURING OVERCOMING FEAR OF SOMEONE POWERFUL

Aardema, V., Dillon, D. (Ill.). & Dillon, L. (Ill.). (1977). *Who's in rabbit's house?* (1977) New York: Dial Books.

Bottner, B. & Rathmann, P. (Ill.). (1992). *Bootsie Barker bites.* New York: G. P. Putnam's Sons.

Browne, A. (1984). *Willy the wimp.* New York: Alfred A. Knopf.

Carlson, N, (1983). *Loudmouth George and the sixth-grade bully.* Minneapolis: Carolrhoda Books.

De paola, T. (1973). *Andy (that's my name).* Englewood Cliffs, NJ: Prentice-Hall.

Galdone, P. (1973). *The three billy goats gruff.* New York: Clarion Books.

Keats, E. J. (1969). *Goggles.* New York: Collier Books.

Kellogg, S. (1973). *The island of the Skog.* New York: Dial Books.

Lester, H. & Munsinger, L. (Ill.). (1988). *Tacky the penguin.* Boston: Houghton Mifflin.

Maddern, E. & Kennaway, A. (Ill.). (1993). *Rainbow bird.* Boston: Little Brown.

Mahy, M., Tseng, J. (Ill.)., & Tseng, M. (Ill.). (1990). *The seven Chinese brothers.* New York: Scholastic.

Rosenberg, L. & Gammell, S. (Ill.). (1993). *Monster mama.* New York: Philomel Books.

Ross, T. (1987). *Stone soup.* New York: Dial.

Wilson, S. (1985). *Beware the dragons.* New York: Harper & Row.

Wolkstein, D. & Brown, M. (Ill.). (1981). *The banza.* New York: Dial Books.

I Don't Like You!
(Personality Clashes)

Many rejected children misread the social cues; in particular, they tend to assume that their peers are approaching them with hostile intentions and, in turn, respond with aggression. (Ramsey, 1991, p. 142)

PERSONALITY CLASHES IN THE EARLY CHILDHOOD CLASSROOM

Aggression breeds aggression as we have learned only too well in adult life. If someone is mean to us, we tend to give back what we receive. Young children have the same problem with negative behavior as do adults. Their plight is even more magnified because of their inexperience. What should they do when someone approaches them in a seemingly hostile manner? Many youngsters strike out as their first response.

On the other hand, if one child approaches another in obvious friendship, the second child usually reciprocates. What makes the difference? Why is one child liked and another disliked? If we knew the answer, we could help children change their attitudes toward one another. If preschoolers could learn how to convert their feelings of dislike into appreciation for each other, think what a marvelous key they would possess for unlocking interpersonal barriers in their adult lives. This chapter looks at personality clashes, their causes, and their possible transformation.

Children's attitudes of dislike toward another child are based on the same three grounds as those of most adults. They do not like someone because they feel 1) they are different from them; 2) they are better than them; or 3) they treat people badly. Such reasons merely lie underneath the perceptions or feelings on the part of the child. This chapter shows how each of these justifications for disliking someone can be transformed, allowing children to like one another and get along together in the classroom.

As you read this chapter put yourself in the place of the young child. Do you have negative feelings for another person based on similar reasons? Sometimes these reasons are hidden so deeply we do not recognize them. We understand, though, that all human beings everywhere display the same emotions of anger, distress, contempt, fear, jealousy, guilt, excitement, joy, and affection—and for the same reasons.

BECAUSE THEY ARE "DIFFERENT"

People we perceive as being different from ourselves sometimes make us uneasy. Why do they look so different from me? Why do they act so differently? How can I understand them if they are not like me? I feel uncomfortable when they are around. What will they do to me? What if more of them come? Are they going to take over? Will I lose my identity? People who harbor these thoughts express fear of the unknown, a very strong emotion. When acted upon, this fear has caused wars, riots, and armed aggression by adults.

What about young children? Do they harbor such feelings? Some do, and some do not. For the most part, children aged three to five have not yet developed prejudices against other children on the basis of differences because their own cognition has not matured enough for them to conceptualize differences as older children do. Younger children, especially, do not seem to notice that

Young children have not yet developed prejudices against other children on the basis of differences.

their peers are of a different sex, race, color, religion, or economic status. Even when such differences are pointed out by older peers or adults, many three-year-olds do not seem to process such information.

Little by little this recognition develops. Its first evidence in the preschool classroom is often the development of same-gender groups in the play areas: girls in the housekeeping area, boys in the block area. Even these groups are fluid and not all that stable. Throughout the preschool years most children continue to play with one another in harmony, based on the fact that they are all children together, not because of similarities or differences.

Only when children act differently—for example, like an outsider—are they treated differently. A newcomer to the classroom sometimes receives hostile treatment at first because she acts differently. If this child knows how to blend in, then the others usually accept her regardless of her skin color, hair color, language, or clothing. On the other hand, children may pick on a regular member of the class who acts differently—perhaps retreating like a victim, or losing his explosive temper easily. Such children act like a magnet to certain other youngsters, unwittingly drawing their attention until a conflict occurs.

Differences of race or skin color come to be recognized by young children mainly from behavior by their peers, siblings, families, or even their teachers toward children exhibiting "differences." Youngsters then may imitate the behavior of those they respect, especially if they see them acting hostilely toward people who have different skin colors or speak a different language. However, if preschool teachers treat all of their youngsters with the same respect and good humor, they can usually defuse most attitudes of prejudice brought into the classroom from the outside.

Use your own matter-of-fact acceptance of every child as your best defense against negative attitudes toward others. They are all good children. They have all come to your class to grow and learn. They may be short, tall, fat, thin, bouncy, slow, blond, black-haired, brown-skinned, hearing-impaired, loud, shy, happy, awkward, or playful—an exciting conglomeration of young human beings whom you enjoy. Your cheerful acceptance shows each of them how delighted you are to have them there. They, in turn, will reflect the same feeling back to you. They will love being there and being around you.

If you do not pick up that good feeling from the children, you may need to change your own attitude. Make a list of all the children in your class, and after each name write down, "I like him or her because...." Are there some children that you cannot find a reason to like? Put these names on separate cards and spend three days jotting down positive things that you observe for each of them, such as:

1. Saying "hello" when they come in the morning
2. Hanging up their jackets without being told
3. Playing for ten minutes without a fight
4. Putting two blocks on the shelf during cleanup
5. Drinking their milk without a spill
6. Spending the whole playground period without punching anyone

Then demonstrate to each of these children both verbally and nonverbally how much you appreciate such things. Say "thanks," as often as you can. Smile, smile, smile whenever possible. Clap your hands and click your heels, too! Why not? The turnaround in attitude such actions can bring may surprise you. Then you will be ready to help children in the classroom change any of their negative attitudes toward one another.

Focus on Likenesses

Think a minute about likenesses. We realize that young children do not focus on differences until we point them out. Why should we point them out? What we have in common binds us together as human beings. How are children everywhere alike? We should be thinking about these similarities. They all eat food; they all speak a language; they all wear clothes; they all like to have fun;

they all have favorite stories, colors, or songs. To point out that Umeko eats different food than Nancy is not necessary or even appropriate.

We make a mistake in our curriculum when we feature the differences in other cultures. We may assume that children from these cultures who are in our classrooms will feel proud if we point out how different their customs are. Instead, they often feel uncomfortable and perhaps not quite as good as everyone else. Only when everyone in the class shares their customs do many of these children feel at ease.

Bring in some old magazines or grocery store ads and have children cut out pictures of the foods they like to eat. Have duplicates of the magazines or ads, and instruct the children to paste the pictures on a big mural with their names beside each of the pictures. Mount the mural on the wall and then point out who likes the same food. Children often express surprise and delight to see that others like the same things they do.

If rice was one of the favorites, you will want to read the book *Everybody Cooks Rice* (Dooley, 1991). Then be prepared to cook one of the rice dishes discovered by Carrie as she goes around her multiethnic neighborhood looking for her little brother. Instead, she finds everyone cooking rice of one kind or another: fried rice, peas and rice, yellow rice, basmati rice, white rice, and creole rice. Recipes for each kind of rice appear at the end of the story. This book is an excellent example of paying attention to likenesses rather than differences in cultures. Other picture books featuring food experiences appear in *Picture Book Storytelling: Literature Activities for Young Children* (Beaty, 1994).

Put out several pairs of chopsticks in the housekeeping corner along with other eating implements, so that the children can incorporate them into their dramatic play. They might start trying to pick up small pieces of sponge (pretend food) from a bowl. If you have a chopstick expert in class, have him teach the others (including you) how to use them. Read the book *Cleversticks* (Ashley, 1991), about the fun Ling Sung has teaching the children and teachers in his preschool how to eat with chopsticks. Then one day put out a pair of chopsticks at each place setting when sticky rice is being served for lunch or snacks and let everybody dig in.

We all have another commonality: living quarters. They may not look the same, but they serve the same purpose. Houses, apartments, cottages, mobile homes, and pueblos give each of us a place where we can rest our heads at night. Read *Paul and Sebastian* (Escudie, 1988) so your children can see pictures of Paul's green trailer with blue curtains and Sebastian's blue apartment with green curtains. The adults in this story, not the boys, are the ones having trouble over differences. Each boy's mother does not like the other little boy because he is different, living in a different kind of dwelling. But when the boys get lost and mixed up in the dark, the mothers finally learn how much alike the boys really are.

In *Space Travellers* (Wild, 1992), homeless city dwellers do the best they can in some strange living quarters, indeed. Zac and his mother Mandy sleep in a rocket that stands in the middle of a park playground. Zac loves to imagine traveling to outer space every night when he climbs into his sleeping bag at the top of the rocket. Your children may want to share photos of their own homes, or magazine pictures of the kind of house they would like to live in.

You can incorporate many other activities that feature children's similarities into the curriculum. Mount a row of sheets of colored construction paper on the wall at the children's eye level. Have them put their names, initials, or scribbles on their favorite colors. Afterward, read their names according to their favorite color. New friendships among children sometimes begin simply on the basis of shared favorites like this. Give each child a crepe paper streamer of one of the colors they have chosen, and let them twirl it around to music. Later they can make a belt or headband out of it. You also may want to read the book *Color Dance* (Jonas, 1989), showing two Caucasian girls, an African-American girl, and a boy dancing with transparent colored cloths. Or, use colored cellophane instead. Have children sign up for the various colors available. Then read off the names of everyone who wants red or blue or yellow or orange. They can cut out circular pieces to be pasted on the frames for the cardboard glasses you have cut out for each. Wrap the frame as a band around the head of each child and clip or staple the frames together. Then have all the "reds" parade around to music; all the "blues" together, and so forth. They also will enjoy hearing the Ezra Jack Keats story *Goggles* (1969) when they have their own pair.

Have children make requests for your book-reading period. Mount the dust jackets of several books on the wall of the Story Center with a sign-up sheet under each for the children to request their favorite stories. Children like to know that other children love to hear their favorite book, too. When you read the story tell which children requested it. This is the time to include multiethnic books showing children of various ethnic and racial groups doing everyday things together, such as *All Kinds of Families*, (Simon, 1976) (getting a haircut, having a party, playing instruments, getting a letter, being ill, having a wedding); *The Day of the Rainbow*, (Craft, 1991) (in the hot city, dropping books, skating, getting on bus, losing and finding things); *Music, Music for Everyone*, (Williams, 1984), (practicing musical instruments, playing for a party); *Pretend You're a Cat*, (Marzollo, 1990), (pretend to be a cat, a dog, a fish, a bee, a chick, a bird, a squirrel, a pig, a cow, a horse, a snake).

Children enjoy music of all kinds. Mount another sign-up sheet in the music center for songs your children would like to sing. Have them sign up for as many songs as they want. Be sure to read off the names of the children who requested each of the songs. First, though, you should teach children some new I-like-you songs that you have made up, by singing them together over and over to favorite tunes. Make up your own or use the following:

I Like Your Smile
(Tune: "Hokey Pokey")

I like (name)'s great big smile!
I like (his or her) happy face!
I like (his or her) swinging style,

The way (he or she) keep(s) it all in place!
(He or she) makes me feel so happy,
And (he or she) turn(s) me inside out!
That's what it's all about!

Sit down ahead of time if you plan to use the following song, and write out some rhyming words to the first name of every child in your class. The children will appreciate hearing their own personal verses. If you can't think of a good rhyme, do it together with the children, and they are sure to come up with something original.

There Was a Neat Boy (Girl)
(Tune: "Michael Finnegan")

There was a neat *boy* (girl)
His name was *Larry* (or Rob; or Jessica)
He was fun and *not contrary* (not a snob; never mess-ica)
He had a pet *you could not carry* (I heard it sob) (that couldn't say yes-ica)
That neat *boy* (girl) named *Larry, very* (Rob, throb) (Jessica, confess-ica)

Brand New Shoes
(Tune: "This Is the Way We Go to School")

Barbara Bradley's (name) got brand new shoes,
Brand new shoes, brand new shoes.
Barbara Bradley's (name) got brand new shoes,
Show us what they *look like.*
                    sound like.
                    jump like.
                    run like.

Let's Give a Clap
(Tune: "Go In and Out the Windows")

Let's give a clap for _____ (name) (clap!)
Let's give a clap for _____ (name) (clap!)
Let's give a clap for _____ (name) (clap!)
As we have done before.

I Like the Way
(Tune: "The Grand Old Duke of York")

I like the way _____ (name) walks,
I like the way he (or she) talks.
I like the way he (or she) flaps his (or her) wings
And never forgets to squawk. SQUAWK! SQUAWK!

This should be fun. It also should be valuable in your effort to accept each of the children unconditionally, and in helping the other children do the same when they see that they are all included in these enjoyable activities. Some other favorite tunes you may want to use to make up your own verses include:

"When the Saints Go Marching In"
"Kookaburra"
"Twinkle, Twinkle, Little Star"
"Row, Row, Row Your Boat"
"London Bridge Is Falling Down"
"Skip to My Lou"
"He's Got the Whole World In His Hands"

Most of your children also have in common parents or caregivers who think they are beautiful. Are they really? Of course they are. Read together *Am I Beautiful?* (Minarik, 1992), about the baby hippo who goes around asking each of the other animals if they think he is beautiful until he finally gets the answer he is waiting for. For each of your children, mount a photo framed in colored glitter on a poster labeled "Our Beautiful Children."

What about your children's parents? What do your children think about them? Most children, of course, wish their parents were just like everyone else's. The little boy in *Weird Parents* (Wood, 1990), is no different, even though they lavish affection on him with their outrageous antics. He finally comes to accept them as they are.

Such books and activities help children who have trouble liking one another realize that they actually are not all that different from one another. In fact, they are not really different at all.

BECAUSE THEY ARE "BETTER"

Secondly, children (and other people) do not like someone if they believe that the other person is somehow better than they are and therefore receives privileges that they do not. What is "better?" We know this as jealousy: "He always gets the biggest piece." "She gets to stay up later than me." "His presents are always better than mine." "She has nicer clothes than me." "My mother likes him better." "She is better looking than me." "The teacher chooses him for all the good things." Have you heard any of these complaints recently? If they come from your children at home, they are reflecting sibling rivalry. In the preschool they spring from feelings of jealousy of one child toward another.

You know that one child is not better than another. How can you help your children understand this, especially when they are in the throes of *experiencing* jealousy? Simply telling a child he or she is just as good as someone else does not do the trick. Jealousy springs from a feeling within, a feeling of powerlessness. Words can soothe but not correct the situation. The child must *experience* a change of heart either directly or vicariously.

Reading stories about characters who have the same kinds of feelings in similar situations helps young children begin to understand their own emotions and why they must change them. As Ramsey (1991, p. 168) points out:

> *Children's books are a primary vehicle for this kind*
> *of teaching. By engaging children in stories, we*
> *enable our young readers and listeners to empathize*
> *with different experiences and points of view and*
> *experience a wide range of social dilemmas.*

Sibling Rivalry

Jealousy often begins at home with sibling rivalry. An older sibling becomes jealous when a new baby comes into the home because she no longer receives the undivided attention of her parents. The new baby is now the primary focus. Older siblings battle over possessions, control, and advantages because they perceive someone else getting more than they do. In some cases, this rivalry turns into real dislike of one sibling for another.

If you plan to read a book about jealous characters to classroom youngsters who have this problem, you may want to start with sibling rivalry because you will often strike a familiar chord. If children can become aware of what is happening in their own lives at home, they will more likely make the connection with classroom conflicts.

In *Sam Is My Half Brother*, (Boyd, 1990), Hessie looks forward to visiting her daddy and stepmother every summer. The story focuses on her first visit after her half brother Sam is born. She is not at all happy about sharing her time with Sam and all his demands for attention, until she and her daddy go through a photo album of her early days, and she comes to realize that now she can be a big sister. After reading this book to a child with jealousy problems, talk with her about how Hessie felt, how her father and stepmother felt, and how Sam felt. Would your child also like to make a photo album about activities she and others are involved with in the classroom? Would she like to take the photos?

In *She Come Bringing Me That Little Baby Girl,* (Greenfield, 1974), Kevin, an African-American boy, is really upset when his mother comes home from the hospital with a baby girl in her arms. When he finally realizes that his mother needs him to help her, and his new sister really needs a big brother to look after her, Kevin not only accepts the new baby but even shows her off. Boys can more easily relate to a story with a boy for the main character. Can any of your boys empathize with Kevin?

The Tunnel (Browne, 1989) is a realistic story turned magical about Jack and his sister Rose, who fight and argue all the time. One day fraidy-cat Rose follows her brother to a tunnel made of vine-covered stones. Jack immediately crawls into it, but his frightened sister holds back and waits for him to come out. He does not reappear. She then realizes, scared or not, she will have to go in and find him. It is a long, dark, scary crawl. She finds him in a strange magical forest where he has been turned to stone. Throwing her arms around the stone boy, she weeps in anguish, which brings him back to life. Thus they are able to return to the real world together as friends. Your children may not be able to verbalize the hidden meanings in this story, but at some deeper level they will understand about the power of love and the need to find it within oneself, if you spend time afterward talking with them about it. As Ramsey (1991, p. 70) points out:

> Books with these themes can provide a way for children to talk about their sibling relations, especially if they find them troubling. They also illustrate the fact that relationships do not have to be destroyed by conflict and misunderstanding, which is a common assumption among young children.

Story Reenactment

A more direct way to experience the jealousy problems of a book character is through *story re-enactment*, informal acting out of a story you have read or told to the children. Children actually take the roles of storybook characters and can feel their emotions. They choose whatever character role they want, with more than one child playing the same role. The teacher narrates the story, allowing the different characters to speak their lines, or act their parts, any way they want. The children who do not choose a character become the audience, for this type of play benefits the children themselves, not an outside audience.

Most important of all, repeat story re-enactments over and over as long as the children remain interested. Each time children get to choose their roles, trying the same role, or a different role, or being part of the audience. Ishee and Goldhaber (1990, p. 74) tell how their children performed *The Three Bears* twenty-seven times in four days! For children to gain the most from such performances, they need to enact their roles again and again.

This is the most important part. Many repetitions help children. For many children it is necessary to watch a play numerous times before making that first gesture of pretense within the play. For others, repetition allows an opportunity to elaborate and expand on the story as presented, to take on a variety of roles, and to assume major responsibility for a role. (Ishee & Goldhaber, 1990, p. 74)

Folk- and fairy tales make especially good stories for story re-enactment. Children remember these tales easily because they have simplicity, repetition of actions, and brief dialogue. Furthermore, the characters in fairy tales have one-dimensional personalities, representing certain types that children can easily identify with. The youngsters can become different characters at different times: the good sister, the bad sister, the handsome prince, the ugly troll, the fairy godmother, or the witch.

Choose a folk story about jealousy and read it to your children. Do they like it? If so, read it again and again. When you think the children really know the story well, you can begin your story re-enactment. The following guidelines will help you and the children become involved in this exciting new venture:

 FIGURE 5.1

Guidelines for Creating a Story Reenactment

1. Choose a folk story you and the children already know well.
2. Inform the children about the characters in the play and ask who would like to play each role.
3. Allow as many children as want to play a role at the same time.
4. Play any role not selected by the children.
5. Everyone else in the classroom should be the audience.
6. Use a minimum of costumes and props, or none if possible.
7. Take the role of the narrator yourself until children become very familiar with story re-enactment.
8. When finished with the play, have everyone applaud each character in turn, and the audience also.
9. Perform the drama as many times as the children want, selecting characters each time.

(From *Picture Book Storytelling* (Beaty, 1994, pp. 136–138.)

A good folk story about competition and jealousy to reenact is *Anancy and Mr. Dry-Bone* (French, 1991). Mr. Dry-Bone, a rich man, lives in a big house at the top of a hill. Anancy, a poor man, lives in a small house at the foot of the hill. They both want to marry Miss Louise. Miss Louise, a clever and beautiful girl, lives on the other side of the hill. She has never in her life laughed, so she will marry the first man who makes her laugh.

The story features black people and animal characters in a Caribbean island setting with striking black-and-white illustrations and contrasting sunset skies and animal colors. Children are delighted with Mr. Dry-Bone's conjuring tricks that do not make Miss Louise even crack a smile. But everyone cracks up when Anancy appears in his hilarious animal-parts costume, making Miss Louise and even Mr. Dry-Bone laugh until the tears roll down.

You really do not need costumes or props, but the children playing Anancy's role enjoy getting something they can imagine as the Tiger's jogging suit, the Dog's hunting hat, the Alligator's other shoes, the Monkey's tie, and the Parrot's feathers when they ask each animal for something to wear to visit Miss Louise. You can use colored scarves or paper streamers. The simpler, the better.

You do not need to discuss the meaning of the story with the youngsters; the story speaks for itself. Your children learn meanings deep within themselves when they take on different roles. Although they may not be able to verbalize "the moral of the story," young children learn intuitively that people have very different attitudes sometimes and that everyone chooses the way he or she wants to be. Psychologist Bruno Bettelheim discusses this point in his classic book *The Uses of Enchantment: The Meaning and Importance of Fairy Tales* (1976, p. 10):

> *A child's choices are based, not so much on right versus wrong, as on who arouses his sympathy and who his antipathy. The more simple and straightforward a good character, the easier it is for a child to identify with it and to reject the bad other. The child identifies with the good hero not because of his goodness, but because the hero's condition makes a deep positive appeal to him. The question for the child is not "Do I want to be good?" but "Who do I want to be like?"*

Your children will ask this question too. When they become involved in story re-enactment, they actually will *experience* the feeling of jealousy from a different perspective, which is truly "other-esteem." Furthermore, when you look at something from a new perspective, you can actually learn to change the way you handle it in real life.

But the special wonder of the *Anancy and Mr. Dry-Bone* story is its unique focus on humor and how it touches all the characters: Miss Louise, who desperately wants to laugh; Anancy, the hero, who is naturally funny; and even Mr. Dry-Bone, the villain, who has to laugh in spite of himself. They all would concur with Mark Twain who declared: "Against the assault of laughter, nothing can stand" (Ayres, 1987, p. 108).

Nothing will stand in your classroom either, not even conflict, if you can get the children in conflict to laugh. When children become intense and irritated with one another, often you can defuse a strained situation by whispering some sort of nonsense in their ears. Something like: "Oh, Kojo! How could you!" or "PonponponPONsa!" if you know that will tickle their funny bones. Of course, *you* need to be lighthearted and childlike, too. Are you?

BECAUSE THEY TREAT A PERSON BADLY

Thirdly, children dislike one another because one treats the other badly. Picking on someone, calling him names, teasing her, messing up his constructions, pushing her around—all these actions make children dislike the instigator. Why does one child treat another like this? Sometimes she herself has been treated in a similar fashion. Sometimes a child struggling for control over others uses these tactics, as discussed in Chapter Four. Some children even try to make friends through such means. Many such children just do not know any better, you may decide. If only they knew how it feels to be on the receiving end of such actions, they might stop misbehaving. Then others would not dislike them, and their life in the classroom would change completely.

Role-Playing Animal Actions

Get all of your children involved in learning how teasing and negative actions feel by having them portray animals engaged in arguments. Down through the ages animals have represented certain human characteristics. For example, Aesop's fables show certain animals acting like foolish humans. Throughout the world people have attributed similar characteristics to the same animal:

Sly as a fox
Brave as a lion
Wise as an owl
Slow as a turtle

Emotions also can be attributed to animals, as the picture book *Sometimes I feel Like a Mouse: A Book About Feelings,* (Modesitt, 1992) tells us. The animals in this book demonstrate the feelings of:

shy: hiding mouse
bold: stomping elephant
sad: howling wolf
happy: singing canary
scared: trembling rabbit
brave: galloping horse

excited: skittering squirrel
calm: floating swan
mad: roaring lion
ashamed: drooping dog
proud: soaring eagle

Obtain pictures of as many of these animals as possible from magazines or teacher-supply stores. Duplicate two copies of each animal picture and give one each to a pair of your children. During small group time have these children stand up and demonstrate their animal natures. Can they make the animal noises? Can they hunch their shoulders and scrunch up their faces to look like the animals? Some children can even wiggle their noses or twitch their ears.

Some teachers prefer to use animal hand puppets. You can purchase hot pad gloves in the shape of zebras, lions, tigers, cheetahs, alligators, giraffes, and monkeys, or the children may want to make their own simple paper bag animal puppets with colored marking pens and paste on ears and noses. Now tell your small group of children (no more than six) a brief story about how each of the animals thinks that it is the best of its kind. Afterward, have the pairs of children portray their animals and argue over which one of them is best. Each pair can do this by themselves or in front of the small group.

Call a time out and ask each child how he felt and how he thought his partner felt during the argument. Did any of the children convert their conflicts to positive feelings? Did any get into actual physical fighting? Next time you meet in

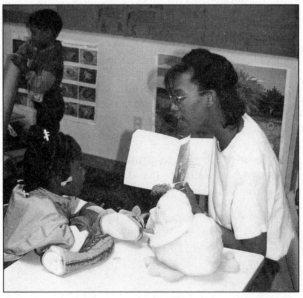

Do a lighthearted reading of a story about animals in conflict.

small groups have children choose an animal, but this time mix up the pairs. Once again tell your story and then have the pairs argue over which one is better. Finally, have the children relate how they felt and how they thought their partner felt. Were they accurate in picking up feelings? Are they getting better at other-esteem? End each session by doing a lighthearted reading of a story about animals in conflict such as: *Boris Bad Enough* (Kraus, 1976), *The Butter Battle Book* (Dr. Seuss, 1984), *The Gingham Dog and the Calico Cat* (Field, 1990), *Tusk Tusk* (McKee, 1990), *Two Greedy Bears* (Ginsburg, 1976), and *Uproar on Hollercat Hill* (Marzollo, 1980).

Adults often hear "I don't like you!" in places where young children play. Perhaps, from now on, you will hear it only in fun in your own classroom. Once children have learned how their imaginary animals feel when bad things happen to them, they may be more sensitive to other children in the classroom. They will have slip-ups, of course, because no one is more dynamic than young children. When a child needs to express strong emotions, have them use the animal puppets. If someone picks on someone else, have the child transfer the teasing to a puppet. Put a puppet on your own hand now and then to get into the fray yourself. If you make it lighthearted enough, you can defuse many of the children's negative emotions.

These are a few of the methods for decreasing personality clashes in the classroom:

 FIGURE 5.2

Decreasing Personality Clashes in the Classroom

1. Help children feel comfortable with peers of different gender, race, culture, skin color, and appearance by showing your own acceptance and focusing on likenesses, rather than differences in stories, songs, cooking, and themselves. (self-esteem)
2. Help children feel that they are not better than each another through stories and story re-enactment. (self-esteem and other-esteem)
3. Help children stop treating others badly by teaching them empathy through role-playing animal emotions. (other-esteem)

TYPICAL PERSONALITY CLASH

Like the rest of us, some children will always have personality clashes with others they feel are different, or better, or behaving badly. Nevertheless, the attractive classroom activities you provide to promote camaraderie among the youngsters will have positive results. Surprisingly children can be jealous of one another one day and best friends the next. Children who "go at" one another ferociously with animal puppets may be the ones who end up block building together in perfect harmony. Your stories, puppets, and dramatizations can be the key for changing perceptions, although they may take a while to sink in. Case #5 looks at a typical boy-girl teasing situation. To an outsider the girl may appear as the victim. The teacher, however, knows that both Geena and Randy often "ask for it." See what you think.

Conflict-Conversion Questions

1. What's happening _____ (child's name)?
2. How does _____ (other child) feel?
3. What will make him (or her) feel better?

#5. The Case of the Terrible Teaser

Setting: Randy, a five-year-old, often picks on Geena Winch, who lives in his neighborhood. He likes to torment her by calling her "witch" or "carrot top," and pinches her when she is not looking. In response, instead of crying, Geena, a thin, agile four-year-old with long, tangled, fiery red hair, calls him names (much louder) and kicks him. Sometimes she takes his things and hides them. Today she is playing in the housekeeping area with another girl piling all the plastic fruit into a collander. Randy sneaks up behind her, pinches her, and runs. She runs after him, catches him, gives him a swift kick and yells "DUM-DUM!" right in front of the teacher. The kick seems to hurt Randy as he limps away, but he does not cry. This very lighthearted teacher has fun with the children and often gently teases them.

Teacher: *Randy, Geena, what's happening? Come over here and let's talk about it.* (Teacher takes them both by the hand and leads them over to a quiet corner where they all sit on the floor.) *Tell me about it, Randy.*

Randy: *Geena kicked me. You saw her. She just ran after me and kicked me, and called me "Dum-Dum." I didn't do anything. She's always kicking people. She took my red crayon, too.*

Teacher: *Tell me what happened, Geena.*

Geena: (Tears are beginning to run down her face, but she puts her head down and won't speak.)

Teacher: *Geena?* (no answer) *All right, Randy, you tell me how you think Geena feels about this.*

Randy: (with surprise) *Geena? Geena? What about me? She kicked me!*

Teacher: *Yes. That's what you said. Now tell me how you feel Geena feels about it.*

Randy: (grumpily) *I don't know.*

Teacher: *Look at Geena, Randy, and tell me how she feels.*

Randy: (shrugs) *She's crying. I guess she feels bad.*

Teacher: *Randy thinks you feel bad, Geena. Do you feel bad?* (She nods her head.) *Now tell me what happened, Geena.*

Geena: (sniffing) *Randy pinched me again. He's done it three times this morning. So I kicked him! And he called me a witch, too.*

Teacher: *Okay, Geena. You say that Randy pinched you and called you a name. How do you think he feels, Geena?*

Geena: *I bet he's sorry now cause I kicked him hard!*

Teacher: *All right. You have both been hurting each other, pinching, kicking, and name-calling, and you both feel bad. You know I can't let the children here hurt one another. So I'm asking you to stop the pinching and name-calling and kicking. Okay? But I would like you to think about what would make the other person feel better. You first, Randy. You said you think that Geena feels bad. Now what do you think would make her feel better?*

Randy: *If she would stop taking my things.*

Teacher: *Is that why she feels bad, Randy? Think about how she feels, Randy. What would make her feel better?*

Randy: *I don't know.*

Teacher: *Well, you think about it while I ask Geena. Geena, what do you think would make Randy feel better?*

Geena: *He feels good when he calls me names.*

Teacher: *Is that right, Randy, does that make you feel good, when you call Geena names?*

Randy: *I like to call her names 'cause it gets her mad.*

Teacher: *Ohhh, so you're a big teaser, are you? Well, name-calling hurts people just like kicks and pinches when it's done on purpose to make them mad. But when it's done in fun, it might make the other person feel better, especially if they do it, too. What do you think, Geena?*

Geena: *I would feel good if I called him names.*

Teacher: *But how do you think he would feel, Geena? Would you both feel good by calling each other names in fun?* (Both look at one another, and nod. This answer puzzles the teacher at first, and she does not know what she should do. Then she decides.) *Would you like to hear a story about name-calling? Then you can tell me if you would feel good about calling each other names.* (The teacher reads *Fighting Words*, Merriam, 1992, about a boy in the country and a girl in the city who say they hate one another because they both get to do things that the other cannot do. So they come together for a fight—with words. The book shows them as giants running through the country, the city, and the zoo calling each other funny names: klutz, dimwit, cuckoo, dodo, grouse, booby. The teacher says each of these words in a high or low comical voice until Geena and Randy begin to laugh.)

Teacher: *Now it's your turn, you two. I'm going to read this book again, and you, Geena, will be the girl, and you the boy, Randy. I'll whisper the names they call each other, and you shout them out, all right?* (They shout out the names until everyone in the class gathers around, and all end up laughing.) *Okay, everyone back to work now… shoo! Geena and Randy, if you want to call each other names, you come and get this book, okay? Then you can do it together. Like the kids in the book. Agreed? Okay, one last name to seal the bargain. Geena? Randy?*

Geena: *Poppycock!* (giggles)

Randy: *Claptrap!* (laughs)

Teacher: *Fine. Sounds just like the kids in the book. Now shake hands on it.* (They shake.)

Positive-Feelings Activity: This time the teacher decides not to hold a positive-feelings activity with the rest of the children. She decides that this fun type of name calling would be better kept private between Geena and Randy. She also wants to see if they will actually use the book as she suggests, or if they will go back to their hurtful tormenting.

TEACHER'S ACTIONS, CASE #5

The way the conflict turned out surprised this teacher. She knew the teasing between the two children in the classroom was only the tip of the iceberg, and much more went on in the neighborhood. When she remembered a new book, *Fighting Words*, (Merriam, 1992), that describes an almost identical situation, she decided to see how these children would respond. She knew if she could get them to laugh about the names used, this might defuse the situation. However, if they had not been able to relax and see the humor in the names, she would have asked them to think about a different way of helping each other feel better. Without such a book, a teacher could do a puppet play about name-calling or use two plastic animals.

This teacher realized that children may say to one another, "I don't like you!" but not mean it literally. Researchers tend to agree with this belief. Shantz (1987, p. 301) reports from one study that, among preschoolers "mutual friends are more quarrelsome, and mutual quarrelers are more friendly than the average."

The children's book *Fighting Words* reflects this same point of view. Nevertheless, a quarrel is a conflict, and a conflict of any kind can be a learning situation for all involved. Whether they are friends or enemies, young children need to learn to empathize with another's feelings and thus convert their conflicts to mutual positive feelings.

IDEAS + IN CHAPTER 5

Personality Clash Activities

1. Treat all children with the same respect and good humor.
2. Accept all children in a lighthearted, matter-of-fact way, no matter how they look or act.
3. For children that you have difficulty liking, make a note of positive things you observe them doing.
4. Show children verbally (say "thanks") and nonverbally (smile) that you appreciate them.
5. Feature things that are familiar, not very different, about different cultures represented in your program.
6. Have children cut out and paste on a mural pictures of foods they like.
7. Read *Everybody Cooks Rice* and cook a rice dish for the children.
8. Put out chopsticks along with other eating implements in the housekeeping area.
9. Have a child chopsticks expert teach others how to use them.
10. Have children cut out magazine pictures of houses they would like to live in.
11. Mount a row of different colored paper sheets on the wall and have children write (scribble) their names or initials on their favorite colors.

12. Give each child a crepe-paper streamer of their favorite colors and let them twirl it around to music.
13. Make "glasses" with colored cellophane and cardboard frames.
14. Mount dust jackets of books to the wall and have children sign up for their favorite story.
15. Mount names of songs on the wall and have children sign up for favorites.
16. Include multiethnic books showing children of various ethnic groups doing everyday things together.
17. Write out words to, and sing new I-like-you songs that you have made up using the children's names.
18. Write out some rhyming words for the names of every child in your class.
19. Mount each child's photo, framed in colored glitter, on a poster entitled Our Beautiful Children.
20. Read stories about characters experiencing sibling rivalry.
21. Spend time afterward talking about how the characters felt.
22. Choose a folktale about jealousy that you have read before and have the children choose characters in a story re-enactment.
23. Make children in conflict laugh by whispering some sort of nonsense in both children's ears.
24. Have pairs of children pretend to be animals engaged in arguments.
25. Have children demonstrate emotional characteristics of certain animals.
26. Use animal hand puppets to show them pretending to be better than each other.
27. Afterward, have children tell how they felt and how they feel the other child felt during the argument.
28. Have children express strong emotions through animal puppets.

TRY IT YOURSELF

1. What would you do if a personality clash between two of your youngsters caused conflict in the classroom? Try your method and see if it works.
2. If several of the children in your classroom come from a Hispanic culture, in what specific ways can you try to integrate their culture into the mainstream American culture by having the children focus on likenesses?
3. In "The Case of the Terrible Teaser" do you believe the teacher addressed the situation adequately? What would you have done in this situation? Why?
4. Use one of the picture books mentioned with a small group of children and do a book extension activity based on the theme of the book. Report the results.
5. How has jealousy or sibling rivalry affected any of the children in your class (or in your experience)? How can you deal with it to produce mutual positive feelings?

REFERENCES CITED

Ayres, A. (Ed.). (1987). *The wit and wisdom of Mark Twain*. New York: Harper & Row.

Beaty, J. J. (1994). *Picture book storytelling: Literature activities for young children*. Fort Worth, TX: Harcourt Brace.

Bettelheim, B. (1976). *The uses of enchantment: The meaning and importance of fairy tales*. New York: Alfred A. Knopf.

Ishee, N. & Goldhaber, J. (1990). Story re-enactment: Let the play begin! *Young Children, 45*(3), 70–75.

Modesitt, J. and Spowart, R. (Ill.). (1992). *Sometimes I feel like a mouse: A book about feelings*. New York: Scholastic.

Ramsey, P. G. (1991). *Making friends in school: Promoting peer relationships in early childhood*. New York: Teachers College Press.

Shantz, C. U. (1987). Conflicts between children. *Child Development, 58*, 283–505.

OTHER SOURCES

Bernat, V. (1993). Teaching peace. *Young Children, 48*(3), 36–39.

Clark, L., DeWolf, S., & Clark, C. (1992). Teaching teachers to avoid having culturally assaultive classrooms, *Young Children, 47*(5), 4–9.

Prutzman, P, Stern, L., Burger, M. L., & Bodenhamer, G. (1988). *The friendly classroom for a small planet*. Philadelphia: New Society Publishers.

Wichert, S. (1989). *Keeping the peace: Practicing cooperation and conflict resolution with preschoolers*. Philadelphia: New Society Publishers.

CHILDREN'S PICTURE BOOKS

Aardema, V. & Brown, M. (Ill.). (1984). *Oh, Kojo! How could you!* New York: Dial Books.

Ashley, B. & Brazell, D. (Ill.). (1991). *Cleversticks*. New York: Crown.

Boyd, L. (1990). *Sam Is my half brother*. New York: Puffin.

Browne, A. (1989). *The tunnel*. New York: Alfred A. Knopf.

Craft, R. & Daly, N. (Ill.). (1991). *The day of the rainbow*. New York: Puffin.

Dooley, N. & Thornton, P. J. (Ill.). (1991). *Everybody cooks rice*. Minneapolis: Carolrhoda Books.

Escudie, R. & Wensell, U. (Ill.). (1988). *Paul and Sebastian*. Brooklyn, NY: Kane/Miller.

Field, E. & Street, J. (Ill.). (1990). *The gingham dog and the calico cat*. New York: Philomel Books.

French, F. (1991). *Anancy and Mr. Dry-Bone*. Boston: Little Brown.

Ginsburg, M., Aruego, J., & Dewey, A. (Ill.). (1976). *Two greedy bears*. New York: Macmillan.

Greenfield, E. & Steptoe, J. (Ill.). (1974). *She come bringing me that little baby girl*. Philadelphia: Lippincott.

Jonas, A. (1989). *Color dance*. New York: Greenwillow Books.

Keats, E. J. (1969). *Goggles*. New York: Collier Books.

Kraus, R., Aruego, J., & Dewey, A. (Ill.). (1976). *Boris bad enough*. New York: Simon & Schuster.

Marzollo, J. & Kellogg, S. (Ill.). (1980). *Uproar on Hollercat Hill.* New York: Dial Books.

Marzollo, J. & Pinkney, J. (Ill.). (1990). *Pretend you're a cat.* New York: Dial Books.

McKee, D. (1990). *Tusk Tusk.* Brooklyn, NY: Kane/Miller.

Merriam, E. & Small, D. (Ill.). (1992). *Fighting words.* New York: Morrow.

Minarik, E. H. & Abolafia, Y. (Ill.). (1992). *Am I beautiful?* New York: Greenwillow Books.

Seuss, Dr. (1984). *The butter battle book.* New York: Random House.

Simon, N. & Lasker, J. (Ill.). (1976). *All kinds of families.* Chicago: Albert Whitman.

Wild, M. & Rogers, G. (Ill.). (1992). *Space travellers.* New York: Scholastic.

Williams, V. B. (1984). *Music, music for everyone.* New York: Mulberry.

Wood, A. (1990). *Weird parents.* New York: Dial Books.

Why Won't You Let Me?

(Access Struggles)

Interactions in preschool classrooms are short, so children are constantly having to gain entry into new groups. This process is made more difficult because children who are already engaged with each other tend to protect their interactive space and reject newcomers. (Ramsey, 1991, p. 27)

ACCESS CONFLICTS IN THE EARLY CHILDHOOD CLASSROOM

The fluid nature of preschool children's interactions with one another often impresses adults watching a classroom of youngsters. There is a continuous ebb and flow of children, sometimes one at a time, sometimes in pairs or groups, who engage in a play activity, leave it, enter another activity, leave it, and so on. Why do they move around like this instead of staying put? Why are a few content to play together in one group, while others cannot find any group where they are accepted?

Welcome to the wonderful world of preschool children! You will learn first-hand that the younger the child, the shorter the attention span and the briefer the play episode. Ramsey's comment, quoted above, holds true: because young children have such brief interactions, they continuously have to gain entry into new groups. Many children have little difficulty interacting with new playmates. A few, however, have not yet "learned the ropes" for entering groups. Their bumbling attempts to gain access to the play of others often lead to their rejection. This rejection, in turn, may lead to such negative reactions as withdrawing from others or disrupting their activities. These few may even complain to the teacher. "Josh won't let me play! I wanna play with the blocks, and Josh won't let me!" These phrases are the words and chorus of the most common preschool melody: "Why won't you let me?" No matter what you do, no matter how you handle the situation, this particular song seems to linger on. Only the names change.

For this you should be thankful. This common preschool conflict—gaining access to ongoing play—ranks as perhaps the most important conflict of all for youngsters *to learn to handle on their own.* Although possession disputes over toys and materials happen more frequently, the most critical learning opportunities that young children must handle are play-access struggles with other children. Such conflicts teach profound lessons in getting along with others: how to watch and wait, when to initiate contact, how to learn what is going on in the play, how to blend in with the group, what to say to avoid rejection, what to do when rejected. These crucial lessons repeat over and over during free play. Researcher William A. Corsaro, (1979, p. 330), notes that a nursery school is like an adult party in many respects:

> at which there are generally several clusters of
> participants (who usually know one another) dis-
> persed in various areas of the setting. The partici-
> pants, somewhat like the young child in the
> nursery school, often feel there is a need to circu-
> late from one group to another. When party mem-
> bers find themselves alone, for whatever reason,
> they, very much like the children in the nursery
> school, have a strong desire to gain access into an
> ongoing conversation or activity.

Sound familiar? Adults, however, have the advantage of having developed over the years some successful group-entry strategies which the young children are just now beginning to learn. We should be thankful that our children have these real life opportunities to learn the social skills they will need to carry them successfully through life. Most preschoolers learn these skills on their own through trial and error. For those children who are having difficulty learning group-entry skills, this chapter can help.

For teachers who believe they should be the ones to resolve children's group-access problems by insisting that groups allow any child who wants to enter, they need to remember the reason children enroll in preschool: to grow, develop, and learn new skills. Children learn social skills, such as group entry, by trial and error, and by making attempts on their own. Teachers who use adult power to force a group to accept an outsider do nothing to promote children learning these important social skills.

Over the years, child development researchers have observed that preschool children use certain group-entry strategies in a particular sequence, and most of

 FIGURE 6.1

Child Group-Entry Strategies Checklist

Child _____   Observer _____

Group Play Type/Theme _____   Date _____

(**Directions:** Check any of the following behaviors that you observe for one child trying to enter one play episode)

_____ Hovers silently near the group

_____ Mimics the play behavior of the group

_____ Makes a group-oriented statement

_____ Enters the group successfully

_____ Asks a question or refers to self ("Can I play?")

_____ Is rejected by the group but tries again

_____ Makes claim or aggressive statement
       ("I was here first!" or "That's my hat!")

_____ Disrupts play physically

_____ Is rejected by the group and does not try again

_____ Complains to teacher; calls for teacher intervention

_____ Other

---

them eventually achieve success. Other strategies yield less successful results, and some tactics almost always lead to rejection by the play group (Ramsey, 1991). Figure 6.1 shows the most common strategies individual children use to gain access to ongoing play. Do your children use any of these strategies? A teacher should note which children are successful in entering groups on their own and what strategies they use to do so.

Unsuccessful children also try particular tactics to gain access, but often meet with failure. Who in your class usually cannot gain entry and what strategies do they try? Use the following checklist to observe children trying to enter ongoing play, and become familiar with what works and what does not work for your children.

KINDS OF GROUP PLAY

Look over the activities in progress during your free play periods to see what may attract a child currently unengaged in play. A small group of children may be involved in *dramatic play*, a spontaneous group pretending activity with a theme, such as cooking an imaginary meal, visiting the doctor, taking babies for an outing, building a highway for the trucks, or skiing down a block ramp. Other children may be playing together with the *puppets*. Still others may be working together on a group *puzzle* or playing with cutout storybook characters on a *felt-board*. Two children may be sorting out colored buttons and weighing them with a balance in the science discovery center. Four others could be gathered around the *water table*, filling plastic bottles, and squirting out the water.

In this typical free play scenario, a few children may be at loose ends, unengaged in any of the ongoing activities, but looking them over and perhaps making an attempt to enter one or another of them. Other children may drift away from the activity they started and try to gain access to another play group that looks more interesting. Using the *Child Group-Entry Strategies Checklist* (Figure 6.1) as a guide, observe what happens: what strategies does each child use in his or her attempt to gain entry? Does he try more than one strategy? Is he accepted or rejected? What does he do if rejected? Does he try again using the same or a different strategy? Does he succeed?

OBSERVATION RESULTS

We can learn many things about our children and their development of social skills through such observations. What did you find out? Even one day of observation will yield important insights into what happens with children in their play with others. Did you find that outsiders have real difficulty entering ongoing play the first time they tried? Did you learn that children almost always refuse a direct verbal request to enter the play (for example, "Can I play?")?

The nonverbal and indirect strategies children use at ages three to five in trying to gain access to ongoing play sometimes surprise observers. Why do they not simply tell the players directly what they want to do or why they should be a part of the group?

Then we remember that the language development and thinking abilities of preschool children are completely different from older children. Preschool children do not have the verbal competence of older children or adults. In addition, they think quite differently. Not only do they focus on themselves almost exclusively, but they have difficulty at first in conceptualizing things from another person's perspective. As a result, young children learn a different set of group-entry strategies to gain access to ongoing play. Most children learn such skills on their own through trial and error, which is as it should be, but a few youngsters may need your help to succeed in entering group play.

GROUP-ENTRY STRATEGIES THAT WORK

Sociologists have long studied such *access rituals* among children of various ages who try to enter play groups. They did not always understand why certain strategies worked for certain age groups, but they accurately recorded what happened. Meanwhile, child psychologists also observed children's group play with an eye toward interpreting the interactions. These meticulous studies enable us to describe successful and unsuccessful group-entry strategies among preschoolers.

Play consolidates or disintegrates constantly in preschool play groups, without much rhyme or reason. Youngsters wanting to enter the play of others usually hesitate at first. Perhaps they know from experience they will probably be rejected on their first try. Research has found that over half of preschoolers' entry efforts meet resistance or rejection on their initial attempt. (Shantz, 1987, p. 293)

This tendency to resist or reject may reflect the fact that children engaged in ongoing play know from experience how easily group play can be disrupted; therefore, they try to keep outsiders away once the play has started. As Corsaro (1979, p. 330) notes:

> *Interaction in the nursery school is fragile, and ongoing activities can break down with even minimal disruption.*

The youngsters simply try to protect their activity from disruption. The younger the children at play, (for example, three- and four-year-olds), the more likely they will actually refuse entry. Older children (aged seven and eight) who want to keep their play intact simply ignore the entry attempts of outsiders (Shantz, 1987, p. 293).

What strategies work best? The first three items on the *Child Group-Entry Strategies Checklist* (Figure 6.1), used in that particular sequence, have proved the most successful tactics with young children. Often, a child needs *more than one strategy* to gain group access, and such strategies need to be *tried in a particular order*. The three strategies are:

1. Hovers silently near the group
2. Mimics play behavior of the group
3. Makes a group-oriented statement

How is it with your children? Obviously, different groups of children may react somewhat differently. Many child development researchers over the years have recorded these particular strategies, however, or something very similar as being the most successful tactics for preschoolers. (Corsaro, 1979; Dodge, 1983; Shantz, 1987; Ramsey, 1991) Teachers and student teachers should have this information in order to help unsuccessful children learn group-entry skills.

Why should these specific strategies in this particular sequence work for so many young children? The first two consist of nonverbal and indirect methods. *Hovers silently near the group* means the outsider child looks things over without calling attention to herself. Corsaro (1979, p. 332) believes that:

> *Since the children come to expect that initial responses are going to be negative, they may develop more indirect (and multiple sequence) strategies...*

To gain access to ongoing play, an outsider can learn to mimic the play behavior of the group.

The play group usually does not interfere with an outsider who merely hovers nearby. As this child comes to understand the play, she can make another more definite move: *Mimics the play behavior of the group*. Without saying a word, the outsider can begins to integrate herself into the group. She may silently take on a role in the pretend play she is witnessing, such as getting plastic food items for the pretend meal or picking up a baby doll for the visit to the doctor.

If group members accept this strategy, she may eventually go a step further: *Makes a group-oriented statement*. She may say something like: "I'm cooking potatoes for supper" or "My baby needs a shot, too." If no child objects, she knows she has successfully entered the group and can continue her play.

On the other hand, the players may reject her at the outset even when she tries to enter unobtrusively. Over half of all preschoolers meet rejection on their initial entry attempts. In that case, she should not give up, but try again a little later. Children who make repeated attempts to enter the same play group are often successful. As (1987, p. 293) Shantz notes:

> *Children who try again to enter ongoing play*
> *often succeed. Between 35%-65% are eventually*
> *accepted into the group.*

GROUP-ENTRY STRATEGIES THAT DO NOT WORK

Not every strategy works for the outsider, as you may have noticed when you used the *Child Group-Entry Strategies Checklist*. The classroom staff must be aware of efforts that frequently do not work for young children. Three such strategies include:

1. Asks a question or refers to self
2. Makes a claim or an aggressive statement
3. Disrupts play physically

Because the indirect, nonverbal approach, which focuses on the play and not the players, succeeds most frequently, asking a direct question such as "Can I play?" will surely fail. The other children try to protect the play they have started and almost invariably reply "No." A claim such as "I was here first!" or "That's my baby doll!" only makes the players tighten their ranks against an intruder. Wouldn't you?

Disrupting the ongoing activity by "crashing the party," taking one of the play materials, pushing someone aside, or breaking down a block structure, not only earns the disrupter an almost automatic rejection, but also usually ends the play for everyone. Furthermore, the others remember the disruptive child's actions, and often ostracize her and prevent her from entering all subsequent play.

The child becomes caught in a cycle of rejection because she has not learned how to enter ongoing play unobtrusively.

THE TEACHER'S ROLE

Although young children learn group-entry skills best on their own, the teacher still plays an important role. Because a large part of the daily activities of the program consists of free play, the teacher can expect a great deal of entering and exiting of play groups. How smoothly this proceeds is ultimately up to the teacher.

However, the teacher should not force a group to admit an outsider when they are opposed to it. Obviously, adults can force preschool youngsters to do what they want them to do, but child development programs should strive to allow the children to learn on their own. If teachers intervene too often, the children will allow them to make all the decisions. This may create a smooth-running program, but it gives children little or no real opportunity to grow and develop on their own.

Instead, a teacher's active involvement in group play and entry problems should include:

1. Providing materials and time for group free play, especially pretending activities.
2. Observing who has learned how to enter groups unobtrusively and who has not.
3. Coaching children who need help entering groups on their own.
4. Using conflict-conversion strategies with the few children who disrupt play with physical or verbal aggression.

PROVIDING MATERIALS AND TIME FOR GROUP FREE PLAY, ESPECIALLY PRETENDING ACTIVITIES

A preschool classroom revolves around learning centers such as blocks, books, dramatic play, sand or water play, computers, writing, science, math, manipulatives, music, art, and large motor activities. During free play, children choose one or another of the activities to pursue. After play has started, some children may shift from one group to another. Some activities accommodate such shifting more easily than others. Groups that involve dramatic play with pretending and role-playing often try to stay closed to outsiders once the play begins. These groups tend to attract the most outsiders and thus have the most access struggles.

To alleviate this problem the classroom can provide a number of pretend play activities. Having only one dramatic play area increases chances for conflict because so many children will want to play there at one time. Instead, consider having two permanent dramatic play areas to accommodate a house setting, and perhaps an office, or store setting. In addition, you can provide prop boxes containing play hats, clothing, and various paraphernalia such as: doctor's office, fire station, bus station, repair shop, supermarket, shoe store, or restaurant.

The block building center should contain enough space and unit blocks, as well as toy truck and people accessories, to accommodate several children at one time. Also, consider having a sand table for pretend play with a nearby shelf full of miniature toy people, trucks, cars, planes, farm animals, zoo animals, and dinosaurs. Pretend play also occurs in doll houses (with furniture and people), lofts, and large motor climbers. What other areas for pretend play can you create?

Children love to pretend with story characters from their favorite books. Buy additional paperback copies of their favorites, cut out the characters, mount them on cardboard with sandpaper backing, and let children play with them on homemade feltboards. Simple books with clear pictures of the characters against a white background work best. For example, from the book *I Went Walking* (Williams, 1989) cut out the little boy and all of the animals he saw on his walk: black cat, brown horse, red cow, green duck, pink pig, and yellow dog. Make individual feltboards by gluing squares of felt from hobby shops to squares of cardboard. Keep the characters in a manila envelope with the front cover of the book pasted on it.

Children love to pretend about book stories. Cut out other book adventures, such as *Amanda's Dinosaur* (Orr, 1988), and let children make up adventures of their own. Mount the cutouts of Wendy and her mother on cardboard, as well as the Australian creatures she knows, such as an emu, a kangaroo, a chicken, a parrot, a calf, and a fox. Include the dinosaur egg and several pictures of her dinosaur as it grows bigger. Make as many feltboard character stories as needed. Simple and inexpensive, but exciting, they add pretend activities to your curriculum. Ensure that at least two children share one feltboard to encourage child interaction.

Children aged three to five engage more frequently in pretend play on their own than most other activities. Pretend play serves the important function of teaching children how to get along with others: how to enter groups successfully, how to take roles and play them, how to negotiate for what they want, how to compromise when they cannot get their own way, how to take turns, how to wait for a turn, how to lead and to follow, how to communicate, and how to cooperate with others.

Expect conflicts to occur as children struggle to satisfy their own needs (self-esteem) while accommodating the needs of others (other-esteem). Remember to welcome such conflicts as learning opportunities for the children. Strive to help them resolve such conflicts on their own. Use the conflict-conversion strategies only with the few who try to enter play so aggressively they harm others or materials. Other children who see how such conflict conversions work may develop other-esteem through observation. Then the positive-feelings activities you use can further reinforce the idea that concern for others' feelings can convert conflict to positive feelings.

Because pretending activities make good learning situations for conflict conversion, be sure to allow enough time for children to become deeply involved in pretending play. When you stock your classroom with sufficient materials and give the children enough time to play, most children will resolve the access struggles on their own and develop "other-esteem."

OBSERVING TO SEE WHO HAS LEARNED TO ENTER GROUPS AND WHO HAS NOT

Use the *Child Group-Entry Strategies Checklist* (Fig. 6.1) during the free play period to observe which children try to enter play groups, as is discussed on page 110. Observe one child at a time, following this child until he finally settles into play. Then focus on another child. To observe most of the children may take several days. If you eventually find that a number of children use the first three strategies in one form or another (that is, hovers, mimics, or makes group-oriented statements), feel positive about their learning these social skills on their own.

Some children may surprise you by successfully entering a group asking unrelated questions, referring to self, or making a claim. Although these entry strategies are often rejected, some children get away with them for a while. Watch what happens next. Children who enter ongoing play like this may not really understand what the group is doing and thus may cause its eventual disintegration. To succeed in entering ongoing play, a child must have a clear idea of the group's frame of reference in order to add to the play.

You may observe that other children do not need to use group-entry strategies at all because they started playing together in the first place and stayed together for the entire period. Other children who do not use these strategies may be new or shy youngsters who have not yet gained enough confidence to try integrating into group play. Still others may be children whose social play skills have not progressed from the levels of solitary or parallel play.

> *The development of social play is very much age related, and it can thus be observed by the preschool child-care worker in a particular sequence as children progress from solitary play through parallel play to group play. Age-related development thus signifies that the child's social skill level depends upon her cognitive, language, and emotional maturity. It also assumes that the older a child is, the more experience she has probably had with social contacts. (Beaty, 1994, p. 115)*

The youngest children often begin by playing by themselves in a preschool classroom. Child development specialists call this *solitary play*. As they mature and gain confidence in themselves and their surroundings, these youngsters may pursue *parallel play* in which they play next to other children but do not play with them. Parallel play often occurs in the block center where a single child builds his own building next to several children erecting a structure together. Parallel play makes up a great deal of free play in early childhood classrooms. It resembles a sort of "hovering" play maneuver next to other children and may evolve eventually into group play.

The most mature play occurs when children form a group to accomplish a task or play out a particular theme, which is known as *cooperative* or *group play.* Some children aged three to five may not reach the group play stage in your program. Child development is highly individual, and the teacher should not push a young child into experiences he is not ready for. Let him pursue his solitary or parallel activities. When he is ready he will make his own entry attempts or signal that he needs your help.

COACHING CHILDREN WHO NEED HELP ENTERING GROUPS ON THEIR OWN

After completing your observations, you will have a better idea of where most of the children stand in group play development. You may have identified one or two who try to become involved in the play of others but do not succeed. Others may try to enter groups forcefully but only succeed in breaking up the play. You should not take such children by the hand and insert them into ongoing play, but you can offer these youngsters effective help.

Take such children aside, one at a time, and ask them about the group they are trying to enter. Do they know what the play is about? If not, ask them to stand near the group, watching and listening to what happens. Then instruct them to come back and tell you about the play. Next, ask them how they could help the group feel better about their play. This focuses the child's thoughts and feelings away from herself and toward empathizing with the group.

If she says that the players are taking their babies to the doctor's office for shots, you might ask her: "How can you help them in their play?" She may answer: "I can take my baby, too." Coach her to get one of the dolls from the housekeeping area and take it to "get a shot" with the others. She should not ask permission or say anything at first, just go in and play with the others as if she is part of the group. Watch and see what happens. If this fails, have her play with her doll next to the others and try again to enter their play a little later.

Giving another example, if Roger complains to you that "Angelo won't let me play trucks with him!" ask Roger to find out how Angelo is playing trucks, and if he says "He's driving his truck on a block road," you might suggest that Roger try building a block road next to Angelo's and drive his own truck on it.

In most of these situations you are helping the children learn how to enter group play on their own. Use this rule of thumb in group-access struggles: do not intervene in the group unless a child causes harm to another child or the materials.

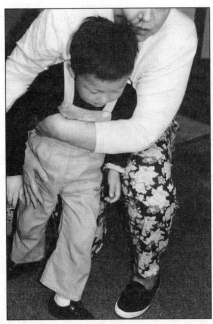

*Teachers can coach children who need help
entering a group on their own.*

Instead, coach the entering child to find out how the group plays, how he might play
in the same way, and then encourage him to try it—more than once, if necessary.

You may find one exception to this rule, however. A shy or new child who
will not try anything on her own, may require your support (but not force). Gently
take the child by the hand and go over and stand near a group to watch their play.
Ask the child what she thinks is happening and how she might contribute to it. If the
children are playing store, for instance, you might say, "Debbie, shall we get our
purses and buy something in Jamie's store? What do you want to buy?" Once the
child becomes immersed in the play, you can withdraw unobtrusively. On the other
hand, the group may decide not to accept Debbie or anyone else, which is their right.
In that case, suggest to Debbie that she play nearby and that you can try again
together tomorrow.

USING CONFLICT-CONVERSION STRATEGIES WITH A CHILD WHO DISRUPTS PLAY THROUGH PHYSICAL OR VERBAL AGGRESSION

If a group-entry conflict gets out of hand, you may need to intervene. If children fight, cry, or harm materials, you should stop the aggression and take the two

children aside for conflict conversion. When more than two are involved, talk with only two: the outsider who tried to enter the group forcibly and one of the children who tried to prevent him from entering. Blame neither one of the children because that is not the issue in preschool conflicts. Conflicts naturally occur in the preschool classroom and can be used to teach powerful lessons on how to get along with others.

Case #6 below, "The Case of the Missing Red Telephone," represents a typical group-entry conflict. The conflict-conversion questions are:

Conflict-Conversion Questions

1. What's happening, _____ (child's name)?
2. How does _____ (other child) feel?
3. What will make him (or her) feel better?

#6. The Case of the Missing Red Telephone

Setting: In this particular inner-city classroom, twenty rambunctious children create a number of short-lived conflicts usually resolved by the children themselves. The teacher tries to keep a tight but respectful rein on the children so things do not get out of hand. She believes that their lives are already chaotic and they need to let off steam in the program within controlled limits. She has used other-esteem conflict conversion previously, which works for her. The children often try to control their space and activities by keeping others out. The teacher supports their right to this privacy. In Case 6, Shaneika and Paula accuse Quentin, one of the most disruptive children, of stealing a red telephone from the housekeeping area where they are playing. Both girls run after Quentin and hit him with their purses.

Teacher: *Shaneika, Paula, Quentin! Slow down. Come over here with me. Yes, right now!* (The children allow teacher to lead them to a quiet corner where they all sit down on pillows.) *Girls, I can't allow you to hit anyone with your purses like that!*

Shaneika: *Quentin stole our red telephone and he won't give it back!*

Quentin: *I did not!*

Paula: *Yes, you did, Quentin! I saw you!*

Quentin: *I did not!*

Teacher: *Where is the telephone now?* (no answer) *Do you know where it is, girls?* (no answer) *Quentin?* (no answer) *When did all of this happen, girls? I don't see the telephone in Quentin's hands.* (no answer) *So I guess the telephone is missing, right?* (Girls nod.) *Well, what are we going to do about it? Quentin, you give me your ideas first. What shall we do about it?*

Quentin: (shrugs)

Teacher: *What do you think will make the girls feel better, Quentin?*

Quentin: *If they had the red telephone.*

Teacher: *If they had the red telephone. Is that right?* (The girls nod.) *But nobody knows where it is. What do you think would make Quentin feel better, girls?*

Shaneika: *If he could play with us. But we don't want him to. He always takes things.*

Teacher: *Is that what this is all about? You want to play with the girls and they won't let you, Quentin?* (Quentin shrugs.) *The girls have a right to play by themselves, don't you remember? We always let people choose where they want to play, and then other children can play with them only if they give permission, remember? Girls, is there any way Quentin can play with you?*

Shaneika: *No. We don't want him to.*

Teacher: *What about you, Paula? Can you think of a way?*

Paula: *He could play with us if he didn't come in our house.*

Teacher: *He could play with you if he didn't come in the housekeeping area. How could he play, then?*

Quentin: *I could telephone them.*

Teacher: *You could telephone them! Would that work for you girls? Would you let Quentin play by telephoning you?* (Girls nod.) *Quentin, what a great idea! You can telephone them from anywhere in the classroom! All right. Everyone agreed? Let everyone give a "five" all around. Now we need the red telephone. Will you look for it, Quentin?* (He nods.)

Positive-Feelings Activity: Just after lunch and before this morning class goes home, the teacher always reads them a story and then lets the children choose a book from her duplicate lending library to take home. If she has intervened in a conflict, she uses this story period for a positive feelings activity as well. On this particular morning she reads *I'm Calling Molly,* (Kurtz, 1990) because the story describes a little African-American boy, Christopher, who plays with Molly, his next-door neighbor, except when she plays with her friend Rebekah. Then they won't let Christopher play, so he calls her on his red telephone. Has Quentin possibly seen this story? The teacher thinks he has. After she has finished reading the story, she asks Quentin, Shaneika, and Paula to tell their own red telephone story.

TEACHER'S ACTIONS, CASE #6

This teacher never knows how these conflict conversions will turn out, but she is happy if all of the child participants are happy. Quentin seems positive about an outcome for the first time, as he has never been allowed to play with the girls before. Once they made their decision to let him phone them, the red telephone mysteriously appeared, as the teacher suspected it would. Although her usual rule of thumb is to talk with only two children in conflict, she felt she needed to involve both girls since both were part of the conflict.

Teachers, teacher assistants, and student teachers ought to adapt the conflict-conversion technique presented in this text to their own situation. They know their children and what works or does not work for them. Teachers who have tried this other-esteem, conflict-conversion technique say it works surprisingly well with disruptive children where nothing else has succeeded. Once the children are calmed down, they seem to respond well to thinking of something that will make the other child feel better. This feels much better to them than being blamed or punished for their actions. Yet they must still answer for the consequences of their actions. The conversion to other-esteem helps "set things right" for themselves and the others involved.

The teacher in Case #6 noted she had not realized Quentin had a group-entry conflict. Previously she had seen him taking things that belonged to others and hiding them. He had the reputation in the classroom of stealing and being a child the others did not like. Now she realized he may have been struggling to find a way to play with others, but did not know how. Using a toy telephone resolved the immediate situation, but she decided that coaching Quentin on a one-to-one basis on how to enter an ongoing group might be necessary if his disruptive behavior continued.

How have these techniques worked with your children? Do certain children respond more readily than others? What adaptations have you made in converting conflicts to other-esteem? Each teacher must adjust her conflict management methods to the children and the situations she encounters. Mutual positive feelings eventually can emerge if she treats the children with respect and the conflict as a learning opportunity.

IDEAS + IN CHAPTER 6

Group-Entry Activities

1. Provide a number of pretend play activities.
2. Have two permanent dramatic play areas to accommodate a house setting and perhaps an office or a store.
3. Have enough space, blocks, and toy vehicles and people in the block area for several children to play at once.

4.   Have a sand table for pretend play with toy people, animals, and vehicles.
5.   Use lofts and large motor climbers for pretend play.
6.   Have feltboards with cutouts of book characters for pretend play.
7.   Have at least two children at a time use a single feltboard.
8.   Be sure to allow enough time for children to become deeply involved in pretend play.
9.   Observe one child at a time trying to enter ongoing play by using the Child Group-Entry Strategies Checklist.
10.   Do not push the youngest children into group experiences they are not ready for.
11.   Let young children pursue solitary or parallel play on their own.
12.   Take unsuccessful children aside and ask them about the group they are trying to enter.
13.   Have them stand near the group and watch to see what is happening.
14.   Ask them how they can help the group in their play.
15.   If they are still rejected, have them do parallel play next to the group, and try again later to enter it.
16.   Do not intervene with a group unless a child has caused harm to another child or the materials.
17.   Take a shy child by the hand and coach her step by step on how to enter the group.
18.   Coach children on a one-to-one basis on how to enter an ongoing group if nothing else works.
19.   Each teacher must adjust her conflict management methods to the children and the situations she encounters.

TRY IT YOURSELF

1.   Based on your observations, what is the main reason for children's inability to gain access to play groups in your program? Why do you think this is so?
2.   What were the successful strategies your children used as observed on the *Group-Entry Tactics Checklist*? How can you apply this information to help children who have been unsuccessful in entering ongoing groups? Report on the results.
3.   What is the teacher's role in helping children gain access to an ongoing group in your program? Is it better to intervene or to allow children to resolve the problem on their own? Why?
4.   How can pretending help a child who has trouble entering ongoing play? Give two examples of pretending that have worked for you or your children.
5.   Use the conflict-conversion strategy with a disruptive child who has been denied access to a group. Did you have to adapt it to your circumstances in any way? How? Why?

REFERENCES CITED

Beaty, J. J. (1994). *Observing development of the young child*. New York: Merrill/Macmillan.

Beaty, J. J. (1994). *Picture book storytelling: Literature activities for young children*. Fort Worth, TX: Harcourt Brace.

Corsaro, W. A. (1979). 'We're friends, right?' Children's use of access rituals in a nursery school. *Language in Society, 8*, 315–336.

Dodge, K. A., Schlundt, D. C., Schocken, I., & Delugach, J. D. (1983). Social competence and children's sociometric status: The role of peer group entry strategies. *Merrill-Palmer Quarterly, 29*(3), 309–336.

Ramsey, P. G. (1991). *Making friends in school: Promoting peer relationships in early childhood*. New York: Teachers College Press.

Shantz, C. U. (1987). Conflicts between children. *Child Development, 58*, 283–505

OTHER SOURCES

Hay, D. F. (1984). Social conflict in early childhood. *Annals of Child Development, 1*, 1–44.

Heidemann, S. & Hewitt, D. (1992). *Pathways to play: Developing play skills in young children*. St. Paul, MN: Redleaf Press.

Kemple, K. M. (1991). Preschool children's peer acceptance and social interaction. *Young Children, 46*(5), 47–54.

LeBlanc, L. M. (1989). Let's play: Teaching social skills. *Day Care and Early Education, 16*(3), 28–31.

CHILDREN'S PICTURE BOOKS ABOUT ACCESS STRUGGLES

Alexander, M. (1975). *I'll be the horse, if you'll play with me*. New York: Dial Books.

Alexander, M. (1981). *Marty McGee's space lab, no girls allowed*. New York: Dial Books.

Barton, J. (1991). *The happy hedgehog band*. Cambridge, MA: Candlewick Press.

De paola, T. (1975). *Strega Nona*. Englewood Cliff, NJ: Prentice-Hall.

Havill, J. (1989). *Jamaica tag-along*. Boston: Houghton Mifflin.

Kurtz, J. & Trivas, I. (Ill.). (1990). *I'm calling Molly*. Niles, IL: Albert Whitman.

Lloyd, E. (1978). *Nini at carnival*. New York: Thomas Y. Crowell.

Orr, W. & Campbell, G. (Ill.). (1988). *Amanda's dinosaur*. New York: Scholastic.

Williams, S. & Vivas, J. (Ill.). (1989). *I went walking*. San Diego, CA: Harcourt Brace.

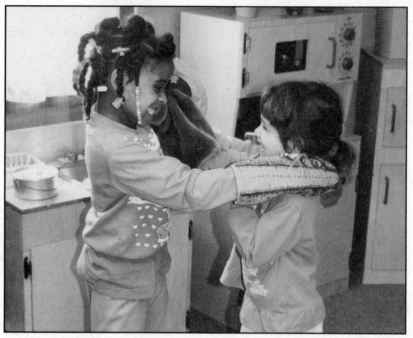

Bang, Bang, You're Dead!

(Aggressive Dramatic Play)

Superhero play can be bewildering and frustrating to teachers. We see its necessity for children as a way for them to feel powerful in a scary world, yet we also try to maintain a safe, caring environment. Sometimes, meeting both of these needs seems impossible. (Gronlund, 1992, p. 25)

SUPERHERO PLAY IN THE PRESCHOOL CLASSROOM

Dramatic play is often the keystone of the activities in a preschool classroom, which is as it should be. Young children use such unrehearsed pretend play as the principal way to learn about themselves, their peers, and the world around them. They take on pretend roles spontaneously in the dramatic play center or house-keeping area, becoming mother, father, baby, firefighter, police officer, doctor, bus driver, or anyone else who takes their fancy at that moment.

Dramatic play like this gives children the opportunity to try out the real-life roles they see around them. Through such free play they begin to understand what it is like to be a mother or a father. They see things from different perspectives, trying on for size the roles they may eventually play as adults. This type of pretend play reaches its peak during the preschool years, giving youngsters an unequaled opportunity to try out the new social skills they learn. Because this spontaneous play naturally leads to conflicts, children also get a chance to try out different conflict-resolution techniques, eventually learning which ones work best for them. Then come the superheroes.

"Cowabunga, dudes!" The Teenage Mutant Ninja Turtles have arrived! Or Superman, or Batman, or Wonder Woman, or Darth Vader, or the Terminator, the Power Rangers, or G.I Joe! "Crash! Bam! Pow!" Welcome to the world of super-hero play! Your children, especially the boys, may burst into the classroom flash-ing karate chops or shouting the latest superhero's challenge, scattering other children left and right as they imitate their heroes.

Is this dramatic play? And if it is, what can it possibly teach the children? That violence resolves conflict? That people can be controlled by force? Is this what we want for our children? What does it all mean, and how should you deal with it? The children get so caught up in the play both physically and emotionally that it seems real to them, then someone gets hurt, cries, and voices suddenly hush. Now you must deal with the consequences of superhero play. What will you do?

Across the country in day care centers, preschool classrooms, Head Starts, and prekindergartens alike, teachers, teacher assistants, and student teachers repeatedly must confront our society's latest media craze: the superhero. No one can escape it, it seems. Everywhere you look television programs, movies, video cassettes, records, and comic books feature the latest superheroes. This media bar-rage receives support from a merchandising blitz of toys, dolls, weapons, games, costumes, T-shirts, lunch boxes, beach towels, and even food in the image of the heroes: "Bang, bang, you're dead!"

This sort of play is nothing new for young children. Although the super-heroes themselves may be new, the play is not. Some children have always grav-itated to a type of pretend play that features power roles: cops and robbers, cowboys and Indians, pirates, monsters, space invaders, or war play. The power itself attracts the players. Because the roles preschool youngsters play become almost real to them, such powerful roles are alluring, indeed.

We remember from the power struggles in Chapter Four that all people instinctively strive for the power to make a difference. Young children are the most powerless of all in their adult-controlled world. Many of them jump at the chance to take on the roles of powerful superheroes. Some of us, in fact, call this kind of play *power role play* rather than dramatic play.

TO BAN OR NOT TO BAN

Many teachers quickly reply that no matter what its name, such play harms children, and they ban it in their classrooms. They feel that children have enough violence to cope with in the world around them, and do not need more in their play, which is perfectly logical adult reasoning. This logic does not, however, take into account the underlying psychological reasons for children's attraction to superhero play.

When children play out the roles and situations they see around them, they not only try to make sense of their world, but they also subconsciously try to deal with some very strong emotions, including fear. Children fear going to the doctor and getting a shot. Thus, "doctor play" and "giving shots" make up some of the most popular dramatic play themes in preschool classrooms because they have a therapeutic function. Children nervously give shots to the baby dolls, saying, "Hold still. This won't hurt. Are you okay?" They act out their own fears in a truly therapeutic way. Most teachers would not consider banning this type of play, even though children pretend to cause pain.

In like manner, children subconsciously attempt to play out their fears about the violence they see or experience in the world around them through superhero *power role play*. This safety valve allows them to work through and blow off strong emotions of all kinds.

Whether or not they live in the inner city, youngsters today see muggings, murders, beatings, robberies, and sexual abuse frequently on television news programs. All this violence can be very frightening. What are they to make of it all?

The violence in the world also affects adults, who too often blow off steam by striking out with words or physical abuse at those who cannot strike back at them—their children. Out-of-control adults in children's lives loom as the most scary of all for the youngsters. But nothing can hurt a superhero. They will take revenge on the "bad guys." No wonder our children so quickly embrace these power roles. No wonder that violent superhero play has increased so dramatically in the preschool classroom.

Preschool teachers have every right to ban superhero play in their classrooms if it cannot be controlled. However, first they need to be clear about what they are doing: they are refusing to allow children to act out a therapeutic drama that may help them deal with fear.

Because fear is such a strong emotion, only powerful pretend play can overcome it. Superheroes indeed make powerful pretend characters, but they can easily get out-of-control and lead to conflict. Superheroes and their adversaries often get carried away with overly-aggressive behavior toward one another. What starts as play can end as fighting with someone getting hurt. Teachers complain, more than anything else, about the tendency of superhero play to get out of hand. It may be therapeutic for the superheroes, but what about the children who end up as victims? And what about the teachers in charge? Should there be constant teacher intervention to help children deal with their fears? Is it possible to bring this power role play under control so that its positive benefits will be realized?

CONTROLLING SUPERHERO PLAY

Many teachers sanction superhero play in the classroom if it can be kept under control. They realize that anything that attracts such intense interest on the part of their children can be used to help children grow and develop. Just as with classroom conflict, superhero play is not in itself bad, but can provide a natural learning opportunity if controlled. Can this be achieved?

Our goal for children is for them to learn self-control, to be able to control their own behavior. Teachers have experimented with several ways to help children achieve these goals. When teachers spend most of their time trying to control superhero play, they do little to reduce its aggressiveness and much to make it permanently dependent on teacher-supervision.

Just as children will allow you to resolve their conflicts for them, they also will allow you to supervise superhero play if you want this role. Most teachers prefer that the children themselves learn to control this play, just as they do with other free play activities and any other conflicts that arise. When teachers try to control superhero play, it loses little of its aggressive nature. When children control their own actions, however, the play can become calmer and less rowdy. It behooves us, therefore, to try one or more of the suggestions given below to see what works for us.

  FIGURE 7.1

Helping Children to Control Superhero Play

1. Become familiar with the superhero play which occurs in your program.
2. Help children focus on the positive aspects of the superheroes.
3. Set limits for superhero play and enforce them consistently.
4. Convert superhero role play to play with miniature power models.
5. Help children to role-play powerful storybook heroes in place of television heroes.

BECOMING FAMILIAR WITH THE SUPERHERO PLAY WHICH OCCURS IN YOUR PROGRAM

Do you know what actually happens when the Ninja Turtles take over? In order to bring about positive results from this phenomenon, the classroom staff needs to take a close look at the play itself. Some teachers report that such play has become overly aggressive, rough, and out of control in recent years. The play does not follow a plot but consists mostly of repetitive moves or actions. How is it in your classroom? One kindergarten teacher noted:

> *As I watched more closely, I saw that most of the kicking and karate chopping was indeed an attempt at "fake fighting." Unfortunately, the amount of skill necessary for controlling such gross-motor movements is not well developed in kindergartners, so injuries occurred. With the advent of the Ninja Turtles movie, I was able to introduce the concept of stuntmen and -women who practice very carefully planned fake fights. A simple reminder of "Fight like they did in the movie," was all that was needed most of the time. (Gronlund, 1992, p. 23)*

Standing on one foot and swinging the other foot in a fake kick was not all that easy.

Gronlund's children had fun practicing their stuntman fake fighting several steps away from one another as an exercise out on the playground. Chopping through the air with an arm and hand extended, but stopping quickly, interested the children and helped them develop motor skills. Standing on one foot and swinging with the other one in a fake kick, without hitting anything, posed a challenge for the children. Those who mastered the maneuver agreed to use it only outside and away from others so that no injury could occur. This play provided, in fact, an excellent lesson in balance and control that some children then tried using in fake kicks with soccer balls.

The children (both boys and girls) who mastered these moves felt very good about themselves and very powerful as they realized that their heroes also used power and control. That was the key, as far as the teachers were concerned: power with control. The children understood they could get carried away with their power moves and actually hurt themselves or somebody else. Too much power was a bad thing. They liked finding a way to control it, and the fact that their teachers had learned about their heroes and allowed this activity delighted the children. The teachers, on the other hand, breathed a sigh of relief when they realized that the children could control superhero play. They agreed with the Idaho early childhood specialists (Pena, French & Holmes, 1987, p. 14) who wrote:

> *The attraction to power and the need for children to experience power in appropriate ways is the key to the issue. Too much power can be as detrimental and frightening as too little.*

HELPING CHILDREN FOCUS ON THE POSITIVE ASPECTS OF THE SUPERHEROES

Teachers have begun watching television cartoons and programs to learn about the superheroes. They jot down all of the positive traits that the characters exhibit, such as helping people in need, being brave, being honest, and preventing bad things from happening. Then they can talk intelligently with their children about their heroes' good points and how they might behave in certain situations. Children often are surprised and delighted that their teachers know about such things, and afterwards are more willing to try out less violent actions in their play.

Superheroes resemble fairy-tale characters in being one-dimensional: usually they are all good or all bad. Because they portray their natures so clearly, the children easily take on these roles. Superheroes often attract young children with their physical power, but you can help them discover other positive aspects. They may not know that these heroes also act with courage, help people in need, deal fairly, bring justice, and try to keep the peace. Children sometimes get so busy zapping the bad guys they just have not noticed these positive traits.

Is their hero brave? How does he or she demonstrate bravery? Is their character honest? What makes him honest? Does their hero help people? How? Can they pretend to help people when they play the role? Talk about these traits with the children. How can their hero demonstrate honesty, for example? Child development specialists point out that:

> *Superhero play helps children create a way to experiment with ideals and values. It enables children to make concrete ideals which our society prizes but which are abstract and difficult to grasp, such as honor, justice, courage, honesty, and mercy. (Kostelnik, Whiren, & Stein, 1986, p. 5)*

You may have noted that children also take the villain's role. How can that possibly help them? The villains in these dramas are always bad and always suffer defeat. Good triumphs over evil. Children often switch roles to see how it feels to be the bad guy. Although bad characters also have power, the superheroes fight them until the inevitable defeat. Psychologist Bruno Bettelheim discusses this bad dilemma as it relates to children identifying with the roles in fairy tales:

> *The child identifies with the good hero not because of his goodness, but because the hero's condition makes a deep positive appeal to him. The question for the child is not "Do I want to be good?" but "Who do I want to be like?" The child decides this on the basis of projecting himself whole-heartedly into one character. If this fairy-tale character is a very good person, then the child decides that he wants to be good, too. (Bettelheim, 1976, p. 10)*

Some children always seem to take the role of the villain in superhero play, just as some children frequently call attention to themselves with inappropriate behavior. Can such roles help these children? They can if the teacher spends time talking to individuals and small groups about their roles. She can talk about consequences and feelings: what happens when the villain misbehaves during superhero play; why does he act that way; how does the villain feels about his actions; and how do the superheroes feel about the villain's actions. Then the teacher can suggest the children try role reversals, which allow everyone a chance to be a hero and a villain.

Children who want to be like their superheroes can learn from your discussions that superheroes have more than strength. As they watch the television programs they can look for such qualities on their own. As they try out these traits in their superhero play, children not only learn new and important aspects of their heroes, but often they also tone down the wildness of their play.

SETTING LIMITS FOR SUPERHERO PLAY AND ENFORCING THEM CONSISTENTLY

Superhero play can adhere to the same limits you set for all behavior in your program, as long as you enforce them consistently. Children are not allowed to hurt one another or themselves, or to damage materials. They understand from experience that someone will intervene if they overstep these bounds. Firm intervention often serves as a reminder that we do not do things here that hurt one another. If aggressive interactions cause out-of-control behavior, an adult will intervene to convert the conflict to other-esteem.

In addition to these regular limits, teachers must determine time and space limits for superhero play. Some programs limit such play to recess or outdoor play periods. If you have indoor space, such as a gymnasium, available for running or expansive movements, superhero play may be allowed there as well. If superhero play seems to dominate the free play period to the exclusion of other activities, you may need to limit it to once a week. Rules you already have established restricting toy guns and weapons should apply to superhero play, too.

CONVERTING SUPERHERO ROLE PLAY TO PLAY WITH MINIATURE POWER MODELS

Some teachers have discovered another outlet for the powerful energies created by superheroes: playing with the heroes in miniature form. You can eliminate most of the undesirable features of superhero play—running, shouting, frenzied physical actions—when it is played on a tabletop. The characters from television programs generally are available in a variety of sizes ranging from twelve-inch dolls to two-inch miniatures. Vehicles and animals associated with the characters also can add realism to the play.

Some teachers store these figures in the block center for floor play with unit block constructions. Others keep the figures in the manipulative area for tabletop play with Legos or other table blocks. Still others use superhero miniatures in a sand table with vehicles. The teacher can limit the number of children playing at one time by the number of chairs put out.

Just as we provide tabletop space for other beneficial activities, providing a table for superhero play will allow children to realize the many social, emotional,

cognitive, and linguistic benefits possible from this
activity. (Johnston, 1987, pp. 16–17)

HELPING CHILDREN TO ROLE-PLAY POWERFUL STORYBOOK HEROES

If children are so strongly attracted to heroes and love to act out their heroes' roles, then we need to consider introducing the youngsters to heroes other than those they see on television. Wonderful bigger-than-life heroes abound in American folklore: Pecos Bill, the cowboy; Paul Bunyan, the giant lumberjack; Johnny Appleseed, the pioneer treeplanter; John Henry, the African-American steel-driving man. Jack-tales from England and the Appalachian mountain country tell rip-roaring stories of the young boy Jack who overcomes not only giants but dragons. The South African tale about a black boy who defeats the terrible monster Abiyoyo depicts still another hero worth knowing. All of these heroes come alive in dramatic picture books that you can share with the children.

What about girls? To get them started, read them *Amazing Grace* (Hoffman, 1991) about the exciting African-American girl, Grace, who spends her days acting out heroic roles: Joan of Arc, Anansi the Spider, a pirate, an African explorer, the Indian Hiawatha, or Aladdin and his wonderful lamp. The realistic full-page

Help children role-play powerful storybook heroes.

illustrations of Grace role-playing each of her heroes will send your girls to the dramatic play area to find dress-up clothes to use just as Grace did.

You, then, should play the role of Grace's grandmother who reads or tells stories to Grace about real or imagined heroes, encouraging Grace to dress up and play the roles herself. Read the following books to stimulate preschool girls and boys to role-play storybook heroes.

Paul Bunyan, (Kellogg, 1984) has every page of this large book filled with rambunctious illustrations. They show Paul wrestling with a giant grizzly bear, combing his beard with a pine tree, defeating the monstrous Gumberoos inside their den, making a giant flapjack griddle so big it has to be greased by his crew skating across it with bacon. They also depict Paul digging out the Great Lakes so that Vermont maple syrup can be sent to his camp, and Babe, his giant blue ox, who eats all the snow from the six-year blizzard so they can get across the Rockies and over to the Pacific Ocean.

If your children want to role-play Paul Bunyan as a superhero, be sure to read them the story several times until they know it by heart. Then have them re-enact the story following the "Guidelines for Creating a Story Re-enactment" (Figure 5.1). These will help them choose their characters and act out their roles when the time comes: Paul Bunyan, the blue ox, Babe, his logging crew, and the Gumberoos. You will know Paul Bunyan has become a favorite when you see his adventures being role-played by the children on their own during superhero play.

The Girl Who Loved Wild Horses, by Paul Goble, recounts a Native American legend about a Plains Indian girl who loves horses so much that she spends most of her time with the horses of her village until a fierce thunderstorm drives them far away to where a wonderful spotted stallion rules. She and her horses become part of his band, returning to her village once a year to bring the people a colt as a gift and receiving from them woven blankets, decorated saddles, and eagle feathers. One year she does not return, but instead the people see a beautiful mare galloping beside the mighty stallion. They say she surely has become a wild horse herself. Dramatic illustrations in Native American art fill the pages, helping children feel the fury of the storm, the pride of the stallion, and the bravery of the girl.

If your girls especially want to re-enact this story, then let them name the girl, the stallion, and the horse characters. Give them blankets to wrap around themselves and feathers to wear in their hair. Boys, of course, can participate if they want to, taking any of the roles—just as girls can enact the roles of male heroes.

Diego (Winter, 1991) tells the story of a real-life hero, the Mexican artist Diego Rivera, who became one of the greatest mural painters in the world. His life about a boy who loves to draw anything, anywhere—unfolds simply like a legend. It describes how an Indian healer named Antonia makes Diego well as a boy when he is dying; how he plays with wild animals and can talk to them; how he covers every surface around him with drawings in colored chalk; how he becomes famous painting the life of the people on the walls and ceilings of buildings all over Mexico.

The illustrations, like framed paintings on every page, can help your children re-enact this unusual story. They will need to take the roles of Diego, his mother and father, the healer Antonia, his pet parrot, the people at fiestas, the workers in the fields, and the soldiers. For props they can use a paintbrush, a small stepladder, farmers' sombreros, fiesta masks, or nothing at all but their imaginations.

Abiyoyo, (Seeger, 1986) narrates a South African legend about a little black boy and his father who together defeat the giant monster Abiyoyo before he eats up all the people in the village. The boy goes around the village playing his ukelele—clink, clunk, clonk—until the people make him "take that thing out of here." His father goes around the village with his magic wand, making things disappear: Zoop! Zoop! So the people force them both to leave the village and live on the other side of the village wall. One day the giant monster Abiyoyo appears, frightening everyone with his long fingernails, slobbery teeth, stinking feet, and matted hair. The people flee in terror, but the little boy grabs his father's hand and pulls him out to face the giant. The boy plays his ukelele faster and faster. The monster dances round and round until he finally falls to the ground. Zoop! goes the father's magic wand, and Abiyoyo disappears. The villagers bring back the two as heroes and all dance together singing the song "Abiyoyo." Children love to re-enact this story as you read or say the words describing the monster. Some want to use a real ukelele or wand, but others love to pretend. Everyone can sing the "Abiyoyo" song as the different monsters dance until they all fall down.

Give children many opportunities to learn about heroes other than those they see on television. Then help them to re-enact the dramas told in picture books. Other suggestions for storybook hero re-enactments can be found in this author's text *Picture Book Storytelling: Literature Activities for Young Children* (Beaty, 1994). Leave the storybooks out where the children can look at them in their free time, and fill the dramatic play area with boxes of clothes and props to fit the stories. You will know that storybook heroes have caught on when children pretend to be these superheroes on their own.

INTERVENING IN SUPERHERO PLAY

By following the suggestions described above, many teachers find that superhero play becomes less violent and more controlled. Sometimes, however, adults must intervene as they do with other conflicts in the classroom. When children overstep the limits and hurt others, themselves, or materials, an adult needs to intervene. When children get carried away with their roles, and fake fighting becomes real fighting, teachers need to step in. When running in the classroom gets out of hand or chasing on the playground leads to crying, adults should step in.

Children's faces can alert a teacher to possible conflict before it gets out of hand. When smiles disappear and frowns or signs of anxiety spread across children's faces, superhero play has lost its fun. You may need to redirect to something less rambunctious. "Time for the Ninja Turtles to sit down and have a drink of superjuice," you can say, or, "The space invaders need to refuel their spaceships

Children's faces can alert a teacher to possible conflict before it gets out of hand.

over in the block corner. Can you find the plastic hoses that squirt out space fuel from the block batteries?" Redirecting aggressive dramatic play by doing your own pretending works like magic with young children, who enjoy having the teacher enter their fantasy world.

When interpersonal clashes get out of hand, try to draw aside no more than two of the principal children involved if possible, even though others may have participated. Sometimes the teacher finds it impossible to convert the conflict to other-esteem, at least not immediately, as in Case 7, but she must try.

Conflict-Conversion Questions

1. What's happening _____ (child's name)?
2. How does _____ (other child) feel?
3. What will make him (or her) feel better?

#7. The Case of the Unyielding Monster

Setting: In this nursery school classroom of twenty four-year-olds, superhero play occurs almost daily. The teachers themselves were tired of Ninja Turtles, so they read hero stories to the children and did story re-enactment with the tales that the children like best of all. One of the favorites was *Abiyoyo.* Everyone wanted to be the father with the magic wand or the little boy with the ukelele who went around making everyone dance, even the monster. One of the teachers brought a ukelele, adding realism to the drama. The teachers knew that their storybook heroes had really caught on when the children began playing out the drama on their own. The role of the monster, Abiyoyo, was also popular, but some of the children played it too realistically. Charles stomped around so ferociously that he frightened some of the children. He would not dance to the ukelele at all but only stomped around and scared people. When it was Jonathan's turn to be the father, he whacked Charles several times with his magic wand, trying to get him to lie down, but Charles just kept coming towards him with his arms flailing and pushed him backwards. A fight ensued with both boys hitting each other and ending up crying. While the teacher took Charles and Jonathan aside, the assistant teacher took the other children over to the book center to listen to a story.

Teacher: *All right, Charles and Jonathan, that's enough. Let's stop the hitting. Come on over here. Let's sit down on these pillows and get quiet. (Boys sit down and finally stop crying.) Tell me what happened, Jonathan. Can you talk about it now?*

Jonathan: *Charles won't lie down. He won't lie down like he's supposed to. He just tries to push everybody around. He doesn't know how to play good!*

Charles: *I know how to play good. I'm the monster Abiyoyo. He always pushes people.*

Teacher: *Let's let Jonathan finish, Charles. You say that Charles won't lie down and that he was pushing. Is that right? (Jonathan nods.) Now you tell me what happened, Charles.*

Charles: *I punched Jonathan because he hit me with his magic wand. He kept hitting me, so I had to punch him out.*

Teacher: *How do you think he felt, Charles, when he hit you with his magic wand?*

Charles: *I think he's the one who doesn't know how to play good. You're not supposed to hit people with the magic wand. You're supposed to say "Zoop!" and they disappear.*

Teacher: *Yes, that's what happens in the story. So how do you think Jonathan felt when he hit you?*

Charles: *I think he felt mixed up.*

Teacher: *Is that right, Jonathan, did you feel mixed up?* (Jonathan shrugs.) *Tell me, Jonathan, how do you think Charles felt when he kept pushing you?*

Jonathan: *He's the one who felt mixed up. He was supposed to disappear when I said "Zoop!"*

Teacher: *So you both felt mixed up. Sounds like you both played your roles a little different than the story, didn't you? That's okay if the other person knows what you're doing. Sounds to me like Charles didn't hear you say "Zoop!," Jonathan, so he didn't disappear. And, Charles, it sounds to me like Jonathan tried to make you disappear by hitting you with the wand when you didn't stop pushing him. That's not what happens in the* Abiyoyo *story, is it? Well, what can you do to make each other feel better, now that it's over? How about you, Jonathan? What will make Charles feel better? Got any ideas?*

Jonathan: *You should make him stop being the monster.*

Teacher: *Well, I like you children to play these roles on your own. I don't want to be the one who tells people what role they can play. What will make Charles feel better, Jonathan? That's what I'm wondering about now. What will make him feel better? Look at him. What will put a smile on his face? Got any ideas?*

Jonathan: *He could use my magic wand when it's his turn to be the father.*

Teacher: *Well, that's very nice of you, Jonathan. Would that make you feel better, Charles, to use Jonathan's magic wand?*

Charles: *I don't want it.*

Teacher: *You don't want it? Well, what would make you feel better?*

Charles: *Nothing.*

Teacher: *Nothing? You're just not in the mood to feel better? Okay. Well, Charles, what do you think would make Jonathan feel better?*

Charles: *If he would disappear. He's trying to make me disappear. But he would feel better if he disappeared!*

Teacher: *He doesn't look like he would feel better if he disappeared. Would you, Jonathan? And I know I would feel bad if you both disappeared. Can we do something together to make all of us feel better?*

Jonathan: *Read the story again.*

Teacher: *Read* Abiyoyo *again? Okay. Is that all right with you Charles? Get the book, then, and bring it back here and I'll read it to both of you. Then we'll get this story straight, so nobody is mixed up. Okay?*

Positive Feelings Activity This teacher is not certain that the conflict is really converted. She has an idea that it was not about being mixed up, but rather that the children got carried away and the play degenerated into a shoving and hitting match. Preschoolers often play this way, but she does not want bad feelings between the two boys to last, so she decides to read *Little Critter's THIS IS MY FRIEND,* by Mayer (1989) to all the children just before they go home. This very simple story describes two children who do things to each other in friendship, but often they end up as misunderstandings. Even though they fight, in the end they remain friends. This time the teacher does not ask Charles and Jonathan to tell how they made each other feel better. Like this story, their conflict could have been a misunderstanding that cannot really be explained in words, just in feelings that may not be clear even to them. If the teacher did not have a book about friendship, she could have done a brief puppet play for the positive-feelings activity.

How do you manage superhero play in your classroom? If you ban it altogether you may be missing a powerful learning opportunity for the children in how to deal with fear and the use of power. Without limits, such play can get out of hand very quickly and require constant adult supervision. This chapter has presented a middle ground: superhero play with built-in controls of time, space, size, and types of heroes for children to experience as they take on pretend roles in order to learn more about themselves. As Johnston points out in *Harnessing the Power of Superheroes: An Alternative View* (1987, p. 16):

> Star Wars *hero Luke Skywalker learned from his mentor that the Force contained both Good and Evil. Luke had to learn to control the Evil in order to realize the Good. Superhero play is much like the Force; and like Luke Skywalker, we must learn to control the negative aspects of superhero fantasy play in order for children to realize its many benefits.*

IDEAS + IN CHAPTER 7

Aggressive Dramatic Play Activities

1. The classroom staff needs to take a close look at superhero play in order to bring about positive results.
2. Introduce the concept of movie stuntmen who practice planned fake fights.
3. Do fake fighting like stuntman do as an exercise on the playground.
4. Fake kicking with soccer balls provides an excellent lesson in balance and control.
5. Watch television programs about superheroes and jot down the positive traits of the characters.
6. Talk with children about their heroes' good points and the consequences of the villains' actions.
7. Have children look for these qualities in television programs.
8. Set limits for superhero play and enforce them consistently.
9. If aggressive interaction causes out-of-control behavior, then intervene with conflict-conversion techniques.
10. Set time and space limits for superhero play.
11. Apply rules you have already set restricting toy guns and weapons to superhero play as well.
12. Have children play with miniature superheroes as a tabletop or sand table activity.
13. Introduce children to bigger-than-life American folk heroes like Paul Bunyan, Pecos Bill, Johnny Appleseed, and John Henry.
14. Read Amazing Grace (Hoffman, 1991) and have dress-up clothes in the Dramatic Play Center to use as Grace did.
15. Read *Paul Bunyan* (Kellogg, 1986) and have children do a story re-enactment.
16. Read *The Girl Who Loved Wild Horses* (Goble, 1978) and have your girls name the girl and horse characters before they re-enact the story.
17. Read *Diego* (Winter, 1991) and help children re-enact this story about the famous Mexican painter Diego Rivera.
18. Read *Abiyoyo* (Seeger, 1986) and have children re-enact this monster story.
19. Fill the dramatic play area with boxes of clothes and props to fit each story.
20. Intervene when fake fighting becomes real fighting and chasing causes crying.
21. You may need to redirect this play when smiles disappear and anxiety spreads across children's faces.
22. Redirect aggressive dramatic play by doing your own pretending. This works like magic with young children.

TRY IT YOURSELF

1. What kinds of superhero pretending have occurred with children you have been involved with? How does this compare with the description in this chapter?
2. Name two effective ways that caregivers can deal with violent overtones in dramatic play? Use one with children and discuss the results.
3. How could you use space stories as a basis for superhero play in your classroom? What might children gain from this? Try it and see.
4. In "The Case of the Unyielding Monster" how would you have handled the conflict conversion with a child like Charles who resisted being "converted"? What would you do then for a positive feelings activity?
5. Observe superhero play in a preschool classroom. Would you ban such play from your classroom? Give three reasons why or why not.

REFERENCES CITED

Beaty, J. J. (1994). *Picture book storytelling: Literature activities for young children.* Fort Worth, TX: Harcourt Brace.

Bettelheim, B. (1976). *The uses of enchantment: The meaning and importance of fairy tales.* New York: Alfred A. Knopf.

Gronlund, G. (1992). Coping with ninja turtle play in my kindergarten classroom. *Young Children, 48*(1), 21–25.

Johnston, J. M. (1987). Harnessing the power of superheroes: An alternative view. *Day Care and Early Education, 15*(1), 15–17.

Kostelnick, M. J., Whiren, A. O., and Stein, L. C. (1986). Living with he-man: Managing superhero fantasy play. *Young Children, 41*(4), 3–9.

Pena, S., French, J., and Holmes, R. (1987). A look at superheroes: Some issues and guidelines. *Day Care and Early Education, 15*(1), 10–14.

OTHER SOURCES

Carlsson–Paige, N. & Levin, D. E. (1985). *Helping young children understand peace, war, and the Nuclear threat.* Washington, DC: National Association for the Education of Young Children.

Carlsson–Paige, N. & Levin, D. E. (1987). *The war play dilemma: Balancing needs and values in the early childhood classroom.* New York: Teachers College Press.

Harbin, J. & Miller, D. (1991). Violent play behavior and language of four-year-old boys: The significance of teacher mediation. *Early Child Development and Care, 75,* 79–86.

Ishee, N. & Goldhaber, J. (1990). Story re-enactment: Let the play begin! *Young Children, 45,*(3), 70–75.

Jones, C. B. (1991). Creative dramatics: A way to modify aggressive behavior. *Early Child Development and Care, 73,* 43–52.

McCracken, J. B. (Ed.). (1986). *Reducing stress in young children's lives.* Washington, DC: National Association for the Education of Young Children.

Wichert, S. (1989). *Keeping the peace: Practicing cooperation and conflict resolution with preschoolers*. Philadelphia: New Society Publishers.

CHILDREN'S BOOKS ABOUT SUPERHEROES

Clements, A. & Yoshi, (Ill.). (1988). *Big Al*. Saxonville, MA: Picture Book Studio.
Cohen, M. & Hoban, L. (Ill.). (1981). *Jim meets the thing*. New York: Greenwillow Books.
De Paola, T. (1975). *Strega Nona*. Englewood Cliffs, NJ: Prentice-Hall.
French, F. (1991). *Anancy and Mr. Dry-Bone*. Boston: Little Brown.
Goble, P. (1978). *The girl who loved wild horses*. Scarsdale, NY: Bradbury Press.
Haley, G. E. (1979). *The green man*. New York: Charles Scribner's Sons.
Haley, G. E. (1986). *Jack and the bean tree*. New York: Crown.
Haley, G. E. (1988). *Jack and the fire dragon*. New York: Crown.
Hoffman, M. & Binch, C. (Ill.). (1991). *Amazing Grace*. New York: Dial Books.
Keats, E. J. (1965). *John Henry, an American legend*. New York: Alfred A. Knopf.
Kellogg, S. (1984). *Paul Bunyan*. New York: Morrow.
Kellogg, S. (1986). *Pecos Bill*. New York: Morrow.
Kellogg, S. (1988). *Johnny Appleseed*. New York: Morrow.
Kent, J. (1981). *The scribble monster*. San Diego, CA: Harcourt Brace Jovanovich.
Mayer, M. (1989). *Little critter's THIS IS MY FRIEND*. New York: A Golden Book.
McDermott, G. (1972). *Anansi the spider*. New York: Holt, Rinehart and Winston.
McDermott, G. (1992). *Zomo the rabbit*. San Diego, CA: Harcourt Brace Jovanovich.
McDermott, G. (1993). *Raven*. San Diego, CA: Harcourt Brace.
Seeger, P. & Hays, M. (Ill.). (1986). *Abiyoyo*. New York: Macmillan.
Winter, J. & Winter, J. (Ill.). (1991). *Diego*. New York: Alfred A. Knopf.

Don't Call Me Stupid!
(Name-Calling Conflicts)

Children, like adults, want to feel good about themselves, so anything that does not reinforce a positive self-image is hurtful. The child who calls other children unpleasant names has found a way of hurting them. (Essa, 1990, p. 76)

NAME-CALLING CONFLICTS IN THE PRESCHOOL CLASSROOM

Most of us remember the old childhood chant: "Sticks and stones will break my bones but names will never hurt me." We also realize, even as we did as children, that unpleasant names *do* hurt. They can hurt the ego of the child just as much as kicks and punches. Happily this sort of conflict does not happen as often as possession disputes or access struggles in most preschool classrooms. Nevertheless, verbal aggression is unacceptable behavior and must be dealt with by the classroom staff. Even names called in fun often leave behind bad feelings.

What names are called in your classroom? Do children call them in fun or out of frustration? Before we can begin to deal with this conflict, we must first observe it when it happens. Several aspects of name-calling need to be considered in order to help children convert it to acceptable behavior. Observe what happens when name-calling takes place, keeping the following questions in mind.

 FIGURE 8.1

Name-Calling Observation Questions

1. How is the name-calling being done by the caller?
2. Who calls and who is being called the names?
3. When and where does the name-calling occur?
4. How does the recipient respond to the name-calling?
5. What provokes the name-calling?

HOW NAME-CALLING IS DONE

Your first clues about the name-calling itself will be nonverbal ones. What does the caller's face look like when she says the name? Is she smiling? Is she frowning? Does she look angry? How does her voice sound? Is it loud? Is it singsongy? Does it sound angry? Does she mutter under her breath? Does she say the name only once, or does she repeat it several times, or is it part of an argument? How far away is the caller from the victim? Is he up close or at a distance? Does the caller look around to see if you or another adult has noticed?

If the name-caller is smiling, perhaps he is just teasing or doing it in fun although it will not necessarily be received in this way by the recipient. Because we help children to develop empathy—the ability to feel as another feels—the caller himself will need, at some point, to learn how it feels to be called a name. If the caller frowns and uses a loud or angry-sounding voice, she probably is using name-calling as a weapon, just as another child might hit or push. On the other hand, if the name caller quickly looks around to see whether an adult has noticed, she might be trying to gain attention in an inappropriate manner.

Observe yet another aspect of name-calling: the name itself. Does it fit its recipient in any way, or is it a generic sort of name such as "stupid," "dummy," or "dumbell" which is called out to anyone. Names such as "crybaby," "fatty," or "bully" are more often used with children who are perceived to have these specific characteristics. Children do not use racial epithets as frequently in early childhood classrooms, perhaps because many preschoolers have not yet learned to classify their peers by race or ethnic group. Swearing, like name-calling, occurs more frequently than formerly because of its increased acceptance on television and in society at large. If children hear swearing in the home they may imitate it in the classroom or child development center.

IDENTIFYING WHO THE CALLERS AND RECIPIENTS ARE

The teacher must determine whether one child seems to do most of the name-calling or if others become involved. Sometimes name callers come from a neighborhood or a home where they hear older children or adults using verbal abuse. Other classroom peers may not attack verbally unless someone initiates it.

Who are the recipients? Does the same child always seem to bear the brunt of the name caller's verbal aggression, or are other children also being victimized? Some aggressive youngsters seem to pick on the same child over and over, teasing him with names, perhaps because they can be sure of his response. On the other hand, friends sometimes call one another unpleasant names in friendly teasing. This inappropriate behavior in the classroom sets the stage for others to follow suit. You may not need to intervene personally in this case. Sometimes merely reading a story to the children involved about a similar situation will be sufficient.

Harry and Willy and Carrothead, (Caseley, 1991) is a picture book that describes three friends: Harry, who wears a prosthesis for his left hand, but is not ridiculed by the other children because he is not embarrassed about it; Oscar, a boy with red hair, who is called "Carrothead" by his friend Willy; and Willy, who does not realize that he hurts Oscar when he calls him "Carrothead." The story helps all three boys learn that unpleasant names can hurt even when used in fun.

WHEN AND WHERE NAME-CALLING OCCURS

Observe the name-calling situation as much as possible and take note of when and where it happens. Does it usually occur every morning when the children pour into the classroom from their buses? Perhaps something happened on the bus ride to trigger it. Talk to the bus driver and find out. Or, does name-calling happen mainly during free play when children mill around the room, interacting with peers and engaging in activities? Sometimes name-calling occurs at lunch when certain children sit next to one another. There, you may decide to change the seating.

Other name-calling may occur when you are not nearby, such as out on the playground, where youngsters tend to be more boisterous. The bathroom serves as another location for name-calling, whether you are present or not. Recipients or tale tellers quickly let you know all about it.

THE RECIPIENT'S RESPONSE TO NAME-CALLING

Teachers, teacher assistants, and student teachers should take note of how the recipient responds to name-calling. If he pays no attention and goes about his business, the name-calling usually stops. If the caller intends to tease, ridicule, hurt, or embarrass someone but fails, then he usually stops. Classroom adults sometimes can help recipients of name-calling by suggesting that they ignore it.

Some recipients, on the other hand, strike out against the caller with their own physical or verbal aggression. You may need to intervene by stopping the hurtful behavior and then helping the children involved with conflict-conversion strategies. Teachers find it more difficult to help the child who withdraws but does not express his hurt openly—like Oscar, the boy called "Carrothead." Some children like the nicknames they are called, because it makes them part of the group. If you pick up that a certain child does not feel this way, then use conflict conversion with this child and the name caller to help them both learn how the other feels.

If children can learn to ignore name-calling, it often stops.

THE CAUSES OF NAME-CALLING

Sometimes observations reveal the cause for the name-calling, sometimes not. Some children call one another names when they are angry. Others may use name-calling as a habitual way of dealing with anything unpleasant. They deal with their bad feelings by trying to make someone else feel bad. Observing them may not reveal why they are feel the way they do, but when children use name-calling habitually for no obvious reason, it is probably prompted by their own negative feelings.

Becoming aware of causes and trigger events may help you deal with name-calling, especially if dealing with the cause will eliminate the name-calling.

PREVENTION OF NAME-CALLING CONFLICTS

Once you observe the children involved in name-calling, learn as much about it as possible and begin to take preventive measures in the classroom. Teachers who have gathered observational data based on the five questions posed in Figure 8.1, *Name-Calling Observation Questions*, often plan preventive activities around the types of name-calling they have identified.

 FIGURE 8.2

Kinds of Name-Calling and Preventive Activities to Deal with Them

Teasing; in fun	Books; story re-enactment; animal puppets; feltboard characters
Power; attention getting	Ignoring; praising; regain sense of power through tasks
Anger; frustration	Substitute words or actions

TEASING NAMES

Children who name call in fun or to tease can learn how it feels to be on the receiving end through books and story re-enactments. An excellent book to read, not just to name callers but to the entire class, is *Don't Call Me Names!* (Cole, 1990). Foxy Mike and piggy Joe plague little froggie Nell, always teasing her with "Nell, Nell, dumbbell," or "Nell's as green as a lima bean." Her porcupine friend Amy stands up to the boys when they call her names, giving the same back to them instead of running home and hiding, like Nell. Finally, during the Costume Day parade, Nell, dressed as a monster, confronts Mike and Joe and frightens them away from teasing little mouse Nicky.

If children enjoy this story, they will want you to read it over and over. Make it fun for them by reading the dialogue in different comical voices for each speaker. When children know the story by heart and can tell it back to you, get them started on story re-enactment as described in Chapters Five and Seven. The characters to be dramatized are Nell, Amy, Nicky, Mike, and Joe. Write down each name and who will play each part. As many children as want to can play each part at the same time. You, as the narrator, will read the story to keep things going. Everyone else can be the audience. When it is time for each character to speak, you can whisper their lines or they can make up their own. Let them have fun with the name-calling, making up any names they wish. More than one child may speak for the same character.

Most children want to repeat this exciting activity many times, which the teacher should allow. Encourage the children to play different characters as often as they wish. In this way they actually will experience how it feels to call names as well as being called names. Does anyone notice that Amy is not afraid of being called names by Mike and Joe? Do they see how she deals with it?

If children really get caught up in story re-enactment like this, you may want to bring in animal hand puppets (you can use hot-pad gloves) to represent the characters. Other name-calling books that can be dramatized include: *Fighting Words* (Merriam, 1992; see Chapter 5); *Move Over, Twerp* (Alexander, 1981; see Chapter 2); *Willy the Wimp* (Browne, 1984), *Oliver Button Is a Sissy* (De Paola, 1979), *Bootsie Barker Bites* (Bottner, 1992); and *Emily Umily* (Corrigan, 1984). The characters in these books overcome their name-calling plight in several ways, as shown in Figure 8.3.

 FIGURE 8.3

Book Characters' Ways of Overcoming Name-Calling

Don't Call Me Names: call names to the name callers
dress like a monster and scare them
do not run and hide

Fighting Words: call each other funny names

Move Over, Twerp: stand up to the big boys
wear a Supertwerp T-shirt

Willy the Wimp: build up strength and defend friends

Oliver Button Is a Sissy: practice hard and dance in a talent show

Bootsie Barker Bites: scare Bootsie in the same way she scares the
girl narrator

Emily Umily: learn to chant an "um" sound and teach the
other kids how

Young children usually enjoy the books you read to them, but often they do not get the point or cannot articulate it. Preschoolers, after all, have not progressed beyond the beginning stages of their cognitive development and sometimes need help understanding cause and effect or logical thought. In story re-enactment where they take the actual roles of the characters, your youngsters will begin to develop real insights about how children can overcome a bad situation. You also can talk to them about these abstract ideas, but not everyone will understand. Often, children gain awareness and understanding by frequent repetition of concrete, hands-on activities.

Preschoolers also enjoy a similar activity, playing with feltboard characters cut out from the books they like best. Make such characters from extra paperback copies of the books as previously described. Cut out the characters, laminate them or mount them on cardboard, glue on a sandpaper backing, and encourage children to play out their roles by placing the characters on stand-up feltboards. To make your own feltboards, obtain squares of felt from a fabric store or hobby shop and glue them onto double squares of cardboard, folded in two to stand on their own. Keep the characters, along with a copy of the book, in a labeled manila envelope on the shelves of your story center for children to play with on their own.

A good paperback book to cut out felt characters from is *A Porcupine Named Fluffy* (Lester, 1986). Here the dilemma focuses on the funny, inappropriate names of the characters: Fluffy is a porcupine who is not very fluffy, and Hippo is a rhinoceros!

What if playing with name-calling characters encourages the children to name call more than ever in the classroom? As long as it is in fun and not hurtful, let them get it out of their systems but within limits. Children enjoy saying aloud the outlandish names used by the storybook characters. If they want to name call in the classroom, have them do so in pairs as long as both agree. Or, encourage them to do it with the cutout characters you have created for feltboard play, for doll play in the housekeeping area, or for toy people play in the block center.

POWER NAMES; ATTENTION GETTING

Name-calling also involves a lack of power to make a difference, often felt by children with poor self-images. These youngsters (who are also discussed in Chapter Four) bully other children and demonstrate their supposed power over others by calling them unpleasant names. These names may also be used by some of the children who try to gain attention in inappropriate ways (see Chapter Three).

Children discover early on that words have power. By age two even toddlers are familiar with the most powerful word in the English language: No! Indeed, they find it surprising that such an interesting word has such a startling effect on the adults around them. They soon discover a number of ways to get responses from their caregivers simply by saying "No."

Children can have their puppets call each other funny "power names."

Articulate children often discover the power of name-calling when they want to get their own way. Sometimes they learn it from members of their household or from television. Sometimes they just stumble on it by themselves. They can see by the response of others how powerful names are: "Stupid!" "Dummy!" "Frog face!" "Lazy dumbbell!" or swear words. The youngest children usually do not even know what such names mean. The meanings are immaterial. To them, the response they get alone counts.

A few parents even allow their children to call *them* such names. How then can caregivers expect the youngsters to behave differently in preschool? We can, of course, and we must. Preschoolers in a group situation can learn how to get along with others in harmony, verbally as well as physically. If they need power in order to feel good about themselves, then you can help them to regain a sense of power by putting them in charge of a meaningful classroom task as discussed in Chapter Four. First, though, they need to discover that they cannot impose their will on others through name-calling.

Name-calling works as a power ploy only when someone responds. If everyone involved ignores it, it eventually stops. You must begin with yourself. Do not respond to the name-calling. Do not make eye contact with the caller. Help the recipient to ignore the names being called. Go over to the recipient if necessary and give him support. Stand between him and the name caller. Put an arm around him and lead him to another area if this seems appropriate. Ask him to perform a task for you in another room. With no one to pester, the caller will have to stop. Continue this behavior for as long as possible. Only if the calling becomes screaming or hurtful will you need to intervene using the conflict-conversion strategies.

Otherwise, wait until after the name-calling has stopped before you approach the caller. Watch to see what appropriate verbal behavior he eventually demonstrates. When you notice something, no matter how small, approach the caller and commend him for his new behavior. "Oh, Anthony, what good words you are using to tell Darnell about the story! What else is the Gingerbread Man doing?"

Children who use name-calling as a power ploy may also need to learn other more appropriate ways to make their words powerful. In what ways are words especially powerful in your classroom? Make a list of the specific ways that you, your staff, and the children use words to make a difference on a daily basis. Does your list include any of the following?

 FIGURE 8.4

Using Words to Make a Difference in the Classroom

Greeting adults and children
Calling names for attendance and answering
Doing "show and tell" at circle time
Telling the activity choice for free play
Giving directions for new activity
Asking for volunteers to help
Reminding children about cleanup time
Reading and telling stories
Leading a transition action chant
Talking about feelings during conflict conversion
Doing a positive-feelings activity
Tape recording favorite words
Doing a story re-enactment

Can your name caller be involved in one of these activities? If she likes to call out names, ask her to call attendance for you in the morning. Then thank her for saying the names so loudly and clearly. Instead of announcing, "Five minutes till cleanup time," to the entire class, have your name caller go around to individual children and remind each of them personally. Does she have favorite words she likes to say? Have her make a tape recording of them and play them back to the others during circle time. What other appropriate name-calling activities can you think of?

ANGRY NAMES

Some children use name-calling when they are frustrated or angry at someone. They may have learned this strategy at home, or from children in the neighborhood.

Name-calling can become a habit just as biting can for certain children when they become too frustrated to speak, and bad habits are not all that easy to break. If they are well established, only some effort on the part of the name caller will alter this behavior. As Mark Twain pointed out about adult habits:

> *Habit is habit and not to be flung out of the window by any man, but coaxed downstairs a step at a time. (Twain, 1990)*

How can you coax your name-calling children down their steps? First, help them to realize that words hurt as much as punches. You may need to intervene with them when they lash out in anger with words, just as you do with a child who bites. After they have calmed down enough to take part in conflict conversion, help them to develop empathy by asking your second question: "How does Roger feel, Tony? Look at his face. How do you think he feels?" When Tony hears what his victim has to say about him, he may consider changing his ways. Let the children work out their own solutions as you do with other conflicts where intervention is necessary. Later, however, you may want to involve this child with activities to help him break his habit.

Such activities can include substituting more appropriate words for the unpleasant names she uses. If saying powerful but hurtful names gives the child relief from her frustrations, just as swearing does for adults, then help the child use some substitute words with epithet puppets. What are epithet puppets? They are name-calling hand puppets that you put aside for upset children. Keep several puppets in a special place for use when children become upset. They can put on their puppets and have their puppets call each other funny "power names." Eve Merriam's picture book *Fighting Words* (1992) is a rich source for wonderful-sounding name-calling words such as:

oaf	*dolt*	*buffoon*	*blockhead*
lummox	*ninny*	*dodo*	*blunderbuss*
grouse	*kinkajou*	*fluke*	*bilge water*
claptrap	*poppycock*	*malarkey*	*balderdash*

Another source of nonsensical names is Dr. Seuss's story "Too Many Daves" from his book *The Sneetches and Other Stories* (1961). Mrs. McCave has twenty-three sons, all named Dave, in this rhyming tale, and she wishes she had named them something else instead. She goes into a long rhyming list of twenty-three other nonsensical names: from Bodkin Van Horn to Zanzibar Buck-Buck McFate. Let your children roll these rollicking monikers off their tongues with their epithet puppets.

Make a game of it with frustrated children. They can use the words only with puppets. If they cannot find anyone to use an epithet-puppet with, have them put one on each of their own two hands and call the names at themselves. How will they learn the names? You can make a tape recording of them. Or, they can learn them by hearing you read the books. Tell such children that on days when they are feeling out of sorts, they should carry the puppets around with them, to let off steam with their epithet-puppet words whenever they feel the need.

The words themselves sound so silly to the children that the words alone should perk up their spirits. Even the word *epithet* provides a comic relief for frustrated youngsters. If they habitually express anger verbally, these words can make a positive difference in their lives.

Another method for taking the sting out of hurtful names is to have the name callers engage in substitute activities such as a pretend fight with plastic dinosaurs on a tabletop. They can have their dinosaurs call each other names, too, if this helps. The dinosaurs' real names sound impressive enough to be power words in anyone's vocabulary:

Stegosaurus	*Triceratops*	*Iguanodon*
Brontosaurus	*Ankylosaurus*	*Tyrannosaurus rex*

Preschool children love to learn and say such multisyllabic names. They will help you pronounce the names of the beasts in picture books such as *Count-A-Saurus* (Blumenthal, 1989) and *Dinosaur Cousins?* (Most, 1987). But if you find that children also use dinosaur names to frighten others, as Bootsie Barker does in *Bootsie Barker Bites* (Bottner, 1992), then you should read them this story about the little girl narrator who overcomes Bootsie's verbal threats by finally telling her that she (the narrator) is now a *paleontologist* ready to dig up Bootsie's bones!

BEING A POSITIVE WORD MODEL YOURSELF

The words you use with the children are the most powerful words of all in the preschool classroom. Obviously, you yourself are not a name caller, but is the language you use around the children *responsive* or *restrictive?* Recent research has looked at the language of caregivers as a method for assessing their performance. Findings show that:

> *Caregiver language provides significant insight into caregiving behavior in general. The more closely we investigate a caregiver's language, the more clearly we know that person's caregiving behavior and style. (Stone, 1993, pp. 12–13.)*

Responsive language describes the most positive category of caregiver language. It shows "positive regard for children and a respect for and acceptance of their individual ideas and feelings" (Stone, 1993, p. 13). She gives examples, such as a teacher saying to a child in a conflict situation: "Hitting hurts. I can't allow you to hurt anyone." Such responsive language exemplifies nutrient or integrative power as discussed in Chapter Four.

At the opposite extreme, *restrictive language* involves "teacher control through such power-assertion methods as issuing unnecessary or disrespectful commands, threats, punishments, and criticisms." For instance, the teacher using restrictive language in the above example might say to the child: "Don't hit him. Be a good boy" (Stone, 1993, p. 13). Restrictive language like this illustrates exploitive, manipulative, or competitive power also as described in Chapter Four.

According to this research, caregivers who use responsive language primarily have children who demonstrate higher self-esteem and fewer discipline problems than those whose caregivers use mostly commands and threats. If we want our children to use words appropriately, we must be appropriate behavior models ourselves. Children imitate what they see and hear around them. Many youngsters get started down the name-calling road in the first place when someone in their environment uses name-calling as a threat or punishment. We can begin to help them overcome this habit by speaking to them with respect and by avoiding commands, threats, and criticisms. The teacher in Case #8 needs to think about her own use of words before she can truly help children to convert conflict in name-calling situations.

Conflict-Conversion Questions

1. What's happening _____ (child's name)?
2. How does _____ (other child) feel?
3. What will make him (or her) feel better?

#8. The Case of the Loose-Tongued Teacher

Setting: Barbara, a new teacher, has a prekindergarten class of twenty four- and five-year-olds. All year long the children have been testing her, she feels, as well as interacting too roughly with one another. She hears other teachers say that more children are misbehaving than ever before. She is determined to get her children settled down before the year ends, but so far her efforts have been unsuccessful.

Then she attends an in-service training session that presents "conflict conversion" as a technique to help the children themselves convert their own conflicts to feelings of other-esteem. She decides to give the new technique a try with Jason, the "terror of the prekindergarten." Jason does everything he can possibly think of to upset her and the other children. He runs, yells, pushes, takes toys, and has now gotten into a habit of name-calling. She has tried to stop him from calling the children "stupid," but her efforts just seem to incite him. Recently he has started calling everyone "puke face," and parents are complaining.

Marguerita: *Teacher, Jason called me puke face again. I wasn't even doing anything to him.*

Teacher: *Jason, come over here a minute. Yes, right now. Come here. I want to talk to you.* (Jason saunters over to Library Corner where teacher is standing with Marguerita.) *Now tell me what happened, Jason.*

Jason: *Nothing happened.*

Teacher: *Marguerita tells me that you called her puke face. Did you?* (no answer) *Did you call her that name?* (no answer) *What are we going to do with you, Jason? You're always causing trouble! How would you like it if I went around calling you puke face?* (no answer) *Well, Marguerita, you tell me what happened if Jason isn't going to say anything.*

Marguerita: *I was sitting at the art table and Jason came over and called me puke face.*

Jason: *You hit me first, Marguerita. You're always hitting me!*

Marguerita: *Well, you took my red crayon. You're always taking my crayons!*

Teacher: *All right. Let's think about how each other feels. How does Marguerita feel, Jason? How do you think she feels when you call her puke face?* (no answer) *Come on, Jason, you have lots to say to the children. Now let's hear from you. How is she feeling?*

(no answer) *Well, I'm going to stand right here until you can tell me about how she feels.* (no answer) *Listen, Jason, if you think you're going to get the best of me, you've got another think coming! We're going to stand right here all day until you tell me how Marguerita feels.* (no answer from Jason; Marguerita starts to cry.) *You want to know something, Jason? You are not going to go around this classroom calling names! Now speak up, how does Marguerita feel?*

Jason: (under his breath) *She's a puke face.*

Teacher: *What did you say? Did you call her a name? You know, Jason, you're not a very nice boy. I want you to sit over on that chair until you can tell me how Marguerita feels. Look what you've done to her. She's crying now.*

TEACHER'S ACTIONS, CASE #8

This teacher, first of all, needs to recognize that the words *she* uses in dealing with the children carry the most power in the preschool classroom. As you look at Case #8, try to pick out some of the power words and phrases that Barbara is using. Did you find any of the following:

Come over here

Yes, right now

Puke face

You're always causing trouble

Puke face

Puke face

You have lots to say

I'm going to stand right here

Listen, Jason

If you think you're going to get the best of me, you've got another think coming

We're going to stand right here all day

You are not going to go around this classroom calling names

Now speak up

You're not a very nice boy

I want you to sit over on that chair

Look what you've done to her

The teacher's language would be classified by early childhood researchers as *restrictive* because it contains commands, threats, and criticisms, and lacks respect for Jason. Does the teacher have to pay any respect to Jason because he is, as she notes, "the terror of the pre kindergarten"?

If we are truly sincere about helping children convert conflicts to other-esteem, then we must take the original step discussed in Chapter One by *changing our mind-set about children and conflict*. First of all, Barbara needs to rethink her own feelings about Jason. Jason is not a "terror," nor is he "always causing trouble," nor is he "not a very nice boy." These judgmental words express the teacher's own feelings of anger or irritation with Jason. Instead, Barbara must think of Jason as simply a young boy. As a preschool child, he has come to her class to grow and learn. He needs to learn how to get along with other children, and he needs Barbara's help in this regard.

Barbara should also rethink her feelings about conflict, because conflict between children is not the same as "always causing trouble." Conflict provides an opportunity for children to learn about their feelings and other children's feelings in order to convert them to other-esteem. Barbara can help children make this conversion if she steps back from the conflict and gets the children involved in developing empathy. Her voice and her words need to express calmness to the children, not commands, irritation, or name-calling.

Children repeat the words and phrases they hear around them. Jason already has picked up one of Barbara's phrases. She says to him: *You're always causing trouble!* and Jason says to Marguerita: *You're always hitting me!* Jason also continues to use his name-calling word, "puke face." After all, he has heard his teacher use it three times in this incident.

How would you use the suggestions offered in this chapter to convert the strong feelings experienced by Jason and Marguerita? Teachers are also human beings and have strong feelings, too. This teacher sounds as though she has reached the limits of her patience with Jason. Her good intentions to use conflict conversion have been thwarted by the adversarial situation she has set up inadvertently with Jason on one side and herself on the other. What can she do now?

She still can step back from the conflict and become a mediator. After all Jason and Marguerita have the conflict, not Jason and herself. Perhaps Barbara could change her mind-set about Jason by taking the incident less seriously and becoming more lighthearted. Children respond well to lighthearted teachers. They do not respond well to blame or criticism. After all, Jason is not bad and his actions are not bad, but they are inappropriate. If they are hurting someone, they should be stopped. They can be stopped just as easily, and perhaps more effectively, if the teacher displays more lightheartedness.

At heart, Barbara remains a creative teacher. She may lack experience, but she is willing to try new things. When her interaction with Jason reached an impasse, she finally stepped back and rethought her options. She had an uneasy feeling that this time she had brought the conflict on herself. Thus, she decided to try to undo the damage by getting both Jason and herself out of their adversarial mode.

She took two purple mittens out of her spare mitten box, put one on her hand and pasted peel-off circles for eyes on the top of the mitten and a line of circles for a mouth in the open palm of the mitten. Then she gave Jason the other mitten and the peel-off sheet of circles to make his own puppet. She told him, "Now we are going to have a 'whisper contest' with our puppets. Just you and me. I'm going to whisper all the names I can think of at your puppet, and you whisper your names back at mine. Ready? Go! Your puppet is a loudmouthed brontosaurus!"

This method worked. Jason caught on immediately and soon whispered back the most ferocious names he could make up. Before they had finished, both Jason and his teacher shook with laughter, and the bad feelings vanished.

Later Barbara decided she needed to learn much more about Jason's name-calling and other inappropriate behavior before she could help him to convert it. Was it done as teasing or attention getting or in frustration? Did Jason start the conflict or did he respond this way to what other children did to him? Until she had such information, her intervention might never work with Jason or any of the children. She decided to take time during free play when the children were busy to make objective observations for several days using the Observation Questions on page 26 as her guide. Then she would know what to do next. She had a strong feeling that Margie Carter's comment about child discipline was right on the mark:

> *A good deal of teacher training on child guidance*
> *focuses on* discipline techniques. *For me, this is*
> *one of the last steps in the teacher learning process.*
> *Teachers have some other very important work to do*
> *first. (Carter, 1992, p. 46)*

Barbara's observations of Jason turned up some surprising results. She found that Jason's running, yelling, pushing, taking toys, and name-calling actually had little to do with trying to upset her and the other children, but related a great deal to his inability to join in with other children at play. To make connections with his peers, Jason interfered with their play and activities. He would hang back until everyone was occupied and then make his disruptive moves. When the children pushed him away, he would strike back or call them names.

Barbara decided to defuse the situation by having the children work in preselected pairs for several days. She could see that Jason needed a great deal of positive attention before he settled down with a partner. She wondered if Jason might need to develop a stronger self-esteem before conflict conversion could be really effective for him. Her readings about child development seemed to point in this direction:

> *Children learn both social and cognitive skills*
> *best if they learn self-esteem at the same time.*
> *Children who like themselves and feel esteemed by*
> *others do not have to act rebellious or sullen.*
> *(Stone, 1978, p. 6)*

On the other hand, she realized that she needed to control her own tongue, and not let children's disruptive behavior personally affect her. Then, with practice, she could make other-esteem conflict conversion a natural part of her own repertoire. As Barbara read more about children's behavior, she especially liked Stone's commentary:

> *Discipline depends in part on [an] adult's own skills*
> *and good conduct. It depends on whether our teach-*
> *ing combines caring with control. This is hard, espe-*
> *cially with difficult children. It demands a lot of us.*
> *Good discipline is not just punishment or enforcing*
> *rules. It is liking children and letting them see that*
> *they are liked. It is caring enough about them to pro-*
> *vide good, clear rules for their protection. (Stone,*
> *1978, p. 6)*

Because she really liked the children and enjoyed her teaching, Barbara promised herself that her own loose tongue would have only positive things to say to children from now on.

IDEAS + IN CHAPTER 8

Name-Calling Activities

1. Step back from the children and observe what happens when name-calling takes place.
2. Read a story to an individual about a similar situation.
3. If name-calling occurs as children enter the room in the morning, talk to bus drivers to find out if something on the bus caused it.
4. Suggest to recipients that they ignore name-calling.
5. Use conflict-conversion techniques to help the name caller and the recipient find out how each other feels.
6. Become aware of causes and trigger events to help eliminate name-calling.
7. Use story re-enactment to show children who name call in fun how it feels to be on the receiving end.
8. When it is time for each character to speak, whisper their lines or let them make up their own.
9. Bring in animal hand puppets to represent characters in books.
10. Have children play with feltboard characters cut out of the paperback books they like the best.
11. Have children use pretend name-calling in pairs with feltboard characters, dolls, or figures.
12. Help name callers regain a sense of power by putting them in charge of an activity.
13. Do not respond to name-calling or make eye contact with the caller.
14. Give attention to the recipient and help him to ignore the caller.
15. Ask the recipient to perform a task for you in another room.
16. Commend the caller when he uses good words.
17. Make a list of specific ways words can be used to make a difference in your class.
18. Involve your name caller in one of these activities, such as calling names for attendance.
19. Have the caller tape record his favorite words.
20. Help children break the name-calling habit by using epithet puppets and funny names.
21. Occupy name callers with substitute activities such as a pretend fight with miniature dinosaurs.

22. Help children overcome the name-calling habit by speaking with respect to them yourself, avoiding commands, threats, and criticisms.
23. Do not become part of children's conflicts yourself.
24. Be more lighthearted as children do not respond well to criticism.
25. Have a whisper contest with the name-caller using mitten puppets.

TRY IT YOURSELF

1. Use the Name-Calling Observation Questions (Figure 8.1) to observe and record the name-calling that goes on in your classroom for three days. What are the results?
2. List two activities you can use with children, based on your observation results? Record the results of using these activities. (Use hypothetical cases if you are not in a classroom.)
3. Are you a positive role model in the use of words? Tape record yourself as you interact with children. What kinds of words do you use? Are they responsive or restrictive?
4. In "The Case of the Loose-Tongued Teacher," how else could Barbara have handled the situation? How would you have handled it?
5. What "other very important work" does Carter's quote refer to? How has this occurred in your classroom?

REFERENCES CITED

Carter, M. (1992). Disciplinarians or transformers? Training teachers for conflict resolution. *Child Care Information Exchange, 84,* 46–51.

Essa, E. L. (1990). *A practical guide to solving preschool behavior problems.* Albany, NY: Delmar Publishers.

Stone, J. (1993). Caregiver and teacher language—Responsive or restrictive? *Young Children, 48* (4), 12–18.

Stone, J. G. (1978). *A guide to discipline.* Washington, DC: National Association for the Education of Young Children.

Twain, Mark (1990). *The wit and wisdom of Mark Twain.* Philadelphia: Running Press.

OTHER SOURCES

Harbin, J. & Miller, D. (1991). Violent play behavior and language of four-year-old boys: The significance of teacher mediation. *Early Child Development and Care, 75,* 79–86.

Jones, C. B. (1991). Creative dramatics: A way to modify aggressive behavior. *Early Child Development and Care, 73,* 43–52.

Saifer, S. (1990). *Practical solutions to practically every problem: The early childhood teacher's manual.* St. Paul, MN: Redleaf Press.

CHILDREN'S BOOKS ABOUT NAME-CALLING

Alexander, M. (1971). *Sabrina.* New York: Dial Books.

Alexander, M. (1981). *Move over, twerp.* New York: Dial Books.

Blumenthal, N. & Kaufman, R. J. (Ill.). (1989). *Count-a-saurus.* New York: Macmillan.

Bottner, B. & Rathman, P. (Ill.). (1992). *Bootsie Barker bites.* New York: G. P. Putnam's Sons.

Browne, A. (1984). *Willy the wimp.* New York: Alfred A. Knopf.

Caseley, J. (1991). *Harry and Willy and Carrothead.* New York: Greenwillow Books.

Cole, J. & Munsinger, L. (Ill.). (1990). *Don't call me names!* New York: Random House.

Corrigan, K. & van Kampen, V. (Ill.). (1984). *Emily Umily.* Toronto, Canada: Annick Press.

Crary, E. & Megale, M. (Ill.). (1983). *My name is not dummy.* Seattle, WA: Parenting Press.

De Paola, T. (1979). *Oliver Button is a sissy.* San Diego, CA: Harcourt Brace Jovanovich.

Lester, H. & Munsinger, L. (Ill.). (1986). *A porcupine named Fluffy.* Boston: Houghton Mifflin.

Merriam, E. & Small, D. (Ill.). (1992). *Fighting words.* New York: Morrow Junior Books.

Most, B. (1987). *Dinosaur cousins?* San Diego, CA: Harcourt Brace.

Seuss, Dr. (1961). *The sneetches and other stories.* New York: Random House.

Surat, M. M. & Vo-Dinh Mai. (Ill.). (1983). *Angel child, dragon child.* New York: Scholastic.

It's Not My Fault!
(Blaming Conflicts)

Always acknowledge a fault frankly. This will throw those in authority off guard and give you an opportunity to commit more. (Mark Twain, in Ayres, 1987, p. 6)

BLAMING CONFLICTS IN PRESCHOOL PROGRAMS

Despite Mark Twain's tongue-in-cheek advice about taking the blame, most young children proclaim their innocence and accuse someone else—loudly, frequently, and whenever things go wrong:

She did it!
It's his fault!
She took my toy!
He's the one who did it!
It wasn't my fault!
Look what you made me do!

Whether or not they are the ones to blame, young children vociferously deny their guilt and vigorously blame someone else when things go wrong. Surely, if youngsters actually owned up to their misdeeds, they would throw those in authority off guard. But that's not the way of the young child's world. Why preschoolers act as they do in this regard has been examined by child researchers from Piaget (1932) to Damon (1988) and beyond. Yet we remain only on the threshold of understanding the dynamics of guilt, innocence, blame, punishment, and moral development.

This chapter regards blaming disputes somewhat differently from the other conflict situations discussed thus far. Blaming conflicts with preschool children often involve a third-party, the teacher, or another classroom adult. In one instance, children who blame one another bring their conflict to the adult to resolve. In another, the adult uses a conflict-conversion strategy with the antagonists and finds them trying to blame one another. Look back at the cases in some of the previous chapters for typical examples:

#1. "The Case of the Purple Cape": Luis blames Sam for making him fall in their struggle over the Superman cape. Sam denies making him fall, saying he fell because he pulled too hard (see page 35).

#3. "The Case of the Bothersome Child": Alex blames Frankie for knocking down his building. Frankie denies this, saying Alex's building got in the way of his truck (see page 58).

#4 "The Case of the Tricycle Takeover": George blames Adam for pushing him over. Adam denies it, saying he fell over by himself. All Adam did was to give the trike a push (see page 78).

#6 "The Case of the Missing Red Telephone": Shaneika blames Quentin for stealing the telephone. Quentin denies taking it, but later he finds it (see page 120).

In each of these cases, as well as almost every other case involving blame in the preschool classroom, the intuitive response on the part of the child who feels blamed seems to be denial ("I didn't do it,") followed by throwing the blame back onto the first child ("It's his fault!"). Why do children behave this way? Do they really believe they are not at fault? Are they afraid they will be punished if they admit guilt? Are they just being defensive? And why blame the other child? Do they really believe he or she did the misdeed? Or, are they just trying to find a scapegoat for something they actually did? This nearly universal behavior on the part of children from a wide variety of backgrounds and cultures suggests that perhaps blame and guilt have their origins in child development itself.

MORAL DEVELOPMENT OF THE YOUNG CHILD

Guilt and innocence, as well as blame and denial, are part of what researchers consider *moral development*. Just as children grow and develop physically, cognitively, socially, emotionally, and creatively in a sequence of stages, they also develop morally. This development occurs both from within and from outside the child: by the development of emotions and cognition within as they mature and by the social interactions they experience around them.

Just what comprises morality? Hard to define, morality has been outlined by child development researcher William Damon to include:

> 1. *An evaluative orientation toward actions and events that distinguishes the good from the bad and prescribes conduct consistent with the good.*
> 2. *A sense of obligation toward standards shared by a social collective.*
> 3. *A concern for the welfare of others, the rights of others, and a commitment to honesty in interpersonal dealings and to the fair resolution of conflicts. (Adapted from Damon, 1988, p. 5)*

The prosocial aspects of morality involve justice, mercy, kindness, honesty, caring, and helping. Immoral acts often include lying, cheating, stealing, deceiving, and harming. With violations of morality there is a price to pay, in the form of shame, guilt, contempt, fear, or outrage (Damon, 1988, p. 5) The most important aspect of children's morality, however, for the teacher to keep in mind is that *morality for young children may be completely different than morality for adults.*

The young child's level of *thinking* and *understanding* differs greatly from mature adult thinking. Preschoolers often make mistakes about the size, number, and importance of things because they can see only one aspect of them at a time. For instance, they think that a tall narrow glass holds more milk than a short wide glass because it "looks bigger." Youngsters also believe, because of their egocentric point of view, that they cause events that happen to them, such as parents' quarrels. When parents take out their own frustrations on their children, it actually confirms what the children already believe.

In like manner, young children operate morally from an entirely different perspective than adults. What adults consider important may have little or no significance in the lives of young children. Acts that represent dishonesty and cheating to adults may, in fact, represent honor and helping to children. Children eventually learn adult morality in a series of stages as they develop emotionally and cognitively through interactions with people. But adults have difficulty seeing things from a child's perspective, and in understanding why children act as they do when they should "know better."

Jean Piaget described how adult authority forms the basis for children's first understanding of right and wrong. His findings suggest that children possess two kinds of morality, rather than one. "The first is an adult-oriented morality of unilateral respect for adult codes and sanctions.... But the other morality of the child is a peer-oriented morality of cooperation and exchange between children and their playmates" (Damon, 1983, p. 134). Both of these codes of behavior operate at the same time in the lives of children. In early childhood, power and authority rest strictly in the hands of the adult. Whatever the adult says, goes. But at the same time, when young children interact with peers, they behave in a more give-and-take, cooperative manner.

The teacher may be the authority figure whose word is law for preschool children. However, children still seem to get into trouble and often do things

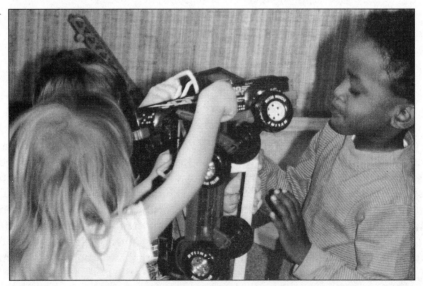

Children learn about fair play and justice as they interact with one another.

that surely they "know" are wrong, and for which they will be punished. Why is this?

Damon's work on children's understanding of authority may give a possible answer, explaining why preschool children can stand in awe of adult authority but still cannot seem to obey it consistently. He discovered "the curious fact that preschool children cannot differentiate their own perspective on rules and commands from the adult perspective" (Edwards, 1986, p. 163).

Damon found that preschool youngsters in the earliest stage of moral development (that is, aged four and under) believe that the authority's desires are the same as their own. They seem to see parents and perhaps teachers as an extension of themselves. Thus they subconsciously either revise their wants to conform with those of the authority figure, or convert the authority's commands into their own desires.

In other words, Adam sees nothing wrong with trying to take the tricycle away from George in Case #4, giving him a hard push when he does not give it up. Adam wants the tricycle, so of course the authority figure also would want him to have it. The fact that George fell is too bad but is not Adam's fault. After all, George was the one on the trike. He fell by himself. If he had given Adam the trike, he would not have fallen. Such reasoning may lie behind much of the denial and blaming that occurs in preschool classrooms.

JUSTICE IN CHILDREN'S RELATIONSHIPS WITH PEERS

Peer-oriented morality, the second kind of children's morality, focuses not on authority, but on justice. As children interact with peers in the classroom and on the playground, they encounter many problems centered around fairness and justice. Who goes first? When is it Betty's turn to use the trike? Who gets the biggest piece? What happens when three children want to play the role of mother?

Children learn to come up with their own standards of fair play and justice as they interact with one another. If they break one of their own unwritten rules, others quickly and loudly inform them of their error: "That's not fair! Paul took the biggest piece and it's not his birthday!" If they disregard the rules entirely, other children may not play with them or may bar them from their play.

Whereas children's adult-oriented morality operates on power, based on whatever the adult says, their peer-oriented morality is based more on reciprocity, cooperation, and equality. Piaget (In Damon, 1983, p. 134) views this child-based morality as the real origin of morality. Children learn moral judgment through reciprocal exchanges, such as sharing materials and taking turns. As children grow older, the cooperative standards of peer morality eventually replace the authoritarian standards of adult morality altogether.

Children's views of justice not only differ from those of adults, but they also develop and change with age and experience. Damon's (1983, p. 135) studies show that children's concepts of justice fit into a developmental sequence similar to their concepts of authority (Table 9.1). Other researchers, using Damon's procedures, have found the same developmental progression among children in Israel, Europe, Puerto Rico, and Canada.

In the research the children were asked to distribute candy among themselves as a reward for making bracelets. The youngest preschoolers at the first level could focus on only one child's perspective at a time. They would give a piece of candy to a peer saying, "He wants it," or "He's my friend." Young school-age children, on the other hand, chose strict equality as the basis for their distribution because they were able to see more than one child's perspective and wanted to avoid conflicts (Edwards, 1988, p. 166).

Preschool teachers need to be aware of these differences in perception of social justice between themselves and their children. They should give children every opportunity to settle their own conflicts, and intervene only when absolutely necessary. The conflict conversion strategies they use should take into account these different perspectives of justice. The children involved should be the ones to decide how to help the other child feel better, based on their own perception of justice whenever possible.

 ### TABLE 9.1   DAMON'S EARLY POSITIVE-JUSTICE LEVELS

Level 0–A (Age 4 and under)

> Children's choices come from a wish that an act occur; "I should get it because I want to have it."

Level 0–B (Ages 4–5)

> Choices reflect desires, justified on the basis of the physical characteristics of persons; "We should get the most because we're girls."

Level 1–A (Ages 5–7)

> Choices based on strict equality in actions (everyone gets the same), which prevents conflict.

Level 1–B (Ages 6–9)

> Choices based on the notion of reciprocity, that persons should be paid back in kind for doing good or bad things.

(Adapted from Damon, 1983, p. 136)

THE EARLY MORAL EMOTIONS: EMPATHY, SHAME, AND GUILT

For morality of either kind to develop and operate the way it has up to now, another important development within the child must have occurred: the forming of the moral emotions, empathy, shame, and guilt. These strong emotions help children to feel good or bad about things, and thus help them to learn a sense of right and wrong. Interactions with others trigger feelings within a child that influence her to act in a certain way. Then new feelings arise, helping her to appraise her actions. If she did right, she feels good. If she did wrong, she feels bad.

Child development specialist Jerome Kagan and a number of other early childhood researchers believe human *emotions* rather than reasoning underlie the development of morality everywhere. Kagan (1984) discusses the following core emotions:

1. *fear of punishment, social disapproval, or failure*
2. *empathy toward those in distress*
3. *guilt over one's own callous or irresponsible behavior*
4. *"ennui" from the oversatiation of a desire*
5. *anxiety over the awareness of inconsistency between one's beliefs and one's actions*

These emotions are shared by people around the world. If these represent the motivating forces for everyone in the development of morality, then we must first examine the development of children's moral emotions rather than their reasoning or logic when we consider their response during blaming conflicts.

Empathy

Empathy has been described as the basis for the conflict-conversion technique used throughout this text. If children can learn to feel the way other children feel (other-esteem) they are more likely to help them. Thus, empathy, is essential to a child's development of the prosocial aspects of morality: justice, mercy, kindness, honesty, caring, and helping.

At birth, children can already react with empathy to emotional situations around them. Babies cry when they hear other infants crying. Toddlers respond to others in distress by trying to comfort them with a favorite "blankie" or cuddly toy. Preschoolers process nonverbal cues in the faces, voices, and body language of authority figures that tell them precisely how these adults feel. When asked how the other child feels in a conflict-conversion situation, many preschoolers can pinpoint the exact emotion. However, although every child may be capable of responding with empathy, not all of them do. Damon (1988, p. 18) notes:

> *Like the capacity for empathy itself, such individ-*
> *ual differences in empathic responding show up*
> *very early in life. Children as young as one and*
> *two respond differently to others' distress.*
> *Moreover, these differences between individual*
> *children endure, at least through the early child-*
> *hood years.*

Can positive interactions with teachers, children, and materials in a preschool program help a child respond with empathy? This author believes that they can, that children this young can learn to recognize emotions in others, can empathize with them, and can even verbalize these emotions.

Can you yourself empathize with the children in your class based on your own childhood experiences? How did you feel when you were blamed or punished? As a role model for the children in your program, you set the emotional tone, both verbal and nonverbal, by being empathic in your own interactions with the children.

Shame

Adults too often try to suppress the emotional outbursts of young children, because they are afraid of emotions, especially their own. They fear that if they give in to emotions, they will get out of control. Thus, they try to prevent not only themselves, but also their children, from expressing emotions. They may impress this point of view on their youngsters with ridicule, warnings, scoldings, and sometimes punishments: "You're not afraid of that dog, are you? I'm surprised at you! A big boy like you shouldn't be afraid of such a little dog!" "Now, stop that crying! You're too old to cry!" "What? You're afraid of a little needle like that? You should be ashamed of yourself, a big girl like you!" "Stop it right now, or you're going to get a spanking!"

Such confrontations not only may prevent emotions from being expressed by children, but they also may promote the development of a powerful negative moral emotion, shame. "Shame," according to Damon (1988, p. 21), "is a feeling of embarrassment that is experienced when one fails to act in accord with perceived behavioral standards." Although the capacity for shame is inherited, its appearance in the lives of young children often results from being humiliated by parents or caregivers.

Toilet training, for example, has the potential for developing deep shame. Children already have the capacity to be embarrassed when they have an accident, even though they may lack sufficient bladder control to prevent it. If, in addition to their own bad feelings, adults also scold or humiliate them, a deep reservoir of shame may well develop.

Some parents and cultures also use ridicule to discipline and control, which is a powerful tool. In these families and cultures, an entire set of mores has evolved, to avoid ridicule, embarrassment, humiliation, and shame. This is called "saving face." People in cultures that practice saving face go to great lengths to avoid blame or anything that can be construed as bringing shame to a person. Some people will even say "yes" to a request they know they cannot fulfill rather than answer "no" and lose face. In these cultures, it is considered better not to admit the truth rather than tell a "shameful" truth and lose face.

As a teacher in a preschool program, you should be aware of the cultural differences among your children that may include saving face as an accepted way to deal with blaming conflicts. On the other hand, keep in mind that many young children of every culture try to avoid taking the blame for something they have done. They may deny it or blame someone else. To them, they have not lied but made an intuitive effort to save face. If they know they will be punished, most children will try to deny their guilt.

Guilt

As children grow and develop, they experience the emotion of shame, whether or not an outside conflict takes place. This eventually evolves into a new feeling: guilt. Once guilt develops, an adult authority figure need not blame the child for a wrongdoing. The child blames herself. We say she has developed a "guilty conscience." Whereas shame seems to develop from an outside stimulus during the toddler years (18 to 30 months), guilt appears during the preschool years (three to five) as an internal emotional reaction.

Psychologist Eric Erikson's classic description of human psychosocial development in his *Eight Ages of Man*, places *guilt* opposite *initiative* as opposing forces in the child's ego development during the preschool years (Erikson, 1963, pp. 270–274). These two forces interact within the child as he struggles to try out new things while at the same time trying to avoid mistakes that make him feel guilty. According to Erikson, if the child can achieve a balance in these opposing forces, his self-image develops in a positive direction. If not, the child may emerge from the preschool years with a poor self-concept and a reluctance to try out new things. No wonder young children avoid blame at all costs!

You as a preschool teacher, teacher assistant, or student teacher can play an instrumental role here, supporting and assisting young children in their struggle to find a balance within themselves as they interact with you and their peers. During the preschool years, children's interactions with peers and authority figures lay a foundation for their moral development.

ROLE OF THE PRESCHOOL TEACHER IN CHILDREN'S DEVELOPMENT OF EMPATHY, SHAME, AND GUILT

Children live in the world of feelings long before they live in the world of words. Unless the adults in their lives have taught them to suppress these feelings, most preschoolers express emotions openly through sounds, actions, and nonverbal signals. They laugh and shout spontaneously, cry easily, and wear their feelings very close to the surface. Just look at their faces while they paint, sing, role play, or argue.

Two of the strongest emotions associated with moral development, empathy and shame, have already made an appearance in their lives, as we have noted. The third, guilt, has begun to develop. Our task in the preschool classroom consists of helping children maintain a balance in the development of this powerful trio of human emotions: empathy, shame, and guilt.

We want youngsters to develop empathy so they can feel what others feel (other-esteem) and thus will want to bring joy and happiness to others. We understand that shame and guilt function to keep children from performing harmful or immoral acts against others. On the other hand, we want youngsters to feel good about themselves and their actions (self-esteem), and not feel overwhelmed when they make mistakes or fail to live up to their own or others' expectations.

Conflicts involving blame and the denial of guilt create effective learning opportunities for our children and ourselves to address the necessary balance of these emotions. In order to help children deal with the strong feelings engendered by blaming conflicts, we have a threefold task:

We must help children maintain a balance in their development of empathy, shame, and guilt.

1. To help children recognize what emotion they are feeling through sensory exploration
2. To help children recognize the feelings of others in blaming conflicts
3. To help children find ways to convert blaming conflicts to other-esteem

HELPING CHILDREN RECOGNIZE THEIR EMOTIONS THROUGH SENSORY EXPLORATION

What emotions do preschool children feel? Just like adults, preschool youngsters also experience many of the following feelings and their polar opposites:

happy—sad	happy—angry
brave-fearful	friendly—hostile
delighted—embarrassed	interested—bored
proud—ashamed	innocent—guilty
amiable—jealous	joyful—sorrowful
calm—upset	certain—confused

Because preschoolers have not yet developed verbal skills as they will have in a few years, they may not be able to tell you in words what they feel. Therefore, early childhood programs must provide youngsters with other means for exploring and expressing feelings, as mentioned in Chapter One.

Children of this age have just passed through the sensory-motor stage of their development, and have reached the peak of their ability to use sensory powers to explore the world around them. By focusing on sensory activities involving color, sound, and movement, preschool teachers can open an exciting new avenue of emotional experiences for their youngsters. Children not only learn about color, sound, and movement, but they also can learn the words to describe what they feel through these experiences.

Color

We often first engage children with color through cognitive activities. We ask them to "learn your colors"—that is, to learn the names of the colors and how to distinguish one from another. We forget that young children already have an emotional connection with colors. They may not know the names of colors, but they know how they feel about them. These emotional aspects of colors can help your children express strong feelings and later verbalize them. As Stephen Lehane notes in his book *The Creative Child* (1979, p. 114):

> *For most three-year-olds, the naming of colors sets*
> *off feelings and images associated with experiences*

that have touched them deeply. In short, kids use
colors to communicate emotions in much the same
way adults use such figures of speech as "green
with envy" or "he's feeling blue."

Children have strong emotional reactions to colors. They find certain colors fascinating and others uninteresting. They do not necessarily respond to the traditional meanings that society gives for particular colors (red for anger or danger; black for sadness or depression.) Young children have their own individual feelings about the colors they like and use. As Clare Cherry notes in her book *Creative Art for the Developing Child* (1972, p. 12):

We must remember that a child's perceptions are
not the same as those of an adult. In all probabil-
ity, he really covered the picture with black paint
because black paint, especially tempera, is so
emphatic and opaque and positive. Using it makes
him feel quite important.

How do you feel about colors? Or, perhaps, the better question is: how do colors make you feel? Do you find certain colors happy and joyful, others gloomy and depressing, or exciting and adventurous? We often choose clothing, flowers, food, furniture, and houses on the basis of color and the way certain colors make us feel. Young children, too, can express their emotions through their interaction with colors.

It is up to you to set the stage. Provide the children in your center with all sorts of activities using paints (tempera, fingerpaints, watercolors), crayons, markers, pens, pencils, pastels, chalk, food coloring, colored construction paper, crepe paper, colored cellophane, glitter, confetti, peel-off stickers, and any other color materials you can obtain. Put them on the shelves of your activity areas along with paper, glue, scissors, brushes, and markers. Keep one or two easels well stocked and active every day. Talk about colors with the children.

Read books and sing songs about colors. Ask the children what colors make them feel happy, sad, calm, excited. The picture book *Kinda Blue*, by Ann Grifalconi (1993) portrays with sensitive pastels and watercolors how young African-American Sissy, feeling blue because she misses her father, has a change of heart when she experiences the colors and feelings of the plants in her Uncle Dan's cornfield. Even corn can be blue! As your children begin to associate feeling words with certain colors, make a note of it. Does Brandon always say that purple makes him feel special, or on some days does he say red? Help children to associate their feelings with colors.

When children are upset or out of sorts, have a "feelings table" they can go to with fingerpaints, crayons, and paper available. Let them swish or scribble out their feelings with colors that they choose. Let them play with colored water in a

The emotional aspects of color can help children express strong feelings and verbalize about them.

plastic pan. Using colors in this way works just as therapeutically as speaking or shedding tears. When you see children putting colors on paper, ask them how the particular colors make them feel, rather than what the picture represents. Most preschoolers have not reached the representational stage of painting pictures, but their scribbles, lines, and colors may well signify feelings.

Have the children also identify a color that makes them feel happy. Then have them close their eyes, take a deep breath, and visualize that color. Can they see it clearly? Give them time. Have them feel its warmth. Let it surround them with happiness. Have it fill them with contentment. Afterwards, the children may want to tell you what their special color looks like, but do not force the issue. Some may want to keep it a secret. If children let you know, be sure that you accept any color they tell you. Remember, black is beautiful, and so is brown and gray.

Read them a book such as *Something Special Within*, by Betts Richter (1978), showing pen-and-ink sketches of different children feeling a pink star of love inside them. Can your children close their eyes and see their own special color inside them like the children in the story? Afterwards, when children feel upset or out of sorts, have them sit quietly on the soft cushions of your story center, close their eyes, and visualize their special color.

Children also find bright colors, like red, very attractive. Read them the book *Red Is Best* by Kathy Stinson (1982), and see how many of them agree with the little girl narrator who believes she can take bigger steps in her red boots and jump higher in her red stockings.

Make up a story with your children about the colors they like best. Let each child tell you his or her favorite color and what the color makes him feel like.

(These can be different from their special color.) Tape-record the story or write it down to make a class book to be read over and over. If some of the children mention purple, gold, black, brown, blue, gray, white, orange, red, pink, green, or yellow as their favorites, read them a poem about their favorite color from the book *Hailstones and Halibut Bones* (O'Neill, 1961). In recognizing colors as feelings like this, you have helped your children discover a new way to communicate feelings.

Sound

Sound is another sensory sensation that attracts young children. Listen to children on the playground when their voices are uninhibited. You will surely hear some shouting, yelling, laughing, giggling, screaming, screeching, cheering, whooping, whispering, murmuring, muttering, grumbling, whining, whimpering, wailing, moaning, and chattering. What does all this mean? You should have now an idea of the range of sounds that children use to express emotions. This range of sounds is much broader than a comparative group of adults would make, for children's emotions lie closer to the surface and therefore are more accessible.

This does not mean you should encourage "playground voices" inside the classroom, but you can use substitute sound makers to help children identify emotions. Put out sound makers such as rhythm band instruments on a table. Have a small group of children at a time go around the table, try each one, then talk about the sounds that the instruments make. They may talk about booming, clicking, clacking, tapping, and tinkling noises at first. Ask them to try each instrument to see what kind of "feeling sound" it makes. Doing this will be something entirely different for most children, but new ideas like this intrigue children because they love being able to use their imaginations and their huge capacity for pretending.

The instruments you use (either purchased or homemade) can include the following, perhaps representing the following emotions:

 FIGURE 9.1

Sound Instruments to Represent Emotions

rhythm sticks, blocks, scrapers: excitement, joy
shakers and rattles: fear, happiness, delight
castanets, triangles, cymbals: surprise, excitement
bells, chimes, gongs: pride, delight, joy
drums, tom-toms, tambourines: pride, anger, bravery

Your children certainly will add to this list with their own feeling words. Sometimes a feeling cannot be expressed by one word: "It makes me feel lowdown," or, "It makes me feel like I can climb up the tallest tree on the playground, or run all the way home without stopping once." Some sounds cannot be explained by one feeling. They may make children feel sad and happy at the same time, as in the picture book *Double-Dip Feelings* (Cain, 1990). Children will find the connection between sound makers and emotions more exciting if they make their own instruments to represent their own feelings. Some simple instruments they or you can make include:

clacking bones: Save the bones from short ribs of beef. Scrape them clean and use pairs for clackers.

sandpaper sticks: Bring in pairs of thick sticks the same size and cut them to the same length. Put glue on the back of sandpaper and glue the sandpaper around each stick.

sandpaper blocks: Take two blocks from the block area and glue sandpaper to one surface of each.

coconut clacker: Obtain coconut, puncture holes in it and drain out the liquid. Saw it in two and pry out the meat. Sand the edges and decorate the outside.

tin can shaker: Bring in tin cans with plastic covers and put dry corn, rice, sand, or nails inside. Tape the cover on tightly and decorate the outside with colored paper or plastic tape.

margarine cup shaker: Make the same as the tin can shaker and decorate the outside with peel-off stickers.

sea shell shakers: Collect sea shells and drill a hole through each (hobby shops do this). String several on a cord or a leather thong.

tennis ball rattle: Make as small hole in a tennis ball and force pebbles or small nails inside. Cover the hole with colored plastic tape and cover the ball with different colored tape.

pop-top rattles: Collect pop tops from cans, string them on a cord, and shake.

pan cover cymbals: Bring in two pan covers of the same size for cymbals.

can top jingle ring: Bring in plastic tops from coffee cans and punch holes around outside. Tie strings of the same length to the top and tie items to bottom of each string to make a jingling sound (nails, pop tops, etc.)

tin can drum: Bring in coffee cans with plastic tops, decorate the cans, and use sticks or ladles for drumsticks.

oatmeal box drum: Bring in an empty oatmeal box, secure the top, and decorate the box.

shoe box banjo: cut four slots at the top of the shoe box ends, string four rubber bands around box, and strum with the thumb. (Adapted from Mandell & Wood, 1957)

What fun you and your children can have with homemade sound makers! At first, children will want to experiment with the sounds they can make. Again, have only one small group at a time use the instruments you put out on a table. This way you can control the level of noise, and the children can hear each instrument clearly. Let them play them to their hearts' content. Then ask them if they can feel the kind of feeling that the instrument makes. Does the swishing of sandpaper blocks sound happy to anyone?

Write down the words they use for a certain instrument. Have other children try the same instrument. Do they "hear" the same feeling? Can they find an instrument that sounds like "surprise"? What about "embarrassed"? What does that sound like? Adults are not accustomed to thinking of colors or sounds in terms of feelings, but children quickly get involved in doing this. After all, everything in their world is new to them.

Movement

Can young children also express their feelings in movement? Think of how they wriggle and squirm with impatience while waiting for lunch to be served or jump for joy when a special day finally arrives. How do preschoolers respond to a new puppy, a fire engine's siren, or the surprise appearance of Mommy? Spontaneous movement is as important a part of preschool children as their voice or their personality.

Do you capitalize on all this energy just waiting to burst forth, or do you groan and wish the kids would settle down and be "normal"? This behavior *is* normal for a preschool child and can be a dynamic learning tool for the teacher or caregiver who is open to imaginative ventures. As Diane Lynch Frazer says in her book *Playdancing* (1991), the three-to-four age group "is the stage when young children engage in the freest, most spontaneous movement explorations. It is perhaps the most important stage for here is laid the very basis for meaningful expression in the child's later development."

Activities which involve expressing emotions through movement can be as simple as walking. Think about all the different ways a person can express his feelings through the simple movement of walking: ambling, sauntering, strolling, shuffling, gliding, stalking, stomping, tramping, trudging, tracking, pacing, striding, marching, tiptoeing. Make some of these movements yourself, and have children guess how you are feeling. Then ask any of them to walk as if they feel happy, sad, proud, or angry.

Other basic movements, such as of running, jumping, leaping, hopping, and kicking, can express other feelings. Read them a story, such as *Jim Meets the Thing* (Cohen, 1981), and ask the children to move in a way that shows how Jim felt about the monster show on television, or how the other children felt when Jim caught the praying mantis. Can some of the children express their feelings through slithering, slinking, duck walking, rolling, or twirling? Hand gestures, leg gestures, and head or shoulder movements can also portray emotions. See if the children can guess how you are feeling when you move your head or your hands a certain way.

Plan an activity that involves the "acting out" of feelings. How can children depict sadness, happiness, or anger? Are there different ways of doing this? Have the children a   ... as many ways to be happy or sad as they can. Perhaps they can guess what feeling is expressed by certain music and then act it out with a hand gesture or a body movement.

For example, try an activity that can be both fun and exciting for children. Let them be an animal that *does not speak*. How can they demonstrate anger or happiness without speaking. Are there other ways to show these emotions? What part of their body can they use? Their head, their foot, their elbow, their little finger? Make up your own game or activity using the body as a way to communicate feelings. Keep it simple.

The movement of our bodies makes up a large part of ourselves and therefore a large part of our self-esteem. When we explore the space around us, we discover the part of the universe that uniquely belongs to us. A child who has just begun to discover what her body can do finds excitement not only in exploring the unlimited possibilities of movement, but also in discovering yet another way to express feelings.

HELPING CHILDREN RECOGNIZE OTHERS' FEELINGS IN BLAMING CONFLICTS

In addition to helping children understand different emotions through the exploration of colors, sounds, and movements, teachers also can assist preschool children to discover the feelings that other youngsters experience when involved in blaming conflicts. Many teachers have found a way for children to connect with the feelings of others (other-esteem) through stories.

Picture-book stories about blaming conflicts can be powerful teaching tools without making their listeners as uncomfortable as real blaming situations do. When the story characters include funny animals as well as children, the youngsters who hear them may open their hearts as well as their minds to the lessons being taught. The teacher should take the role of leading a lighthearted discussion after the story, asking how the children think the story characters felt when they were blamed.

The number of children's picture books on the market today featuring blame taking and fault finding indicates that this is, indeed, a subject close to the hearts of young children. One of the favorite stories, Helen Lester's *It Wasn't My Fault* (1985), depicts bumbling Murdley Gurdson, a little boy who always causes accidents. One day, Murdley goes out for a walk with one shoe on, when someone lays an egg on his head, and a day of buck-passing of hilarious proportions begins. The bird that laid the egg blames the screaming of an aardvark; the aardvark blames a pygmy hippo that stepped on its tail; the pygmy hippo blames a hopping shoe with long ears; and the hopping shoe turns out to be a rabbit that landed in the shoe and became stuck. Whose shoe was it? You guessed it—Murdley's!

The story and the pictures are so much fun they will want to hear and see it again. Be sure to read it only to small groups so that everyone in the group can sit close and see the illustrations. On the second reading ask the children why the animals said that it was not their fault, and blamed another animal. How did these animals feel? Was it *any animal's fault?* Does it matter? The youngsters should consider these important questions because many of their own blaming conflicts reflect the same issue: is anybody really at fault? Does it matter who is at fault? What really does matter in such conflicts? How did Murdley and the animals convert this conflict to other-esteem?

In *Who Sank the Boat?* (Allen, 1982), a cow, a donkey, a sheep, a pig, and a tiny mouse decide to go out in a red rowboat. As each one gets in, the boat almost sinks, and the narrator asks the reader: "Do you know who sank the boat?" The boat finally sinks with a terrific splash as the tiny mouse hops aboard. Was it the fault of the big fat animals or the tiny little mouse? Your children will enjoy this rhyming tale and should have an interesting time deciding who sank the boat as well. The animals do not blame one another. Only the narrator asks the question, leaving it up to the reader to answer.

The Gorilla Did It (Hazen, 1974) shows a little boy illustrated by black-and-white pen sketches with a huge (imaginary?) gorilla in blue. The gorilla creates a mess in the boy's room while he's supposed to be taking a nap. When his mother appears and wants to know who made the mess, the boy says, "The gorilla did it." The mother wants a better answer, so she sends the boy back to think about it. When she reappears the mess is even worse from cleanup attempts the boy and gorilla have made. The boy sticks to his story but adds that the gorilla is sorry and did not mean to do it. The two tried to clean it up, and now they are hungry. Can he give the gorilla a cookie and have one for himself? What can the mother do? She opens the cookie jar and holds it out.

This story poses another moral dilemma for your children. Is the boy telling the truth? Does the mother believe him? Is the gorilla real? Does the mother think it is real? What would your children do in this situation?

These books and others can give your children another perspective on blaming conflicts, helping them to consider how the people or animal characters feel about the situation and what they can do about it. Have the children dictate their own story called "It Wasn't My Fault."

HELPING CHILDREN FIND WAYS TO CONVERT BLAMING CONFLICTS TO OTHER-ESTEEM

You may find yourself dealing with several kinds of blaming conflicts in a preschool program:

1. conflicts in which the child being blamed caused the problem but denies it
2. conflicts in which the child being blamed did not cause the problem and will not take the blame

3. conflicts in which nobody knows who caused the problem or which were caused by a chain of events
4. problems reported by an outsider (tattler) and blamed on someone who may or may not have caused the problem

Do you deal with each of these situations differently, or have you found some common ground? If you follow the conflict-conversion technique proposed by this textbook, then you will find a strong basis on which to consider all of these situations: that *the teacher should not focus on blame* during conflict conversions, no matter what happened nor what the children say.

Just a minute, you may respond. If one child caused a problem between two children, and you know who, should not that child be blamed and punished? No. The conflict-conversion technique based on empathy maintains that *it is a learning situation for both you and the children, not a blaming situation.* The children are important. The conflict is important. The blame is not important.

During the conflict conversion each child learns how the other child feels (other-esteem). Each child then finds a way to make the other child feel better. The children involved in the conflict also have control of the resolution of the conflict. The children end up feeling good and not like victims out for revenge. You yourself end up feeling good, especially when you later find that so-called "trouble-making children" have stopped making trouble. You also learn more about conflict itself, what the children know about feelings, and what creative ways they can invent to help one another feel better.

Still, you may respond, if one child did something bad to another child *on purpose*, should he not be blamed and punished? That used to be the method. But if you agree with this book that conflicts are not bad but create learning opportunities, and that children are not bad, but just sometimes need help in converting conflicts, then you understand that blame is not a part of the problem, nor should it be part of the solution.

Because children involved in blaming conflicts often try to pull you in as a third party, you must be especially careful not to let yourself become a part of the conflict. Children often want you to fix the blame. They want the perpetrator punished. However, you must carefully avoid becoming a part of their conflict by staying out of it emotionally and especially by not blaming anyone.

We recall that morality for young children differs from adult morality. Blame also differs. The child who appears to be at fault in your eyes is usually not at fault at all in her own eyes. Punishment will not resolve the problem, and it will only make the child feel unfairly treated. It may even make her feel like doing the same thing again. On the other hand, conflict conversion based on empathy helps this child to feel what the other child feels, and she learns how to repair the damage by suggesting something to make the other child feel better. She ends up feeling better herself, as well, because the other child does the same for her.

If you do not allow yourself to become part of children's blaming tactics, if you change the conversation when they mention blame, and if you ignore the topic of blame completely, then children will do the same. They will take your lead, and eventually you will find that blame no longer plays an important part in your classroom conflicts.

Tattling

Tattling, or "telling on someone," can also be ignored. Sometimes children who tattle blame a child who did something to them, but often they have simply developed an unfortunate habit of constantly running to the teacher to tell her what another child did wrong. Many children who tattle do so for attention, and they have found that adults respond to it.

Your best approach may be to ignore the tattlers' blaming and change the subject. "Brenda, think of something good to say about Laura, and I'll listen to you," or, "Bobby needs to speak for himself, Brenda." Then you must be sure to help them feel good about themselves for the positive things they do. Sometimes, however, the tale telling describes real conflicts that require the teacher's attention. You may need to observe the situation yourself before you decide how to handle it, as in Case #9.

Conflict-Conversion Questions

1. What's happening _____ (child's name)?
2. How does _____ (other child) feel?
3. What will make him (or her) feel better?

#9. The Case of the Tale-Telling Twosome

Setting: Darnell and Jake are four-year-old boys who play together in their neighborhood and at nursery school. For the most part they get along well together, but when the slightest thing goes wrong one or the other rushes to the teacher or her coworker to blame the other. By observing the boys play together, the teacher notes that they both have short tempers and do not try to work out the conflict. Instead, they immediately run to the adult in charge. Today Jake complains about Darnell taking his truck as they play together on a block road they have built.

Jake: *Teacher, Darnell took my truck and won't let me have it back.*

Teacher: *Jake, did you ask him about it? Did you ask him to give it back to you?*

Jake: *No. He never gives things back.*

Teacher: *Maybe the way you ask him doesn't sound good to him. What could you say to him?*

Jake: *You tell him. He won't listen to me.*

Teacher: *In this classroom, Jake, we like children to solve their own problems if they can. I see you playing with Darnell every day. I think he will listen to what you say. What will you say to him about the truck?*

Jake: (loudly to teacher) *"You took my truck, Darnell! Give it back to me right now!"*

Teacher: *Listen to how that sounds, Jake, if I shout at you: "You took my truck, Jake! Give it back right now!" How does that sound? Would you give me back the truck if I asked you like that?*

Jake: *But I don't have the truck. Darnell does.*

Teacher: *All right. You ask Darnell to give you the truck. Make your voice sound friendly, Jake. When we sound friendly to another person, that person is usually friendly to us.* (Jake goes over to Darnell and asks him. Darnell looks up, sees the teacher watching, and so hands the truck to Jake. They resume playing, but soon Darnell complains to the teacher that Jake took his truck.)

Teacher: *Jake and Darnell, you need to solve your truck problems on your own, not with me always telling you what to do. How are you going to*

	do it? How are you going to play together with trucks without the teacher always interfering?
Darnell:	*My mom always makes Jake give me my truck when he takes it.*
Teacher:	*This is nursery school, Darnell, not home. There are eighteen children who want to play together. All of you need to find ways to play without fighting over toys. How are you going to do it, boys? What could you do by yourself when the other one takes your truck? What about you, Darnell? What could you do?*
Darnell:	*I could take his truck.*
Teacher:	*How would he feel about that, Darnell? Would that solve the problem?* (Darnell shakes his head.) *What else could you do, Darnell?*
Darnell:	*I could stop playing with him.*
Teacher:	*How would that make him feel, Darnell? Would that solve the problem?*
Darnell:	*He would probably feel mad. But maybe he wouldn't take my truck the next time.*
Teacher:	*Do you want to try that, Jake and Darnell? If one of you takes the other's truck, then you'll stop playing?* (The boys look at each other and nod.) *All right. Do you have your own trucks now? Okay. Let's see if you can play together without taking each other's truck. If it happens, then the play stops. Agreed? Let's shake on it.* (The boys shake.)

TEACHER'S ACTIONS, CASE #9

The boys finish the play period without taking each other's trucks, so the teacher decides not to call attention to this conflict by having a positive-feelings activity on this particular day. She wants to wait and see if they will be able to play peacefully in the days to come. Another day she might do a puppet play about taking toys, and if Jake and Darnell want to contribute by telling how they solved their problems, they can. Their solution might not work for everyone. It might not even work for them on another day.

There is so much a teacher does not know about children's situations at home and in the neighborhood, but this teacher realizes she can help children solve problems in this classroom environment. She must listen to what children have to say, let them know if things are handled differently here than outside of class, and then involve them in their own conflict conversions.

She could have ignored the tale telling of the boys because it created more of a nuisance than a problem. She could have made one boy give the truck to the other. Or, she could have put the trucks away. None of these solutions, however, would have helped the boys to handle their own future conflicts. She knows that many attempts on her part may be necessary to help each boy really focus on the feelings of the other boy or to understand that the problem is theirs and requires their own solution.

You have made a good start if children have resolved conflicts on their own in your program, guided by the respectful way you treat everyone. However, the conflict-conversion technique itself, repeated over and over, truly does build the children's conflict-resolution skills. Children need to be taught how to handle conflict in the classroom again and again. Once they truly get the idea, you will hear them repeating your own words to one another: "How does Robbie feel?" "What will make Laura feel better?" "It doesn't matter whose fault it is." "We're talking about feelings, not blaming."

Repetition is the key, for as Mark Twain reminds us:

> *Any person who's got anything worthwhile to say*
> *will be heard if he only says it often enough.*
> *(Mark Twain in Ayres, 1987, p. 197)*

IDEAS + IN CHAPTER 9

Blaming Conflict Activities

1. Provide all sorts of color activities using paints, crayons, markers, chalk, etcetera.
2. Talk about colors and read books and sing songs about colors and feelings.

3. Have a "feelings table" where children can go and express their strong feelings through the use of colors.
4. Have children identify and visualize a color that makes them feel happy.
5. Let each child tell his favorite color and what it makes him feel like. Tape–record it.
6. Use sound makers to help children identify emotions.
7. Ask children to try rhythm band instruments to see what kind of "feeling sounds" they make.
8. Have children make their own instruments to represent their own feelings.
9. Write down the words the children use for certain instruments.
10. Have children guess how you feel from your movements alone. Then have them walk as if they feel happy, sad, proud, angry.
11. Read *Jim Meets the Thing* (Cohen, 1981) and ask the children to move in a way that shows how Jim felt.
12. Have children demonstrate through movement as many ways as they can to act happy or sad.
13. Use stories to help children understand the feelings of others.
14. Lead a lighthearted discussion after reading a story about how the children think the characters felt when they were blamed.
15. In *It Wasn't My Fault* (Lester, 1985) have children talk about why the animals blamed one another and who really was at fault.
16. In *The Gorilla Did It* (Hazen, 1974) ask if the boy told the truth and if his mother believed him.
17. Have the children compose their own story called "It Wasn't My Fault."

TRY IT YOURSELF

1. Can you think of an example of yourself being drawn into a blaming dispute by children? What did you do? How did it turn out?
2. Has moral development in children changed since you were a preschooler or is it the same? Give specific examples to support your position.
3. How can you use color, sound, and movement to help children recognize the emotions of happiness and sadness? Give examples for each. Use one with children and record the results.
4. How would you have handled Case #9 with Jake and Darnell? Observe children in your center who often tell tales on one another. How is this handled? What are the results?
5. Write out a case study similar to those in Chapters Two–Nine, that features a teacher and two children involved in a blaming conflict. Include a positive-feelings activity.

REFERENCES CITED

Ayres, A. (Ed.). (1987). *The wit and wisdom of Mark Twain.* New York: Harper & Row.

Cherry, C. (1972). *Creative art for the developing child.* Belmont, CA: Fearon Publishers.

Cratty, B. J. (1986). *Perceptual and motor development in infants and children.* Englewood Cliffs, NJ: Prentice-Hall.

Damon, W. (1988). *The moral child: Nurturing children's natural moral growth.* New York: The Free Press.

Damon, W. (1983). *Social and personality development: Infancy through adolescence.* New York: W. W. Norton.

Edwards, C. P. (1986). *Promoting social and moral development in young children: Creative approaches for the classroom.* New York: Teachers College Press.

Erikson, E. (1963). *Childhood and society.* New York: W. W. Norton.

Frazer, D. L. (1991). *Playdancing.* Princeton, NJ: Princeton Book Co.

Kagan, J. (1984). *The nature of the child.* New York: Basic Books.

Lehane, S.(1979). *The creative child: How to encourage the natural creativity of your preschooler.* Englewood Cliffs, NJ: Prentice-Hall, Inc.

Mandell, M. & Wood, R. E. (1957). *Make your own musical instruments.* New York: Sterling Publishing Co.

Piaget, J. (1948). *The moral judgment of the child.* Glencoe, Il: The Free Press (Originally published in 1932).

CHILDREN'S BOOKS ABOUT BLAMING CONFLICTS

Aardema, V. & Dillon, L. and D. (Ill.). (1975). *Why mosquitoes buzz in people's ears.* New York: Dial Books.

Allen, P. (1982). *Who sank the boat?* New York: Coward-McCann.

Cain, B. S. & Patterson, A. (Ill.). (1990). *Double-dip feelings.* New York: Imagination Press.

Cohen, M. & Hoban, L. (Ill.). (1981). *Jim meets the thing.* New York: Greenwillow Books.

Furtado, J. & Joos, F. (Ill.). (1992). *Sorry, Miss Folio!* Brooklyn, NY: Kane/Miller.

Grifalconi, A. (1993). *Kinda blue.* Boston: Little Brown.

Hazen, B. S. & Cruz, R. (Ill.). (1974). *The gorilla did it.* New York: Macmillan.

Johnson, D. (1993). *Your dad was just like you.* New York: Macmillan.

Lester, H. & Mansinger, L. (Ill.). (1985). *It wasn't my fault.* Boston: Houghton Mifflin.

Marzollo, J. & Kellogg, S. (Ill.). (1980). *Uproar on Hollercat Hill.* New York: Dial Books.

O'Neill, M. & Weisgard, L. (Ill.). (1961). *Hailstones and halibut bones.* Garden City, NY: Doubleday.

Polacco, P. (1992). *Chicken Sunday.* New York: Philomel.

Richter, B. & Jacaobsen, A. (Ill.). (1978). *Something special within.* Marina del Rey, CA: DeVorss.

Rovetch, L. (1991). *Trigwater did it.* New York: Puffin.

Sharmat, M. W. & McPhail, D. (Ill.). (1978). *A big fat enormous lie.* New York: E. P. Dutton.

Stevens, K. & Bowler, R. (Ill.). (1985). *The beast in the bathtub.* New York: Harper & Row.

Stinson, K. & Lewis, R. B. (Ill.) 1982). *Red is best.* Toronto, Canada: Annick Press.

It Works!

For all the talk you hear about knowledge being such a wonderful thing, instinct is worth forty of it for real unerringness. (Twain, Tom Sawyer Abroad, 1894)

CHILDREN OF TOMORROW'S WORLD

A new millennium is almost upon us. What will it bring us? Perhaps a time of great harmony and goodwill, starting with young children. They have been the innocent victims of our civilization's surge of violence. Now they can show us how easily conflicts can be transformed into good feelings. What children can accomplish in the preschool classroom, we can accomplish in our own lives.

Head Start teachers in Columbia, Missouri, for example, experienced immediate success using other-esteem conflict conversion with out-of-control children for whom nothing else seemed to work. While the teachers did not need to use it for every dispute, even used once or twice a week it reminded the children of the need to consider others. The director noted:

> *We are practicing the conversion technique so that*
> *the children have a background for use when the*
> *occasion arises. With practice we hope that empa-*
> *thy will become a part of our children's method of*
> *dealing with daily conflicts. (Worstell, 1993)*

TO TRY OR NOT TO TRY

To find a solution for conflicts—especially one that would assist preschool teachers to help children find their own solutions would be wonderful, but—and there is always a "but"—most people have difficulty trying something new. Change is not all that comfortable for many of us. We can think of more reasons not to change than we can for making a change.

However, a number of teachers in the early childhood field have used the conflict-conversion technique discussed in this text. Some of them had resistance to it at first. They felt it had merit, *but* hesitated to spend time giving it a try. They had to overcome a number of objections before they agreed to try it. It is important for us to consider these objections carefully.

 FIGURE 10.1

Objections to Using Conflict Conversion

1. It is too time consuming.
2. One teacher alone is not free enough to use it.
3. It is too idealistic.
4. Teachers and children do not verbalize enough to use it.
5. We already use it.

IT IS TOO TIME CONSUMING

With numerous classroom activities operating simultaneously, and with twenty or more lively youngsters scampering about, the busy preschool teacher and assistant have only a limited amount of time to spend with individual children. Many teachers feel they cannot take time out from an entire class for one child. Thus, the only time they spend on conflicts is used to stop any conflict quickly and send the children involved to a "time-out chair." A teacher with this point of view often rejects any sort of conflict-resolution procedure which appears to take longer than this.

At first glance, this text's conflict-conversion technique seems to take more time than merely stopping a conflict and sending a child to time out. However, as teachers reconsider their action and its results, they realize that time out in itself does not resolve the problem. It may stop the conflict for the moment, but it does not address the problem. The same conflict frequently recurs, often started by the same child. Time out, in fact, does not really *help* the child at all but seems instead to act as a punishment that often makes him feel more belligerent than he was to start with. In truth, time out helps only the teacher, and then only briefly, by getting the child out of the way for the moment. It is a teacher solution for a child problem. Thus a time out does not address the issues involved in the conflict nor help the child learn to deal with them.

As teachers begin to reconsider the way they deal with conflicts in their classroom, most come to realize that time out wastes time. Even more than that, the use of time out places a damper of veiled threat and implied blame and shame over all the children and their actions. It does not resolve conflicts but seems to say: "If the teacher catches you doing something wrong, you will be punished by being sent to the time-out chair. Then you will have to sit in front of the whole class for everyone to see." Do we want such a message hanging over the heads of three-, four-, and five-year-old children?

After a time out, the problem that created the conflict still exists. The children were not allowed to resolve it on their own, nor did an adult help them convert it to other-esteem. Instead, the teacher took it upon herself to put an "end" to the conflict by sending one of the children to time out. Then she told him that he could rejoin the group when he could act better. Even those teachers who spent time talking with the children involved before they reentered the group had no real assurance that the children would, in fact, "act better." Whether or not they acted better, most children did not feel better.

Teachers who come to realize what happens with time out in their classrooms may agree to try the conflict-conversion technique described in this text. They will:

1. At first it takes longer to speak with two children but not that much longer.
2. It is more time efficient in the long run because the children involved do not repeat their conflict as often.
3. It gives all the children a more positive attitude when they find they are not blamed or punished, and are in charge of helping one another feel better.

Another important result is that the attitude on the part of the teachers changes. They no longer have to "get after" children who often misbehave. As they use the conversion technique to teach children to empathize with one another, they themselves begin to empathize with the misbehaving children and see things from an entirely different perspective. Finally, the number of conflicts in the classroom decreases dramatically. Almost all of the children seem to learn other-esteem from the conflict-conversion experiences of only a few. The teachers in the Columbia Head Start classrooms, for instance, found that they needed to use the conversion technique less frequently because children's serious conflicts decreased:

> *For the general group we use it once or twice a week. At the moment we have an extremely hostile child and we are using it every day, sometimes two or three times. It appears to be helping. He has not hit someone since we introduced it. (Worstell, 1993)*

Is this conversion technique too time consuming? Teachers who have tried it answer, "No way!" The time expended could not be better spent by both children and teachers.

ONE TEACHER ALONE IS NOT FREE ENOUGH TO USE IT

At first glance a single teacher in a classroom full of children would not seem to have enough time to deal with two children in conflict. What will happen to the other children if she takes time to ask the three conflict-conversion questions and listen for the answers?

Teachers who operate their programs on an exclusively teacher-initiated basis may indeed have trouble doing anything other than standing in front of the children and being in command. Most preschool teachers, however, have found a more successful method for implementing their curriculum goals. They arrange the physical environment of the classroom into learning centers that respond directly to the children's needs and interests. Then they allow the children to make activity choices and pursue their interests on their own in the learning centers. These teachers act as facilitators who can work with individuals who need special help, once the other children are busy with activities.

Teachers who have not set up the physical environment "to do the teaching" like this, miss an exceptional opportunity to help children develop independence, initiative, and creativity by interacting with materials and other children on their own. In addition, they deprive the children of chances to explore new activities and practice untested skills by themselves. (See Beaty, *Preschool Appropriate Practices*, 1992.)

Teachers who have set up their classrooms to do the teaching will find that they always have freedom to intervene in conflicts using the conversion technique discussed in this text.

IT IS TOO IDEALISTIC

Sometimes ideas can appear overwhelming to people reading them or hearing them for the first time. They may ask, "Can this new idea really be applied to my situation?" Sometimes the written word does not even seem practical, particularly in an action setting. Have you ever attempted to put together a new toy with a written set of directions?

On the other hand, the conflict conversion technique described here is natural, spontaneous, and simple. If the teacher or caregiver herself has a friendly personality, she will find this technique to be "user friendly." Most of us want to feel good, to be joyful, and to *pursue* happiness. We need to treat interpersonal conflict more lightheartedly rather than so seriously or idealistically.

Although emotions are sometimes hard to pin down, children enjoy tapping into them and working with them. A simple process like this, which identifies and transforms feelings, not only enhances our own well-being, but also that of the young lives in our care.

The author contends that this strategy strengthens communication between the teacher and the child because it develops a relationship of support and trust as well as an understanding between children through its emphasis on other-esteem. We must ask ourselves: Is the conflict-conversion process really idealistic or simply a natural way to respond to interpersonal confrontations? Those who have used it declare it brings a welcome release from their own dilemma of how to communicate with children who use inappropriate behavior.

TEACHERS AND CHILDREN DO NOT VERBALIZE ENOUGH TO USE IT

Often we find difficulty expressing our emotions verbally to one another, yet when we do not want our feelings to surface, they come boiling out, embarrassing us. We "lose our cool." Is it any wonder that adults seem reluctant or uncomfortable or even threatened by the use of emotion?

The Western world has struggled to understand human emotion and its control for many years. Much of its nature still eludes and confuses us, scientists and laymen alike. Now we have the additional challenges of cultural and ethnic diversity in our society, and the increasing emergence of violent behavior in our homes, schools, and communities. How can verbalizing feelings really change any of this?

The author maintains that the best method of communication with children is through feelings. Any child, regardless of cultural or socioeconomic diversity, regardless of language or lack of language, lives in the world of feelings. He can respond to anyone who supports him and relates to him through feelings, which is all he really knows.

Thus, a teacher or caregiver who uses the conflict-conversion process can bridge these differences and help the children and herself find a common ground to resolve the conflicts through verbalizing feelings. "How do you feel?" "How does the other person feel?" "What will make him (or her) feel better?" The natural bond of feelings can bring the adult world and the child world closer together. Children respond to the opportunity to be part of a conflict solution by verbalizing their feelings. They have the capability, and furthermore, they enjoy doing so. If you make verbalizing feelings fun for them, you also will find it enjoyable for yourself.

On the other hand, an early childhood professional in North Carolina who is excited about using the conversion technique still has this concern:

> So many of the children do not verbalize well. Very
> rarely do I hear them verbalize feelings. Our area
> has children who have very weak communication
> skills. Some of their teachers are equally weak and
> do not provide good role models. I can see that
> teachers who use this method will have to develop
> communication skills themselves. (Novik, 1993)

It is exciting to realize that converting conflicts to other-esteem also may make teachers better role models? Everyone has feelings, whether or not they verbalize them. Think of how many ways feelings can be communicated: by looks, movement, sound, colors, songs, pictures, *and words*. Teachers can use these means one at a time to help children communicate their feelings: "How do you feel? Point to the picture. Make a face. Move your body. Yes, we call that feeling being *happy*. Can you say *happy*? Now, how do you think Maria feels? Look at her face. Show me how she feels."

You, as well as the children, can enjoy discovering words and activities to express this natural emotional part of every human being, adult and child. Start from what you know, where you are, and where the children seem to be, and explore ways to use this simple concept of verbalizing emotions and thus converting conflicts to positive feelings and other-esteem.

WE ALREADY USE IT

This conflict-conversion technique seems to bear certain similarities to conflict-resolution strategies already in use by some programs. However, you may find important differences. A number of programs use a technique in which the teacher stops the disruptive child and asks her why she is doing what she is doing. For example, the teacher might say: "Brenda, tell me why you are hitting Melissa."

On the other hand, in other-esteem conflict conversion, the teacher carefully asks *both* of the children, not just one, to state *what* is happening, not *why* someone is doing something to someone else. For example, the teacher might say, "Brenda, tell me what's going on here," rather than "Why did you hit Melissa?" If the child replies "Melissa took my crayons," the teacher can reflect this reply by saying: "You say that Melissa took your crayons. And, Melissa, you tell me what's happening." Melissa may reply, "Brenda hit me." Now the teacher reflects both points of view in a calm, matter-of-fact way: "So now we know what happened. Brenda says Melissa took her crayons. And Melissa says that Brenda hit her."

In this conflict conversion the teacher has acknowledged what happened and allowed both children to describe their actions. However, the teacher does not use judgmental or blaming comments, such as, "Melissa, you know better than to take someone's crayons. What should you do if you want some crayons?" Or, "Brenda, you know that hitting hurts. What other way could you let Melissa know that she shouldn't take your crayons? Can you say it in words?" Although such a discussion may end the conflict, it does not settle it.

In other-esteem conflict conversion the teacher takes a different direction. She stops talking about what each child did altogether, and instead asks each child how the other feels. She converts the conflict to empathy, helping each child to feel the way the other child feels. She changes the focus of the conflict from what happened and who is at fault to other-esteem.

To facilitate this conversion, the teacher asks Brenda to say how Melissa feels. This question surprises Brenda because she would rather have Melissa punished for taking her crayons. The idea that Melissa has feelings about what happened has not even occurred to her. When asked how Melissa feels, Brenda starts by saying: "But she did it. She took my crayons." The teacher then replies: "Yes, I heard you say that. Now we want to talk about feelings. How do you think Melissa feels? Look at her face. How does she feel?"

In like manner the teacher asks Melissa how Brenda feels. Brenda too is surprised to find that Melissa has feelings about the situation, which may be different from her own.

Finally, the conversion goes one step further, asking each girl what can help the other to feel better. This final step differentiates the conflict-conversion method from most other conflict resolution strategies. Many other resolution strategies ask children how *they feel*, but not how the other child feels.

This technique has a special advantage because it helps end the conflict on an especially positive note. Later, the teacher presents a positive-feelings activity to share with the other children how the children in conflict helped one another feel better.

By following this technique the teacher does not *resolve* the conflict. She does not act as a mediator. Instead she helps children to *convert* the conflict to positive feelings and other-esteem. She acts as a transformer. She does not blame or punish.

She helps the children themselves transform the confrontation to good feelings all around. Furthermore, she helps children focus on the emotional aspects of conflict, rather than the cognitive aspects, for she believes:

> *People don't learn social lessons cognitively; they learn them affectively, by emotionally processing and anchoring lessons learned from intense experiences. (Clark, DeWolf & Clark, 1992, p. 6)*

Think about the conflict-resolution technique you presently use. Does it change confrontation to positive feelings? If so, congratulations, for you know how well it works. If not, will you consider using other-esteem conflict conversion? It really works.

TRY IT YOURSELF

1. Do you think this conflict-conversion technique consumes too much time for the busy classroom teacher to use? Defend your position by your own experience if possible.
2. Explain in some detail how one prekindergarten teacher who is all alone in the classroom would be able to use this conflict resolution technique, based on your experience.

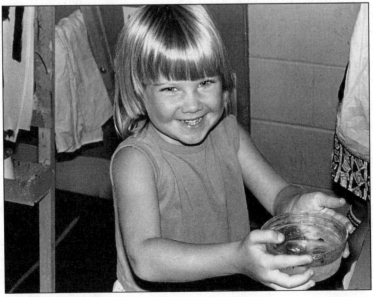

Try it, you'll like it!

3. Is this conflict-conversion technique too idealistic? Why or why not? Give examples.
4. Can children verbalize their emotions as asked for in this technique? If so, how? Use the technique with a nonverbal child and discuss the results.
5. How does this conflict-conversion technique resemble other conflict-resolution strategies being used in the preschool today? How does it differ? Which techniques have you used and what were the results?

REFERENCES CITED

Beaty, J. J. (1992). *Preschool appropriate practices*. Fort Worth, TX: Harcourt Brace Jovanovich.

Clark, L., DeWolf, S., and Clark, C. (1992). Teaching teachers to avoid having culturally assaultive classrooms. *Young Children, 47*, 5, 4–9.

Novick, S. (1993). Interview. Charlotte, NC.

Twain, Mark. (1894). *Tom Sawyer abroad*, New York: Harper & Brothers.

Worstell, G. (1993). Interview. Columbia, MO.

OTHER SOURCES

Carter, M. (1992). Disciplinarians or transformers? Training teachers for conflict resolution. *Child Care Information Exchange, 84*, 46–51.

Hohmann, M., Banet, B. & Weikart, D. (1979). *Young children in action*. Ypsilanti, MI: The High/Scope Press.

Ramsey, P. G. (1991). *Making friends in school: Promoting peer relationships in early childhood*. New York: Teachers College Press.

Children's Book Index

INDEX

GROWING

A Woman's Guide to Career Satisfaction

GROWING

A Woman's Guide to Career Satisfaction

by
Elmer H. Burack
Maryann Albrecht
Helene Seitler

LIFETIME LEARNING PUBLICATIONS • Belmont, California

A Division of Wadsworth, Inc.

Developmental editing: Sylvia Williams
Copyediting: Sylvia Stein
Design: Wendy C. Calmenson
Illustrations: Mary Burkhardt
Production editing and proofreading: Suzanne Pfeiffer Williams

Printed in the United States of America

2 3 4 5 6 7 8 9 10—84 83 82 81

Library of Congress Cataloging in Publication Data

Burack, Elmer H
    Growing, a woman's guide to career satisfaction.

    Bibliography: p.
    1. Vocational guidance for women—United States.
2. Job satisfaction.   I. Albrecht, Maryann H.,
joint author.   II. Seitler, Helene, joint author.
III. Title.
HF5382.5.U5B87   650.1′4′024042   80-11990
ISBN 0-534-97990-4

To Jeff, Stephanie, and David
—M. A.

To our friends, associates, and s̹
who are the living examples
and inspiration for Growing.

To the many special people
who continue to be part of
my growing.

Contents

PART TWO MAKING PLANS 45

PART THREE   MOVING ON—WITH YOUR STYLE   133

PART FOUR   MOVING ON—
WITH YOUR SKILLS   209

Preface

If you're a woman in America today, the odds are you work for a living. More than 50 percent do, and the '80s are moving the figure up fast. This book is for that majority—you—because *Growing* is about work: how to create a career and direct it so that work becomes a happier, better, and more rewarding experience for you.

Let's be specific: If you're a working woman who feels stalled where you are—boxed in, let down, passed by; if you're disappointed or dissatisfied; if, in fact, you've ever answered the question, "What do you do?" with that apologetic little sentence, "Oh, I'm just holding down the usual 9-to-5 job," then you'll find better answers and real help in this book.

Growing is for you if

- you don't have any idea how to go about creating a career

- you have a career and know where you're headed but need help getting there

- you like your career but want new ways of expressing yourself in your work

We want to make working women *career women.* We want to help women explore the new, richer, and more fulfilling options that come with careers, and we know that careers are not just for professionals and executives.

What *is* a career? And how does it differ from a job? A career is work that (1) uses skills you enjoy, (2) in ways that fit and express your personality, (3) in jobs and surroundings you find satisfying and rewarding. It may completely unfold within one organization and potentially involve only job—or different jobs and various employers.

In a way, then, having a career is simply finding a lifestyle that suits you—a better blend between you and your work. We don't think having a career necessarily means months at night school or years getting an advanced degree—although for you it might. We don't think it necessarily means earning a high salary, wearing a Saks suit, or carrying a Halston bag—although for you it might. We don't think it means changing jobs or occupations—although, again, for you it might. *You* are the key.

That's why this book begins and ends with you. And, as you develop ideas, we show you how to work out plans that take you step by step from thinking to doing and how to make reality checks along the way.

After working through the materials in *Growing*, you may find your career will move you up, or out, or across, or just let you settle in for more satisfaction where you are. But whether you're on an assembly line or in a typing pool, at a desk or at a computer, behind a counter or a checkout stand, in a classroom or in an operating room—wherever, whoever—supervisor or trainee, manager or receptionist, service rep, lab tech, bank exec—whatever you are, you'll be moving in your career.

Does it work? Yes. Is it easy? It takes time and thought to develop the career that's right for you, but you'll find it a very satisfying and rewarding investment. We have careers, too, and we know the thought and effort you'll invest as you learn to direct your own career. But we also know the joy that comes with the sure feeling of success. Using this book as a guide, we know you'll accomplish these five goals: You'll discover how to:

- *identify* your values, your style, and your skills

- *develop* career plans that are realistic and right for you

- *implement* your career plans in ways that are realistic and rewarding

- *manage* the direction and timing of your career activities successfully

- *utilize* ways of working and relating to others that fit you and your needs

You will, in other words, be directing not only your career but your life. You will be *growing*. That is our wish for you and our purpose in writing this book. For us this was a very special effort.

The authors

ACKNOWLEDGMENTS

In developing the career materials for *Growing*, we have benefited from lots of helpful people—from many hundreds of women, counselors, and personnel specialists who sought our guidance, used our methods, and were kind enough to report back on their effectiveness. Of course, we learned from each other, too, as the material took on shape and substance over the years of our work. Each of us took on special responsibilities, but the ideas were freely shared, and patient help was generously given as needed. The final product benefited from the career experiences, research, and ideas of all three authors.

There is always a need to acknowledge the support and patience of family and friends who shared our preoccupations and schedules as we created *Growing*. Special thanks also go to those who reviewed earlier drafts of the manuscript.

Growing: How To and When To

Growing is more than a book to read; it is a book to use. You'll use it to create a career and direct it. We view career as work that

- uses skills you enjoy
- in ways that fit and express your personality
- in jobs and surroundings you find satisfying and rewarding

Creating your career is a unique process of growth; directing your career is an exciting process of making choices that is ongoing throughout your life, and this book is designed to bring your career off the pages and into your life.

First, its four parts are developed in a sequence of discussions and activities that will help you to take charge of your career—thus, they are organized to involve you directly. The parts form a resource network, and you'll find each part and chapter add progressively to your understanding. Part One introduces you to the concept of a career and helps you to explore some of your basic preferences in the world of work. The idea of a "career compass" is described, and we show you how to use that compass as a guide for developing career plans, evaluating career activities, and keeping targeted on career matters important to you. Part Two helps you to plan—to understand and develop the foundation of that career. Parts Three and Four focus on style and skills in the broader scene of work and jobs. The intent here is to assure that your career activities are planned *and realized*, so that your style and skills and opportunities blend into occupations, jobs, and work environments. For each section, we've listed some books as special resources. These are books useful for women in a variety of occupations; they can assist you in exploring a sectional topic of special interest or provide a way of understanding, a little more fully, the ways in which women create satisfying careers.

Second, we've used practical devices—sketches, checklists, charts, inventories—all the materials we've found most effective in the courses and training programs we've developed over the years as career counselors.

We've also set out ways of approaching career matters, frameworks, so that you can deal with these in a more objective fashion. These materials are for you, each illustrated with an example and given a page for your own use. You'll be able to gather the information you need about yourself and your career as you search, plan, and reach out for the goals you choose. And you'll be accumulating an invaluable record of your thoughts along the way that will help you during many phases of your career.

Third, we've used as many real-life examples as we can fit into these pages. These are not faceless notes from a file, but rather the life stories of women we have known, worked with, cared about—women whose life experiences we have seen unfold and, for some, helped unfold. Of course, we have changed names or circumstances to a degree; but we share them with you to illustrate what careers are about, to highlight the reality of career activities, and to point to the ideas you will use.

At the end of each part, we've included profiles so that you can "try on" the experiences of a particular woman in a "fitting room" of different ideas and approaches. You can take on her role and consider how you would respond to her situation. Then we comment: you'll find your ideas may not be the same as hers—or ours—and that's all right. Your values, perspectives, and experiences are unique to you; and working through an actual set of circumstances will surely increase your ability to visualize how your-self might deal with career realities. At the same time, you'll be exposed to other viewpoints which you may wish to take into account in the future.

And, finally, we've placed key phrases in the page margins of each chap-ter and checklists at the end that capsule the contents. And, because this book is self-directed and thus controlled by your efforts, we've constructed end-of-section checklists so that you can note personal action items. These checklists, then, can serve as a reference for you—a quick reminder of things you may wish to get back into *Growing*—and as a "memo" for personal actions. We want *Growing* to be for you what it's intended to be: a valuable resource for years to come for the woman who has a career.

HOW TO USE THIS BOOK

Growing is divided into four main parts, each of which builds career inquiry and personal skills in a logical, related way. For your convenience, a detailed listing of all the headings in the book is presented on page 287; you may find this helpful in previewing the contents and locating information of personal interest to you. Depending on your career interests, you may follow one of two different strategies in using this material:

If you find career material a new experience, we suggest you follow the material in the order as developed. This flow of topics and discussions comes out of our experiences with hundreds of women who have a need to start at the beginning of things and work things through in a way that builds slowly and carefully both understanding and acquired skills. A look at page 287 may prove a helpful "preview of coming events."

If, on the other hand, you are already familiar with basic career ideas, have an established career position, or simply know what you want to know, you'll likely want to go straight to the topics of special interest to you, in which case you'll find the list of headings beginning on page 287 especially helpful.

The general structure of the book is as follows:

Part One. Taking Stock. This part is about your values and your skills. Its purpose is to build understanding of your values that heavily influence much of your current activities and career interests. To round out this understanding of self, we help you to take a quick inventory of your skills (Chapter 3) and describe (in Chapter 4) the career compass—the key elements needed for starting to develop a career game plan.

Part Two. Making Plans. This part concerns planning and goals and their connection to careers. Planning forms an integral part of our lives, both personal and professional, though we often aren't fully aware of the elements, let alone how to improve them. Planning (Chapters 5 and 6) sets the stage for goals (Chapters 7 and 8), which in turn form the foundation for starting to erect a specific career plan (Chapters 9 and 10). For women, planning is complicated by a number of factors, of which dual careers and working mothers are among the most pressing (Chapter 11).

Part Three. Moving On—with Your Style. In this part, we discuss work, the work environment, and some practical ways of thinking about career possibilities and dealing with the problems that emerge. Your work needs to be related to your style (Chapter 13); thus, gaining familiarity with what you want in your work environment is essential (Chapter 14). Difficult situations are bound to arise as you seek to deal with your work situation and make career progress (Chapter 15), so that knowing some workable ways of dealing with problem situations will prove helpful (Chapters 16–18).

Part Four. Moving On—with Your Skills. This part is concerned with your skills revisited and with establishing career strategies. The need for awareness of one's skills is never ending because this is a dynamic process and all capabilities are ever changing (Chapters 19 and 20). Thus, we need to know in which directions our best possibilities lie and how to set about to transfer our abilities to take advantage of opportunity—and, of course, further our own career interests as well (Chapter 21). Game plans or strategies are needed so that we are not wasteful of (our previous) time or resources. The concluding discussion (Chapter 22) seeks to share with you some useful ideas in firming up a workable program for your career advancement.

GROWING

A Woman's Guide to Career Satisfaction

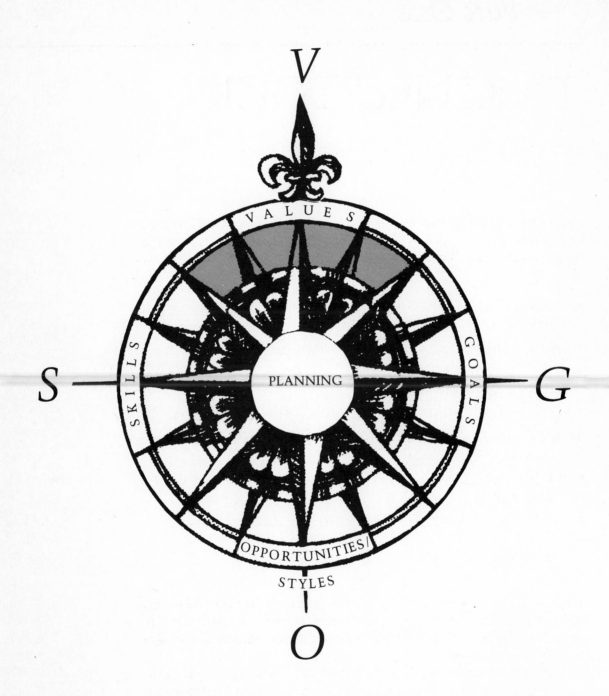

TAKING STOCK

Careers begin when you gather information about yourself and the reality around you and use some helpful ways of organizing that information. Part One helps you gather that information. It shows you:

- How to discover what's important to you, your values, for your career

- How to bring those values to your career decisions

- How your values blend with those of work associates, or, at times, create points of conflict

- How your values can change in the course of your life/career

- What a career style is and how it can help you create or choose a better working environment

- What your skill preferences are—in all areas of your work and life experience

- How to gain a sense of direction from the *career compass*

Women with many different backgrounds and career needs have used this material, but each subject area stands by itself and assumes little prior knowledge. The areas you choose to focus on, reread—or skip —are your decisions.

There are good ways to find out what you enjoy doing and becoming. In this part we present three simple and explicit inventories to help you in your process of self-discovery. You will see that many of the answers about what you enjoy doing were inside of and around you all along, and that you only needed to bring them into clearer focus.

Later parts show you how to use that information to nourish your career in ways that you find productive and rewarding. You will see that your work can become a way of expressing and fulfilling you and your values and that with discovery there's a sense of self-directedness—a feeling that you finally know where and how to direct your talents in ways of working that best express your personal preferences. It's like letting yourself in on a very satisfying secret —the secret of where you, your capabilities, and your potential really fit into the world of work. Each of the parts of *Growing* helps you enrich that sense of self-direction.

Careers start from NOW. This short Part One invites you to a kind of encounter with yourself, and starts you on your way to making your career real—and satisfying.

1

Discovering Your Values: What's There Inside

Sure I know what I want out of life . . . and what kind of person I want to be, too. But I don't think I can just list out on a piece of paper what all my values are!

LYNN

Never thought about it. I enjoy many of the things I'm doing and hate other parts of my work, but I don't know why.

BECKY

Lynn is a bright young woman and pretty verbal, but it's not surprising that she thought she couldn't put her values down on paper. Becky has always thought of her work as "just a job." Although she hopes something better will come along, she hasn't thought of what that means for her. Your values play an important, often central, role in career decisions; but your awareness of just what they are and how strong their influence is may be minimal.

What are values?

In contrast to your attitudes about what's important at a particular time of your life, values are more enduring and specific. Your values express your belief that a certain act, goal, or behavior on your part is preferred by you —often values are supported by generally held values in society. For example, general values in society are implied when we say, "It's the proper thing to do" or "I'm 'entitled' to a vacation . . . I worked hard enough this year." If you agree, those *values* refer to your beliefs and express your preference(s) for particular activities, choices, or goals in your life. And in this sense, your values represent real needs and desires on your part. Your values are an extremely important part of your career planning and a powerful influence on your career choices.

5

THE POWER OF VALUES

Why values are powerful

The concept of values is a powerful notion because it tells you that career thinking and career actions are part of a patterned design that shapes your work goals, *even* if you are not fully aware of its details or intricacies.

A greater awareness of the values you hold can help lead you to better career decisions. You can become more aware of the unseen forces that guide you and, at the same time, can make a *conscious* decision as to alternative directions you may choose to pursue. For example, a strongly held value about a sense of accomplishment can have a great influence on the type of career you seek and the type of challenge you seek in current work activity. Realizing how strong the value is helps you reach out for what you find rewarding and also helps you understand more fully the actions of those around you.

VALUE CONFLICTS

Differing values can cause conflict

Values are held by everyone. The strongest values of supervisors, managers, or other officials in your organization may be different from yours or may even be in direct conflict with your values. Even if values are agreed upon and completely shared with your supervisor, the means of satisfying these values or the relative importance assigned to them may differ. For example, both of you may believe strongly in self-respect. You may feel that self-respect is best achieved by working for an ethical employer. Your supervisor, however, while sharing this value, may have many different interests at stake in her job—monetary benefits, for instance—and she may be prepared to look aside or play down various unethical company actions or practices. A conflict in values is bound to exist. Understanding the whys and hows of that conflict can help you manage your career and take appropriate action, when necessary. Part Three of *Growing* shows how that's done.

CHANGE IN VALUES

Your values and beliefs are shaped by past experiences that may have long faded from your conscious thought. However, it's important to realize that even values are not cast in concrete. If your beliefs are exposed to compelling evidence or new information, your values can and do change. Realistically, however, values tend to change slowly, and this is appropriate, since they are so much a part of your inner being.

Time itself is an inevitable changer. You are not the same person today as you were a year ago, and next year you and your values, your plans and priorities, may change, too. Career planners have learned that many people move through various phases as they grow older and as their circumstances change.

Values do change

For example, a woman's needs and preferences at age 20, both in her career and in her personal life, are likely to differ from her needs and preferences at age 40—or age 50. At 20, she may be attempting to find herself and to seek out mentors. At 30, she may be growing—developing at work and perhaps raising a family, too. At 40, she may have achieved some career goals, but others, not sought before, may become more important. It is important, then, to "touch base" periodically—to see if, in fact, important value shifts have taken place.

How age changes values

THE ROKEACH VALUES SCALE

Since your values play such an important role in your life decisions and career satisfaction, we want you to be able to surface yours, to be aware of them and to be comfortable about them. As our friend Lynn learned, you *can* put them down on paper and target them to a rewarding career choice.

Surfacing your own values

In the spirit of becoming better acquainted with yourself, then, complete—and enjoy—the following values inventory. It was devised by Milton Rokeach, and it's a good one. As you see, there are two lists to be ranked. Rokeach calls one *terminal values*—"ends" or "goals," the kind of life or kind of person that you want to be, that you *value*. The other he calls *instrumental values*—"means" or "doing," the way you'd like to act to achieve what you want, the kind of behavior in yourself *you* value.

Note that what you'll be doing is to rank in importance the 18 items in each scale from those most important to you (number 1, 2, etc.) to those least important (number 16, 17, 18). Those 18 cover a range of choices, but if you want to add something in either column that doesn't seem to fit under any of the 18 headings, go right ahead. Just be sure to give it a number and rank along with the rest. A good way to start is to scan the list first. What's important for you will give you a sense of "that's me"—you may want to check off those phrases and then figure out your rankings.

You're probably surprised to discover that these phrases well describe some of your strongest feelings about what you want to do or be. By the way, it's not uncommon at all to have only a few core values, or many. And, as you discovered, there are some way down on your list that you just can't seem to relate to at all; they hold little meaning for you. However, if none seems to stand out, it may be that you've had an overly tiring or a busy day. Try again another time—or look at the "Tips on Value Hunting" near the end of this chapter before returning to the scale.

THE ROKEACH VALUE SCALES

There are two sets of scales on this page; rank each list separately (1, 2, 3, 4 . . . 18) in terms of its relative importance to you.

TERMINAL VALUES	RANK	INSTRUMENTAL VALUES	RANK
A comfortable life (a prosperous life)	⎯⎯	Ambitious (hard-working, aspiring)	⎯⎯
An exciting life (a stimulating, active life)	⎯⎯	Broadminded (open-minded)	⎯⎯
A sense of accomplishment (lasting contribution)	⎯⎯	Capable (competent, effective)	⎯⎯
A world at peace (free of war and conflict)	⎯⎯	Cheerful (lighthearted, joyful)	⎯⎯
Equality (brotherhood, equal opportunity for all)	⎯⎯	Clean (neat, tidy)	
A world of beauty (beauty of nature and the arts)	⎯⎯	Courageous (standing up for your beliefs)	⎯⎯
Family security (taking care of loved ones)	⎯⎯	Forgiving (willing to pardon others)	⎯⎯
Freedom (independence, free choice)	⎯⎯	Helpful (working for the welfare of others)	⎯⎯
Happiness (contentedness)	⎯⎯	Honest (sincere, truthful)	⎯⎯
Inner harmony (freedom from inner conflict)	⎯⎯	Imaginative (daring, creative)	⎯⎯
Mature love (sexual and spiritual intimacy)	⎯⎯	Independent (self-reliant, self-sufficient)	⎯⎯
National security (protection from attack)		Intellectual (intelligent, reflective)	⎯⎯
Pleasure (an enjoyable, leisurely life)	⎯⎯	Logical (consistent, rational)	
Salvation (saved, eternal life)	⎯⎯	Loving (affectionate, tender)	⎯⎯
Self-respect (self-esteem)		Obedient (dutiful, respectful)	⎯⎯
Social recognition (respect, admiration)	⎯⎯	Polite (courteous, well-mannered)	⎯⎯
True friendship (close companionship	⎯⎯	Responsible (dependable, reliable)	
Wisdom (a mature understanding of life)	⎯⎯	Self-controlled (restrained, self-disciplined)	⎯⎯

HOW TO INTERPRET YOUR RESULTS

You have ranked the items in each of the two lists. You can see now that the *terminal values* (goals) list, as we suggested, is broad and deals mostly with ends—what you want from life and yourself. The *instrumental values* (means or ways of reaching a goal) list is more specific and deals with means; it tells you the relative importance of different actions for you. With the information you have now gathered about yourself, there are some comparisons you can make, with useful results:

Interpreting your values—terminal and instrumental

1. Look over each list separately to gain a better idea of your own priorities.
2. Look at each list side by side to see if there are possible points of difference, even conflicts, in your rankings as well as points of mutual support.

HOW TO COMPARE RANKINGS: A REAL-LIFE EXAMPLE

Let's look at Diane's rankings from this values inventory. We've listed just her first five choices on each list, but you'll see how comparing worked for her.

COMPARING VALUES—DIANE'S EXAMPLE

TERMINAL VALUES	RANK	INSTRUMENTAL VALUES	RANK
Wisdom	1	Courageous	1
Freedom	2	Honest	2
A world at peace	3	Capable	3
Family security	4	Ambitious	4
An exciting life	5	Responsible	5

Diane placed high importance on the terminal values of wisdom and freedom. Because she greatly valued her freedom of action, she wanted a career and a job where she called the shots. She bristled under a strong, authoritarian boss and was willing to change positions, employer, pay, or even location for this highly regarded terminal value. She was literally courageous in her actions, an instrumental value, prepared as she was to take a position on her work and assert herself. Yet she also saw honesty, her number two instrumental value, as an important way of conducting herself and as a quality she admired in those around her. Unhappy where she was, she wanted to make a career change that would bring her greater satisfaction.

Diane's set of terminal and instrumental values are a powerful combination. For some employers, they might represent a potential threat: freedom, insight (wisdom), and directness (courage, honesty) are not always acceptable and/or easy to live with. What Diane learned about herself from looking honestly at her scales of values has led her to think more carefully about her own career plans. She got some ideas and jotted them down:

(1) Seek or make a realistic fit with any new employer; (2) go for jobs where I can use my skills to add personal insight; (3) get control over my own work; (4) avoid highly competitive environments—they aren't comfortable for me. If I can't avoid them, learn to handle competition.

Combining values to advantage

Note how, in this example, the most important interpretations occurred when both scales were looked at together: Diane's insights came when she thought about how she could combine terminal values—where she was going and the things valued in her life—with the ways of getting there. Someone who valued the same terminal values but put a stronger emphasis on the instrumental values of obedience and broadmindedness would find a different way to direct her career, regardless of her skills. Diane found her new position—developing products (and people)—was a wise career move. Of course, she also had to locate the right industry and develop her skills to put it all together. But she started with values.

Suzi's examples

Another example may help to crystalize what you've learned about values and their meaning for a career. Suzi, another friend of ours, was thinking about quitting her job as an art instructor in high school because she didn't seem to "fit in." She wasn't advancing. For years, her colleagues had tried to persuade her to get a master's degree or write some article in order to move ahead, or maybe even make some strong demands—get involved in the politics of it all. Suzi hadn't wanted to do any of that (and didn't). But now she was wondering why she *didn't* care. She was beginning to feel pretty out of place when she talked with us.

Suzi loved to teach and to create the art pieces she called "Rock People" —combinations of rock and paint that she crafted and sold nationally. She wasn't convinced she should quit teaching and just handle "Rock People" full time. Still, she wondered what was wrong with her that she cared so little about her professional advancement or development.

When Suzi checked out her values, the answer seemed obvious. The values that seemed to influence her choices were these twelve:

COMPARING VALUES—SUZI'S EXAMPLES

TERMINAL VALUES	RANK	INSTRUMENTAL VALUES	RANK
A world of beauty	1	Imaginative	1
A comfortable life	2	Independent	2
A world at peace	3	Cheerful	3
Pleasure	4	Loving	4
Self-respect	5	Capable	5
Excitement	6	Self-controlled	6

Here's what she discovered:

I like . . . teaching and creating art because I love beauty and the excitement of kids, travel, and business. My money from "Rock People" brings me the pleasures and comfort I want from life.

I like to do that by . . . using my imagination and being my own boss —hiring people that are pleasant and cheerful and that I can be friends with.

How Suzi's values interrelate

I can see that my values for goals and means interrelate. Look at my occupation and business, my scheduling, desire for a roomy office with a stimulating office-mate who will talk art and swap stories. I even picked a city school for the variety it brings! Why, this is all me! No way am I going to quit because I don't "fit in." I fit in all right, but I'm just not an eager-beaver achievement type. I know now why I am who I am. I think I'll work with that. I feel a little freer to do what I want—travel, be creative, teach, stabilize the business, buy a summer cottage on a lake. I've wanted to do those things but just kept worrying about my career. I think I'm doing fine. What I *want* to do and find meaningful *is* my career.

OBSERVATIONS ON YOURSELF

You'll find you can look back now and make *some* judgments about yourself by assessing your own response to the Rokeach Values Scales. Be as honest as Diane; the insight you gain will pay off—not just in successfully using

Assessing your own values

this resource material but in making satisfying choices for your own career.
Here you go:

OBSERVATIONS ON MYSELF

My observations on my terminal values (What's at the top? At the bottom? What does it all say about me?) I like: _____

_____

_____

My observations on my instrumental values. I like to do things by: _____

_____

_____

_____

Other observations, comparing my terminal and instrumental values (goals and means). Here's what I notice about me: _____

_____

_____

_____

My observations, putting it all together. Describe any type of work, employer, behavior, or environment that you should seek out, create, or avoid: _____

_____

_____

_____

TIPS ON VALUE HUNTING

Perhaps you'd like to explore your combination of values and the ways they help you fashion your life in a little more detail. Or perhaps you're having problems putting it all together. Just having some time, peace, and quiet to explore it all helps. Completing the chapter on career style will help you see your values more clearly. But one or more of the following techniques may also help. They encourage you to visualize, reflect on, or think through your values in different ways. Try any that seem to provide an interesting way for you to learn about your interests and preferences.

Three further ways to discover your values

1. All in a Day's Work

Could be that you're so busy at work that you don't really notice *what* you're doing, or how. For the next few days, try to become more aware of what you're saying and doing and how you respond to your niche and the others around you. Take some time to think back on it every once in a while and at the end of the day. Do you see how *what* you do and *how* you feel reflect your values?

2. Think About a New Job

Perhaps you're caught up in a pretty rigid schedule and haven't had much time to think about yourself lately or to do the kinds of things you'd really enjoy. Well, "try" a new job. Pretend you could pick *any* job you wanted. Any job, even a "glamorous" job. What would it be? Picture yourself doing that job. What are you doing on a typical day? What's the work place like? Whom do you see around you? Take about ten minutes to really picture yourself going through the working day. "Daydream" about it.

Now come back from your "glamour" job. Think about your "day-dream" or speculations or possibilities. What do they tell you about your preferences and values?

3. Take a Friend Along

Perhaps you're so used to your lifestyle and work that it's hard to see your values; they just blend into your routine as a matter of fact. Pretend a favorite relative or friend is visiting you—or has just visited you. "Take them along" as you visualize your day. What is it they would notice about you that's different from their other friends or relatives? In what ways are you the same and different from other people you work with, care for, or see around you? Got any ideas? Jot them down.

You've got one start now in your process of self-discovery. Hang on to the information about your values which you've just put down and be ready to refer to it as you go on to discover more: your style, your skills—and how all of these can go together to help you make your career plans.

USING A CHECKLIST

The checklist that follows is one you'll find at the end of each chapter. It's a kind of summary, but it's much more: It gives you a chance to remind yourself of an idea that's especially important for you and to make some decisions about what you want to do. In the space headed "My ideas and action steps," jot down tentative ideas or plans. Items on the checklist cover some of the important points in each chapter and may help to spark some ideas. Use the space for a record of any whats, whens, and hows that come to mind. In later chapters, we'll show you how to sift through ideas from each chapter and how to pull them together to form career goals and plans that will be meaningful, realistic, and rewarding for you. That process starts with ideas—not necessarily a lot of ideas, just some beginning ideas that seem important to you for now.

Using a checklist

ACTION CHECKLIST FOR CHAPTER 1

Checklist	*My Ideas and Action Steps*	*Date*
√ Values are powerful and affect career decisions.		
√ Values express beliefs and needs central to my life or work.		
√ Values can conflict or blend with those of others.		
√ Values can change in their relative importance for me.		
√ Values express my goals (terminal values).		
√ Values indicate ways I prefer to reach out for my goals (instrumental values).		
√ Values combine and create patterns that outline my preferences.		
√ Being aware of my values and their patterns allows me to direct my skills to work that is personally satisfying.		

2

Getting a Glimpse of Your Career Style

I just dread driving down there. The pay can't make up for the madhouse. Rush rush rush! No time for each other, my bosses, or even a chance for a decent lunch. I'm bushed at the end of each day. We need more help. Until then, it's peck, peck, peck, until I feel like a hen instead of a typist. Half of the time I end up yelling at someone. And by the time I get home. . . .

MARSHA

Nobody's trying. Nobody's involved. Nobody seems to care about their work. Seems like we're all waiting for retirement, and that's a long way down the line. Those of us that care about getting out good work, looking good, or making something of ourselves have to bear up under the others. Think you're so special, they tell us. Well, maybe we are! And maybe all of us should treat each other a little more special too. . . .

JESSICA

You know, I love it—not just the work—the whole atmosphere. Everyone cares and it shows. No matter how busy, somebody takes a second to smile, see how you're doing or what you need to get going. And people really care about their work, too . . . I get twice as much done as I used to. . . .

EDNA

Marsha, Jessica, and Edna are expressing their career styles and their work styles and the frustrations (and satisfactions) that come from trying to negotiate a better fit between their style and their work environment. But the chances are that, like their values, they don't know what their career and work styles are. Justly famous as American women may be for recognizing style, we've found they have little insight into their own career and style —and what these can mean in making career decisions.

What a career style is

What is a career style? A career involves doing more of the things you enjoy doing—that fit between you—your values, skills, and work take you from a job into a career. Your career *style* identifies the way you prefer to approach that work. It helps you to identify in a *general* way what it is about a work environment that is satisfying and productive for you. Your career style is your *general* approach to work that is related to your values and will "travel" with you to all the jobs and positions you'll hold over the years of your career. Of course, careers are also carried out in a *specific* work environment. You'll be interested in how you can translate your career style into a work style, a natural way of approaching the day-by-day doing of a specific job in a specific working environment with its people, tools, space, and expectations.

For example, Suzi, the artist discussed in the last chapter, had a career style that emphasized pleasant and pretty surroundings, lots of stimulating conversations about art, and a desire for compatible work associates and flexible work arrangements. How all of that translates into the day-by-day *doing* of a specific job is *work style*. Suzi did her job with great variety, lots of coffee breaks, field trips, business trips, being a faculty "peacemaker," finding new teaching methods, and spending lots of time "mothering" students. Get the idea?

Your career style defines your general approach to work—an approach that is meaningful and desired by you because it is shaped by the patterns of strongly held values. Your work style helps you bring these preferences to the opportunities and limitations provided by a specific job. Knowing your career style and your work style will help you create a better fit between you, your work, and your work environment. Realistically, you'll have to compromise some of the work style elements or related items to fit into real-world situations, but it's important to have a solid point of departure before any cutting and trimming take place.

Other chapters in *Growing* will help you identify your career style and link it to the career goals you'll be making along the way. Here let's look at how you bring your career style to your daily responsibilities. Let's identify your work style.

YOUR WORK AS YOUR STYLE

Your work, after all, is day-by-day doing—*your* doing. How you go about your work expresses not just your skills but your values and your personality to others. Your career style affects you and often influences your career activities in important ways. It's not just *what* you do, then, that makes a career meaningful and rewarding. The *whos, wheres,* and *hows* of your work are also important, and your career goals may include a desire for ways of working that weave more of your personal preferences into the day-by-day reality of your career.

How knowing your style can help

What you're looking for are more comfortable, adaptive, enjoyable ways of blending work and self. That's *work style*—a unique set of ways of working with and responding to your job surroundings, associates, and experiences which enrich your career.

Knowing your work style should enable you to understand better

- What you do at work

- The ways you prefer to carry out your work

- What changes might strengthen your career potential

- How you reach out to others and how they behave toward you

- How you like the climate of your work or what it is about your work climate that you like

HOW YOUR WORK AFFECTS YOU

Work means not just money but a way of communicating a sense of who you are, a way of enriching your growth and maturity. Time spent at work is an important part of the human experience—an experience that shapes the quality of one's total life.

Every year people spend some 2100 hours in their job or work activities. That's just about the amount of time most adults get for sleeping in a year. It far exceeds any other single activity of our lives. The time we spend in that work experience, and its quality, affect us as maturing, healthy, and satisfied women. In fact, most of the comments heard off the job are *not* about the job itself. Most comments, like those repeated at the head of this chapter, reveal how different kinds of work, surroundings, and people influence our lives and can even make up for a poor work experience.

How work affects you

People, places, and events from many sources blend into the work scene, and that mix affects your thinking, feeling, and doing. Awareness puts career behavior front and center. Your career planning will include a concern for your career style and the growth and space you'll need as you branch up or out or dig a little deeper into your career. Growing space is not easy to create. You'll need an understanding of both your own style and your own values to help you bring a sense of yourself to your career.

TWO REAL-LIFE EXAMPLES

What Marsha did

Consider Marsha and Jessica again and how career style made a difference.

Marsha decided *not* to quit. She really liked the work but not the working experience her job had become. She knew she wanted more stability, harmony, and peace within her office scene. Unfortunately, when more typists were added, the work and the pressure continued to pile up. Marsha wondered how she'd ever get settled down so she could really just concentrate on her work and some training programs instead of her churning stomach. But at least she realized that her problem had to do with her career style and its fit with her work environment, not her career choice. She knew she had to learn how to plan for a period of steady digging in and try to make her job environment change.

Jessica's problems

Jessica, on the other hand, finally became the supervisor of her group. Her concern for others and for "getting the job done" made her a strong leader. Still, she, too, had her share of adjustment problems. Jessica didn't realize that her new position meant a different balance between her own needs for self-expression and her new responsibilities for hearing and evaluating the opinions of other group members. Expressing her feelings now seemed to make everyone else hold back and accuse her of using the promotion to get her own way. "How come," she asked, "*I* can't have an opinion all of a sudden?"

She could, but first she had to learn when and how to express her concern—how to fit *her* style into her new career activities and environment. Change goes easier when you have a sense of your style, a sense of direction, and the plans that can bring that style to both your career and work activities.

DISCOVERING YOUR CAREER STYLE

Your preferences matter

To discover your unique work style, you need to find out what your preferences are. Like discovering your values, it's a matter of looking inside and being honest about what you are and what you like. That's basic. Later chapters will pick up on the preferences you have and help you to establish the goals, plans, and methods that will create a better blend of self and work.

A PERSONAL INVENTORY OF WORK AND WORK STYLE

Your own work style inventory

The work and work style inventory that follows will help you explore the preferences and possibilities that can enrich your current work and/or the work activities you plan for the future.

WORK AND WORK STYLE INVENTORY

This inventory reminds you of many of the activities that are part of your job. Think about your work. Then scan the list and check any activities that you do now and also check the activities you want to do more often.

	WHAT I DO RIGHT NOW	WHAT I WANT TO DO MORE OFTEN
Planning out the day	✓	
Sticking to a schedule	✓	
Finding time for others		✓
Handling my moods		✓
Handling my reactions to the moods of others		✓
Lunch/break times	✓	
Getting involved		
Working faster or better		✓
Taking care of equipment		
Sharing work/equipment		
Getting organized	✓	
Starting or finishing tough projects		✓
Getting drudge work done		✓
Getting more training		
Gossip/reputations		
Asking for help/giving help		✓
Asking about work/careers/benefits/pay		
Stepping up to problems	✓	✓
Loyalties to the firm/work crew		
Changing the job a little		

	WHAT I DO RIGHT NOW	WHAT I WANT TO DO MORE OFTEN
Getting a sense of priorities	✓	—
Doing more on my own/ independence	—	✓
Accepting responsibility	✓	✓
Promotions	—	—
Handling competition	—	✓
Handling mistakes	—	✓
Speaking up in a group	—	✓
Travel	—	✓
Transfers	—	

Work and non-work activities often interrelate or enrich each other. Sometimes they provide us with opportunities to express ourselves in different ways. What do you do now, or want to do more often, in terms of non-work activities, the personal you?

	WHAT I DO RIGHT NOW	WHAT I WANT TO DO MORE OFTEN
Hobbies	—	✓
Recreation	✓	—
Education	✓	✓
Training	—	✓
Religion	—	—
Politics	—	✓
Volunteer work	—	✓
Finances	—	✓
Home care	—	—
Relationships: Friends	✓	✓
Neighbors	—	—
Spouse	—	—
Children	—	—
Relatives	—	—

Now look over the phrases you just listed. Check the ones that will also help boost your career or enrich your work. Doing more of these activities will help you strengthen and advance your current career, and, if they relate to your core values, they will help you strengthen your career style, regardless of the job you hold. In later chapters, we'll show you how to check activities with core values and how to blend together all your planning.

OBSERVATIONS ON YOUR STYLE

Just as you did with your inventory on values, make some observations now about your work style. Take a look again at all of the phrases you have checked. Which are presently part of your work activities or goals—a part you'd like to enlarge and do more of? List here the ones most important to you, maybe five to ten you really most enjoy.

Assessing your style

Your work and work style list is the beginning for any plans you might make later. Developing those career plans takes some time, thought, and planning techniques. But now you may have a better sense of who you are and where you want to go by way of your work styles. Other sections of *Growing* will help you fine tune that style.

OBSERVATIONS ON YOUR STYLE

What I like and would like to do more of:

1. _____

2. _____

3. _____

4. _____

5. _____

6. _____

7. _____

8. _____

9. _____

10. _____

Career style:
work expressed
through
personality

As you can see, your style is a part of your work activities. Your style expresses your preferences concerning what you feel is important in your career activities or your working environment. Your career style is your work expressed through your personality. Your work style is how you bring those preferences to a specific job, location, and work associates.

ACTION CHECKLIST FOR CHAPTER 2

Checklist	*My Ideas and Action Steps*	*Date*

√ A career style is the way you prefer to work.

√ Your work style brings your career style to your specific job, working environment, and work associates.

√ Some of your work preferences are related to strongly held values.

√ Those preferences are the core of your career style.

√ Knowing your career and work style helps you create a happier work environment. It makes work a more natural expression of your personality.

3

Assessing Your Skills, Present and
Potential: A Quick Inventory

> *I'm not sure what my skills are. I went to junior col-*
> *lege—but any way you look at it, my talents are no big*
> *deal. No way would I try to have what you call a*
> *career. . . .*
>
> MARILYNN

> *I've got more skills than a skillsaw—at least the way I*
> *think of skills. So what are they worth to me? I'm*
> *sitting here doing a good job selling annuities to work-*
> *ing women. It pays all right, but I don't much like it.*
> *And it seems to me that it doesn't take much skill. Just*
> *a lot of time. . . .*
>
> RONNIE

Most of us think of *skills* as a word describing something we do to "get the
job done." That's how we'll use it in this book. Simply stated, skills are
abilities you put into use: the ability to type, take shorthand, or use a
transcribing machine (secretarial skills); the ability to program a computer
(data-processing skills); the ability to persuade people to buy a product or
service (sales skills); the ability to operate specific kinds of adding and calculating machines (bookkeeping skills); the ability to administer treatments
and medicines (nursing skills).

THE THREE ELEMENTS OF SKILL SETS

All these different skill sets are made up of just three elements: information
(data), people, and things. This is important to keep in mind. The *Dictionary
of Occupational Titles*, which we'll explore in Part Three, and much of the

What skills are

23

Kinds of skills

information in it, is based on this simple premise: *Every job requires a worker to function in relation to data, people, and things in varying degrees.*

But there are lots of different skills that relate to data, people, and things. They are not just what some people call "hard skills"—manual or business skills—but skills called "soft skills," skills at getting along with people. Examples are how well you understand others or can plan out a work schedule. In other words, there are many kinds of skills.

Skills are what you can do. And it's in this sense that Marilynn may underestimate herself and Ronnie misunderstand herself. Like them, you have lots of skills. You need to have some idea of what your actual skills are, hard or soft, so that you can match them with your values and your style —and ultimately with the jobs and industries that fit your preferences.

A PERSONAL SKILLS INVENTORY

Discovering your skills

Specific job skills can become the building blocks of your future in the world of work. To explore your potential for specific job skills, we're going to ask you to think of all the things you do in your life experience—not just your current work activities, but also your hobbies, recreational activities you enjoy, basic things you do to keep your life in order. All of these can provide insight into specific career skill potentials. Please think through each of these different aspects and consider the value of that particular skill to you. to you.

SKILLS INVENTORY

	Who, me? No way—that's not for me!	Well, I do that stuff—but certainly not for a living.	That's something I enjoy doing, once in a while.	Never thought about it in terms of a career skill, but it just might make sense.	Yes, I can see how that fits into some of my career goals—I'm going to look further into it.	I already do this, but I sure could do more and, chances are, get more career satisfaction from it!
PHYSICAL SKILLS Using my hands to 1. build things						

	Who, me? No way—that's not for me!	*Well, I do that stuff—but certainly not for a living.*	*That's something I enjoy doing, once in a while.*	*Never thought about it in terms of a career skill, but it just might make sense.*	*Yes, I can see how that fits into some of my career goals—I'm going to look further into it.*	*I already do this, but I sure could do more and, chances are, get more career satisfaction from it!*
2. operate tools and equipment						
3. fix and repair things						
4. create artistic things						
5. grow things						
Using my body to 6. do athletic things						
7. carry out physical tasks (lifting, moving, etc.)						
8. do outdoor activities						
Using my physical senses (sight, hearing, smell, taste, touch) to 9. evaluate						
10. observe (watch over or supervise)						
11. examine						
MENTAL SKILLS						
Using words to 12. influence others in speaking						
13. influence others in writing						
14. teach or instruct						
15. communicate socially						
Using numbers to 16. prepare budgets						

	Who, me? No way—that's not for me!	Well, I do that stuff—but certainly not for a living.	That's something I enjoy doing, once in a while.	Never thought about it in terms of a career skill, but it just might make sense.	Yes, I can see how that fits into some of my career goals—I'm going to look further into it.	I already do this, but I sure could do more and, chances are, get more career satisfaction from it!
17. keep financial books and records						
18. manage money and investments						
19. count and control things						
20. apply logic						
21. compute						
Using analytical logic to 22. solve problems						
23. research information						
24. analyze information						
25. classify information or objects						
26. make comparisons						
27. evaluate						
28. follow through on projects						
Using intuition to 29. show insight						
30. perceive important issues						
31. visualize things						
32. demonstrate sensitivity						
33. demonstrate foresight						

	Who, me? No way—that's not for me!	*Well, I do that stuff—but certainly not for a living.*	*That's something I enjoy doing, once in a while.*	*Never thought about it in terms of a career skill, but it just might make sense.*	*Yes, I can see how that fits into some of my career goals—I'm going to look further into it.*	*I already do this, but I sure could do more and, chances are, get more career satisfaction from it!*
CREATIVE SKILLS						
Using thoughts and words to						
34. write creatively						
35. be artistic, as in painting, crafts, music						
36. be imaginative and innovative						
37. design						
38. decorate						
39. think up new processes and procedures						
40. invent						
LEADERSHIP SKILLS						
Using personality to						
41. speak before groups						
42. assume responsibility						
43. influence and direct others						
44. get things organized						
45. start new projects						
46. create new acquaintanceships/ friendships						

	Who, me? No way—that's not for me!	*Well, I do that stuff—but certainly not for a living.*	*That's something I enjoy doing, once in a while.*	*Never thought about it in terms of a career skill, but it just might make sense.*	*Yes, I can see how that fits into some of my career goals—I'm going to look further into it.*	*I already do this, but I sure could do more and, chances are, get more career satisfaction from it!*
47. persuade						
48. motivate myself and others						
HELPING SKILLS						
Using skills to 49. take care of others						
50. guide and direct						
51. serve						
52. listen and counsel						
53. heal or cure						
54. teach						

OBSERVATIONS ON YOUR SKILLS

Assessing your skills

You now have some quite specific information about your skills. You may never have realized what some of them are. In Part Three of this book, we'll explore these in depth and show you how to link them to work, industries, and jobs. But for now, you can make some observations.

OBSERVATIONS ON YOUR SKILLS

Of the five skills listed (physical, mental, creative, leadership, and helping), the ones I am most experienced in. _____

Which ones, regardless of experience or my degree of skill, I most *like to do* (list the skills you enjoy using):

1. _____   2. _____

3. _____   4. _____

5. _____   6. _____

7. _____   8. _____

9. _____   10. _____

11. _____   12. _____

13. _____   14. _____

15. _____   16. _____

At this point, you have a quick survey of the skills you've tried out and/or enjoy. It will take time and thought to pull together your skills, work preferences, and values so that your career takes a sense of direction that's realistic and right for you. That sense of direction will come from your career compass. The following chapter shows how that compass will "pull together" your thoughts and reflections.

ACTION CHECKLIST FOR CHAPTER 3

Checklist	*My Ideas and Action Steps*	*Date*
√ All skills have elements tied to data, people, things.		
√ Personal skills inventories are based on all your life experiences.		
√ Skills have differing values to you.		
√ Many skill categories exist that have proven helpful in inventories.		
√ Where do you stand on these? physical skills — hands, body, physical senses		
mental skills — words, numbers, logic, intuition		
creative skills		
leadership skills		
helping skills		

4

Constructing Your Career Compass

You talk about a sense of direction. How do I go about getting that? It really sounds like a difficult, but satisfying, chore is ahead of me.

MEG

I have some idea about my values—and about my career style, too. But I don't know about careers in general. The whole idea of a career sounds exciting and a bit mysterious—almost as if it's something designed for other people. But not for me. . . .

CLEO

Careers *are* exciting, but there's nothing mysterious about them at all. And they're not for "other" people. You'll become aware of what you want, learn to get your career launched, and find realistic ways of reaching a better blend of you and work.

Careers need not be mysterious

Careers take you into the future. They are lived and constantly experienced and project you into a future of your own choosing. They take you into a situation that is much more than simply a job. Moving into your career means doing more of the kinds of things you value. A career brings together work, relationships with others, opportunity, and challenge. It usually involves developing and using your abilities. So career planning may mean doing better in your current job or preparing for new work possibilities. Careers mean having a better feeling about yourself and your work, regardless of which direction you choose.

A CAREER COMPASS

Gaining a sense of direction

Cleo's feeling about a career being mysterious probably meant she didn't have as clear a concept of a career as she did about her values and her career style. To begin planning, she needs a sense of direction, something specific

30

she can turn to for help or to use as a guide. That's why we've constructed a career compass.

Think of it this way. Your future career is somewhere out there on the horizon. Your present career plans and activities take you there. You might rocket straight through to your goal, stop to plan or replan, or adjust your speed and style to fit any special needs or preferences that come up. You might even choose to drift around for a while. However, it helps to have a *sense of direction.* That's what a career compass is all about. It helps to have a plan that will keep you "on track" as you reach for your goals.

A way to keep you on track

Just remember, the goals and the plans are yours. Even when you sift through the concerned advice of superiors, co-workers, or well-intentioned friends, relatives, or neighbors who say, "If I were you. . . ," you have the final word on the direction your career will take. You take charge of your career!

It also helps to remember that career plans, like people, change. That's why they're put on paper, not carved in marble. Your career can, and will, shift with newer understandings, opportunities, and life circumstances. The career compass developed for this resource material shows you how to maintain your sense of direction even when you shift your career activities to fit the important events and people in your life. Figuring out what you want, getting it, and doing more of what you want in ways that are realistic and important to you are what careers and career planning are all about.

Even if you shift directions

GETTING YOUR ACT TOGETHER

An expression commonly heard these days is "getting your act together," and this surely applies to career planning. Personal career planning has four acts—or as we've designed it, four points of a compass. Like a play, the acts have to be carefully executed so that they blend together and are seen as part of a common whole. The four acts—our compass points—revolve around you and include your values, skills, goals, and opportunities. Your planning pulls them together to assist you in forming your career plans. The four points on the compass are illustrated on the following page.

And a way to get your act together

Career planning and thinking thus form a compass—or a play in which all four acts are changing in character or are capable of being changed. It's as if you are constantly changing the lines of the script, yet it must all come together in unity at the end of the play. As you think of staging this play of your career, think of the play as your self—the true center of your career compass. Your goals, opportunities, values, and abilities all act to draw the needle of your career compass to different directions or areas at different times.

With you as the center

YOUR CAREER COMPASS

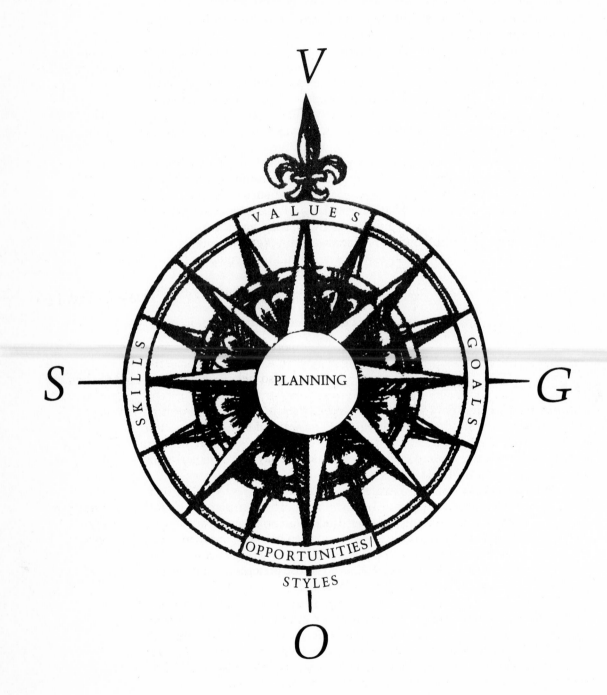

POINTS ON THE COMPASS AND CHANGE

Your abilities and skills can and do change in response to training, schooling, or just getting more work experience.

The four career compass points

Your opportunities keep changing as the demand for particular skills keeps shifting in your organization, or when some sections of the country provide new employment opportunities while opportunities lessen in other sections, or as the characteristics of the work force or population change.

Your career goals change, too, but usually more slowly. Not surprisingly, career goals shift with such things as age, family circumstances, or the changing national scene.

Your values, interests, and needs probably change most slowly over time, but they do change as you gain experience and wisdom and meet with some disappointments and failures, but with some successes, too. Much more will be said about these points later, but now the important thing to keep in mind is that the career compass will help you "put your act together" so that all of the key parts *reinforce and support each other.*

HOW YOUR CAREER COMPASS HELPS

Each of the four components we've described—the compass points—influences your career and may become more important at different times. Skills and opportunities do shift to meet changes in us, in others, or in the work world. Your career compass, therefore, can also help you to understand, organize, and plan a better fit between your career style and broader career activities. That kind of career planning takes your whole person into account. It helps you locate your own effective ways of strengthening performances, handling "people problems," or moving toward a good working environment. All of that empowers you to make the day-by-day experiences of your career more satisfying.

Your compass can deal with change

Enriching your career can change your work habits, your work associates, your work equipment, your work activities. Those changes each call for some internal direction to guide you through growing space you'll need during different phases of your career. You need to balance your own needs for self-expression and accomplishment with deeper appreciation of your career responsibilities. You also need to relate those preferences and goals to your skills and the opportunities you have at work.

And still give steady directions

Getting all this together can be a trying and difficult process, especially when other personal, family, community, or professional concerns enter into the picture. Yet, you can focus that picture a little more clearly through the lens of your career compass. Its design allows you to integrate your career preferences and skills and balance them against other responsibilities, while at the same time it keeps you on a steady career course.

Feeling the sense of direction and of making plans, big or small, that *You're ready* help develop your career starts with you—and with this compass, which *for planning* shows you how to maintain your sense of direction even when you shift your career activities to fit the important events and people in your life. Figuring out what you want, getting there, and doing more of what you want in ways that are realistic and important to you are what careers and career planning are all about. You will have to provide the patience, thought, and effort as you move on to planning—the next section of this book.

ACTION CHECKLIST FOR CHAPTER 4

Checklist	*My Ideas and Action Steps*	*Date*
✓ Career compasses provide a sense of direction.		
✓ Values, skills, goals, and opportunities must blend — need to "get this act together."		
✓ The points on the *compass* — values, skills, goals, and opportunities — do change.		
✓ When changes take place, new directions, action steps, learning, skill development, or business associates may be indicated.		

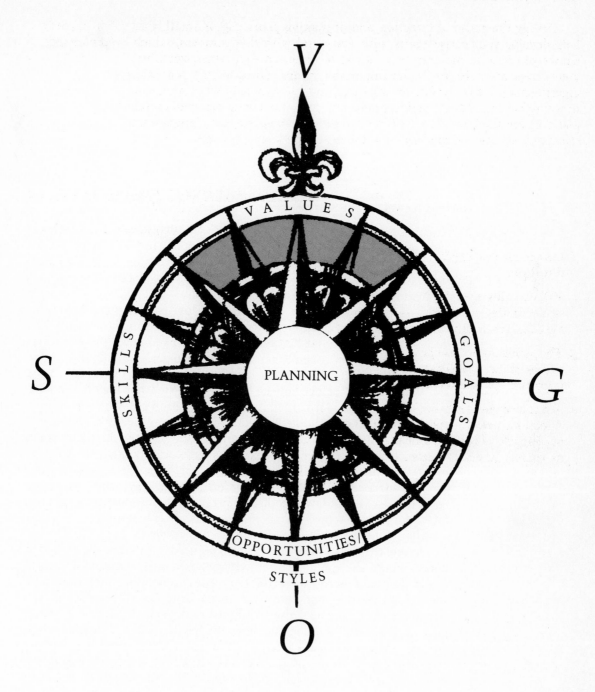

PROFILES FOR PART ONE

Amanda Newell and Sherri Johnson

Amanda Newell—The Story

Amanda Newell is a 48-year-old recent widow. She has always worked and knows she must continue to work—which is fine with her since she has always enjoyed and found excitement in discussing trips with potential travelers. For years she has been a travel agent in a small agency in a suburban community. She'd "chosen" the job—and loved it—because it had some "perks" despite the relatively low pay: she got travel discounts and some even applied to her husband. Thus they traveled a good deal—a real-life goal for her. She and her husband never placed money and security as top goals. When she was younger, Amanda had undertaken a rather extensive "career search" on her own. A value inventory she found in one of her college books interested her greatly, and she worked it through—it turned out to be Rokeach's. "An exciting life" was her number one choice. For her, it was exemplified in traveling.

She now has some decisions to make: she has two relatively small insurance policies from her husband, a small contractor who had always insisted he just didn't "believe in insurance." She also has one child: a son, 24, married with one child and one on the way, who is about to enter his last year of law school. The pregnancy was unexpected and had forced his wife to stop working. She had been his chief means of support —although he works weekends as a taxicab driver.

At one time, Amanda's friends had pointed out that, if she cashed in both policies, she could take her lifelong "dream trip" around the world —and they said there was certainly nothing to hold her back from this, the culmination of her desire for an exciting life. Now she has the freedom to do what she'd always wanted to do—and her husband would have been pleased. But does she have the freedom? She remembers that, years ago when she had eagerly viewed her career possibilities, "an exciting life" and "freedom" had been her first and second choices in the values scales inventory she had taken. The trip seems to fit these choices of "terminal values." The book is still on the shelf and shows that she had also put "independent" and "responsible" as her first and second choices for "instrumental values."

Complicating Amanda's situation is another factor—for five years now, her boss has held out to her a standing offer to come into the small firm as a partner. She is good at her job; he is older and wants to do less; and he thinks that this would be fine for both of them. She has refused whenever he brought the matter up. She wants her freedom and her exciting life—plenty of time to travel, not being tied down with the responsibility of being an owner at Christmas or during summer vacations, when she herself likes to "get away."

Questions for You

1. How did the terminal values of "an exciting life" and "freedom" and the instrumental values of "independent" and "responsible" guide Amanda's earlier career activities?

2. What new complications have entered the picture at age 48 that seemed far distant or even "non-existent" at an earlier point?

3. What new interpretations may Amanda (have to) attach to her values in the light of the situation now confronting her, that is, what kind of newer thinking must she introduce that will still be in harmony with her values—yet be responsive to her situation?

4. What practical approaches might she consider?

Our Comments

At an earlier point in Amanda's life, the values of "an exciting life" and "freedom" sought a workable outcome in the light of skills she possessed, the then-existing family situation, and the opportunities available. Being in a small town and with a husband tied down to his business (and area) clearly narrowed her choices of "what" and "where." She'd "chosen" the travel agent job because it was available, within driving distance, and had the *promise* of being interesting because it tied in with things Amanda likes to do—and has some skills in doing. Intelligent search—and luck—both play roles in the job search process. Hopefully, most of the emphasis is on the former and the latter (luck) is just that little bit extra that sometimes creates an opportunity. Things worked out for Amanda—her work was interesting, her child was growing up and pursuing his interests and life in a way rewarding to him and to them. Her husband was actively engaged in his business and apparently generated enough income so that, by pooling their funds, they were able to pursue their mutual interest of travel—an experience which further reinforced her travel expertise! But all that changed—and this is natural and to be expected—it's life. Her challenge is to regroup, to think things through in the light of her new circumstances.

Amanda realizes that she is suddenly in doubt about what she really wants. She finds that, in spite of her good friends' advice, she is not that eager to take the big round-the-world trip; she finds she is thinking about her son—and about her own future. She realizes she does not want to be a burden to him; she recognizes that she and her husband have worked hard all their lives but never made "retirement" a paramount matter. Who would take care of her if she were really ill—or really old? How will her son finish law school now that her daughter-in-law will have to stop work—at least for six months?

Amanda has sense enough to think carefully about what she does. She took a workshop in career counseling and found herself again taking the same values inventory she took years ago. "An exciting life" is no longer her first choice; no one is more surprised than she to realize she has written down "family security." On the other hand, her number two choice is still "freedom." But she realizes, with some shock, that freedom now means something else to her: as defined in the scale, "independence, free choice," she realizes that now, as a widow of 48, freedom means "not being dependent on any other person"—especially her son —for her care and welfare. She wants to do this for herself, she thinks; she does not want to hinder him in any way. This is terribly important to her.

Postscript: Amanda took one of the policies and bought a share of the travel agency. She will forego the big trip for a piece of the business —and a good chance to become sole owner within a few years. She turned the other policy over to her son to help meet his tuition payments for the final year of law school. As she viewed the future, she even had some thoughts about managing to sit with the youngsters if their parents went away on a trip.

Amanda's values have changed—even as in the matter of "freedom" her actual definition of one value. But she accepts these changes and feels that she has arrived at a workable basis for dealing with her career situation.

Sherri Johnson—The Story

Sherri is only 21; but she is certainly a working woman. She has been working since she was 12! She began in the school cafeteria, and all through junior and senior high school she worked in the cafeteria. After school or nights, she also worked at a fast-food counter not far from her home. She is just finishing a college prep course at a community college. She wants to continue at the state university 90 miles away and become a math teacher since she has received great encouragement from her teacher regarding her math abilities. She'd like most of all to be a college professor, but would "settle" for work in which she could bring together abilities and interest.

Her circumstances are such that she must now work for at least one year to pay for college tuition and room and board—it's too far away for her to live at home. She has always helped support her family and feels she wants to and must do this. Her mother works on an assembly line nearby; over the years, she has cared for a mostly invalid grandfather (in a wheelchair) when her mother was away on either the swing or the night shift. She has three younger brothers, for whom she provided total care: sending them off to school, getting meals, making and mending clothes, fixing toys, tutoring, and entertaining them. Sherri is so immersed in her problems that the only work she can see herself qualified for is her job at the fast-food store. Even though she can now be an assistant manager if she works full time, her salary will be relatively low so that she cannot save much money after she has contributed toward her family. Thus she feels trapped and depressed. At home, her mother, whom she greatly loves as a mother—and a tired, hard-pressed worker —has little sympathy for her. Her mother says she should have stuck in high school and community college to practical courses: "If math was her favorite subject, she should have taken accounting and other business skills—and always kept her typing up so she could be a good secretary to someone."

Only her grandfather has a stubborn faith in her: "That girl can do anything she sets her mind to," he always says. But her mother says this is only because she's his only granddaughter. Sherri is quite enterprising and, though her young life has been taken up with work, brothers, grandfather, and house chores, she managed to do other things as well.

Sherri knows she needs some help in getting a "handle" on things —she turned to one of her teachers who had had many years of practical work experience before coming into the school system. Shirley Murphy, the teacher, had a long "conference-type discussion" with Sherri and advised her to try to take stock of her interests—things she found pleasing and others perhaps that she really wanted to do—and also to think about her skills and abilities. "Why not list out things you have done and then we'll try to see what they say about your abilities?" At last Sherri felt a bit more at ease with things, knowing that at least she was onto something that might lighten the burden.

Questions

1. Sherri didn't have the benefit of a skills inventory listing but was starting off with things she had actually accomplished; then she and Shirley Murphy were going to analyze them. What can Sherri list and what do these suggest regarding her skills?

2. What role was Shirley Murphy playing in these activities?

3. If you were to try to sort out some of Sherri's interests, goals, and

opportunities—shorter term and longer term—what might these be?

4. After completing these analyses, do you think that Sherri can be a bit more at ease regarding future possibilities? Why?

Our Comments

The questions for the Sherri Johnson situation are to assist in sorting things out in a pragmatic way, to take advantage of resources that are available and attainable. Finding a teacher with the "right" background and a good relationship with Sherri was part of the pragmatism. Shirley Murphy's background crossed the work, school, and feminine aspects of Sherri's situation. Shirley thus represented a resource *and* a sounding board for Sherri. Sherri's "homework assignment"—a listing of activities—was a practical way to get her started thinking about these things in a more systematic fashion, and, despite her tender years, the list was impressive:

Activity	*Implication*
School Finished prep program	— "Stick-to-itiveness" Aptitude for college work
Math courses	— Math competency (especially with teacher's comments) Analytical abilities (use in computer work, systems, elsewhere?)
Home	— Child caring; tutoring, care of handicapped; organizing household work — Self-organization to get it all accomplished
Work	— Familiarity with food operations; ability, potentially at managerial level Green thumb Selling ability—corsages for prom Physical energy

The list of possible goals and time frames put together by Sherri Johnson and Shirley Murphy are as follows:

Work possibilities, career opportunities and goals	Short run—"Say, in the next year or two"	Long(er) run—"Say, next 2–4 years"	Over 4 years
Food management			✓
Food service		✓	✓
Floral business			✓
Teaching (math)			✓
Assistant manager, food store	✓		
Day care	✓	✓	
Computer/data analysis	✓		

Note that many of these tend to fall into the long-term career picture and would require frequent review. Yet, at this point, the press of immediate economic and family circumstances sets the priorities—so Sherri set out to cope in the best fashion possible with these, but with an eye to the future (bringing together goals, opportunity, values, skills). Admittedly, Sherri faces a tough decision; but in the light of what she's already confronted and successfully overcome, the outlook for her is reasonably positive. She must deal with her interests in a realistic but hopeful fashion. Sherri has expressed a desire for possible teaching (longer range goal), but must deal with shorter run economic necessities. Although she may have the ability to work effectively as assistant manager in the fast-food store, she may have better short(er) run potentials for income in an occupation such as computers and/or data analysis, where she can use her analytical abilities. Because of her attachment and sense of obligation to her family, she'll have to keep her options open.

ADDITIONAL RESOURCES

Part One: Taking Stock

BOLLES, RICHARD N. *The Three Boxes of Life and How to Get Out of Them.* Berkeley, Calif.: Ten Speed Press, 1978. Placing work in the perspective of a lifetime and one's needs for education and recreation.

FLACH, FREDERIC F. *Choices.* New York: Bantam Books, 1971. How to increase the effectiveness of personal choices.

NEWMAN, MILDRED, and BERKOWITZ, BERNARD. *How to Be Your Own Best Friend.* New York: Ballantine Books, 1978. A reassuring look at self-insight as a guiding force in life.

ROGERS, CARL R. *On Becoming a Person.* Boston: Houghton Mifflin, 1961. The philosophy and process of being a person.

SCHWARTZ, FELICE N., SCHIFTER, MARGARET H., and GILLOTTI, SUSAN S. *How to Go to Work When Your Husband Is Against It, Your Children Aren't Old Enough, and There's Nothing You Can Do Anyhow.* New York: Simon and Schuster, 1973. Tips on entering the labor force.

SHEEHY, GAIL. *Passages.* New York: Bantam Books, 1977. A presentation of the crises of adult life.

TERKEL, STUDS. *Working.* New York: Avon, 1975. A documentary look at people, their work, and their feelings about their work.

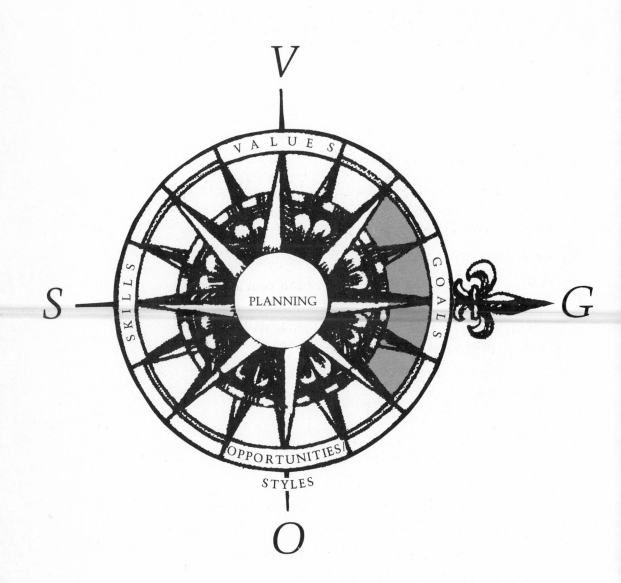

Part Two

MAKING PLANS

Planning can help you to bring more satisfaction and happiness into your career and also assist you in doing things faster, better, or more effectively. Planning takes you from goals to reality. It pulls together information to form goals and to organize realistic ways to reach those goals. Part Two helps you create career plans. It helps you:

- Understand the meaning and purpose of planning
- Verify your own planning experience and your ability to do sound planning
- Learn how the specifics of a career change with time
- Set career goals and prepare paths to get there
- Begin to make your own planning strategies so that values, goals, skills, and opportunities—the four points of your compass— come together to serve the "center"—you

"Failing to plan is planning to fail." You have done planning if you have:

- Prepared a list of things to buy or a reminder list of things to do
- Talked to a friend about things you'd like to do on the weekend
- Made notes to remind the boss about this or that
- Arranged a purchase for future delivery

Some people may say that these rather obvious or ordinary events shouldn't be glorified by calling them "planning." Our experience is entirely different: we have found that the ability to make plans, whether small daily ones or important long-range ones, is paramount to individual success. The purpose of Part Two is to convince you how crucial planning is. Remember, *all career thinking and self-assessment* rests on the assumption that *you are willing to accept the possibilities for improvement in your personal life that planning can provide.*

The central message of this whole career-planning approach, then, is that *you take charge of your career.* There are many well wishers, quite sincere in their motives, who encourage you to do this or that. Organizations, too, will often make an honest and determined effort to assist you. But, when all is said and done, you've got to be your own person and be sufficiently organized and directed to proceed by your own compass. If your thinking is clear, if you have some directional notion of where you want to go with your career and some workable ideas of how to make it happen, then you'll find your employer and associates can really be helpful.

5

Understanding What Planning Means

There are lots of job openings where I work—good, higher-level jobs, too. The trouble is they always want somebody with more experience or education in such and such an area. I'll never get that promotion.

HELEN

If Helen understood what planning was, she might not feel so discouraged. What is common to all planned events is that they

What planning is

- Take place in the future

- Satisfy a purpose or need

- Have been thought about in advance

- Have required consideration of alternatives

- Have involved a choice

Admittedly, the quality of planning, the working it through, and the results vary from person to person; but we've all done planning. And we can be certain Helen has, too. Sure, she's discouraged, but some observation on her part would convince Helen that there seems to be a regular and periodic pattern of promotional opportunities in her unit *and* that these often require credentials, experience, or training beyond what she now has. Adding all that up, she could plan for her promotion. Helen could go out and prepare herself by taking a few courses or by participating in one of the company's after-hours training programs. For the moment, she's going no place because she's waiting for opportunity instead of observing, checking it out, and planning for it. No one's going to hand her opportunity packaged with a red ribbon.

47

SIX FUNDAMENTAL QUESTIONS OF PLANNING

Six questions to ask

In Helen's case, her package just won't arrive, that is, it won't unless she starts doing some planning—planning that begins by asking herself the six fundamental questions of planning:

- WHAT?
- WHY?
- HOW?
- WHERE?
- WHO?
- WHEN?

The questions Helen needs to ask

For Helen these questions are:

1. WHAT qualifications are necessary for the promotion *I* want?

2. WHY are those skills necessary or important for me to build?

3. HOW, specifically, can I acquire those skills or abilities—what alternatives are available to me?

4. WHERE can I get the necessary resources, training, or experience?

5. WHO can guide me along the way, give me feedback to help me stay on track?

6. WHEN will I begin?

The function of planning

By answering these six fundamental questions, Helen is able to complete the function of planning, which is to *transform purpose into action.*

Our preliminary observations and our preliminary example, Helen, have been provided to convince you that all of us have some level of planning experience and ability and that we can build readily on experiences that most of us have.

How planning can pay off

However, so far, you've had to take it on faith that planning can provide a more satisfying, perhaps better, life. Consider for a moment, then, the common, almost daily experience of purchasing milk. A little comparison shopping will likely tell you that your preferred brand is available for 3 cents less per gallon at another store. (Comparison shopping is, in effect, an answer to the "where" planning question.) Consumer groups claim that careful comparison shopping (planning) can save 5 to 10 percent on annual food bills—and that could be a savings of $500 or more a year.

But not all planning has such specific or immediate payoffs. Sometimes we don't see the fruits of our planning efforts until years later, and sometimes the changes created are very subtle.

*Now — or
years later*

A CASE FOR PLANNING

It is appropriate now to crystalize this planning idea within the context of career thinking, for planning is indispensable for successful career progress—the type of progress that is satisfying because you know you have done everything possible to maximize realization of your career opportunities. When you plan:

*Planning is the
context of
careers*

1. *You have more time to consider more alternatives.* For example, if you are in your last year of school and wait until after graduation to begin looking for a job, you may find there aren't any left. By planning ahead, you could have begun interviewing for jobs while you were still in school and avoided the rush of summer job applicants —probably recent graduates like yourself.

*Four key ideas
for career
planning*

2. *You can gain a better understanding of yourself and can learn more about a work situation and its possibilities.* For example, in planning your career, you will have to think about the types of talents, skills, and interests you possess, as well as the kinds of people and activities you like or dislike. To plan a career, you have to know yourself. Career planning also means that you will have to gain more information about job opportunities and requirements and work trends.

You gain time

*You learn
about yourself
and jobs*

3. *You will reduce risks and chances for failure or even disaster.* Bad decisions cost money and time. They mean frustration and often lost opportunity. Although planning doesn't eliminate uncertainty, good planning builds in practical ways to deal with uncertainties. These practical techniques include preparing alternate plans "in case" things don't work and understanding trial-error correction approaches. After all, the plan "A" may work, but you may discover it's not the best plan for you. It's always important to prepare alternative approaches and to generate adequate and useful information as you plan so that your approach is practical and helpful for you and can be easily adapted as you try things out.

*You reduce
risks and plan
alternatives*

4. *You will be in a better position to deal with a situation that doesn't work out as you expected.* For example, let's say that you are suddenly fired from your job or you don't like the people where you work. If you have planned out in advance some alternative courses

*You can deal
with the
unexpected*

of action, you won't be left "out in the cold," not knowing what to do or where to turn. Planning can save valuable time, reduce unnecessary tensions, and often lead to better choices or results.

PLANNING AND CHOICE

Planning ahead increases choices

The more time you can wedge between where you are now and where you want to go or what you want to be, the greater the choices you'll have. Shown in the diagram is a cone on its side. Think of this cone as a kind of tunnel that gets smaller as you go from left to right. That's exactly what happens when you don't start planning your career or your alternatives early enough: the choices keep narrowing to a point where there is no choice —and possibly no opportunity either.

The Planning Cone Exercise

Try your hand at the Planning Cone Exercise with a simple example like vacation. Think about the last vacation you took out of town. What were your alternatives when you first thought about it? What were they two or three months later? If you had neglected advance arrangements, you might have found yourself trying to find a friend who could have "put you up for the night" or running out of money instead of reaching your destination.

Do you see how planning makes a difference? Your idea of what you wanted to do shifted as you considered places, budget, other needs and plans, as well as your feelings about what you really wanted to do. It also shifted as the event drew near and the options were reduced. You probably went over your plans several times, checked them out with other people, and had some alternative plans and strategies for handling bad weather or money problems.

By thinking carefully about a vacation or some other example of personal planning, we better understand our personal likes and dislikes, the importance of pleasing others, and how the attractiveness and excitement of visiting new places (or friends or family) are all factors in our planning. By realizing all that's involved and thinking about past vacations, we improve our choices and can plan an even better vacation next year.

Similarly, in a career context, planning brings us to a better understanding of ourselves for the activities we enjoy, situations to avoid or to deal with more effectively, or simply places an emphasis on the need for more information.

Career planning can be focused by using the career compass. That compass outlines the information you need: your values, goals, opportunities, and skills. Like any other kind of planning, you may find you have all the information you need to get started or you may want to get more information or check out some ideas before you get started. Different chapters and parts of this book are designed to help out all around. Part Four, for example, provides information on targeting skills to occupations and jobs; and Part

CONE EXERCISE

My vacation situation: _____

_____

Time

Date when
first planned: _____   Months later: _____   Date vacation
                                                                 time actually
Choices then: _____   Choices were: _____   scheduled: _____

_____   _____

_____   _____

_____   _____

Note how the darkened circles are reduced in size as the event, your vacation, is approached.
If my vacation had first been planned (date)_____ , my choice might have been:_____

_____

_____

Three helps you explore the idea of career style in greater detail. There are even chapters on setting goals, solving practical problems, and working out dual career and working parent strategies. As in any type of planning, you start with what you know. Your ideas and interests focus in as you gather more information. The career compass helps you keep that focus while you gather information and plan. It also helps to maintain that focus as different events in your life change the relative importance of an idea or it tells you that it's time to adjust or fine-tune that plan.

At this point, you probably realize that planning is an activity you do often—almost every day, in fact. Planning lets you reach out for the important things in your life in ways that are easier and more effective.

PLANNING: SUMMARY THOUGHTS

Good planning: careful, practical, and worth it

Careful planning doesn't eliminate uncertainty, but good planning does reduce risks and disasters. Wise planning recognizes its own incompleteness regarding information and future events. Thus, planning in practical ways deals with the uncertainties. These practical techniques of planning include contingency or alternate plans, trial-error-correction approaches, and development of better information sources.

ACTION CHECKLIST FOR CHAPTER 5

Checklist	*My Ideas and Action Steps*	*Date*
√ Planning completeness involves five elements that deal with the future, satisfy purpose(s), take place in advance, consider alternatives, and involve choice.		
√ The six basic questions of planning must be answered sooner or later: what, why, how, who, where, and when?		
√ Planning can economize on your time and funds—and reduce final frustrations by helping to develop alternatives, improving understanding of self, reducing risks, and dealing with the unexpected.		
√ Planning involves all your compass points: skills, goals, values, and opportunities.		

6

Changing Career Stages for Today's Women

I know it's a new decade—and I should "feel free" to try to get wherever I want to go in any job. But I don't. And I'm only 34. It's just that every time I think about changing—just asking to change—well, I get cold feet. I was just brought up to feel that women don't push or try new things, I guess. . . .

MARGARET

There are major social changes that affect the female population today. These changes can be seen in the work force, lifestyles, types of jobs held, family relationships, and the like. They have had an enormous effect on the idea of career stages and thus on the kinds of plans women need to make.

Gail Sheehy, in her book *Passages*, described a number of these career-lifestyle stages and some representative situations confronting women at different periods in their lives. We have encountered a number of similar situations in our counseling and workshop experiences, and the following are representative of a wide range of career–life stage situations.

FIVE CAREER-LIFE SITUATIONS

Marilyn, 50 years old, felt that it was finally her turn to follow her interests. Her youngest child, Billy, Jr., was in high school; and Bill, Sr., a bank executive, earned a comfortable living, enough to take care of Marilyn and the needs of their children in school. This wasn't enough for Marilyn. She had received her B.A. in Spanish at 21, worked a few years in an office before marrying, and quit work when she became pregnant with her first child. Subsequently, she devoted almost 25 years to her family.

Marilyn — reentry woman

Marilyn's case is typical of many women who are *reentering* the work force. Immersed in traditional values of women's roles in the homes, typical

53

jobs, and acceptable patterns of behavior, these women are usually in their late thirties and forties. Many of these women are seeking new challenges in their lives. They are approaching the work world with the determination and zest often associated with young men at the early stages of their careers.

Marilyn, in an extended period of thinking about possibilities for herself, searched and experimented with various job situations. She returned to school for a real estate license, but she found she didn't like the work because of long hours on weekends and nights. Eventually she found a job as an inside salesperson for a large pharmaceutical company. With pleasant surroundings, interesting people, and regular hours, this job proved to be well suited to Marilyn's needs.

Betty Lou — a young vice-president

Betty Lou's career progress was remarkable, considering her move to an officer's position in her company before age 40. She had been one of the youngest people in her company to become vice-president—and the first woman. A few people remarked, "It was EEO. Besides, she's black." As a matter of fact, Betty Lou's well-established credentials had long been recognized; she had done an outstanding job as a lower-level manager, had been elected president of a local personnel association, had presented a paper at the annual meeting of a professional association, and had been nominated as one of the ten top "Young Women of the Year."

Betty Lou worked extremely hard and often took her work home with her. She and her husband, a successful lawyer, had worked out an effective living-working relationship which they felt gave them "the best of both possible worlds."

Dorothy and her promotion

Dorothy's situation represents another phase of a career-life cycle, one experienced commonly by women. Dorothy, 36 years old, single, a clerk-secretary in a regional insurance office, had worked for her current employer for five years.

Since she enjoyed her independence, she had chosen not to marry. She earned enough to take care of all her basic needs and to travel on her vacations, something she liked very much.

On a number of occasions, Dorothy was asked to work with company service representatives, inside salespeople, and actuaries because of her abilities with figures. She had a series of discussions with the office manager regarding her job progress, yet she felt disappointed in terms of a promotion or transfer to another department.

Finally, Dorothy resolved to talk with the officer in charge of the office-support services. After lengthy discussion of her career goals and the road-blocks to these goals, Dorothy found in this officer an emphatic supporter who "reviewed" her situation with the office manager. She got the promotion she wanted!

Another woman, Juanita, who had successfully balanced work and family life, was now thinking about more of a career. Juanita was 29 years old, married, with three young children. She met her husband, Carl, while both were working at a mail order company.

Juanita earned an associate of arts degree at age 20 from a community college. After graduation, she started looking for a job but was unable to find anything that pleased her. She wanted to move out of her parents' home, but her parents insisted that she live with them: "We don't want to be worrying every night about what's happening to you."

Juanita found a job as an order clerk with a large mail order company. After she had been employed two years, her supervisor mentioned that she had heard of an opening in the purchasing department. "Frankly," said the supervisor, "yours is a dead-end situation. My position is the top of the line, and I expect to be working here for a long time. Why don't you apply for the purchasing department job?" Juanita applied and was placed in a training classification, merchandise buyer C.

After six months she was promoted to the B level classification after successfully completing her training. She worked with a number of people in the merchandising department, one of whom was Carl. They started dating and were married a short time later. When the children arrived, Juanita took brief maternity leaves. When she returned to work, she arranged child care with a neighbor.

Since Juanita and Carl needed the extra income, she continued to work and, in fact, enjoyed her many friends, discounts, company events, and secure job. She had the feeling, nevertheless, that she was capable of more responsible work. And yet she was undecided whether to take a chance and talk to the manager about her goals.

Ruth graduated from college in accounting when she was 22. She worked full time with a public accounting firm where she had worked summers while attending college.

Ruth's father, Herman, was a retail merchant. After working in a department store for almost 20 years, he quit and started his own business when he was 45. He worked hard and was fairly successful. Her father often talked to Ruth about his previous job with the department store, the present business, situations he had encountered and how he had dealt with problems. Frequently, he talked to Ruth about the importance and attractiveness of being independent, not permitting people to "push you around."

After her first year with the public accounting firm, Ruth received a substantial pay raise as a result of her performance evaluation. Although she was young, with little experience, the partners in the firm felt she had an excellent chance for a partnership. But Ruth felt conflict between her own experience and her father's advice.

*Juanita —
marriage, a
career, and
advancement*

*Ruth's
conflicts about
independence*

A COMMENTARY ON CHANGING CAREERS

Although these five examples offer incomplete risk patterns of female careers, they do represent features that almost everyone faces as she seeks to define a career for herself:

Features career women face in common

1. Each woman felt varying degrees of career and job mobility, depending on family obligations and other responsibilities. However, it is important to note that restrictions on mobility are sometimes psychological and based on ideas from the past that are no longer relevant or on misunderstandings rather than being related to the real needs of current responsibilities. Some of the women had the fear of moving into areas of work or responsibility distant from their background or upbringing.

2. While work values are changing, these women were brought up to play a more traditional role and felt threatened when they wanted to make changes in their lives.

3. Each of these women could have benefited greatly from networks and from mentors, female or male, who could act as sounding boards or sources of thoughtful advice at critical points in her career.

4. These women were in work situations where career progress often depended on a major time and energy commitment by an individual. Many organizations have a kind of open-ended work week for people who have taken on senior responsibilities. These people find it difficult at times to limit themselves to a 40-, 50-, or even 55-hour work week.

It is imperative to recognize that mobility, style, values, networks, mentors, energy—all of these—comprise only half of the career planning approach. The second half is, of course, the organizational setting in which an individual experiences her career aspirations.

ORGANIZATIONAL CAREER MANAGEMENT AND INDIVIDUAL CAREER PLANNING

The organization's viewpoint on individual careers

So far we have been concerned only with careers of individuals, but we can't ignore the fact that organizations and managers also have a viewpoint or perspective on careers. This viewpoint may or may not be supportive of individual goals and objectives. There are really two major approaches to careers: *individual career planning* and *organizational career management.*

Individual and organizational needs can both be met

The primary point to recognize as an individual career planner is that your manager or other company people view career considerations *within the framework of organizational requirements.* This means that the enterprise must assign its first priorities to continuity, profits, and renewal of its talent and capabilities. Thus, individual careers can become a means of achieving valued results for an organization at the same time that they meet individual career planning requirements.

The problem is that the organization can offer no more than the types of jobs it possesses and can provide only the possibilities for growth and individual satisfactions that are tied to its markets and customers. Nevertheless, the requirements of many people may be met by what the organization offers, and growing numbers of organizations are now devoting much time and money in support of career-related activity and human resource development. You are on center stage and the first priorities go to you in individual career planning. In organizational career management, obviously, first priorities go to the company's problems and concerns for its future.

It is *your responsibility*, then, to find the kind of organization that provides the environment, people, and work that you find personally satisfying. There is a remarkably large area in which individual and organization can meet on common ground and be supportive of each other's needs and requirements for the future. Yet viewpoints are different, and a woman planning a career must look at both company and self in order best to understand potentially different viewpoints on career matters. While you are primarily responsible for your career development and satisfaction, remember that the organization is charged with providing the environment, the attitudes, and the resources that enhance an employee's satisfaction. In planning career options, a woman thus needs to explore and determine those organizations that attend to human resource needs—and maximize her probable gain by doing so. She also needs to consider her interests and ability to benefit from what the organization can offer and what she can learn to do through work as opposed to other opportunities in her life.

Finding the right organization— your responsibility

But the organization has responsibilities, too

DEVELOPING A BASIC SKILL INVENTORY

Individual career planning requires a close look at yourself in terms of your abilities and your desire to change in order to move into other areas of the work world. The purpose of this section is to help you develop an initial inventory of basic skills, learning styles, and personal objectives in seven different areas.

The scoring represents your impression (or how you feel about these items) as you see them today. Now, it's time for you to complete An Initial Inventory of Basic Skills.

AN INITIAL INVENTORY OF BASIC SKILLS

Goals? Drives? Ambitions? Where am I going? How much do I really want to change things and move forward in the world of work? For each of the following questions, rate yourself on the following scale:

9–10   Exceptional, certain
7–8   Quite well, rather strong
5–6   O.K., fairly strong, fairly often
2–4   Some doubts, seldom
0   Undecided

A. *Ambition*

1. How exact are your goals regarding business or work?

   0 1 2 3 4 5 6 7 8 9 10

2. To what extent do the goals you have selected challenge your utmost ability?

   0 1 2 3 4 5 6 7 8 9 10

3. To what extent are you prepared to break out of your routines, even make sacrifices, in order to move toward your career goals?

   0 1 2 3 4 5 6 7 8 9 10

4. How confident are you of your ability to move forward toward your career goals?

   0 1 2 3 4 5 6 7 8 9 10

5. How thoroughly have you worked out a plan for attaining your career goals?

   0 1 2 3 4 5 6 7 8 9 10

   Total number of points   _____

B. *Drive, Self-Starting Ability*

1. To what extent do you go beyond that which is immediately required?

   0 1 2 3 4 5 6 7 8 9 10

2. How often do you seek out additional work?

   0 1 2 3 4 5 6 7 8 9 10

3. How much stick-to-itiveness do you have on difficult tasks?

   0 1 2 3 4 5 6 7 8 9 10

4. To what extent are you willing to gather all the necessary details for problem solving or decision making?

   0 1 2 3 4 5 6 7 8 9 10

5. To what extent do you strive for the best solution to a problem rather than just an acceptable solution?

   0 1 2 3 4 5 6 7 8 9 10

   Total number of points

C. *Learning Style, Approach*

1. To what extent do you seek out new learning?   0 1 2 3 4 5 6 7 8 9 10

2. To what extent can you shut out distracting matters?   0 1 2 3 4 5 6 7 8 9 10

3. Can you easily grasp new ideas?   0 1 2 3 4 5 6 7 8 9 10

4. How often do you consider a number of viewpoints when dealing with problems or situations?   0 1 2 3 4 5 6 7 8 9 10

5. How well do you organize items for thought, analysis, and/or discussion?   0 1 2 3 4 5 6 7 8 9 10

    Total number of points   _____

D. *Problem-Solving Style*

1. Can you regularly bring together different ideas or information sources without too much difficulty?   0 1 2 3 4 5 6 7 8 9 10

2. How often do you hang in and stay with a problem?   0 1 2 3 4 5 6 7 8 9 10

3. Do you find it easy to stay calm, even under difficult conditions?   0 1 2 3 4 5 6 7 8 9 10

4. Do you often think of alternative ways to solve a problem?   0 1 2 3 4 5 6 7 8 9 10

5. Do you find it easy to make a final decision?   0 1 2 3 4 5 6 7 8 9 10

    Total number of points   _____

E. *Relationships with Other People*

1. To what extent are you willing to discuss feelings—yours or theirs—with others?   0 1 2 3 4 5 6 7 8 9 10

2. To what extent are you trusting of others?   0 1 2 3 4 5 6 7 8 9 10

3. Are you willing to accept or sometimes even seek out constructive criticism?   0 1 2 3 4 5 6 7 8 9 10

4. Can you accept conflict and initial disagreement between yourself and others?   0 1 2 3 4 5 6 7 8 9 10

5. Do you think you have a good insight and understanding of others?   0 1 2 3 4 5 6 7 8 9 10

    Total number of points   _____

_____

F. Management Potential

1. Do you think you are willing to take on responsibility?   0 1 2 3 4 5 6 7 8 9 10

2. Are you prepared to make important decisions yourself?   0 1 2 3 4 5 6 7 8 9 10

3. Do you like to involve others in decisions?   0 1 2 3 4 5 6 7 8 9 10

4. Do you like to use personal skills and persuasion to help others?   0 1 2 3 4 5 6 7 8 9 10

5. To what extent are you willing to let others do work rather than doing it all yourself?   0 1 2 3 4 5 6 7 8 9 10

     Total number of points   _____

G. Supervisory Skills

1. Can you make decisions that may affect other people's work?   0 1 2 3 4 5 6 7 8 9 10

2. Do you show an active, continuing concern for subordinates?   0 1 2 3 4 5 6 7 8 9 10

3. Can you get a message across to other people?   0 1 2 3 4 5 6 7 8 9 10

4. Are you comfortable working with many different kinds of people?   0 1 2 3 4 5 6 7 8 9 10

5. To what extent can you work without a great deal of support from others?   0 1 2 3 4 5 6 7 8 9 10

     Total number of points   _____

REALITY CHECKING

When you have completed your initial scoring of this inventory, let's look at those items in which you had doubts before continuing. When you work through these types of listings by yourself, it is natural to be uncertain about how to handle certain items, perhaps because you simply haven't thought about these items before or in such specific terms. It is often helpful to discuss some of these points with friends or co-workers you trust or even to give them a blank scale and ask them to rate you on certain points. This process is called *reality checking*. Many women find this procedure so helpful that they like to get others (not always the same person) to rate them on all the items in this inventory. It has also proven helpful to discuss why you rated a particular area "strong" or "okay." True, there are risks in doing this because you may expose some of your personal sensitivities. But if help is provided in supportive fashion, the results are useful. The more realistic the

Women can benefit from networks and mentors, who
may act as sounding boards.

information (both as we see it and objective viewers see us), the greater the
help in career planning and thinking.

In each of areas A through G, your score could range from 0 to 50. Any
area score below 25 is indicative of an opportunity for you to do skills
development. Higher-level jobs often require these abilities, but you should
find out which are emphasized and move accordingly. Scores above 25 indicate areas where you have greater strength and require less development
work. Also, you should check out single items within each area to pinpoint
your most important development needs.

List your score for each area below and describe how satisfied you were with your current personal inventory and your desire to improve:

AREA	SCORE	HAVE YOU REAL-ITY CHECKED?	SATIS-FIED?	WANT TO IMPROVE?
A. Ambition				
B. Drive				
C. Learning				
D. Problem solving				
E. Relationships				
F. Management				
G. Supervision				

Now, for each area that you want to improve, jot down one very specific thing you can do which can help. Understandably, some areas are easier to deal with than others, but don't be frightened if it seems difficult. For areas you would like to improve but which seem "impossible," check around. It's surprising what people can do when they want to do it! Under "ambition," for example, you could find out more about your work or career opportunities in your field. For "management," you could make a list of all the responsibilities you already have. Under "learning," people learn in multiple ways —maybe you want to strengthen reading, listening, or visual skills. It's good to recognize that each of us has a particular learning style so that we are unexpectedly good in reading, watching (as in TV) and interpreting, or listening and interacting with others. It is very desirable to discover your style if you aren't fully aware of what it is. There is, however, another side to this "picture" of learning style. Some jobs by their very nature place great stress on particular styles of learning that may not match yours. You can often learn to exercise some of these other learning approaches in adequate fashion if you really want to. For example, problem-solving skills can be learned in regularly offered workshops and classes.

Perhaps you are a basically quiet person or you like to do things on your own. If you wish to strengthen the area marked "relationships," an awareness of the factors underlying relationships and their contribution to work performance can of itself prove helpful. Remember, at this point the purpose of putting these things down is to get started. More follows.

AREA	SOME SPECIFIC BEHAVIORS TO HELP ME IMPROVE
A. Ambition	
B. Drive	
C. Learning	
D. Problem solving	
E. Relationships	
F. Management	
G. Supervision	

That gives you a general overview of where you are and where you want to be. You don't have to make any *final* decisions on how satisfied you are or how much you want to improve a specific item. Again, this is just to get things started. Think it over for a while. It's likely you'll want to return to some of these areas later on.

You might want to try selecting a specific behavior that is *realistic* and *manageable* for you. Use a *time line* to check yourself on how you are doing. You will be able to see as well as feel a sense of success and accomplishment.

Now that you have taken time to gain some perspective, let's look in more detail at where you are and where you want to be. Let's break it down a little. Look at your good points first. Scan the areas where you scored 25 or more and the questions on which you scored above 5. See where you are really proud of your efforts. List these areas below:

1.
2.
3.

4. _____

5. _____

6. _____

7. _____

Are some of your strengths in one area, such as problem solving or supervisory skills? If so, you have already developed your career orientation in important ways. Check off your key area strengths on the following:

A. Ambition _____
B. Drive _____
C. Learning _____
D. Problem solving _____
E. Relationships _____
F. Management _____
G. Supervision _____

If you find that at this time no particular area seems outstanding yet there is one you wish to develop, treat that area as a target for improvement. However, it's good to recognize that the skill-related areas, such as problem solving and supervisory functions, are the easiest to acquire. Areas such as relationship and learning are more difficult as they require changes in style, approach, or "what seems natural." Many women feel that areas such as ambition and drive are difficult to deal with and may not even be subject to much change. Yet, remarkable accomplishments have been achieved by ordinary people with modest "ambition" or "drive"—but who have been motivated to succeed by a specific problem or circumstance!

Many career specialists feel that building on strengths is important—more so than trying to cover up weaknesses. This building on strengths is probably most important at the start—to get things going. Once things are starting to flow, it becomes possible to consider selectively the strengthening of other points. Thus, your strong points provide a sound foundation for building to meet your future needs.

Now let's take a look at areas where you'd like to improve. Look at the areas where you scored 25 or less and/or questions on which you scored 5 or below. List those items you'd really like to improve upon:

_____   _____

_____   _____

_____   _____

Developing those abilities can help you find more satisfaction in your career. Chapters 7 and 9 in this part of *Growing* will help you evaluate possible payoffs for your career and establish your priorities. The important point for you to realize here is that you, your abilities, and your understanding of all that's needed for your career shift with the experiences of life.

CAREERS OVER TIME

We've stressed through Part One of *Growing* the fact of change: changes in values, changes in opportunities, changes in you. And that is the central point in this chapter on different career stages for women.

You can be virtually certain that key features of your career will change over the course of time, whether you make a decision for change (search or explore alternatives) now or not. Life scientists have found that people move through a series of stages throughout their lives, as we pointed out in Chapter 2. Each stage usually covers a period of from four to six years and represents different life or work needs. Each of these periods in our lives reflects a complex combination of aging, experience, marital situation, personal development, social trends, psychological needs, and personal values.

Key features of your career are bound to change

We can thus anticipate, at least generally, what some of the typical problems or issues may be at particular points in our lives. For example, at roughly 18 to 24 years, we often search for identity, seeking to establish a career. Friendships change quickly and mentors are sought for sympathy or counsel. Between 25 and 44 years, other stages of growth occupy time and concern: developing close and deep relationships (with a spouse or friend) and establishing strong work or organizational commitments; we may form networks of friends. Toward the end of this period, we try to bring about increased security in our personal lives and stability in our work world.

Typical life stages and their concerns

What we have described here are "typical" career stages and characteristic issues, problems, and opportunities that arise over time. But there's nothing really automatic about these things, especially if one is thinking about *improving* her possibilities as much as possible. *Networking* is an example of a positive way in which organization members can improve their career–life stage possibilities. Women can do modest but practical things such as establishing and widening their contacts with and outside of their work activities that can prove instrumental later in gaining "inside" information, advice, help in problem solving, or concrete leads on job opportunities. Networking is a well-established technique that can be of practical assistance to you in building your possibilities and achieving the most that your career–life stages have to offer you.

What is important for you to realize as we go on in Chapter 7 to consider setting career goals is that careers *do* change. That's what our career compass is all about: You shouldn't feel uncomfortable about the need to change or shift directions or to assess realistically how any organization fits your needs.

ACTION CHECKLIST FOR CHAPTER 6

Checklist	*My Ideas and Action Steps*	*Date*
√ The success of individual career planning is importantly dependent on individual awareness of company plans and opportunities.		
√ The content and focus of "points" in the career compass change over time as new situations arise or life/career stages are entered.		
√ Individual career possibilities are supported or limited by the thoroughness of our self-examination.		
√ Reality checking can help to ensure soundness of career thinking and taking full advantage of opportunities.		

7

Learning to Set Goals

I'm planning to finish my B.A. in business administration next year if I possibly can. And then I'm going to try for a job where I can use what I've learned. It's exciting. But it's more than just reaching the goals I wanted for myself . . . it's something else . . . like finding myself again and again and reaching out for what I want.

SANDY

Setting goals is really a form of planning. You remember *goals* as one of the four points of our career compass, which has as it center *you* and your career planning. Goals can be crucial under a difficult set of conditions or changes because they help you stay on track when the going is rough. Goal planning isn't really difficult if the directions are clear and the functions understood, but it does take time. Goals have to be thought about carefully and under quiet, non-stressful conditions to ensure that you end up with a sensible set of goals that are achievable and valued. Establishing goals also takes information about values, skills, and opportunities. Remember all parts of the compass create the compass, support each other, and help in career planning. Goals form the foundation for career planning, and it is impossible to overestimate their importance for virtually all your career-related actions.

Goals are crucial to conserve

It is appropriate again to think of the career compass in the context of goals: Events are constantly changing or shifting in your personal and work life. Increases in the cost of living, new job offers, new friendships, disagreements with associates, and job transfer possibilities are all examples of common events that influence our goal-planning decisions.

It's easy to react emotionally to these situations without adequate reflection as to whether your decisions are correct. This is when the career compass can assist you in (re-)establishing and maintaining direction. You might ask, "Will the offer or action contribute positively and effectively to securing my goals?" Goal planning gives you that sense of direction and a

Goals give direction

67

point of focus. However, planning is an impossible task unless goals are first clarified.

WHAT ARE GOALS?

A simple definition of goals

For purposes of career planning, goals represent specific and valued targets you want to achieve. Setting goals and achieving them enrich your human experience; they make you feel better about yourself, more satisfied, more economically rewarded.

Goals Must Support Your Values

Goals emerge from values

All career *goals* should *contribute to some* of your career-related values, but not necessarily in the same way or with equal effect. In Chapter 1, you discovered a lot about your *terminal* and *instrumental* values. It is worthwhile to review these periodically because goals usually emerge directly from your values. At the very least, values should serve as a reality check to make sure that you haven't proposed goals or (priority) actions that conflict.

If a particular career-related goal doesn't seem to contribute to any of your important values or actually *detracts* from those values, then you need to reexamine those relationships. For instance, if you believe strongly in the terminal value "family security or taking care of loved ones," career goals that lead to frequent and risky job changes might undercut the fulfillment of this value. Therefore, the conscious awareness of what values are important to you is extremely helpful in developing desirable career goals that in turn serve as a compass guide to individual actions and choices.

Goals Must Be Practical

As well as supporting your values, your career goals should include a concern for your opportunities and your skills. Part One has helped you assess some of your values and skills and the way those relate to your work environment. Parts Three and Four enrich those understandings, so that goals are built on a foundation of all the information and understandings you need to make career plans.

Practically speaking, the achievements you seek must be specific enough to allow you to think in concrete terms about how you will achieve them. Goals must also be *realistic, manageable, and obtainable*. Once you have determined what your goals are, you have to be prepared to plan *action steps* that will enable you to *realize* those goals.

Goals should be realistic, manageable, obtainable

Career goals are a compromise between vague generalizations and overly specific objections. Let's clarify this point with an example—Sandy, who spoke at the beginning of the chapter. Sandy has been going to night school for several years to finish a degree started many years ago. She has been working as an administrative assistant in the office of a small manufacturing firm. Sandy has written one of her goals in a set of action steps:

Action steps:

- Get an "A" in my accounting course.

- Successfully finish my B.A. program in business administration next year, in the evening program

- Apply for a transfer and get a position in our accounting department

- Get into work that makes fuller use of my abilities

- Gain a greater sense of personal satisfaction and reward in that part of my life devoted to work

Sandy's specific goals

Values these career goals support:

- Demonstrate to myself that I'm ambitious and can make it on my own and enjoy the accomplishments

- Have a stimulating, active life and be happy, too

How they support her values

In Sandy's situation, *career values* blend into *career goals* and these into action steps; this is the "something else" that Sandy found "exciting"—and, you can be sure, satisfying as well.

Let's pause for a moment with the idea of action steps. Goal achievement doesn't take place unless long-range plans and goal thinking are translated into doing activities—action steps. Action steps keep you on the accomplishment track; they keep you centered in your career values and goals. Most commonly, there are no obvious points where one phase of this planning stops and another begins. The specifics, as well as the details, keep changing as your base of experience shifts in work and in life itself.

Action steps keep you on track

GOAL THINKING: GENERALITIES AND DETAILS

As you mature, it is often possible to think much more concisely about the activities you like, the things you realistically want to do, can and will do—matters of your style and skills.

With little work experience, you lack detail and often think in terms of broad occupational fields: accountant, secretary, nurse, supervisor, or engineer. With experience, you start to think about the elements of work (for example, types of tasks, responsibilities, people, work conditions) which you find attractive.

Goal thinking shifts with experience

The following example shows how your thinking about career goals shifts as you gain experience. Notice that in this diagram, two very different

What Gerri learned

types of situations are pictured: In situation A, Gerri thinks about specific jobs with their functions, tasks, responsibilities, and activities. In situation B, she capitalizes on the experience and identifies job elements that often lead to a satisfying work experience. Examples of these types of work include meeting people, answering questions they have, or telephone contact, convincing people of the merits of your product.

EXPERIENCE BENEFITS GERRI IN HOW TO LOOK AT WORK AND JOBS

SITUATION A: EARLY CAREER VIEW

Gerri chooses a job by thinking about occupations, starting out: "I want to be a . . ."

- Nurse
- X-ray technician
- Secretary
- Sales representative
- Real estate broker
- Marketing manager
- Banker

These are *OCCUPATIONS* with different *FUNCTIONS, TASKS, RESPONSIBILITIES,* and *ACTIVITIES.* Most people start out by choosing occupations with activities they think they will enjoy—yet think in terms of general occupations.

SITUATION B: CAREER/JOB VIEW WITH SOME EXPERIENCE

With experience, Gerri thinks about career possibilities that bring together elements that are right for her. "What kinds of jobs have these features. . . ?"

- Tasks I enjoy
- Appropriate responsibilities
- Activities that fit my career style, such as
  — Meeting people

— Answering questions

— Telephone contacts

— "Selling people" on product

— Action oriented activities, little writing

— Changing situations

These are *SPECIFIC ACTIVITIES* for jobs within one *OCCUPATION.* Finding the right blend of activities and responsibilities helps Gerri find a *JOB* within an occupation—it helps her think things through with company people regarding future career opportunities.

Now try it for yourself, as you did in the work styles inventory in Chapter 2. Out of your general or specific job experiences, identify some work activities that you believe are important to you.

DESIRED WORK ACTIVITIES

Specific elements of work out of my general or specific job experiences I have found satisfying or attractive and like to do.

Rank for Importance
(1, 2, etc.)

1. _____

2. _____

3. _____

4. _____

5. _____

6. _____

_____   _____

7. _____

_____   _____

8. _____

_____   _____

With an idea now what goals are—and an understanding that to set them means reviewing your values as well as thinking again about your career style and skills—you are ready for Chapter 8. That chapter takes a hard look at the difficult problems of establishing career goals and setting out a workable plan.

ACTION CHECKLIST FOR CHAPTER 7

Checklist	*My Ideas and Action Steps*	*Date*
√ Goals emerge from values and thus a clear knowledge of my values is a basic point of departure in career thinking.		
√ Reality checking goals means that they must be realistic, manageable, and obtainable.		
√ Career thinking regarding work possibilities requires that we get down to basic job elements that reflect skills and are supported by personal interests — also priorities must be assigned to these.		
√ Identifying work targets for career requires that skills and interests be combined in creative ways and be listed against the potential for achieving valued goals.		
√ Ultimately, career goals and values require translation into practical, "do-able" steps.		

8

Facing Up to Practical Problems in Goal Planning

I'd like to get at least my college degree—maybe go for more. But you can bet no one's stepped up and handed me any big scholarship for free—and I certainly can't ask my family for money! Besides, I'm not sure what goal I have—after college, I mean. I've got all kinds of problems about this college degree.

MELINDA

I'm just going to have to turn down the company job in California—no matter how great it sounds. I couldn't cope without my friends—and, besides, right now my sister takes care of my two kids during the day. What can I do about child care and the support I want for me and them!

DEE

Our concern thus far has been with career goals, values, personal needs, and priorities. These are important elements for getting started on the right track. But they are seldom the only elements. Most women (and men, too) have other "business" that must be attended to in order to be successful in the career process. Let's consider, then, the potpourri of practical matters and goal-setting problems that are part of the career process. They usually don't go away and they don't solve themselves.

Practical problems that won't go away

PLANNING CAREER GOALS: SOME PRACTICAL PROBLEMS

Your career goals with planned steps for accomplishment may mean periods of job search, special training, or further education. Let's look at some of the problems involved and ways to "plan around" those problems.

"Transition" Money

Whatever these goals are, you are likely to find they have a common denominator: money, which is necessary to fund your goals. Too often, people fail to provide for these needed funds and then find that they don't have enough money to pay for seeing their goal through to accomplishment. That is truly discouraging. So it's prudent to plan in advance the amount of *(extra)* money you'll need in the next few months or years to see yourself through the educational program. If you need more money than the amount you have saved or you receive from your salary, you can apply for federal grants and/or federally sponsored student loans.

The Basic Educational Opportunity Grant (BEOG) offers full-time students funds and the Supplemental Education Opportunity Grant (SEOG) also provides additional funds—modest amounts, perhaps, in the light of educational costs, but helpful nevertheless. Grants, based on need against requirements established by Congress, do not need to be repaid.

Federally Insured Student Loans (FISL) at low interest are offered by private lending institutions, such as banks, to students attending a qualified educational institution. These loans are insured by the government to the lending agency with a maximum loan period of 10 years.

You can request necessary application forms for student grants and loans from vocational and trade schools, community colleges, and universities. Each school offers counseling and forms from the financial aid officer.

Friends and family are possible sources, too, for loans for your worthwhile educational purpose. One suggestion: with the help of an attorney, write an agreement including a promissory note so that no one misunderstands the amount, terms, or repayment schedule.

The source(s) you choose for borrowing "transition" money depends on the reality of your goals, self-confidence, available collateral (property or money used as security for the repayment of a loan), or eligibility for possible student grants and/or loans, and length of time you need to repay a loan.

Education Degrees

Today many employers still use a college degree as a mark of accomplishment or demonstration of potential, yet people are thinking more critically about college and whether the time and cost are a desirable investment. Increasingly, possessing a degree has lost its edge in commanding employment or a better job. Many people have studied for a particular degree without carefully considering whether the knowledge or information accumulated in the process would be truly helpful to them—lead to doing something they really wanted to do—or is even something they are really interested in. The value or worth of education degrees is definitely in transition. For *today*, however, the importance of a degree should not be underplayed.

Certain occupational fields and many jobs require specialized training in the form of a technical, college, or graduate degree. The type and length of schooling required should always be part of your consideration in setting career goals. You may find you're not interested in going back to school to get the required degree training, and you will have to alter your career plans accordingly. Or you may have your heart set on a particular career, realistically within your reach; and you may push yourself to get the additional schooling, even if you don't find the prospect particularly exciting. Remember that your attitude regarding required training tells you something about your career choice. If the idea of getting additional degree training seems extraordinarily difficult or distasteful to you, rethink what it's going to be like once you have established yourself in that career area.

Assess your own attitude about schooling

Adult Learning: The New Model

Growth in the median age of people in the population combined with the constant changes in the work scene have created a new thrust for *adult education*, a perspective built around the idea of *lifelong learning*. It is a form of education where *you* determine what your needs are and select the programming that best meets these requirements. Individual growth needs and changing work demands are leading to a number of new institutional arrangements, courses, programs, and hours when instruction is made available. Programs are sponsored by universities, community colleges, commercial schools, private organizations, and a growing number of employers. These developments in adult learning are important, and many women are taking advantage of one or several of these programs to further their career objectives. You may find you want to be one of them.

Developments in adult education

PLANNING CAREER GOALS: SOME SOCIAL PROBLEMS

Career moves are likely to lead to important changes in your circle of business associates and friends. Making new ties and dropping old ones are typical and to be expected. Thus, career planning goals must also encompass the social side of your life because it is affected by your work and career. Under circumstances where you place great importance on these social ties, any career thinking that leads you to strain or cut these connections must be approached cautiously. Promotion into supervision, for example, can bring about as much of a change in social relationships as a career move to another employer.

Your career affects your personal life

Take, for example, Betty Sun's situation. When offered a promotion to field sales supervisor with her insurance company, she practically jumped at the opportunity. Then Betty found that somehow things "had changed." She greatly valued the friendship of her work associates, people in the field and office. But suddenly their greetings seemed different and they saw each other less frequently. When she did meet with them, their conversations seemed strained and they more frequently disagreed on work-related things. Betty was quite unhappy and started to wonder whether she had been too hasty.

Betty's situation is a common one and emphasizes the importance of thinking through carefully the full range of demands imposed upon you in your targeted job or career. Betty could have been better prepared for what was to happen in her new assignment but really discounted the priorities and value she assigned to the social side of her relationships.

Work Associates, Friendships

*Changing
social
relationships*

Social changes of the nature we've described are exciting and challenging, yet frightening for some people. Each person has to make this analysis for herself. Regardless of your initial reaction to possible change in your life, the analysis should be made so that you are better able to deal with these changes as they occur.

When your planning for career goals indicates a shift in highly valued social relationships, you can handle each change in constructive fashion. If your plans include moving to another employer or to a distant city, for example, you can correspond by phone, plan meetings with friends and even take common vacation times, maintain your valued social relationships, and deal with the situation. If your career plan involves a move into management, recognize that this is often difficult to handle in terms of co-worker friendships. Relationships change. Friends expect changes but still make biting jokes, treat you distantly. You may have to accept some of this "cost" of your career.

Family Hazards

*Family
relationships
can change, too*

Whether you are single or married, you will find that fulfilling career goals usually means changes in your family relationships, responsibilities, and obligations. These are problems that must be faced—but the point is that with thoughtfulness and good planning they can be faced.

DUAL CAREERS

*The problem of
dual careers*

If your pay has been considered extra income to boost the main source derived from a husband or partner, full-time work or increased salary may become a mixed blessing. On the one hand, the extra income is welcome; but, on the other hand, some men who have been the primary source of income may start to feel threatened as their salary becomes relatively less important. Other men may feel bewildered by the increase in self-esteem within the partner/wife.

If you are part of a dual career situation, then career values, goals, and action plans must be thoroughly discussed with your husband/partner so that you both understand and support your mutual priorities. You might also benefit from talking to friends who have experience in dealing with their dual career relationships.

In no way should the notion of a dual career be considered an unsolvable problem. In our experience, however, it does pose one of the greatest challenges in career planning. One suggestion is that anticipating problems likely to arise represents a major, positive step forward in dealing with dual careers. It also means that any conflicts must be discussed carefully and in depth—not just on a personal level but also on the level of career planning.

You'll find more on dual careers and the working parent later in *Growing* and a dual career profile at the end of Part Two.

KIDS

Kids, even more than pets, plants, and possessions, require attention and loving care. They may not get as much if you're in school or working longer hours or have many other things on your mind. Yet many working parents rightfully point out that it's the quality of the time spent and not the quantity of time that counts. Few would argue with this; but you should be prepared for accusations, often from your own children: "You don't care;" "You're always too busy." Children often make great efforts to arouse a working mother's guilt feelings. She has to deal with these feelings.

The needs of children

If your career planning somehow can't include ways for dealing with these questions and your husband, partner, or friends have no helpful advice to offer, it might be best to modify your plans or consider some alternative approaches. Some families have dealt with these situations by using friends or neighbors, known by the children, as sitters. Others have scheduled "family time" where all family members get together on a weekend or evening and simply enjoy each other's company.

Young children can pose special problems. The initial time away from a parent is quite emotional for both mother and child. Waking children up at 6 A.M. to bring them over to a sitter isn't fun; yet kids not only get used to it, they may become much more self-reliant and independent as a result.

SINGLE WORKING PARENTS

The previous discussions on money, social considerations, and kids—and more besides—are all rolled together for the single working parent. The money and economics side of things usually comes up as a major consideration, unfortunately, as a problem. Typically, funds from insurance, court-awarded support, or simply finding yourself holding the bag of responsibility for house and kids spell B-A-D news—and you're under the gun to do something. If you've been working, your income may no longer be enough if your marriage/partner situation has suddenly changed. If you've been working a long time, you've probably worked things out as in the dual career couple, but you don't have any backup system. Career goals have to be approached cautiously because the reality is that you have much to lose if things don't go right. On the other hand, our experience has been that the single working parent often builds a corner for herself with a surrounding wall that's almost impossible to break through. "After all, I know what I've got; but if I take on the new responsibilities (or job), who knows. . . ." Thus, inaction supports more inaction. Clearly, caution in career moves is needed and urged; but if it paralyzes action almost regardless of opportunity, then you need the lift and perspective that reality checking with associates/mentor and careful self-analysis can bring.

KEEPING UP YOUR SPIRITS

There is little to replace a sense of confidence, a sense of moving in the right direction. As you work through *Growing* or try out your plans, your spirits may frequently sag and you may wonder if this career-planning business is all worth it. There are no hard and fast answers to help you over these rough spots other than to assure you that these moments will pass and your career compass will help. On the one hand, it will be necessary to maintain a sense of progress and have established checkpoints or accomplishments that give you solid evidence of movement in the right direction. On the other hand, there is the need to think carefully about the signals, responses, or problems emerging around you (family, friends, work associates) to make sure that you aren't missing something important. Thus, it becomes something of a balancing act to maintain progress, but be sure that the sense of motion you feel *really is progress.*

How are you going to get from where you are to where you want to be? The best answers lie in thinking, planning, and learning. The next section is designed to help you do just that: use your own ambition, drive, desires, and abilities to plan for growth—your growth. And remember, learning transfers. What you learn about solving problems by planning—a genuine skill —will also help you become better at working out your relationships with others and managing your work.

EXPLORING

Exploring careers puts you front and center—your experiences, reflections, and judgments. Understanding this helps you realize that when it comes to career planning, people start at different points, move at different speeds, and reach for different goals. Some people have only general goals; others know exactly what they wish in great detail. Let's take a look at how those ideas of who you are and what you want to do can be nourished and enriched.

THREE GROUPS IN THE CAREER WORLD

In the world of careers and career planning, there are commonly three groups of people; men and women are equal here.

Where you are in the career world

- Those who know
- Those with some notion
- Those who are uncertain

Those Who Know

Some people have a fairly precise idea of where they want to go and/or what they want to do. For them, some assistance in strengthening goal-planning techniques, testing out the reality of their career objectives, and developing some alternatives are what they find to be most important.

You know

Those with Some Notion

Some people have some notion of where they want to go in terms of their career. These people feel more tentative about careers, goals, path-steps, particular jobs, or types of organization for which they would like to work. If this situation best describes your own, then it's likely you would want all of the career-planning goals skills we've described and, in addition, might wish to spend more time in

You have some notion

1. thinking about your values, priorities among them, and how they influence your choice goals

2. expanding your information on path-steps and possible alternatives by:

   - Talking to associates or others who have done similar work

   - Researching business magazines, books, newspapers, and other literature for descriptions and examples of people who have experienced various work situations

   - Planning talks with department heads/supervisors elsewhere in your organization

   - Having discussions with personnel people and career counselors in your organization

   - Having informal discussions with your supervisors

Those Who Are Uncertain

You are
uncertain

Some people are uncertain about their careers. Everything described in Part Two applies here, but your plan of attack may call for some shifting of priorities. This material can't cover all possible contingencies, but a few guidelines may be helpful. Those who give advice often say that you must first know yourself before you plan your career. And you've been making some discoveries. But things don't always work this way. In some cases, career planning is similar to a search for keys that unlock the doors to thoughts you have had regarding work and your future. For others, the search would be mostly wasted because the person has had little need to think about things or exposure to career-related matters is slight.

What should you do if you are uncertain?

1. Don't panic. The situation is common.

2. Initially, place greater emphasis on getting acquainted with yourself. The exercises provided for determining your value priorities and various categories of needs are helpful in this regard—your style and skills, too.

What to do

3. Working through your values and needs provides a basis for setting out some *tentative* goals. However, remember again that this first attempt at setting down career goals is just that, an initial effort with the expectancy that changes will be made, perhaps even substantial ones.

4. Develop more information in two categories:

   • yourself

   • work possibilities

Develop
information

The suggestions for developing more information regarding yourself are exactly those described previously for Group 2 people above. However, you can expect to place greater emphasis on sources of basic life planning or career information. Some companies and communities sponsor "career days." People have a chance to talk to others who are also exploring possibilities for themselves and with career counselors and other professionals in a particular field.

Similar remarks can be made about *work* possibilities and the discussion of Group 2 people above. Talking to people in various lines of business, even undertaking some activities on a part-time basis (for example, real estate sales, writing, free-lance work) can help to qualify your interests further. *It is as important to find out what you don't like as it is to find out what you do like.*

5. Reexamine your initial, tentative career goal statements. It's likely that new or expanded sources of information will lead to modification or major changes in your statements of career objectives.

There is another possible outcome of these self-analyses that may also turn out to be right for you: *a decision for no change in your work situation.* It's possible that, after having examined various work and career alternatives, you feel much better about doing what you are now doing. There's nothing wrong with this conclusion if you've done an adequate job in exploring possibilities.

As a matter of fact, more companies are coming to the realization that having employees who want to do a good job in what they're doing can be an acceptable, even desirable, end in itself. People are being recognized for what they are and what they contribute to the organization and not necessarily on the basis of how high they want to go in it.

ACTION CHECKLIST FOR CHAPTER 8

Checklist	*My Ideas and Action Steps*	*Date*
√ Career goal planning requires resourcefulness and careful thinking regarding the funds needed to make it through and the sources of these.		
√ Career progress often places a new premium on adult learning so that, in the spirit of directing your career, you need to be able to identify and select needed educational experiences.		
√ Career moves usually alter social relations and pose new concerns that require thinking through in advance.		
√ Family responsibilities or assumed duties understandably restrain flexibility but also may lead to complete immobility — is this realistic for you?		
√ The preciseness of career goals varies widely, thus suggesting the areas of the career compass that should be receiving attention first.		

9

Beginning to Plan Your Own Career

My life and interests have been pulling me in many different directions—I just finally decided that, if I was going to get my act together, I had to set some priorities for myself—things I really wanted to do and finally facing the fact that I couldn't do everything.

BETTY

Thus far we have discussed some basic concepts of planning. We have also discussed how those concepts apply to career planning in general, to values clarification, and to the goal-setting process. Now we'd like to focus our attention on how you can utilize all the ideas developed up to this point in planning *your* career.

How to begin building a path

Earlier we said that careers involve people in the present day-to-day work situation as well as in the future. Because of this present and future relationship within a career, each person must build some type of path that takes her from here (the present) to there (the future). The design of that path must account for where the person is today, where she wants to be tomorrow, and what alternatives are available for getting her there.

IDENTIFYING PERSONAL PRIORITIES

Priorities are immediate goals

Priorities are really immediate goals—short-term ones. Priorities are what you would like to achieve right now. Start moving in your career by identifying 10 personal priorities—your very own. These may or may not relate to work, but they are important to you.

To help you get started, let's consider some of those that Betty set down and her ranking of them:

BETTY'S PRIORITIES/SHORT-TERM GOALS

GOALS	RANK
Have a flexible work schedule so that I can schedule at least some of my time myself	5
Maintain my friendships at work	3
Develop enough income so that the kids and I can get into a place with more room	2
Have good income stability	6
Have flexibility on vacation scheduling so that the kids and I can spend time together	4
Be able to keep up my choir membership requiring weekly meetings	7
Maintain my weekly tennis game with friends	8
Get some new clothes now and then without getting guilt feelings	10
Go out now and then	9
Keep the children's love for me	1

List your 10 in the space provided and then rank your priorities from 1 (most important) to 10 (least important).

YOUR PRIORITIES

GOALS	RANK
1. _____	_____
2. _____	_____
3. _____	_____
4. _____	_____
5. _____	_____

6. _____ _____

7. _____ _____

8. _____ _____

9. _____ _____

10. _____ _____

IDENTIFYING WORK PRIORITIES

Now let's look at your work priorities—immediate goals—in the same way you have just considered your personal priorities. They may or may not overlap with personal priorities. Identify below 10 work-related goals that are important to you and then rank them from 1 (most important) to 10 (least important).

RANKING WORK PRIORITIES

WORK PRIORITIES	RANK
_____	_____
_____	_____
_____	_____
_____	_____
_____	_____
_____	_____
_____	_____
_____	_____
_____	_____
_____	_____

Some of your priorities may spring from the ideas and action steps you've already noted at the end of previous chapters. Part One may have given you some thoughts about values, work styles, or skills; and other chapters also may assist you in becoming more aware of what you'd like to achieve. But remember, priorities are immediate—short-term goals. Career goals and career planning will involve all of your goals and priorities and blend them into a unified action plan. Your 10 priorities are a beginning.

COMPARING PRIORITIES

How do your personal and work priorities look compared to each other? Would success in any of your personal priorities lead to success in any work priorities? If so, these goals support each other. For example, one of your personal priorities might be to "increase my income." Success in that personal priority would be supported by work-related goals of "complete a course in accounting" and "being considered for a promotion in my company's accounting department."

Priorities that are supportive

Look at your personal and work priorities again. Circle the personal priorities and work priorities that are supportive of each other.

Do any of your priorities conflict? For example, will fulfilling your personal priority of moving to another city work against your work-related priority of "employment stability?" If you see conflicts in your personal and work priorities, draw a square around those items that conflict.

Priorities that conflict

MAKING PRIORITIES SUPPORTIVE

Now let's do some analysis. If there are conflicts, think through those priorities and your underlying rationale. Look at your ranking again. Are there any changes you would like to make? If so, make them. Perhaps, after looking at your personal and work priorities in balance, you might like to increase the value of some low priority in one column because it is more supportive of a high priority in another column. After examining your lists and making any changes you wish to make, go on to the following exercise.

An analysis of your priorities

Identify five personal and work priorities. Use the boxes on the following pages to show personal and work priorities that *support* each other. Rank your priorities again from 1 to 5. Are these immediate goals *realistic, manageable,* and *obtainable*? It's worth listing and reconsidering any that do *not* support each other, and we've provided space to list those, too.

ANALYZING YOUR PRIORITIES

PERSONAL AND WORK PRIORITIES
THAT SUPPORT EACH OTHER   RANK

_____ _____

_____ _____

_____ _____

_____ _____

_____ _____

_____ _____

_____ _____

PERSONAL AND WORK PRIORITIES THAT DO NOT SUPPORT EACH OTHER	RANK

Now you can see what some of your own priorities are—your immediate and specific goals. Notice, too, how changes in one area of your life can support, conflict with, or be independent of changes in another area of your life.

Although brief, this exercise has asked you to think through personal and work priorities. Because many of us tend to think of each of these independently, it is easy to miss the points where personal and work priorities can reinforce each other or other points where they may be in conflict. Career thinking, good planning, and goal selection require that you be able to surface your priorities, interests, and concerns in both the personal and work areas and that both be considered in a way that can enable you to maximize your personal and professional potentials.

Surfacing your priorities — a must

ACTION CHECKLIST FOR CHAPTER 9

Checklist	*My Ideas and Action Steps*	*Date*

√ Often goals, events, and even opportunities compete with each other so that priorities have to be set as to what comes first.

√ Work and personal priorities require sorting out, yet the two have to be reconciled and conflict resolved.

√ Where personal and work priorities are in direct opposition, resolution may mean trying to think of new alternatives or ways of doing things so that it's not always one or the other.

√ Resolving priorities or developing new alternatives means we must have a good grasp of our "compass points" — opportunities, values, skills, and goals.

10

Designing a Path to Reach Your Goals

Career moves can be tough. When thinking about mine, I got all the help I could. My friend, Dorothy, has a good, realistic head on her, and she encouraged me. I was all set to go for the assistant sales service job, right away. Well, I am going for it—but, thank goodness, I sat down and did some planning first! Because I realized it's going to take me some work and some time to get myself lined up and ready. But that's OK . . . and Dorothy's right . . . I'll get there. . . .

JUNE

When I decided I was going for my real estate license, I just didn't consider all the heavy-duty problems I'd have to deal with—take review courses, get into night school, find transportation, get free time to study. . . . Everything was touch and go and firefighting from day one until I found out enough about it to put it all together.

LEE

Haphazard planning hinders your career potential

A career emerges in the future, but only as a result of plans you carefully make now. Haphazard planning, or not planning, can lead to a waste of your economic resources and result in great frustration. At times it may mean your full career potential is never realized.

Since a career is a process that unfolds during your working years, some type of path must be built so that your career will develop the way you want it to. The design of your path, then, must take into account first where you are today, which you have considered briefly in Part One; second, where you want to go (goals and priorities); and, finally, the paths for getting there—the alternatives available and the choice that seems the best path for you.

Career goals involve chosen job responsibilities and characteristics that you want in the future. Your aspirations may take you to a position with greater responsibility or wider scope of activity in your present organization, in a similar organization, in the same city, or in another geographical area. Your career may mean a wholly different type of work or occupation or reaching out to more of what you want in your present work.

You should not worry about making the "wrong" career choice. There is no such thing as a single, irrevocable career choice. A career is a process that takes place over the entire span of your working years. It is a series of work and work-related experiences linked together by a common tie, you. By developing your career-planning skills, you are more able to give direction to work experiences so that they will be more satisfying for you. And if you choose a path and find out it isn't for you, your career-planning skills will enable you to steer yourself back on the right track. Career planning means removing unnecessary risks and pressures from your future by developing your own sense of direction and taking control of your career.

Plan — don't worry about a "wrong" choice

YOUR PATH: THE CONNECTION BETWEEN TODAY AND TOMORROW

The connection between where you are today and your future career goal is the *path*—the means by which you reach tomorrow's career goals from today's work situation. The path to a better career/work situation may involve training, educational preparation, new areas of reading, contacts with vocational counselors, professional licensing, or moving—to name a few examples.

A path is a means to reach your goals

Thus, the path to success is really a set of subgoals or activities which must be accomplished in order to achieve all of your future career goals. Everybody's path is different because each person starts from a different place. Your path is built completely around your own compass: your values and needs, your skills, your goals, and the opportunities available to you.

To be an assistant sales manager, for example, is a career goal that may involve specific training (path-step) and job changes (path-steps). Those subgoals or future activities for securing the career goal require a *time plan*. Unless you recognize when particular events should take place and develop your plan accordingly, you tend to drift in the present, hoping for the future. The time involved and the number of career paths, of course, depend on how ambitious you are, how much you have to do, where you are starting from, and—sometimes—good fortune.

You need a time plan

REALITY CHECKING

In many cases, however, it helps to get a reality check on any points where you feel more information might reduce some uncertainties. A good friend or business associate whom you trust can be helpful in completing a reality

How to make a reality check

check. There are risks in this process; but you don't have to expose your innermost feelings—just talk about a job objective or an area for skills improvement, topics that tend to be less personal and easier to discuss. Many women find this procedure so helpful that they do a reality check with more than one person to get really adequate and objective feedback.

Another way is to look at what you've actually done—completion of work projects, courses, and so on—to see if you have been able to meet targets on time, as planned. These are concrete checkpoints of accomplishments, both within your organization and outside of it. Further reality checks may even be established through experimentation: trying something out for the first time or doing something differently to see if you can handle it. Finally, be sure to do reality checks often because situations change, and you must be prepared to shift with each change.

DOING A REALITY CHECK WITH A FRIEND

Checking reality with a friend

A little practice in the technique of reality checking can lead to the development of a highly useful skill. For example, consider the following conversation between June, who wants some assistance, and her friend, Dorothy:

JUNE: Hi, Dorothy! What are you having for lunch today?

DOROTHY: Nothing fancy. Made myself a peanut butter and jelly sandwich. Had to really run to make the bus this morning.

JUNE: You know that discussion we were having last week about jobs?

DOROTHY: Sure. You were thinking about some changes.

JUNE: Well, I've got a question or two for you—need some advice from an expert.

DOROTHY: I'm no expert! But I'd like to help by listening.

JUNE: You know, I've been thinking about some of the jobs posted in the office, especially in the sales department.

DOROTHY: So what's the question?

JUNE: Don't rush me—check me out on my thinking. I especially like that assistant sales service type of job. The company is expanding its stores and will need a lot more of these people. Right?

DOROTHY: Makes sense to me. So?

JUNE: Well, I've been here four years . . . worked on three different jobs in the office . . . know the merchandise lines. So I should be able to handle phone complaints.

DOROTHY: That part is true, but what about knowing the sales people and the accounts?

JUNE: I thought of that, too. I already know some of the sales people, and I can get to know the customer accounts once I start working with them.

DOROTHY: But doesn't this sales service type mean something about dealing with complaints?

JUNE: Yes, and that's the point. I've always gotten along with people, and I can "dig in" when I have to.

DOROTHY: Yes, I know; but can you do it without getting people upset?

JUNE: Thanks for the "almost" compliment. But what I'm really wondering about now is the assistant job. Those assistant sales service people must have other responsibilities.

DOROTHY: I know something about that; I worked for one. He had to work with a manager—follow directions but got to do things on his own, too. But now that you mention this assistant thing, I think you could have done a better job.

THE REALITY CHECK AS POSITIVE FEEDBACK

Notice how June started to talk about her tentative career idea with her friend. She began with a general notion of what the job involved, then talked about specific job experiences that should fit in with the assistant's job. Dorothy was used, in a positive way, as a sounding board for ideas and to *reality check* some of the critical abilities needed by June in applying for this position. Also, June stayed away from personality matters and concentrated on abilities, personal strengths, and work needs.

Reality checking is a positive technique

CONSTRUCTING YOUR CAREER PATH

Now we want you to start at constructing a career path for you. The following diagrams will help you along. The starting point (Step 1) is to set down your major career goals and subgoals (Step 2) based on your thinking about planning, values, abilities, and goals from the preceding sections. Then, to create your career paths diagram, you'll put one or more long-range goals on top of the diagram and fill in your subgoals on the steps. The activities involved in completing each subgoal will fit inside on the dotted line (Step 3). That way you can follow your subgoals as they help you reach up to your major goal or look to the right of a subgoal to check on all the activities needed to achieve each one. You'll find an example later in this chapter that

Begin your career path

The three
planning steps   will show you how June filled out her career path diagram. But it is important to realize that your diagram focuses on your goals, subgoals, activities, and all the important reminders you'll need to plan out the ways and timing that are best for you.

TIME AND CHECKPOINTS ON YOUR CAREER PATH

Step 1. Set down your major career goals *and* the time at which you would like to accomplish each goal. These goals could be job accomplishments, major skills development, and/or your future level of work. They are *your* goals:

Goals	*Timing*

Step 2. Set down, in chronological order, the major path steps (subgoals) that have to be accomplished in order for you to reach your major career goals. These are your paths or roads to success. Put down the year (or month, if appropriate) when you expect to achieve these subgoals.

Subgoals or Path-Steps	*Timing*

Step 3. Plot your career path on the practice sheet staircase diagram.

PRACTICE SHEET

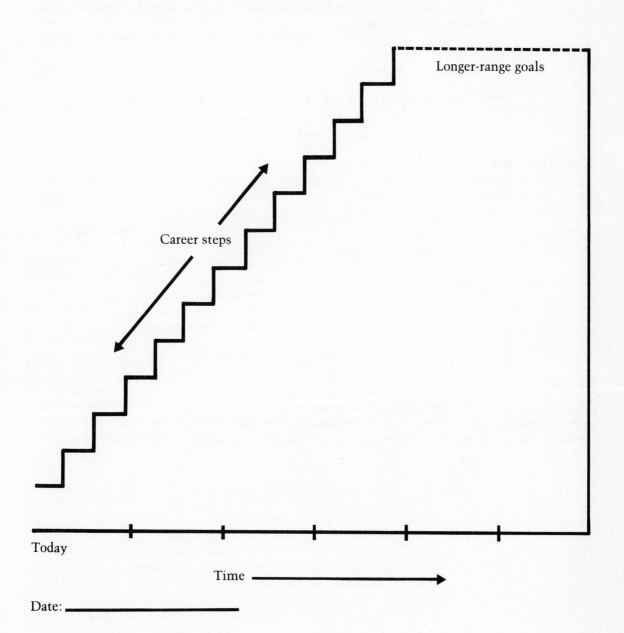

Longer-range goals

Career steps

Today

Time

Date: _____

CHECKPOINT

This is the first time thus far in the book that you've had the opportunity to get some specific career objectives down on paper, together with a time line on how you are going to accomplish these objectives. You may have begun to feel uneasy, particularly if this kind of linear thinking is unfamiliar to you. Many people become uncomfortable with early efforts in using this approach.

First, they are concerned about their choices of goals and ways to achieve them. Second, they are concerned about the technique itself, even whether they are doing it "right." But we've already pointed out, and you already know, that the only right answers are those which make sense and are realistic and right for you. Third, providing yourself with this realistic and adequate information builds your confidence. To give you some assurance about the technique and how well you have begun to apply it, a sample career-path diagram is provided on the opposite page.

How path-steps worked for June

Now you've seen June's path-step (or career steps) example and a portion of her reality-checking process as illustrated in the feedback she got from Dorothy. June checked with a number of other people and concluded that it might be wiser to develop some of her abilities and areas of knowledge *before* applying for one of the assistant sales manager jobs. June varied the time scale at the foundation of her staircase plan based on her best estimate of when to start various activities (path-steps). She decided that starting with a home study course in communications would be a good first step. June knew two people in the sales department. She talked to them about her plans, and they agreed to help her get acquainted with customer accounts.

The last path-step in June's program involved enrolling in a formal management course or workshop. When June talked to her supervisor (Mr. Grant) about her interest in the sales service job, he advised that she take some formal, but practical, course work or study in management as a quick way to learn about key management ideas. Since the company had a tuition reimbursement program, she decided to apply for that benefit before attending a program in the fall. After review, it appeared that the self-development time needed before June should apply for the sales service job was almost a year—a long time, perhaps, but worth it to her.

Lee, of course, had just an idea in the beginning—not a detailed plan. When she started doing everything at once, she realized it was too much too fast; and she really started planning. In fact, she was almost overorganized for a while, considering her free-floating lifestyle. A few weeks of experimenting with her plan and getting more information from other students and brokers gave her the information she needed to plan out the essentials while keeping an eye on her "routine" activities and her need to plan in some free time for travel, "wandering around town," and study. Her final plans are presented later in this chapter. The point is: there's no "right way" to plan. The only right way is to find the answers that make sense and

EXAMPLE: JUNE'S PRACTICE SHEET

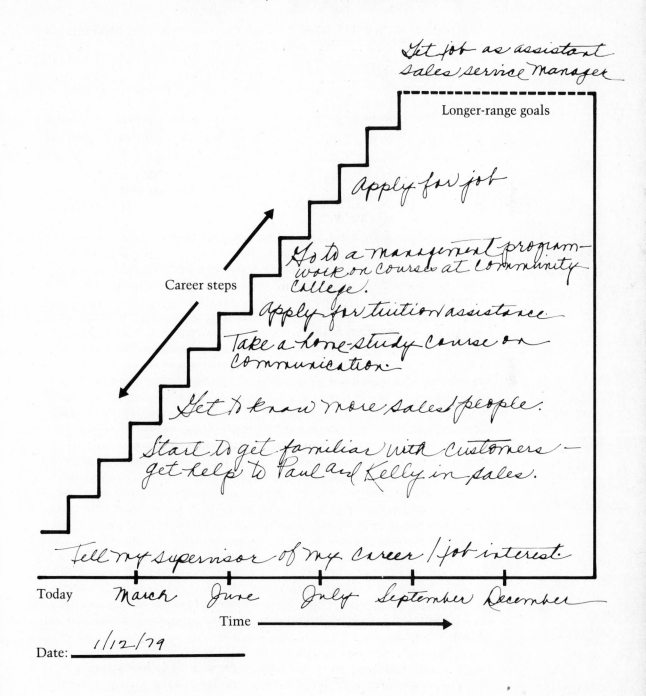

Get job as assistant sales service Manager

Longer-range goals

Apply for job

Career steps

Go to a management program — work on courses at community college.

Apply for tuition assistance.

Take a home-study course on communication.

Get to know more sales people.

Start to get familiar with customers — get help to Paul and Kelly in sales.

Tell my supervisor of my career/job interest.

Today   March   June   July   September   December

Time ⟶

Date: 1/12/79

are realistic and good for you in the sense that they take all of your concerns into account. The information you get from your own thoughts, reflections, reading, and reality checks helps you make a good start in that direction. Your own experiences and reactions will provide more information as you go along, so you can rethink and readjust plans as necessary. They needn't be elaborate—or simple—just workable and right for you.

Before you go on, look back over your goals, path-steps, and staircase with its time bar at the base. Are there places where you want to get more information or do some reality checking? Make a note to yourself to cover any uncertainties about important career steps, and encourage yourself. You're worth it!

DEVELOPING A MORE DETAILED PLAN

Time planning specifics

In this portion of your career, analysis, you are going to develop a more detailed plan for securing your career goals. You must consider two points here: (1) the notion of *alternative* path-steps and (2) the fact that many, many things you do or plan to do are *interwoven* with and affected by other activities and plans (subgoals).

For virtually any career path, there are numerous alternative means of accomplishing the same end. However, it sometimes takes considerable creativity and wisdom or feedback from someone who has been around to identify *practical* alternatives—alternatives that are workable, alternatives that enable you to achieve your goals while considering time, costs, and even the chance of choices not working out. Career counselors, informed friends, and professionals working in your areas of interest represent practical sources of creative alternatives for obtaining job information.

Finding workable alternatives

The critical questions—those that help you decide which alternative to select—are those questions that have to do with *effectiveness* and *efficiency*. The choice of an effective, efficient alternative takes into account economic costs, time, size of the possible payoff (in terms of satisfaction or career goals), and the likelihood that the alternative will indeed achieve your career objective. In short, you want to maximize your probable gains.

Mary's alternatives

The following example helps to illustrate choice among alternatives. Mary is going from St. Louis to Los Angeles for a job interview. Airfare is $240, a bus ticket costs $85, and a train ticket costs $130. If we take into account the cost of food while traveling, the adjusted cost looks like this: air, $240; bus, $105; train, $160. It's important to recognize that any of the three types of transportation could be chosen, depending on the criteria Mary utilizes.

If the only consideration were cost, she'd probably take the bus. If the only consideration were time, she'd fly. If she wanted to see "scenic America" and could leave a little early, she'd probably take the train. In this example, effectiveness and efficiency take into account cost, time, or personal pleasure—with each choice resulting in the achievement of the same goal: getting to Los Angeles for the job interview.

INTERWOVEN OR INTERDEPENDENT ACTIVITY

Typically, things have to be done in a certain sequence or pattern. Stockings are put on before shoes. Warm-up exercises are performed before jogging. Grammar school comes before high school. In a similar fashion, a career goal of "selling houses" may involve several subgoals to be accomplished *before* the first sale can be made. Let's consider Lee as an example. Her subgoals may include attending a review course, passing the real estate licensing exam, and such. Attending a review program in the evening may mean arranging transportation, which in turn may mean purchasing a car. The interconnected sequence would look like this:

Planning steps may be interdependent

Alternatives

Step 1	Arrange transportation ⟍ or ⟋ purchase car
Step 2	Attend ↓ review
Step 3	Take ↓ exam

How Lee's steps were interwoven

A still more complete sequence—say after Lee has arranged transportation for the review course (and decided to buy a car later)—would be as follows:

Step 1	Arrange transportation
	↓
Step 2	Take review course
	↓
Step 3	Take real estate exam
	↓
Step 4	Contact real estate office (Get a job)
	↓
Step 5	Buy used car
	↓
Step 6	Start selling

Occasionally, two things must happen at the same time before you can proceed to the next step, as Lee found:

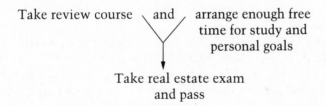

Take review course ⟍ and ⟋ arrange enough free
time for study and
personal goals

↓

Take real estate exam
and pass

ANALYZING YOUR PATH-STEPS

You can see that completing a real estate review course involved several other subgoals and several alternatives once Lee thought about them, like time for study and arranging transportation. Your subgoals may need some additional planning, too. Take three of the most difficult subgoals you listed in Step 2 and plot out any other key or important activities that need to be completed in order successfully to accomplish each of these subgoals.

ANALYZING YOUR PATH-STEPS

THREE HARDEST SUBGOALS	OTHER ACTIVITIES INVOLVED IN THAT SUBGOAL
1. _____	_____
_____	_____
	_____
	_____
	_____
	_____
	_____
2. _____	_____
_____	_____
	_____
	_____
	_____
3. _____	_____
_____	_____
	_____
	_____
	_____

Now make sure your major career path-steps are in the right time sequence. Use the following form to relist them. It's likely that you will need to check the order and estimate the time it will take to accomplish each path step.

MAJOR PATH-STEPS	POSSIBLE ALTERNATIVES (AS NEEDED)	ESTIMATED TIME
_____	_____	_____
_____	_____	_____
_____	_____	_____
_____	_____	_____
_____	_____	_____
_____	_____	_____
_____	_____	_____

For the first time in this book you have put down on paper some concrete career objectives together with a time line that shows when you might hope to accomplish these objectives. You've had a chance, too, to think about reality checking and about whether your career goals and subgoals, as laid out in path-steps, fit in with your own values, style, and skills. You should feel good about yourself, because providing yourself with realistic and adequate information is bound to build your confidence.

Building a path builds confidence

ACTION CHECKLIST FOR CHAPTER 10

Checklist	*My Ideas and Action Steps*	*Date*
√ Career paths have to build a logical and connected basis for taking you from where you are to where you want to go.	_____ _____ _____	_____
√ Career path-steps play out over time so that dates and realistic accomplishments can be spelled out.	_____ _____ _____	_____

√ As your priorities and career plan become more specific in activities and timing, reality checking helps to assure that these are realistic and fully reflective of your possibilities and alternatives.

√ Reality checking means that mentor and network relationships must be built carefully so that these fairly represent and provide inputs by reflecting good information and a wide scope of useful viewpoints.

11

Planning Tips for Dual Careers and the Single Working Mother

You know, right now I can head for home at 3:30. I'm not sure I can do that as the manager of this hotel. And if I can't, I don't know whether I want the job or not. I mean, I love my career and we can sure use the extra money. But I also want to be home before 6, and I don't want a transfer, either. Being a working wife and mother sure isn't easy! How do I figure this out?

ESTHER

It's been five years since I got my divorce—and it's just about taken that long for things to get settled down for me and the kids—and for me to start thinking about my *career.*

HELEN

Dual careers aren't just husband and wife each with commitments to their work. The whole notion of dual careers involves the idea of planning for a career and for personal obligations that involve at least one other person.

Significantly, the single woman who is concerned about meeting family obligations or personal commitments shares many of the concerns of the couple where both individuals work. However, as established previously, the whole burden of making decisions falls on her; and the backup systems —financial support, advice, and the like—are generally weaker.

There are other career dimensions in these situations. The "other" career for the married woman with no children is that of her spouse. The other career(s) for the single working mother is that of younger individual(s) whose learning and maturing towards their careers will need assistance. The married woman with children has multiple careers in her family. Each woman will need to plan her career with a concern for the plans being made by others and the responsibilities involved. Each wants to develop a career plan that is workable and realistic for her in terms of *her* career, personal obligations, and life situation. So, in the broader sense, dual career planning isn't just for two adults; it's for (at least) two people who each have goals and plans. Dual career planning helps to keep things running along in, it is hoped, a reasonably smooth fashion.

Dual careers can run smoothly, although they require extra time, planning, and effort. Energy and planning are needed to maintain the household and keep up with the weekly and seasonal activities that define family life. After a few years of working experience, the working couple or single parent has, of necessity, figured out ways of handling the household routines. These approaches stretch to meet the predictable crises of most households.

SOLVING DUAL CAREER PROBLEMS

Dual careers need formal planning

But career planning can mean shifts in family routine and schedules that at first either look physically impossible or seem to conflict with the activities of other members of the family. That's when formalizing dual career planning and doing lots of reality checking can spot and solve potential problems. This is especially important before commitment, resources, and patience wear thin and bring about "solutions" that weaken individual career directions. Some examples show what we mean.

Early in a Career

Judy: in early career

Judy was a political science major at a local college. She dropped out to "drop into" the local mayor's campaign for state senator. The senator won, and she kept Judy on the payroll to handle local committee work and public relations. When the next election was lost, Judy was out of a job. Now 25 and married, Judy wondered what to do with her career. "I'd love to finish my degree," she told us, "but I've got family responsibilities, too. And Tom wants to go to night school and entertain more often—and what can I possibly do with that degree anyway? Help!"

Managing Career and Kids, Too

Helen: working mother

Helen was a working mother with two children in school—one in fifth grade and the other a sophomore in high school. Helen had been divorced for almost five years and had really found the going tough before the problems with the kids adjusting to the new situation—and she adjusting to hers —had started to settle down. She polished up "older" office skills and picked up a clerk-typist job in the office of a sales representative to keep money coming in. It was a convenient location and gave her a chance to look after her kids and the apartment. But this wasn't going to work out for much longer. First, the income wasn't enough for growing kids. Second, she was just plain bored with the job.

Mid-Career

Esther was a clerk at a local hotel. Originally, she'd wanted to be a teacher; but she married young, moved with her husband, and found the hotel job gave her the flexibility she needed to meet the needs of her growing family (two children). She enjoyed helping the clients, keeping the accounts organized, and "mothering" the staff, too. She was good at her work—so good the manager asked her to take on some extra training. She became an assistant manager and even planned for a career in hotel management. But that's Esther talking at the beginning of this chapter. You can see she knows she has a problem. "A change like that," she kept telling us, "that's a big commitment."

Esther: in mid-career

Sudden Change in Careers

"Guess what? John's been offered a promotion and a salary raise! Terrific? Are you kidding? The job's in Center City. How do I find a job for a pediatric nurse in that place? I looked for two years here before I got a break. Right now, John's thinking of turning the offer down. But who knows when a chance like that will come again? And we'd love Center City. It seems like the right place at the wrong time. Or is it?" Maria couldn't make up her mind. Neither could John.

Maria and John: sudden changes

And you probably know similar stories, which is why some joint planning guides are in order. This chapter will present:

- perspectives that place a career in the context of dual careers and family life

- guidelines that help you plan in ways that are realistic and supportive of two or more careers, or where there is one major career concern (now)—often with family responsibilities.

MULTIPLE CAREERS AND CAREER PLANNING

No one said careers were always easy. The career of a spouse and/or plans of children or other family members can mean that a family has lots of "careers" running simultaneously and independently with lots of last minute juggling to meet the needs of all involved. The dual career family is really the two-, three-, or four-career family.

The "four career" family

Changes in a career or in family circumstances mean readjustments all around, and you may often wonder how you can find some space for *your* career and still maintain family responsibilities. In fact, just thinking about work schedules, school schedules, and vacation plans—let alone recreation programs and day-by-day activities—has discouraged many children and adults in a dual career family from trying new career activities or even thinking about new opportunities.

Reality checks with your VIPs

There's no one way to cope with career changes that occur to you and the VIPs (very important persons) in your life. But some planning can help get all the new beginnings launched in the right directions. Some of that coordination can come by reality checking your career plans and options with your VIPs, especially when those plans require their cooperation and understanding. How much advice and cooperation they can provide depends a lot on the mixes of ages and experience involved. But quite often the reality checks help clarify goals, identify alternatives and new resources, and even tap unsuspected talents. Here's what Judy, Esther, and Maria discovered when they sat down with the family.

Judy's Joint Planning Guide (JPG)

Judy's JPG

We provided Judy with a good solid guide that allowed her to get some insight into her needs and her husband's as well. Pages 105–6 show how she put it all down.

Judy and Tom: solutions with the JPG

Judy and Tom discovered a lot by putting their plans and needs on paper. They found that their beginning careers produced a hectic schedule. Each wanted to bend the family routine and budget to fit in new career activities. When they realized each might end up wanting the car on the same night, they became concerned about handling the pressures of their active social life while fitting in their nighttime courses and shopping chores. That's where the joint planning guide helped. Each person could check plans, sort out limited resources, and meet common needs with unified activities. Judy and Tom used it in ways that worked for them and strengthened their career activities.

In fact, Judy and Tom ended up moving closer to the downtown area, where they found a school that would let them both attend night classes and a location convenient to their work. It seemed sensible to them to do it all at once and "get it over with," although another couple we know took turns advancing their careers so that at least one partner remained flexible while the other faced the inevitable pressures of adjusting to new schedules and demands.

The JPG can help for the future, too

The joint planning guide is meant to help identify mutual goals and spot potential problems. Naturally, solutions will be as varied as the individuals and circumstances involved in modern family life. By the way, the JPG helped Judy and Tom during the next phases of their careers, too. She ended up in public relations work for a local firm. When they both moved West, she switched into a recreation division of an airplane manufacturing firm and now heads the recreational planning and vacation tour department.

JOINT PLANNING GUIDE

INDIVIDUAL
CAREER PLANS

Our Major Goals
1. Judy — Degree in Political Science
2. — explore job possibilities
3. Tom — Courses in transportation management

INDIVIDUAL
CAREER PLANS

Our Subgoals
1. Judy — (Jan.) Begin school 3 nights/week
2. — use local counsellors, check leads
3. Tom — (Sept.) — Start courses
4. — See about further education, jobs

Our Common Career Needs

Information —
Transportation — To and from classes
Skills —
Family activities — Help with household routine
Social —
Financial — Tuition, books, food expenses
Other — Good night school programs (local)

My Personal Career Needs

1. Job hunting — how to look at the options.
2. A quiet place to study/work

His Personal Career Needs

1. Check into course options and career needs before registering

Now go to next page and work out a joint plan.

Ways of Helping Each Other

Tom can have his personnel department
recommend books on job hunting (for Judy)
Judy can pick up registration material
Both agree to a loan, to share weekly shopping.

FURTHER
REALITY
CHECKS

Local bus
and train
routes

Problems We Will Encounter and How We'll Solve Them

Problem(s)	Solutions
1. Transportation	See if schedules can be merged.
2. poor schedules (not enough time together)	Cut down on other social activities

FURTHER
REALITY
CHECKS

Future of
transportation
management
(jobs, salaries,
etc.)

Fall-back Plans for Both of Us

Plan A: In case   of $ problems

then we will   get a loan. Check with bank
now about possibilities.

Plan B: In case   — no good possibilities in
transportation

then we will   look into possibilities in MBA in
related fields (?): air travel (freight)
or city administration (traffic).

When we will review to see how things are going   2 weeks, then monthly
                                                                        date

She's very happy with the fit, and the job involved a plus that both Tom and Judy enjoy: some "traveling weekends."

Esther's Solutions: A Family Matter

Esther's children told her not to worry about the "after-school" baby-sitters. They could generate a list of terrific sitters in no time. In fact, her oldest wanted the job. But her husband mentioned he could switch around his schedule if they wanted. Then he brought up the deeper issues involved. Would she really like to go back for a teaching degree or another degree? Would it help if he found out more about other kinds of management train- *Esther: support* ing? She hadn't expected such support. Then she started to realize that this *from the family* wasn't a go-for-broke decision that had to be made now. She postponed her decision for a few months and talked to people in management and in fields she had considered: teaching, nursing, and social work. Esther finally went into training as a teacher for the handicapped. After several years, she took over as district administrator for special services, a job that still left her "family time" and also combined her skills and values into a better-paying and more exciting career position. Just going over her career plans and action steps with her family helped her find some options she hadn't considered.

Maria's Options

Maria and John found nothing but problems at first. The new city had a surplus of nurses. The special reality checks they devised included an exploration of his career options and hers. But he found he couldn't really refuse this promotion and still move ahead with his firm, although a competitive firm might be looking for "someone like him" in three months. She found that telephone calls to the new location turned up no leads in industry, school, or institutional nursing.

Finally, Maria and John rechecked their values—each of them—and *Maria and* their style, and their skills—and all the kinds of jobs and areas that might *John:* use those skills. It helped. Maria found some new leads that looked promis- *rechecking* ing: orthopedic nursing (a related area) as well as an opening in a private *values helped* institute for corrective eye surgery (broader search). Both jobs meant contact with large numbers of young children. She realized her nursing options weren't limited to hospitals and their clients.

The broader search that came with that insight led to jobs that combined her concern for health, children, and her Spanish "family": director of Red Cross services for the Hispanic and district director for health education to Spanish-speaking students. She also heard of a city opening for a nurse who could help with children brought to the juvenile court for protective custody. She applied for all five jobs and finally accepted the court position.

TIPS ON USING THE JPG

We think you have the general idea on joint planning. There's always a limited amount of time and money, as well as differing needs, styles, skills, and resources. It makes sense to reality check career plans that impact on your relations with the VIPs in your life.

Your own JPG

How much discussion? Who's involved? When? How much can be planned? It's all a matter of personal circumstances (and personal preference), but we can pass along some tips on using the joint planning guide and planning mutual goals. We put a two-page JPG later in the chapter for you to use whenever you need it.

Approach to the JPG

There's no one best way to keep resources and people coordinated. We encourage you to plan your future with the realization that some careers or family routines are fairly stable and need no special coordination—at least right now. Others need to "work it out" as much as possible.

Approaches vary to fit family needs

Even then, approaches may have to vary to fit the needs of different types of youngsters in the family: "Responsible Ralph," for instance, the child who's a natural planner himself; "Mothering Martha," who wants to take on too much; or young "Romantic Roger," who will need lots of support and flexibility as he discovers his idealistic dreams don't always fit reality.

Think over an approach to planning that fits your very own VIPs. But also be sure to cover the basics so your approaches are as realistic and workable as possible for all involved.

Goals for Your JPG

Goals come in all sorts of shapes and sizes, we've learned: king, queen, and junior, and all very important. They can involve long-term commitments or monthly plans. Some are vague and some are specific; some have numbers attached and some speak to quality; some emphasize the social side of work and others, the task dimension of work; some goals emphasize both. All are goals. By all means, try to be as specific as you need to be to get started, but remember: everyone may have different goals or even "no special goal," and some of your very favorite people may lack the courage to mention their hopes. They'll need a little time and experience to get really involved in this business of planning—and that can be perfectly okay.

Specific goals are helpful

Beginnings are launched best when the goal is fixed firmly in sight. VIPs like "Romantic Roger" will find it very comforting to know his goal of an "A in chemistry" and subgoal of "four hours a week of quiet study" also have a family commitment during the initial weeks when stamina, endurance, and motivation are tested against reality. Try to start with goals that are realistic for the person and reach for workable approaches that fit the situation.

COMMON CAREER NEEDS AND WAYS OF HELPING EACH OTHER

Jot down on the JPG what's needed to start and/or maintain career plans; and don't forget the car, time, or money for any new clothes that are a genuine must. Make sure the list is complete. More than one couple covers home, heart, and children with their own efforts and later discovers they haven't planned enough for themselves. Jot down the needs: ways of helping will be obvious.

Jot down everyone's needs

Of course, some VIPs help each other best by leaving the other person 100 percent alone and pushing her/him gently but firmly out the door ("I knew you could do it"). Other partners take on all the challenges with skill, determination, and organization of a full military commander. Just put down some thoughts that seem to make sense for the time being and then give some thought to the following points.

Workable Approaches (Solutions)

Think of your plans as "workable approaches"—or beginnings. Time and constant reevaluation keep careers and plans on course. The first JPG may work well, but "planning the work" means "working the plan." It's a little different to *think* through the new commitments than to *live* through them. For example, we know more than one husband who would cheerfully slay dragons for his wife's career and even cook dinners on end and do dishes but who cannot manage to baby-sit a Saturday morning mélange without lots of frustration spilling all over the family scene. He didn't realize all this until he "tried his wings" at cooking and crowd-sitting. And there are children who thrive and grow on responsibility just as there are those who wilt.

Plans as "workable approaches"

See how initial plans work out and arrange for definite times for reevaluation so there's a time and atmosphere that encourage the "Mothering Martha" to admit she's really a little young to be a mother and a father and a teenager right now. And if Plan A doesn't work out, don't forget that Plans B and C are important, too. You need workable alternatives.

Be flexible: Plan B can replace Plan A

Reality Checks and Workable Alternatives

Reality checks remind you that plans mean choices, and choices mean committing *more* of your time and effort to some experiences and *less* to others. That presents a lot of pluses—and some minuses, too. What are the minuses? What ones are important? How can they best be handled?

Reality questions must be asked

For some, if your plans mean less time spent at home, someone will definitely ask: But what about

- time spent with your spouse?
- the children?
- the housekeeping?
- responsibilities to family and friends?

Good questions. And we can suggest some others:

- If you're making some major career changes, think about the career you're passing up. Are there any important minuses in choosing A and not Z right now? What about the future?
- How about other family activities and plans that might need coordinating, like education, clubs and organizations, religious activities, savings, recreation, the social scene, vacations, time for family and friends?

The bottom line should pay off

Do some hard thinking and reality checking. There is no sense in making major commitments at present if the bottom line looks really unworkable or if the payoffs won't pay off in the ways you want. Balance the risks, plans, and problems—and then develop some ideas that will neutralize the negatives, or even create constructive experiences and alternatives. And have some workable alternatives, too.

Plans B and C and sometimes D are needed as backup. Bring up all the "what ifs" you can think of. What if

- the children get sick and there's an important meeting?
- the whole family objects to our moving?
- I/you hate the new job?
- I/you/we/they find we can't handle the pressure or work involved?

What's Plan B, and what is a backup to that? You'll need to ask all the tough questions you can, especially the one that's basic: what if I/you/we/they "fail"?

What is "failing"?

Or is it "failing" to try some calculated risks and not achieve the goal? Is success the trying, the achieving—the feelings, or the outer accomplishment? Whatever the answer, there will be the times and traumas of not achieving all you'd like. What happens when somebody's plan and career activities journey to a dead end? What might the new plan look like? Think it through *before* you start Plan A. It can and does happen that couples move, expecting to find jobs easily. And it can and does happen that people get fired, too; it can even happen to you and yours. It also can and does happen that people are successful and need to plan ways of handling much more than they bargained for.

Thinking of all the unthinkables now may give you some ideas for establishing a foundation that will help find all the different routes more easily and place setbacks and success in the context of a whole career and life situation. Don't cross that bridge when you come to it; plan the routes and alternatives that will be realistic and workable and allow you to build a foundation for the help, advice, and newer opportunities you might need for Plan B. *Thinking the unthinkable leads to good planning*

As you can see, JPGs are an approach to career planning, one that leads to what is workable right now for you and the VIPs whose personal lives are touched by your career. Your workable approaches and experiences will probably lead to better and more workable plans and alternatives when everyone has learned a little more about their capabilities and limitations and can plan more realistically. The beginnings will be marked by ups and downs and soon settle into a routine. Plan for reevaluation often; and when it's time to hear the negatives, listen with patience and understanding and the questions: *Reevaluate often*

- "Is it still a problem?"

- "What have we learned?"

- "What can we do about it *now?*"

Joint planning puts it all in perspective—the perspective of planning methods *and* plans that fit you and your lifestyle. Try it for major career commitments—your plans and the plans of the VIPs who define your personal life. A JPG just for your use follows on pages 112–13.

One other reminder seems especially important for dual careers: plan for the future, not just a continuation of the past; and consider the future often and with optimism, like Teresa.

Teresa planned to return to work once the kids were in school. With no firm plans except those made long ago to return to work, she found herself hopelessly outdated, so she reached—with profound unhappiness—for Plan B (to go to school) along with some comments like "If it weren't for" . . . "Why didn't I" . . . and "Where's *my* reward for all those years of effort?" marching down the school corridors with her. Plan B worked. Teresa realized she made the choices that seemed right for her 20 years ago and the ones that seemed right for her 5 years ago. Now she's found she didn't really lose 20 years of her career. The skills and maturity gained while raising her family are pluses she's brought to her new job, and she's learning the technical side of her job fast. She figures she's lost 10, not 20 years of her career,

JOINT PLANNING GUIDE

INDIVIDUAL
CAREER PLANS

INDIVIDUAL
CAREER PLANS

Our Major Goals

1. _____
2. _____
3. _____

Our Subgoals

1. _____
2. _____
3. _____
4. _____

Our Common Career Needs

Information _____

Transportation _____

Skills _____

Family activities _____

Social _____

Financial _____

Other _____

My Personal Career Needs

His Personal Career Needs

_____

_____

_____

_____

_____

_____

Now go to next page and work out a joint plan

Ways of Helping Each Other

_____

_____

_____

_____

FURTHER REALITY CHECKS

Problems We Will Encounter and How We'll Solve Them

Problem(s)   *Solutions*

_____   _____

_____   _____

_____   _____

_____   _____

FURTHER REALITY CHECKS

Fall-back Plans for Both of Us

Plan A: In case _____

_____

then we will _____

_____

Plan B: In case _____

_____

then we will _____

_____

_____

When we will review to see how things are going _____
date

and she has another 15 to 20 years before retirement. She's starting a new Plan A now, "head of a division," and figures her workable approaches will include lots of time for grandchildren.

New beginnings	Perspective	Lifetimes	Career times
↓	↓	↓	↓
Our goals	Reality checks	Workable approaches	Workable alternatives

Joint planning puts it all in perspective—the perspective of planning methods *and* plans that fit you and your lifestyle. Try it for major career commitments, yours and the plans of the VIPs that define your personal life.

SINGLE PLANNERS—CHECKLIST

Earlier we pointed out that the single working mother shared some of the career planning concerns of the dual couple model. But, as suggested by Helen's situation referenced previously and the discussions in Chapter 6, the single mother situation is a complex one. For one thing, non-career-specific concerns, like budgets and backup funds, become critical and must receive as much attention as career thinking and planning. No use in dreaming about career opportunities if the reality is a ton of worries regarding bill paying and trying to keep up the morale of kids while you try to get a new act together. Thus, budget planning, the welfare and immediacy of kids' career needs, and careful reality checking can enhance the possibilities of a good career move and lessen the chance that a whole group of new problems will arise. There are no "guarantees" in planning that things will happen as we work them out—but we are lessening the chance of some of the risks and the "dumb" mistakes that happen more frequently than most people realize.

As a result of these considerations, our checklist of hints for the single working mother is a general one. Aside from the items in this list and the career-planning approaches discussed previously, careful attention and time can be given to these specific points.

CHECKLIST: CAREER-PLANNING HINTS FOR THE SINGLE WORKING MOTHER

Major Goals—Clarity and Completeness (check): _____

Goal notes: _____

_____

_____

Subgoals—Spelled out: _____

Goal notes: _____

_____

_____

Career Supporting Needs—Financial, Family, Social, Logistical

Financial: _____

   $ _____ for educational
   programs, books

   $ _____ for backup

   $ _____ for moving

   $ _____ needed to

   "career" us for _____ months

Family: _____

   Career needs for kids

   Support and understanding
   of possible changes

   Family care

   Sitting/kid care

Social: _____

   Friends

   Companionship

   Community

Logistical: _____

   Transportation means

   Time

Problems I'll Encounter in Dealing with Them: _____

Problems/Issues	Solutions
_____	_____
_____	_____
_____	_____
_____	_____

Backup Plans:

If . . .	. . . then I'll
alternate career arrangements	_____
financial	_____
kids	_____
	_____
_____	_____

My career planning _____   Financial ___

Family _____   Social _____

Logistics _____   _____ _____

_____ _____

Reality Checking: Do I have a plan B? (Have I checked out my plans to meet each need?)

ACTION CHECKLIST FOR CHAPTER 11

Checklist	*My Ideas and Action Steps*	*Date*
√ Dual careers (with husband involved) mean that we have to think as two and things have to be worked out with both of our careers in mind.		
√ Dual career thinking means that problems must be realistically anticipated and attempts made to work things out in advance.		
√ Dual careers, single working women, and single mother career planning require that thinking be given over to non-career-specific but still vital planning concerns.		
√ Single working mother career planning may be "damned if you do and damned if you don't"; but if planning doesn't start, nothing is likely to happen.		
√ Single working mother career planning has to place great stress on non-career-specific issues, including budget and family.		

PROFILES FOR PART TWO

Mary Miller, Connie Stewart, Jean Franklin, Joan and Mike Meyers

Part Two of *Growing* has projected you into the framework of a career. You've become aware of the ways in which present activities can lead you into your future career and of the planning guides that will direct and steady you as you reach for that future. The profiles presented next serve the purpose of reinforcing those ideas and of showing you how four women with different career goals planned their careers.

Mary Miller—The Story

Mary Miller is 34 years old. She is a clerk-typist at the college business office, Central Community College. Mary has a 13-year-old son who is to enter high school in the fall. Her husband, Herb, is a machinist at a company that makes various tools for home use.

Mary met Herb when they were attending Central Community College. They married after their graduation. In order to make ends meet, Mary took a part-time job at the school. Three years ago, when her son, Bob, started eating lunch in school, Mary began working more hours —8:30 A.M. to 3:00 P.M. Mary enjoys her job, and she now is considering full-time work and wondering what to do.

It's time for her to take stock of her situation—and she does just that in these steps: (1) Who am I? (2) What is my future work role—the work-type person I'd like to be? (3) What are the means to accomplish my goals? (4) What are some alternatives?

For Mary, her personal information gathering looked like this:
Who am I?

- Associates arts certificate—specialization in secretarial sciences

- About seven years of experience in offices, including three years of nearly full-time work

- Get along well with other people

- Pick up office routines quickly
- Kept budget for department head, was often complimented on my work

What is my future work role—the work-type person I'd like to be?

- Have various friends at school, one of whom qualifies as an executive secretary. Always thought her job sounded very interesting
- Read the local neighborhood newspaper regularly and notice that "executive secretary" frequently appears in the help wanted section
- It occurs to me that this job is a good one for more pay, greater responsibility, and better job options with various employers —just in case "things don't work out" at the college. Also, the title "executive secretary" seems to carry with it some prestige among friends

What are means to accomplish these goals?

- Talk to friend at the college and learn that I will have to be able to do more things than I can now do if I am to qualify for an executive secretary's job—and it will take time
- It appears that I will have to develop new skills in the secretarial sciences involving more schooling and general secretarial experience while working

What are some alternatives?

- Take adult education courses at night or go back to school for one semester full time
- Family can't be without my income for four months (if I go to school full time) and, besides, the college probably wouldn't give me a leave of absence
- Stay at Central Community College or seek another employer
- Check out some of the other departments at the school; learn that at least two have or will be having secretarial openings. For the time being, staying at Central seems more practical, but this should be checked out again later on

Questions for You

1. What was Mary Miller's way of thinking through her goals?

2. How did she relate her goals to her plans for the future?

3. How did the time factor enter into her thinking?

Our Comments

So far, you have been concentrating on a visible future. Now let's stretch your imagination. You may or may not want to change jobs in the future. Thinking of "next jobs" is a good idea for most of us, though. We may want to advance, change firms, try new positions. Just the thought of it stretches our horizons. Try developing a goal plan of your own for a next job that you might like, skills you'd like to strengthen, or skill areas you may wish to improve. Ask the questions Mary asked.

Who are you? What strengths do you have that are an asset in the business world? What skills? What experience? Remember to include those experiences and skills you gained in volunteer and community work, too. Many people don't realize the insights or skills they have gained from completely non-paid situations. Work in parent-teacher groups, scouting, volunteer work in hospitals, funds solicitation, and even arts groups can be major sources of individual skill development. Common areas to consider would be organizing, communicating, working with others/relationships, selling, planning, and craft skills. The fact that these activities may be in a volunteer or non-business setting is not especially important. And remember to glance back at your first inventory for some of your strengths.

What work would you like to undertake, or what type of person would you like to be? Look again at your personal and work goals and your values. Did these exercises help you visualize some future goals? What will it take to achieve this goal? What alternatives exist to get any needed skills or experience?

Map out your general goal plan for the future on the time line that follows. Those goals could be the goals and subgoals filled out in Chapter 10, or you may want to project some longer-range plans for the

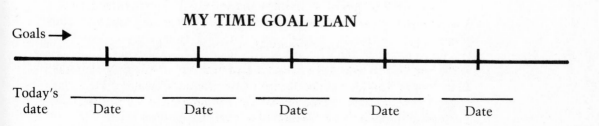

MY TIME GOAL PLAN

Goals →

Today's date _____ _____ _____ _____ _____
          Date   Date   Date   Date   Date

future. Either way, the listing helps to clarify the order and time estimates involved in your planning. It also emphasizes the importance of
each step on a career diagram and puts your ideas in perspective. When
you have completed this, put it aside for a while and then look it over
again to see if you have any new or different ideas.

Connie Stewart—The Story

Connie Stewart began working at Food Flavors, Inc., just after her high
school graduation seven years ago. Her first assignment with the company was "jr. secretary." This was something close to a pool arrangement in which Connie was responsible for taking dictation and doing
typing for twelve people in the research lab.

The work was not particularly difficult, especially after Connie became familiar with the chemical terms and symbols used by the people
in her department. Although her days were hectic with so many people
requiring secretarial support, Connie did not often find herself overbur-
dened with office problems. She seldom had to stay long hours of over-
time, and she never "took her job home." Most all of her evenings and
weekends were spent in activities with friends, out dating, or helping
her folks with chores around the house, where she had continued to live.

Connie's first promotion came shortly after her second anniversary
with the company. Her lab manager, Bob Duncan, had been impressed
with Connie's increasing familiarity with the company's basic work as
well as with its internal policies and procedures. When his friend, Art
Smith, the sales manager, mentioned that he was looking for a new
secretary, Bob said Connie might just be worth interviewing. Actually,
it was this lunchtime conversational accident that got Connie her promotion to management secretary.

For the next three years, Connie reported to Art Smith. At first she
also provided occasional secretarial help to the company's four sales
representatives; but within her first year in sales, the department had
added six more reps. Two more secretaries were brought in to provide
backup for them. Connie's responsibilities centered chiefly around
Smith and his new assistant sales manager.

Connie really enjoyed working in the sales department. She found
that her background in the research lab was most helpful to her understanding of the company's products and the challenges involved in marketing and selling the various colorings, additives, and flavorings they
produced.

Once or twice she even offered an idea for Smith to pass along to a
sales rep. Smith was very flattering to her and frequently remarked
that Connie "could become our first lady product manager." He always
suggested that Connie take advantage of the company's tuition reimbursement program and attend some evening courses related to sales

and marketing, but Connie seemed reluctant to take time from her busy social life. Although she definitely considered herself "involved" in her job and always talked about how much she enjoyed working with Smith and his assistant, Connie did not respond to some of the challenges that were open to her. Once when Smith asked her to rough out a promotional letter to home economics teachers, she declined saying, "Gosh, I can't ever develop that kind of a letter. I'd be forever thinking up what to say. That's a project for Jack or one of the guys in the advertising department."

Another time Smith asked Connie if she would like to represent Food Flavors at a small trade convention in another city, but she declined to do so because it meant two nights out of town and her boyfriend didn't think she should be traveling alone. "I appreciate your asking me, Mr. Smith," she said, "but it just isn't worth arguing about with Bill. Can't Frank or one of the guys go instead?"

None of the jobs she turned down were really crucial to Connie's responsibilities as a management secretary. She continued to expand her knowledge of Food Flavors, Inc., and to refine her secretarial skills. Overall, Smith was very well satisfied with her work. He continued to make comments to Connie about the value of her gaining some additional education and how much more worthwhile it would be for her to think about her career more and her boyfriend less, but Connie always tossed those remarks off as Smith's way of teasing. "I just know you'd like me to turn into one of those totally dedicated, hard-boiled career women," she'd say, "but that's not for me. Someday I'm finally going to hook some nice guy, and then being his wife will be all the 'career' I'll ever need."

Questions for You

1. Is Connie's orientation toward a career more like or unlike that of most women you know? How do you feel about other people (like her boyfriend) shaping Connie's decisions? Who is involved in shaping your decisions?

2. How do you see Mr. Smith's flattery and requests for more involvement on Connie's part? Is he teasing, as Connie thinks, or is he genuinely offering Connie an opportunity for professional development?

3. Connie sees herself as being "involved" with her job. Do you see her that way? Do you think that Connie is familiar with the objectives of her organization or department? Do you think she sees herself anywhere in those objectives? What about you? How familiar are you with the objectives of your boss? Your

department? Your organization? Where do you see yourself fitting into those objectives?

Our Comments

Like many women, Connie seems to be approaching her career on a "Sleeping Beauty" basis. Her job is something she can dream her way through until marriage. What Connie does not seem willing to think about is the scope of her responsibilities within a marriage or a choice not to marry or possibly not to marry for a long time. Regarding the marriage alternative, Connie seems not to be considering the fact that today's economy increasingly calls for a two-income household, that most married women hold paying jobs some time during the course of their marriage, or that almost half of all marriages end in divorce, with the woman increasingly responsible for her own support—and sometimes the support of her children.

Of course, if Connie is allowing others to shape her decisions for her, she can continue to avoid responsibility for what happens to her *in her career*. She will always be able to point to others and say, "If it weren't for . . ."

There is another alternative here that Connie and others often fail to consider. Trying out promising alternatives, even if one fails, can be a perfectly acceptable career strategy so long as it is seen in proper perspective. If an employer, geographic location, or work alternative is tried out as a conscious strategy in individual career thinking, the experience itself can be a positive one even if the results are not satisfying.

Simply recognizing that there are specific limitations on our abilities to anticipate our likes or what might prove to be a satisfying career experience makes this possible. Sometimes it's easier to try out the job or situation since speculation can go on endlessly with no decisions made at all. But in all cases where this approach to careers is taken, the individual must be prepared to accept a specific event that *fails* as a *positive step in eliminating some alternative(s)* and possibly leading to the identification of others.

Often we attribute negative motives to things that other people say. Or, like Connie, we brush off their encouragement with remarks that discount everyone—"Oh, that's just his way of teasing." It would appear that Mr. Smith is, indeed, interested in seeing Connie develop greater skills and expertise. Even if this wasn't the case, however, if Mr. Smith was only manipulating Connie to get additional work without having to pay "professional" level salaries for it, couldn't the expertise be of value to Connie later? By responding to Mr. Smith from a negative, "I can't ever do that" position, Connie isn't giving herself an opportunity to check out reality, to weigh the relationships between effort and potential reward. She could change this by communicating with Mr. Smith

Connie seems to be approaching her career on a Sleeping Beauty basis.

from a more adult perspective—asking him questions that would give her more information on which to base *her own* decisions to accept or reject additional responsibility.

It is difficult to know exactly how much or how little Connie actually knows about the objectives of the company or of her department. It is clear that she doesn't see herself related to those objectives, however. Connie's interest in her work is on a day-to-day basis. Even though she offers an occasional suggestion, she does not follow through herself, nor does she tie her suggestions in to the goals and objectives of those around her. Involvement in a career implies a much more assertive role than the one Connie takes in relationship to her work. Put yourself in Connie's place. What do you think about the issues raised? How would you path the future?

Connie's situation poses some realistic but subtle problems that you may be only partially aware of. Thus, we would like to make some general observations regarding the usefulness of information you may be using in your career thinking and decisions.

Many people are not trained observers and find it quite difficult to see or understand the total picture of organizations, work, people, and external environment. There is a natural tendency to construct their view of an organization, work, and possibilities through the window provided by friends, immediate work associates, rumors, and even one's supervisor. Needless to say, there are likely to be substantial gaps or shortcomings in the scope or depth of this information. Adequate career planning requires that the individual do more than simply gaze through the window constructed for her by immediate associates or sources of information. One who takes charge of her career must learn the art of cultivating new information. Networks of work associates in the organization or in similar positions elsewhere provide some of that perspective. They can provide an important source of information and often help with reality checks and advice. These networks are formed by taking an interest in the new people you meet and keeping track of who does what and who knows what in ways that are useful to you. Take the time to schedule some lunches with co-workers and superiors and even the others across town who have some mutual interests and needs. Keep track of the individuals in your networks (men and women) and reach out to pass along and obtain helpful information. As your career plans take shape, it can help to think about the people you know or would like to meet who will share mutual concerns. You're not necessarily looking for a cohesive group that will meet once a week in a formal way to discuss a "presentation," although a formal group can provide the structure, support, and network you want. The idea is actively to maintain contact with those who can lend reinforcement, advice, tips, or assistance when needed and who will benefit from your help in return. They begin when you take the initiative to write, call, or meet others, offer ideas, and maintain (even written) contact with compatible people. Networks come in all kinds of sizes and shapes to fit most any need, from emergency child care and social help to professional groups that are exclusive and concentrate on career needs and/or the formation of a "women's group." Remember that career networks are a group you choose to support your activities, and remember also that a good working relationship with all your work associates will provide the supportive network you need within your organization. Don't let an exclusive group isolate you from broader career activities. Networks are really commonsense groups and should help you learn more about your present and future careers and facilitate processing of your work, too. Chances are that the future will include the reality of many different career needs and work associates. Flexible, realistic, and concerned individuals in networks can help with the information, support, and advice you need to fit into that future.

Mentors can play a key role in enlarging the view from the window or even helping you to construct wholly new windows. Numerous studies of individual careers have indicated that mentors can be highly supportive of your efforts to develop information, test out alternatives, and/or serve as a sounding board for ideas. This role can be played by a person at work or somebody in your community or personal life. Mentors typically possess a good store of information on work matters, have work experience, have understanding of matters going below surface issues, and are interested in and can relate to you in a friendly and helpful fashion. Mentors provide the specialized information and advice that can lead you further in your career because they understand you, your position, and the path (and problems) of your day-by-day or future career activities.

Jean Franklin—The Story

Jean Franklin was a secretary to the production manager of Atlas Products. Jean originally had been hired at Atlas for one of the production assembly lines, a job she had held for almost two years.

Work on the production line was not difficult, and Jean worked with a good crew. But she often remarked to her mother, "You know, I really like working down at Atlas—they don't act strange or treat me different because I'm black. I really like the other girls. But the work is so boring, I'm going out of my mind!"

When a job was posted for production clerk, Jean applied and was accepted on a trial basis. She performed so well that after three months her job title was officially changed to production clerk and she received a small increase in pay.

Jean finished high school before coming to work at Atlas. As a matter of fact, she had started a program at King Community College; but she was forced to drop out after a year when, unfortunately, her mother had become ill and was herself forced to quit work for a while. Thus, with little money coming in, the responsibility had fallen to Jean to get a job—her assembly job at Atlas.

Now, in the production office, Jean worked into the routine quickly. Before long, other clerks, even the manager's secretary, were seeking her out for advice. The manager's office was located in a corner of the production plant, and many of the problems that came up had to do with production and floor problems that Jean was familiar with.

Jean still brown-bagged her lunch with friends from the production line. One day they talked about jobs and work. Jean indicated that the group in the office was really "super," but that she wanted to do more with her life than file, answer phones, do lookups, and write notes. Jean's friend Martha then asked her, "Well, Jean, if you don't like what you're doing now, what do you want to do?"

For the next week, Martha's question kept popping back into Jean's mind—along with a few more like "What am I prepared to do?" and "How do I get into a 'better' situation?"

One day Jean ran into one of the teachers she had had at King Community College, Mr. Burns. To her surprise, he said he remembered her. He also remarked about the potential he had seen in her and her opportunities for the future.

"Mr. Burns," Jean said, "you're going to be disappointed. All I am is a file clerk."

"Jean, there's nothing wrong with that kind of job. But you do have the potential for much more."

"You know, Mr. Burns, deep down I feel the same way; but I don't seem to be able to get my act together."

"Jean, among other things, I do a lot of counseling at school . . . you know, jobs and careers and all that stuff. Coming to a career decision isn't easy, and it's not just a once-and-for-all decision. Things do change. But there are some pointers I can pass along to you.

"First, know yourself—your abilities, interests, values . . . and your shortcomings.

"Second, identify the work activities that can satisfy you and can keep you reasonably happy and still challenge you to the extent you want to be challenged and have the capacity for challenge. This forms the basis for a career as opposed to just a job or a way to earn a living.

"Third, know your alternatives and the job's opportunities. Think of work experiences and your own personal development activities that can help you realize your career.

"And then, fourth, connect up your job, alternatives, and experiences to make a road map for yourself as if you were traveling by car from one part of a strange city to another—lay out the directions you'd need to get there."

When Jean got home that night, her head was spinning from all the ideas Mr. Burns had passed along. She could see that there was much work ahead of her in even getting to know herself better, let alone finding out about job opportunities, importance of more schooling, and whether there was a future for her at Atlas Products.

Next day Jean asked her boss about future possibilities at Atlas in terms of jobs, promotions, and careers for her. The manager indicated that there were several people he knew who had "broken out" of production into some very important jobs. He sketched out one example:

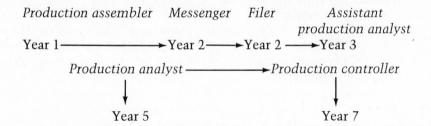

Production assembler   Messenger   Filer   Assistant
*   production analyst*
Year 1 ──────────► Year 2 ──► Year 2 ──► Year 3

Production analyst ──────────► Production controller
         │   │
         ▼   ▼
      Year 5   Year 7

Jean wanted to know whether the person required special training or schooling to move up and how long these things took. The manager then provided a more detailed sketch for such a career path.

POSSIBLE CAREER PATH AT ATLAS PRODUCTS

Production assembler	→	Messenger filer	→	Assistant production analyst	→	Production analyst	→	Production controller

EDUCATION/TRAINING PATH

Night classes	(Basic math (program (Shop (drawings (Scheduling I	Advanced math) program) Scheduling II)	Night classes	On-the-job training (former analyst)	Communication and dealing with people (night classes)
		Production management)	In-house company program	Use of computer (night class)	

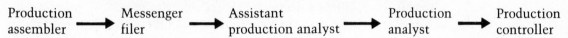

Time
line ──

Year 1   Year 2   Year 2   Year 3   Year 4   Year 5   Year 6

Questions for You

1. What is your interpretation of the dissatisfaction Jean has felt in the production and clerical jobs?

2. Do the jobs Jean has held form some part of her career path? Of what use, if any, have the jobs been to her in furthering her career?

3. What is the difference between jobs and careers? What is the relationship?

4. What is the role of education and training in a career path design?

5. How do personal abilities and interests affect the choice(s) Jean is likely to make for her career?

Our Comments

In both jobs that Jean has held, she has gotten along quite well with the people in her work group and was apparently quite competent. In fact, Jean reached a level of proficiency on both jobs in a very short time. Her dissatisfaction probably comes from the frustration of being able to use only a small part of what she can bring to a job.

These jobs could form a part of Jean's career development. The only question is where we break into the work/individual development process. The key point is where an individual starts to seek out specific experiences against a particular career objective or goal. In other words, we are aware of making conscious choices among jobs, work experiences, education, or training in order to build personal skills, attitudes, or general understanding (perspective). It's probably true that the jobs Jean has held gave her a familiarity with working with people, production methods, and office routines which can prove helpful in the future. To the extent she's unaware of these experiences in relationship to possible future job goals, career processes are not at work. Thus, it is important for Jean to take stock of herself and bring together interests, abilities, opportunity, personal limitations, resources, and so on.

Usually, jobs are thought of as a means of attaining careers. That is, a sequence of jobs forms the path or bridge from a person's current state to a future state where she can make good use of personal abilities and achieve things she values.

A career path can't be built solely around jobs but requires the support of work experiences with other experiences (for example, education) which build new mental or physical skills and abilities.

Jean hasn't fully uncovered her abilities and interests. So far, because of her family situation, she has been largely a victim of circumstances. It appears that Jean could benefit from more schooling, but before going too much further, she should take stock of herself—the kind of evaluating you've undertaken in Part One and Part Two of *Growing*.

Joan and Michael Meyers—The Story

Electrical engineering was an important and rewarding career 15 years ago when Mike Meyers began work with a large computer firm. When the space race ended, Mike was happy to switch to sales and watch his career develop into sales management for a growing region.

Today, Mike is not so happy about his career. He learned firsthand that corporate careers and dual careers have different goals and time frames. His career, his wife's career, and corporate demands seem irreconcilable.

Five years ago, Mike married a young divorcee with two children. Joan was an assistant dean of women for a major university. With careful saving and hard work, Joan and Mike purchased and rebuilt a house and shared a lifestyle of backpacking and fishing that each enjoyed.

After only two years in their new home, Mike was offered a career advancement, a move to a major metropolitan area. Moreover, he was informed that his career would stagnate if he did not make the move. Weighing the 30 remaining years of his work against the family's pleasures, they moved.

At first, the change was traumatic. Expenses far outweighed his salary increase. Their new home was far less desirable than they expected. Recreation was expensive and inconvenient. Joan's new position in a local college proved unexciting. The move forced them to work harder to develop the types of work, growth, recreation, and friendships they had taken for granted. But after three years of effort, they have recaptured their lifestyle and work goals. Even the children are proud of their school and friendships.

Once again, the firm wants Mike to move to a different region of the United States. The move would take them even further from the lifestyle they enjoy and force Joan to begin again in another position. Mike's corporate bosses are firm about the necessity of the move. At his level, job openings are few. He must follow openings on the promotion ladder now or remain frozen in his current job for many years. This would bring him a great loss of respect among his subordinates and signal headquarters to ignore his future advancement. He can only expect to ignore a request like this once or twice in his career with this corporation.

After an initial period of disbelief, grief, and anger, Mike and Joan are ready to consider their response. How would you counsel them to handle this opportunity?

Questions for You

1. What information can Mike and Joan obtain about their careers to help them make this decision?

2. What do you think their options might be?

3. How difficult will it be to move their family? Why?

4. What do you think possible solutions might be?

5. Can you choose a better alternative for this family?

Our Comments

Mike and Joan have run into the reality of modern life. Over 40 percent of wives work, many at positions with potential for advancement. But modern corporate planning has only begun to consider this reality in its career planning.

It sounds as if both careers could benefit from discussions with qualified personnel advisors who can map out potential careers in Mike's corporation and discuss the future of educational growth with Joan. What are his potential moves and for what time periods? What positions is he likely to hold and in what cities? How important is a career to Joan?

How do Joan's needs contribute to their future? Is there a career in education for her? Can she move flexibly with his career? Does one or both have to reconsider job commitments? Perhaps he needs to move to a local company in an area where they would all prefer to live. Perhaps she needs to change her direction to a flexible position with good pay and with opportunity for mobility.

At last notice, Mike, Joan, and the children were exploring all of these possibilities. In fact, they planned their summer vacation in the Midwest and West, an excursion to look at computer firms and local colleges. The children planned to investigate local schools, sports, and social events. They realize that moving every two or three years is unacceptable in terms of happiness for the family.

ADDITIONAL RESOURCES

Part Two: Making Plans

BIRD, CAROLINE. *The Two Paycheck Marriage: How Women at Work Are Changing Life in America.* New York: Rawson, Wade, Publishers, 1979. An examination of the different options working women and couples are using to meet personal and work responsibilities.

BLISS, EDWIN C. *Getting Things Done.* New York: Bantam Books, 1977. Time management and some ideas that make working hours more effective.

CRYSTAL, JOHN, and BOLLES, RICHARD N. *Where Do I Go from Here with My Life? The Crystal Life Planning Manual,* 1976. Excercises that help you identify the work you find enjoyable.

CURTIS, JEAN. *Working Mothers.* Garden City, N.Y.: Doubleday, 1976. An exploration of the alternatives used to meet the family obligations of the working mother.

HALL, FRANCINE S., and HALL, DOUGLAS T. *The Two-Career Couple.* Reading, Mass.: Addison-Wesley Publishing Company, 1979. A presentation of the problems of two-career couples and practical solutions.

HOLLAND, JOHN L. *Making Vocational Choices: A Theory of Careers.* Englewood Cliffs, N.J.: Prentice-Hall. The philosophy of finding work that is interesting and meaningful to the person.

POGREBIN, LETTY COLTEN. *Getting Yours: How to Make the System Work for the Working Woman.* New York: Avon Books, 1975. Some basic understanding and ideas about the competitive job market.

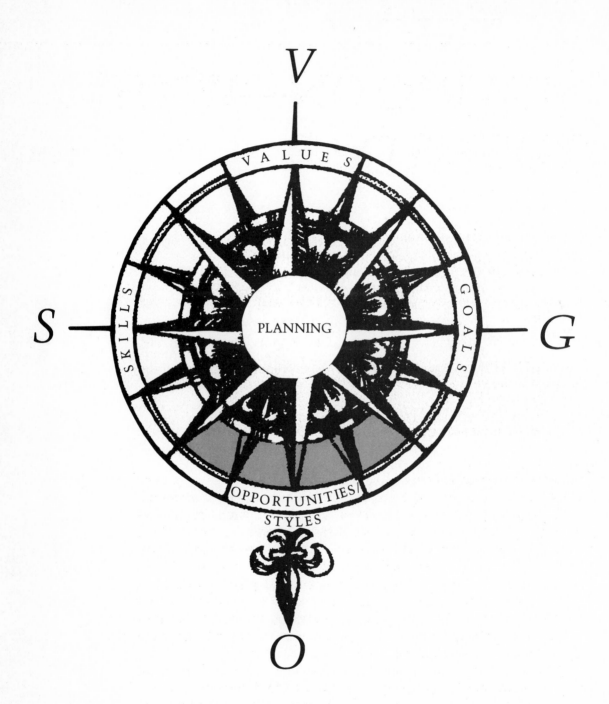

Part Three

MOVING ON—WITH YOUR STYLE

Part Three shows you:

- How to identify your career style and the work environment that suits it
- How to cope with the fears and anxieties that come with change and challenge
- How to enrich your environment with your style
- How to negotiate and exchange as ways to advance your career
- How to reach out successfully to your work associates

Many of the comments we hear off the job are not really about the work itself. Often they reveal how different kinds of work surroundings and different kinds of people influence someone's life and her emotions—and even make up for a poor work experience. These strong individual responses reflect the quality of work life a person seeks—and she seeks that quality because it suits her style.

This part of *Growing*, then, will find you using your career compass to target your career style and to direct activities within your work environment. Learning what your style is and how to use it or modify it to make your career experience more natural and more comfortable—these are the goals of this part.

The steps you take to blend your career style with your work activities may not be giant steps, but you will find them meaningful, for they will enrich your life and give you more of the satisfaction you seek from your career.

12

Recognizing Your Work Environment and How It Fits Your Style

I like my job fine. You might think I'd get bored—doing the same thing at almost the same time every day—even eating with the same bunch every noon. But I kind of like to just work along and get everything done that's on my desk. I don't feel pushed that way. And I take my breaks to read a little or make my grocery list. I just like routine, I guess. . . .

BETH

I get everything done, but I know I have to work like crazy near the end of some days. I get to talking with a friend—or I take a long break fixing my hair. But it all seems to even out, and no one minds as long as the work gets done and done well. Let's face it, this job is boring. Doing the same old thing day after day makes me feel boxed in, sort of. A little goofing off makes the time pass. I guess I'm just going to have to think about a better job. But I sure enjoy the friends I've made here, and I'd hate to get into a position where I felt I was watching the clock every minute like Beth does. . . .

BRENDA

In Chapter 2 of *Growing*, you got a glimpse of your career style. We said that doing more of the things you enjoy doing takes you from a job into a career and that when you understand your own career style, you'll be able to create a better fit between you, your associates, and your work environment. So let's take time now for more than a glimpse: let's understand what career styles means and explore yours in depth. And let's look carefully at what the work environment really consists of.

YOUR WORK ENVIRONMENT

What the work environment is

Your career style really involves the social aspects of your work—literally, what's happening around you. The formal responsibilities, personalities, and skills of people around you—plus policies, methods, and rules—help to define your work responsibilities and influence how and how well you work. They also shape feelings about what you do and where you work. So the work scene is filled with those people, things, and procedures that create an environment for your work activities. The following figure shows some of the forces and considerations that create your work environment.

Each environment is different

Naturally, each person responds differently to all those factors; and each work environment is unique, too. Some activities may affect your job differently from the way they would in other kinds of work. For example, women who have lots of contact with the public probably use more formal ways of dressing, speaking, and organizing their working space compared with those whose work is all in-house. And, of course, each person helps to create her own niche through the ways she relates to others and the work itself.

TWO EXAMPLES OF WORKING STYLES

Let's go back to Beth and Brenda and what they had to say at the beginning of the chapter. They have the same jobs, but just hearing them talk lets us know they express their personalities differently during the same working day.

Beth's work style

Beth types in a word-processing center. Usually arriving early, she checks out her hair, makeup, and jobs for the day before touching base with others in the department and grabbing her usual cup of coffee. Her work proceeds almost nonstop and with the steady rhythm suited to Beth's working style. Her breaks are usually spent at her station planning for family needs. Lunchtime usually finds her with friends or reading a best-seller written by one of her favorite authors. Her career plans include a shift to private secretary work sometime in the future; but she enjoys her current position, benefits, and office crew.

Brenda's work style

Brenda, across the way, is almost an opposite image to Beth. Free-flowing and a little more interested in the unusual, Brenda tries out a lot of different hair, clothes, and work styles. Her station has a variety of messages, pictures, and organizers which change around a lot. She starts out her day with people and visits a lot during breaks and lunchtime. Her working pace is much more varied. Her stops, starts, and interruptions to locate the right materials define part of her work style and give her a little more of the change of pace she wants. Right now, as she says, she feels "boxed in." But she wants to stay put to get a better idea of how her skills can be used in the future.

FORCES THAT AFFECT YOUR WORK ENVIRONMENT

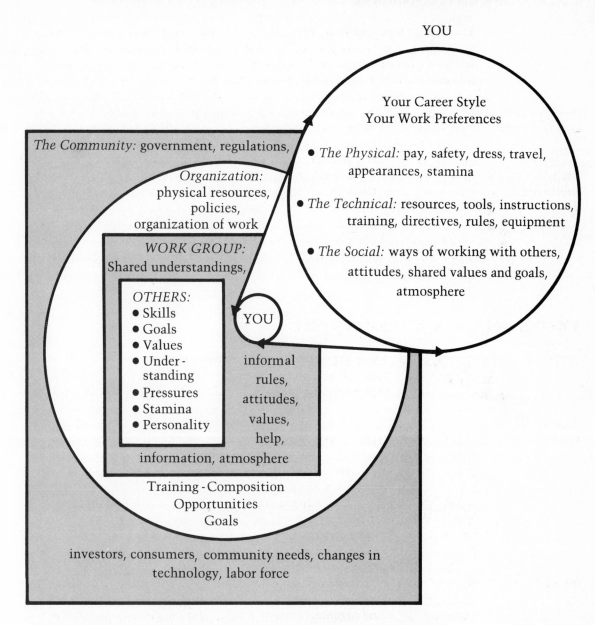

YOU

Your Career Style
Your Work Preferences

- *The Physical:* pay, safety, dress, travel, appearances, stamina

- *The Technical:* resources, tools, instructions, training, directives, rules, equipment

- *The Social:* ways of working with others, attitudes, shared values and goals, atmosphere

The Community: government, regulations,

Organization:
physical resources,
policies,
organization of work

WORK GROUP:
Shared understandings,

OTHERS:
- Skills
- Goals
- Values
- Under-standing
- Pressures
- Stamina
- Personality

YOU

informal
rules,
attitudes,
values,
help,
information, atmosphere

Training - Composition
Opportunities
Goals

investors, consumers, community needs, changes in technology, labor force

Who is getting more out of the job? Both Beth and Brenda like to work; both are competent, and both are glad to have each other around. Beth, however, loves routine work, while Brenda likes the excitement of the unusual. When Brenda is upset or Beth needs someone to cheer her up, the other tends to notice and respond almost automatically. But their style *is*

How their styles differ

different; and, quite naturally, it has different consequences for them in terms of job satisfactions, goals, and the ways others "see" and respond to them—as well as their needs to move on or up in the career world. Project those styles into a different environment and imagine what the effect would be if Beth worked in a noisy, crowded typing pool or Brenda became the only receptionist for a small office.

Your surroundings are important

Visualizing your present or possible work environments brings home the realization that surroundings are an important part of your working life and that there's a variety of highly compatible and incompatible environments for most people. Finding the right job but in the wrong surroundings (for you) provides a fast reminder that your mind, feelings, stamina, work habits, and ways of relating need to be in harmony. Unless there is a change in you, your work, or others around you, there is often a need to shift jobs or rearrange your personal life a bit to fill in the needed or missing pieces. Knowing your own career style and the more specific features of it, your work style, and what is important to you can make the difference between being satisfied or dissatisfied. Knowing your career style can help you reach out to create some realistic, healthful, and satisfying ways of experiencing work.

THE CAREER COMPASS AS A GUIDE TO CAREER STYLE

Career styles express our values

Career styles usually express your basic values in very general ways. Brenda, for example, placed a high premium on "an exciting life" and on "being cheerful." She found a routine work load boring. On the other hand, Beth had strong needs for "inner harmony" and "independence" and was able to organize her work in ways that supported those values and allowed her to express them through her work.

Work styles bring our career styles to a specific work place

Considering career style *and* work style becomes important if, for example, you enjoy your work but not the work place. At such times, you'll need to have a clear idea of your general career preferences so that work-related factors, such as job, work place, and work associates, can be analyzed.

Work style can and does change, depending on your job and the opportunities you have to adjust activities, surroundings, or relationships with others. As another personal strategy, you may decide to maintain your current ways of working but bring more of your personal preferences to different community and home activities. We won't stress the differences between a career style and a work style, knowing you'll appreciate the basic point: It's helpful to recognize what's really important to you and to realize there are different ways of satisfying these desires at work and/or through other activities.

Most of us develop an awareness of our work style after long periods of trial and error, but there are some shortcuts to becoming more aware of how our basic needs can be met and fulfilled in our work environment. The best shortcut we know of comes by using the career compass to target your strongest preferences and to bring a sense of self-direction to work activities. *The compass as a shortcut*

That's done by first identifying what you most want in your work environment, activities, and relationships with associates; then those preferences are checked against your values. Preferences that relate, in an immediate and direct fashion, to your core values define the basics of your career style. Other points of the career compass (skills, goals, and opportunities) assist you in using your style to develop more effective working skills and relationships with others. *Check your preferences against your values*

As you noticed in Part Two, the career compass can also be used to evaluate goals and develop plans that will help stabilize or adjust your career style to current work responsibilities. You can even blend those goals and plans with your broader career plans. The anchor points of your preferences, skills, opportunities, and goals guide broader career activities.

In Part One, we showed you how to create a career compass for use as a planning guide that grows with you and keeps you on target as you chart your future. We want you to see now just how your compass can serve as a guide to your career style. First, take a look at Chapter 4, page 30, to remind yourself of "the" compass and what each of its four points represents.

Now you are ready to see how the compass can adapt to help you identify your preferences, your feelings about your work environment—and can thus bring a sense of self-direction to your day-by-day activities. We've added other information to the career compass to help you in thinking about career style. Note how the compass reflects the "basic you," the "everyday you," the "expressive you," and the "future you." *How the compass gives self-direction*

You can see from this compass how people, places, and events from many sources blend into the work scene. Of course, this mix is going to affect your thinking, feeling, and doing in important ways. Awareness of this mix and just what it means to you puts career behavior front and center. That's what your career style is all about and that's why we want you to do some in-depth thinking about *your* style in Chapter 13.

YOUR CAREER COMPASS AND YOUR CAREER STYLE

GOALS

Future You

Identifying goals in your work environment:
- Ways of working
- Working relationships
- Organizational activities

ABILITIES

Skillful You

Using style to improve and skills to solve work and career concerns:
- Exchanging career help
- Negotiating career concerns

YOU

OPPORTUNITIES

Expressive You

Using common goals, skills, and preferences to build good working relationships with others:
- New associates
- New ways of relating

VALUES

Basic You

Finding ways of working that build on your
- values
- beliefs
- energies
- feelings

ACTION CHECKLIST FOR CHAPTER 12

Checklist	*My Ideas and Action Steps*	*Date*

√ Understanding your career style helps you create a better fit between you, your work associates, and work environment.

√ Work environments differ; not all needs can be met at a particular job.

√ Work styles reflect specifics of career style and contain many different elements that can contribute to a sense of satisfaction and to personal growth.

√ A career style expresses your values for ways of working that you find meaningful.

√ The career compass helps you put your ways of doing things into perspective. It relates them to your values, skills, opportunities, and goals.

13

Knowing What You Want from Your Work Environment

> *I took the QPI, and for once I feel as if I know just what I like and don't like about my work place. It's right up front: I like a good commute. I like a decent schedule. I like a room to work in with lots of color. And nice people, and no smokers, and—well, you get the idea. Those things are very important to me. And that's my style.*
>
> ANN

Two major questions that relate to career style are ones it's worth asking of yourself often during the path-steps you are taking toward your career goals:

1. What do I find meaningful and rewarding? (This will mean rechecking your values in Chapter 1.)

2. How can I do more of it?

For these kinds of questions, a self-inventory built around your preferences helps. You took one to get a glimpse of your work style in Chapter 2. Now let's take one that lets you really think through what you like most and least about your present surroundings. It's the Quick Personal Inventory (QPI) that Ann is talking about above.

A QPI OF YOUR JOB ENVIRONMENT

The QPI helps you locate things you really like or dislike about your surroundings. A reminder list follows to help you think about things that you might otherwise overlook. Be sure to complete this form on your own, thinking only of the preferences that matter to *you.* The inventory helps you look at your work and environment in terms of personal, technical, and

142

social preferences. Some of the things you especially like or dislike might fit into one or more of these categories. You might, for example, really dislike the equipment you're using, either because it's too big to be comfortable for *you* (personal) or because it's not designed to do the job you want it to do (technical) or both. Enter preferences wherever they come to mind.

Looking at your personal, technical, social preferences

Directions for the QPI

In the boxes that follow, fill in the things you really like and dislike about your work right now. Of course, some items may be simple or relatively important—like having a place nearby for a quick snack. Others may be just a part of the working day that can't be avoided right now, like the time it takes to get to work or the fact that you need more working space. Either way, you're just exploring the things, big and small, that you like or dislike —for whatever reason. An example, using Ann, is given in each box.

Exploring what you like and dislike

One more helpful tip: If you find you just can't seem to think of anything you like or dislike a great deal, it may be that nothing in your surroundings is very impressive. On the other hand, it could be that it's just hard for you to visualize your work place and to start evaluating it.

Problems in starting off your inventory can be helped by pretending a close friend or relative is filling out the list for you. Pretending someone who knows you is helping you to fill out this form will remind you of things that are so much a part of your working day that you almost forget about them. Also, the reminder list that follows the QPI can be used to see if anything else comes to mind.

How to get started

The Personal. For starters, the personal includes all the things that involve your mental, physical, and emotional stamina—such as job comfort, the physical environment, the pay, and benefits.

What are you reminded of that affects you personally that you . . .

Really like!	*Really dislike!*

Listing personal likes and dislikes

The Personal—Example from Ann's List

Really like!	*Really dislike!*
Good insurance programs	*Haven't had a good raise in two years*
The freedom I have in scheduling	*Traveling by car in the winter, too long and too scary*
Good cafeteria	*Takes me too long to get the work out, always behind*
Lots of work space	*Unattractive—colors of the walls and work station are blah*
Having coffee at my station	*I bring the job home—worry too much about it*
	Music while I work
	Smokers nearby

The Technical. The technical includes tools and resources, all the rules, instructions, ways of working, opportunities, and equipment that influence how well you can do your job. What is it about the way you work that you . . .

Listing technical likes and dislikes

Really like!	*Really dislike!*

The Technical—Example from Ann's List:

Really like!

Good equipment
Help when we need it

Really dislike!

Unpredictable schedules
No programs for further
training for advancement
I end up with a lot of other
people's work

The Social. The social includes all the relationships among people that affect you or the way you work. The social includes you, everybody else, and what is or isn't happening at work. What is it about people and what's going on that you . . .

Really like!

Really dislike!

Listing social likes and dislikes

The Social—Example from Ann's List:

Really like!	*Really dislike!*
People are concerned about each other	*Too much petty gossip* *Competition about clothes, hairdos, etc.*

Reminder List

Use the reminder list for yourself

Just in case you overlooked something, here's a list of some things, conditions, and activities found at most work places. If one reminds you of something specific that you *really* like or dislike about the place where you work, put that in your notes on the personal, technical, or social lists—wherever it seems best to express your feelings. Don't put down things that are considered important by other people you know but not by you.

This is your reminder list:

Physical surroundings: noise, heat, humidity, light, temperature, attractiveness, comfort, safety, movement

Schedules: daily, weekly, seasonal, vacation, sick days, personal days, travel

Compensation: base salary, bonus, merit pay

Benefits: health insurance, dental insurance, life insurance, retirement plans, stock/annuity options, other compensation programs

Job: equipment, work volume or quality, difficulty of the work, sense of achievement or accomplishment, variety, recognition, co-workers, seeing results/getting feedback, fair division of labor, good atmosphere for work, good atmosphere for friendships

Organizational features: training, authority, bosses, staff, morale, support and help, good opportunities to learn and grow, feedback

YOUR CAREER STYLE: FINDING CORE PREFERENCES

Now what? You've got lists that provide some information about your style —some idea of how your values find expression at work. Those lists also point to some preferences that aren't being met at work, however big or small those preferences may be.

Finding your basic career style

To get a more accurate sense of your own basic career style, take a look again at what you really like and don't like about the current working scene and put those thoughts into some positive and general statements. Later you'll check to see how meaningful and important each is for you. For an example, let's look at Ann's list. The checked items are ones that Ann thinks define her basic career style right now because they relate to the values she identified as very important when she ranked her terminal and instrumental values on the values scales in Part One.

Write down summary of thoughts on your style

ANN'S SUMMARY THOUGHTS

What I want at my work place is . . .

PERSONAL	TECHNICAL	SOCIAL
√ Some freedom in scheduling my work	Good equipment	√ A group of people who care about each other and where I can develop some working friendship
√ Good pay and insurance programs	√ Backup help when I need it	
√ A safe, easy commute	Fair and well-organized schedules	
	√ A chance for more pay, training, and career opportunities	
Access to good food nearby		
A place to work that's colorful, quiet, roomy, neat, and smokeless		

Ann's list defines part of her career style—some of the basic preferences *she* has. Of course, many of these needs are already met where she works; some *can* be met if she plans for them. Others may never be met on the job in general or perhaps on this particular one. For example, Ann may need to satisfy some of her friendship needs off the job. But the needs are important to her and relate, she feels, very strongly to her own broader terminal values

How Ann's style related to her values

of freedom, sense of peace, and inner harmony. Some elements of her style are related more to instrumental values that encourage her to be capable, responsible, and ambitious in her work activities.

Ann noticed the link between many of her work-related likes and dislikes and her values. It reminded her that those kinds of activities and preferences seemed most important to her because they were ways she could express her values at work right now. They started her career style, and that's why she checked them off.

But she wasn't quite sure what to do about elements of her career style that did not fit into her surroundings at present or about items that weren't related to core values and yet were things she liked and disliked. She needed to think more about what she really did want, her opportunities, and some ways of planning how her career style could fit with other career activities. She took items on the *Really dislike* list she felt were important to her and jotted them down as a reminder to think about them again later.

Put down positive statements

Ann's example may give you some idea of how to make more accurate judgments about your own career style. First, look over what you really like and dislike in your work environment and then put these into more general and positive statements, just as Ann did.

MY SUMMARY THOUGHTS

What I want at my work place is . . .

PERSONAL	TECHNICAL	SOCIAL

Now, like Ann, look back at Chapter 1, page 8, and check your rankings of terminal and instrumental values. Jot down below your five highest:

Recall your own values

TERMINAL VALUES (WHAT I WANT FROM LIFE)	INSTRUMENTAL VALUES (VALUES THAT GUIDE MY ACTIONS)
1. _____	_____
2. _____	_____
3. _____	_____
4. _____	_____
5. _____	_____

Use these lists of values to check generally the items on your career style list. Some may line up directly and others won't. For example, a well-organized schedule is important to Ann, but she feels it doesn't really relate in a direct and obvious way to *her* most important values. Sometimes it's hard to see the connections or maybe it's just not part of her basic career style—but she will still keep it in mind when she looks over elements and activities in her work place. You'll find ideas from page 12 helpful here, too.

If you find some items that seem to match or express *your* values, check them off. They're part of your basic career style—general ways of working that express your strongly held values and that you prefer to have in your surroundings, if possible. Of course, as we have learned, surroundings will change and your values may shift; specific ways of expressing these values may change, too. But some basics of your career style are worth thinking through and planning for as your career develops.

Check where your style matches your values

Understanding, organizing, and planning are required to achieve the fit among your career, career style, and surroundings. Sometimes preferences cannot be entirely met and shifts have to be made between personal and work responsibilities. Sometimes your preferences require more realistic assessment and planning. The following chapters provide guidance.

Finding the fit for your style takes planning

ACTION CHECKLIST FOR CHAPTER 13

Checklist	*My Ideas and Action Steps*	*Date*
√ Knowing what you want in your work environment helps you plan for the future.	_____ _____	_____

√ The QPI helps you identify
preferences in the personal,
technical, and social side of work.

√ Preferences that relate strongly to
your values are part of your basic
career style.

√ Some style preferences will be met
in the community; others can
become a part of broader career
plans.

√ Needed changes that build
comfortably on your style can
increase your effectiveness and
productivity.

14

Dealing with the Anxieties that Can Come with Career Changes

Just what I need—another challenge. Finally made friends, got the home–office juggling routine straightened out, and the boss suggests that I transfer to the downtown branch—to the same position, mind you, and also take some courses in finance! "Miriam," he says, with such great confidence, "dig in. Be ready to go up the ladder as the bank grows with local industry." I don't know if I want to dig into new responsibilities or just dig deeper into the comfortable rut I've finally carved out for myself, deserve, and enjoy. The whole thing SCARES ME TO DEATH!

MIRIAM

Every year I surface from the rat race I've created for myself, figure out where the marathon is taking me, and plunge in again. This year I'm trying to ask some different questions. I know what I'm getting out of my planning—and the extra programs and the extra effort. I'm getting the skills I need to stay up with changes in my field and do a super job! But I'm also getting nervous. I can't seem to get the "old me" and the "new me" together yet. The programs make me feel like I should act, talk, and work like someone else. It's not me! Right now I've decided to settle in a little and think things over. What can I do that will help me figure out what's bothering me and whether I'll enjoy some of the changes planned into my future?

JULIE

Stay put? Move? Shift things around a little? Change a lot? Careers direct you to the challenge of handling work responsibilities in new or different

151

Change brings problems

ways. But the opportunity to redirect a career is only an invitation that *you* choose to accept or reject.

Sorting it all out can be easy and obvious or difficult and confusing—or scary. This chapter of *Growing* is addressed to your concerns about the meanings of change in career plans—for you, your career, and your ability to work in ways that are satisfying and productive. We want to help you identify and solve problems that accompany changes in career activities. Your new understandings, we hope, will ease the transition between the present and future of your career.

But transitions can be eased

First, let's examine change—the type of change that comes with career activities. There are good methods for identifying and thinking through the concerns and anxieties that often come with thoughts or plans to redirect career activities.

THINKING THINGS OUT: CAREER CHANGES

Reexamine who you are

Who are you? What can you do? The question raised during job interviews is often re-echoed in the corridors of your mind as you move from youth to adulthood. Sometimes the echoes are strongest during passage from a period of growth in careers. At such times, changes in you, in people around you, or in your work encourage you to reexamine who you want to be and how you can best express yourself as you keep growing—the kind of taking stock you did in Part One. At other times of your adult life, a phase of personal growth encourages you to use work as a way of demonstrating your capabilities to yourself and to others. During these transition periods there is growth through the challenges and opportunities provided by work or home experiences and a newer maturity brought to the job.

EXPLORING NEW HORIZONS

Rethinking "where you are" currently in terms of your career often makes you aware that you have changed over the years. People and problems you have met along the way have sparked changes and influenced your ideas, values, and ways of doing things.

Experience means changes

Growth and change through work itself come with the years of on-the-job reality. Inexperienced workers, for example, usually wish to explore broad opportunities. Then, having learned the basics and gained some confidence in their abilities, they take the time to explore different dimensions of a job. At this point in your career, you may test the depths of work by taking on greater responsibilities, pushing for additional productivity, and/or enlarging your network of office contacts. The only constant for a time is change as you redirect behavior to fit your need for exploration.

When possibilities become limited, experienced but bored individuals also look to see if other jobs or employers will fill the vacuum of their discontent. In later years and different seasons of a life or career, the same person will bring new needs, perspectives, and skills to a work place. Co-workers and supervisors, too, changing with the momentum of their own needs, change the work place outlook. The work itself changes. Newer technologies, schedules, and organizational adaptations challenge you to strengthen or adapt existing skills. You may need help in working through the vague feelings of anxiety that can come with a desire to change.

Desire for change can bring anxiety

CAREER STYLES AND CHANGE

Creating a fit between the social and work dimensions of your career plans requires thinking and some experimenting. As your career plans take shape, look over the action checklists completed for Part Three. Note any changes, large or small, that might sharpen your performance at work. Check those adjustments against your broader career goals. What changes might come first? How will you make these changes? Does a change in one area of your life/work support or conflict with other plans you have? Take some time to smooth out your planning and focus your career compass for a clear direction.

Ideas about your career style can strengthen your career plans

Growing a career means paying more attention to the fit between your-self, your activities, and others. Rethinking your needs and values may cause you to redefine your responsibilities or change the way you relate to people around you. For example, every item of a checklist in Part Three points to changes you might make concerning your career style. Some of these changes might include placing a newer emphasis on yourself as a whole person. Others are concerned with your skills or with your relation-ship to others (social-related goals) in the work place. Your career planning should include a thoughtful look at the style changes you are contemplating and the ways in which emerging patterns in your career style can reinforce each other and strengthen your career plans.

P-L-A-N changes that strengthen your career

1. **Plot the changes**
   Look at your action checklists and jot down some of the changes you feel are important in experiencing and doing work or the ways you and others relate to that work. Those changes aren't necessarily big ones, just ones you feel you want to make.

2. **Look at them**
   Get an overview. See if those changes seem to have a common thread that pulls them together—one area of work or a work habit that calls for attention.

3. **A**djust
   See how the changes you're thinking about fit in with your career values and career goals.

4. **N**otice opportunities
   Plan out any changes that will need some organizing in terms of your present or future career growth.

Planning for changes will help to strengthen needed rearrangements or refocusing of your career activities.

For example, Joan, a young supervisory trainee, used that overview of the goals on the social side of work to good advantage. She found that her checklists referred again and again to ways of coordinating people and work. She checked that insight against the other points on her career compass: her own goals, values, and opportunities. It kept her on target when she determined to stretch her wings and try a new line of work. She felt "as if the job had been designed for me and me for the job" because she was prepared.

You can learn skills that build on strengths and values

Knowing she was choosing work that would put her in charge of a group of people for the first time, Joan hunted around for a chance to practice and build her skills before she actually made the switch. She took on a coordinating job at a local club. While she trained for the technical side of the job at work, she learned to handle groups with the help of more experienced neighbors who shared her interests. That sense of direction made her more ready for her new career step. It also opened up some new interests off the job.

It is not luck that guides a career along and puts the right person in the right place at the right time. The good fortune that turns jobs into careers is the magic of a career compass directing a thoughtful and deeply felt concern for the future. You have already fixed the basic points of that compass around your own needs, values, and skills. Other points have been defined by using an awareness of yourself to identify career goals and opportunities. When put together, the compass directs your steps along the pathway of your future.

Setting the direction of your own personal growth along that pathway simply means checking out your style preferences for patterns, seeing how those changes relate to points on the compass and checking the fit with the reality of broader career plans and current opportunities. Again, out of our experiences, we can offer you some systematic ways to plan and think about change. We call it our "THINK" Model.

The THINK Model

Working involves decisions about *what* to do and *how* to do it and also the discipline of turning your attention and skill to the task at hand. Often the specifics of your job are well established. It is the difficult task or the decision to try something new that makes you feel vulnerable. Sometimes memories of your own past experiences and the collective wisdom of your friends can help support you as you cope with a difficult period of adjustment.

At other times, however, a thoughtful search of the past provides no clues, no revelations, and no feelings of confidence in your ability to confront the unknown. You search for ways to identify the forces that hold you back from becoming more involved with your own career. At such times, you need a method that will help you identify the whys of your uneasiness. *A method of* Although thinking it through involves a willingness to be honest with your- *identifying* self, it also takes a little structure and practice to search the depths of your *your feelings* anxieties, identify specific problems, and decide how to handle them.

One helpful technique is to take your general problem—for example, uneasiness about a possible promotion or transfer—and ask yourself, "Why does that bother me?" Let the reasons for your discontent come to mind. A reality check on your fears can then tell you whether your discontent *Use a reality* springs from a realistic inner warning system or merely a need to get more *check* information, some guidance, or organization as you move through a transition stage. Thinking it through in a focused way involves: (1) taking a few minutes when you are most relaxed, (2) eliminating as many distractions as possible, and (3) talking to yourself freely about whatever is bugging you.

First, focus on the problem and then identify what's bothersome about *Then focus on* it. Do that until you run out of reasons. Then check the reality of your *your problem* concerns and make some plans that will help you cope more effectively with any remaining fears. For those who have trouble getting started, it often helps to *visualize* whatever's bothering you, almost like a picture or a movie. Let's use Bev as an example.

Bev was nervous about her promotion from assembly line worker to supervisor. Once she pictured herself handling that job, she found it fairly easy to discover why a "nice girl" like her was worried about giving directions. Bev used the basic THINK Model that follows as her approach to *Use the THINK* figure out why she was nervous about becoming a supervisor. We've in- *Model* cluded a blank model for your use and Bev's completed model.

Although Bev knew it was the responsibility that bothered her, she didn't realize why it bothered her until she could target her main concerns, check the reality of those fears, and make some plans to help her move more easily into that new position. Of course, Bev might also have decided to stay put for the time being after exploring her options. The point is: The thinking-it-through approach, whether done on paper or from memory, is one good way to tackle vague feelings of anxiety that hold you back because it helps sort out feelings and work out problems. When the next anxiety problem looms for you, try the THINK Model right here in *Growing:* Start at point 1 and move clockwise; when you reach point 5, you're bound to have sorted things out some—and that's a good feeling.

THE THINK MODEL

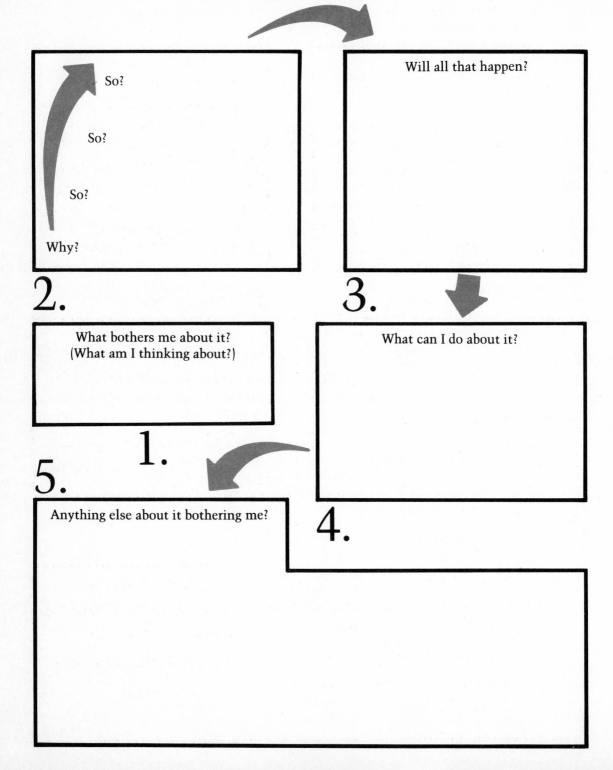

2.

So?

So?

So?

Why?

3.

Will all that happen?

1.

What bothers me about it?
(What am I thinking about?)

4.

What can I do about it?

5.

Anything else about it bothering me?

BEV'S THINK MODEL

2.

So? *I'll be fired.*

So? *Others will suffer, everyone will be mad at me.*

So? *I'll make mistakes.*

Why? *I don't know the job.*

3.

Will all that happen?

Part of it. I don't know anything about the new job. I know I'll make some mistakes, but if I get advice, those mistakes will only inconvenience a few people. And I'm sure I won't get fired over a few mistakes.

1.

What bothers me about it?
(What am I thinking about?)

Responsibility — being promoted.

4.

What can I do about it?

1. ask Mrs. Hayes if she'll help me get started and be around for advice

2. Find out more about what I'll be doing and what happens if I don't do well.

5.

Anything else about it bothering me?

Having people angry at me still bothers me. Thinking it over, I realized that I liked people to be happy. Mrs. Hayes helped me see that was one reason I wanted to be "in charge." But if I like the job I'll have to learn that you can't please everyone all of the time.

COPING WITH SPECIAL FEARS

Fears should be examined

Sometimes a basic fear, like getting fired, seems unrealistic after a quick reality check. But intermediate fears, like making mistakes, are more real and speak to a need for further thought and action. Whatever the reason, the feelings of "Something's wrong" or "I'm really nervous and uptight about this" can flag a time when you need to sift through your feelings and check out the ingredients of fears that tie you down.

Two of the special fears that hold people back are "fear of success" and "fear of failure." That two-edged sword swings especially over the heads of many women who would really like to break out of their shells and try something different.

Fear of Failure

Fear of failure can paralyze

Fear of failure often keeps people on their toes and at peak performance. Their awareness of the consequences of small and not-so-small mistakes encourages them to take a special care with important work. But fear of failure can become a paralyzing force that keeps people from trying new activities or even *thinking* about trying them. As Bev found out, the consequences of "not succeeding" become magnified by irrational and overexaggerated fears. Sometimes inexperience encourages people to underestimate their skills, as well as the understanding guidance they can get from others as they stretch their wings.

Fear of Success

The problems of success can be dealt with

Success has consequences, too, and many people wonder how success in a very different kind of job will change them and the way others "see" and treat them. They envision drastic and irreversible changes in themselves and others as a consequence of a new job. Job changes seldom change princes into frogs or princesses into wicked witches; but they may bring some hectic moments complete with real anxieties, some mistakes, and a few misunderstandings as a person grows into newer responsibilities. Devices such as the THINK Model can help ease the personal transition of career changes.

A fear that holds people back

It also helps to realize that many of the fears that come with career planning are fairly common. Those fears—of success, of failure, or of change itself—emerge from a concern over new or different responsibilities and their impact on work, career style, or personal lives. It is important, therefore, not to let the growing that comes with career planning be choked off by yet another fear: fear of responsibility.

Fear of Responsibility

"The whole thing SCARES ME TO DEATH!"—Miriam

"I'm afraid to take it on. Too much responsibility."—LaVerne

"Represent the group? But that's a lot of responsibility! What will I say to the gang if I can't *convince* the supervisor?"—Ellen

All three of these women are expressing a heartfelt fear of responsibility. And it's a fear that holds people back—often—from what they really want to do and planned to do only to find, as the reality of their plans take form, that they are afraid. Of what?

What is responsibility?

How does it affect you?

The dictionary provides these definitions of forms of the word *responsibility:*

DEFINITIONS OF RESPONSIBILITY

RESPONSIBILITY

Responsive: 1. Giving response

Responsible: 1. Liable to be called upon to answer

2. Quick to respond or react appropriately

2. Able to answer for one's conduct and obligations

Responsibility is, then, by one basic meaning, an act, a *response,* an opportunity to use your skills in an appropriate fashion. But for many people, the word takes on the full force of its other meaning, *responsible:* liable to be called upon to answer. Then it becomes a burden, a weight that wearies body, mind, and emotions. Opportunity? Burden? Both? How is it that people see some responsibilities differently from others?

Two ways to view responsibility

Much of that vision is shaped by worry over accountability, a fear of the consequences of one's behavior and the demand to answer for one's conduct. *But responsibility balances the freedom of shaping and defining work activities.* The words "You are responsible for . . ." are reminders that others are *dependent* on your efforts. Learning to accept that responsibility can be both anxiety-provoking and satisfying.

It can be satisfying

For example, Sally had all the qualifications for her job but no experience when she gave her first sales presentation a year ago. It was a simple presentation, and Sally did well. But consider how she felt then, as compared to now:

Sally's example

Here I was, 15 years younger than anyone else there, representing the company. And a few of the people there asked some tough questions in some nasty ways. I was so afraid about getting the firm a bad contract I could hardly think. I fumbled. I hedged. I stammered. Thankfully, Joan was there to jump in when I felt really lost. I won't forget her praise when I walked out feeling my knees buckling and my palms sweating. Now I know better. Representing the company means everyone is there for backup and advice. I've watched others flounder and recover. I'm more content to do my own best now, and I love coordinating it all—good business for our people and theirs—business that *I* helped put together.

Accepting responsibility comes with practice

Taking on responsibility is a learning process, like learning to drive, getting a party together, or taking care of someone who is ill. It doesn't happen overnight. It comes with practice, coaching, and getting advice and on-the-job training. There are lots of watching eyes and helping hands around—mentors and networks that we'll be talking about. There are also training programs and courses available that use discussions, illustrations, and practice sessions to help people get some experience before the first day of a new position.

Of course, there are often mistakes along the way—yours and the miscalculations of others that make the final product a little less than what was wanted. What then?

Fear of Accountability

Having to account for what you've done

Accountability means you must account. What happened? Why? What was done about it? Those questions come up in most adult situations, from handling finances or the first parking accident to the delays or errors in our work. You forget, misplace, or handle it all wrong. You may need and find a more experienced guide to bail you out or head you in the right direction. Some mistakes may be costly to you and to the organization. There will be other times when there are no actual mistakes but you somehow wish things had turned out a little differently.

You learn from taking risks

For example, Sally made some calculations on a contract, then inflation hit and . . . well, you know the story. Quite human. In accounting for what happened in Sally's organization, however, each person involved learned what went wrong and what went right, and what to do next time around. Some mistakes were in fact "expected." Again, taking risks and bringing your judgment and abilities to bear on a new situation is a learning process —a necessary part of career growth. Accountability often provides a very positive picture of that growth. Welcome these formal and informal discussions as an opportunity to learn from your organizational network. The accounting is a good way to reality check your progress (and strengths) that can soon turn any anxiety you may feel into a solid sense of confidence and pride in your new skills.

CONFIDENCE ABOUT NEW BEGINNINGS

All too often an exaggerated fear keeps people from reaching the fulfillment of their careers. Women feel concern, worry, anxiety, fear. And they ask, Can I do the different? the more demanding? the more responsible?

Questions that come from fears

We hope you've found some ways to find answers, ways that:

And realistic answers

- Help you think through the problems of career change

- Free you from unrealistic fears

- Let you focus on the job requirements and the reality of your own career style

- Relieve your anxieties so that you can examine the premise of new beginnings with confidence in yourself and in those who will work with you

There will be new beginnings whether the answer to an opportunity at hand is yes or no. Changes in yourself, others, technologies, and organizations will reshape the directions of many careers. Most women spend at least 25 years in the labor force, and the changes that come with time, choice, or necessity often expand the questions "Can I do it?" and "Do I want to do it?" to include a concern for their career styles: "How do I fit in?" they ask. "Will I have to change?" "Will I have to give up the ways of working and ways of relating to others that I've come to enjoy?" The following chapters help you resolve those concerns.

New beginnings are a certainty

ACTION CHECKLIST FOR CHAPTER 14

Checklist	*My Ideas and Action Steps*	*Date*
√ Career changes can be planned or come from changes in us, our personal lives, our work environment, or newer technology.		
√ The THINK Model helps you to think through reasons for anxiety; it encourages checking these out and planning a realistic response.		
√ An *unrealistic* fear of failure can keep you from trying something new—it needs to be seen for what it really is.		

√ Fear of success is concern about how change will change work or our personal lives.

√ Fear of responsibility also involves change and a concern for work skills and others.

√ Concern regarding future career activity should lead to planning and reality checking to smooth the way for personal change.

15

Negotiating—One Way to Use Career Style

Every year it's the same old story: "Sorry, Pat, the boss won't okay a raise until profits go up." And I'm tired of the threats and the "pat on the head" when I confront the boss. Maybe I should just threaten to quit—but I'm afraid he'd let me. What do I do now?

PAT

Thelma? She'll work out. But how I don't know. Never had such an uptight partner. Every time I breathe she gets nervous—must think I'm Simon Legree or something. Now I'm getting nervous—and I like people! I'll tell you, this one's something else. If we can't work it out in another month, I'll call it quits and get someone else. Hate to do that, though. Wouldn't look good for me or her, and besides she knows what she's doing. We just can't work together at all. How do I get her to relax so I can relax so we can get the work done. I'd like to be myself without frightening her to death.

ANN

Going from wanting to doing often involves negotiations with others or with the organization. Time, money, and opportunities are limited. People can and do disagree on issues of both major and minor importance. Negotiations help to settle issues and solve problems, with the necessary give and take that can provide an acceptable, workable solution for everyone. Every issue from where to go for the departmental dinner to how to get a promotion usually involves some kind of negotiation—the ability to persuade, the willingness to give a little to get whatever's wanted. Thus, your ability to negotiate is often an important aspect of your career style, and you may wish to develop skill in using it.

Settling issues and solving problems

163

This chapter of *Growing* will help you to understand *power* and its role in negotiations related to careers; to identify your own style of negotiation and learn to use it (more) effectively; and to target career goals that often require negotiations with others.

NEGOTIATIONS AND CAREER STYLE

What negotiation is all about

Let's start with an understanding of what negotiating skills are all about. Negotiation is about helping others understand your needs and preferences and winning their cooperation. To a great extent, negotiation is also what you do during the quiet talks to yourself or the lunchtime strategy sessions that identify the whos and hows of lining up schedules, equipment, promotions, raises, or cooperation.

Negotiation is also about *power*—that is, the ability to influence others. Negotiation is also about exchanging—that is, the ability to give and take. (We'll talk more about exchanging in Chapter 16.) Negotiation is a reality of the working world, and the way people negotiate and use their ability to influence others is a part of their career style. The process looks like this:

POWER/NEGOTIATIONS DIAGRAM

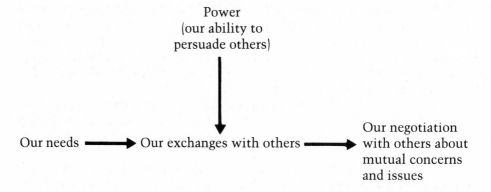

Sometimes negotiation is not difficult. For example, Ann found it wasn't too hard to negotiate some breathing space with Thelma. It just took time, skills, and patience—and sharing some ideas along the way. At other times, negotiation involves every bit of persuasive ability you can muster. It may even involve promises to keep up the good work or to deliver a little more. Pat found this out when she went in to negotiate a hoped-for raise with her boss.

DIFFERENT PEOPLE, DIFFERENT STYLES

Careers involve job responsibilities, as we learned in Chapter 14. These responsibilities include negotiations that affect our work or the work of others. How we engage in these negotiations depends on our style, as well as our values and skills. Your career style can shape negotiations that confront issues head on or instead lead softly into a discussion of shared concerns. Each style can be effective, depending on the circumstances. Consider the way Becky and Leona went about solving their career problems.

Different styles of negotiating

Becky, the Helper

Becky was the sweetheart of the office. Thoughtful and bright, she was called on whenever somebody needed a hand. Her (growing) skills were extended, on request, to older co-workers who had trouble learning the new machines as well as to the inexperienced who needed coaching and encouragement.

Becky, the office "sweetheart"

Success brought about success—and more requests for assistance. People started coming to her more often and asking for her advice. When she wanted help with her own career goals, people returned the favor generously.

Leona, the Expert

Leona was a new supervisor, with a less than enthusiastic group of workers and too many inexperienced hands. She wanted to get her group organized and trained. She started her first meeting with a written agenda and strong statements about the ability of the group and her willingness to help them. She also made it very clear that lateness didn't fit in with *her* career plans or *theirs!* She responded to their unspoken but evident needs for better schedules with the same strong and directive career style.

Leona, the confident leader

Leona worked hard for her group and expected everyone else to pitch in, too. It took about six months before her confident and concerned leadership turned these new and hesitant workers into a group of very capable workers.

It's obvious that Becky and Leona had quite different styles. Yet each was a powerful person who could influence others and negotiate important career activities. Each advanced her own career and also found ways to bring her career style and values to the work at hand.

THE MEANING OF POWER

Power, or the ability to influence others, isn't necessarily push. In fact, the pushy types generally are cut down and made to learn to consider the needs of other people. Leona found out these facts the hard way earlier in her ca-

Power is not push

reer. Her one-sided calls for action, her high-handed threats and occasional outbursts, were greeted with no cooperation. She learned to temper her style with some concern for others and to deliver what was important to her group.

Real power comes from trust

Power isn't simply dress, an arrangement of an office, or even a title on the door. The physical side only sets a stage for action; it doesn't write the script. Real power—the ability to influence and persuade—comes from trust generated by past behavior. Who's talking? What is she like? Can I trust her? Will she come through for me? Will she provide what I need by way of advice and ideas, help, skills, and backup support?

The person with power is the one who can deliver what is needed to the right place and the right people at the right time.

Power is getting the job done, helping others to do the same, generating their trust, and earning that influential reputation.

DISCOVERING YOUR NEGOTIATING STYLE

An inventory of your negotiating style

How all that gets done depends on your negotiating style, the ways you express yourself, create better working arrangements, or get the privileges, perks, and promotions you want.

The following inventory provides some insights about your negotiating style.

NEGOTIATING STYLE INVENTORY

There's no right answer, just different styles. To get an idea of yours, think about what you would do if. . . . Check the response best fitting your approach or handling of the situations.

1. A co-worker wanted to trade equipment with you. The supervisor doesn't care. Your friend suggests she give you her work station, better location, and equipment for your setup. But your equipment is in better shape so you'd like to bring it along and use it.

Do you:

A1. Start out positive and then mention the problems involved? _____

A2. Begin with the issue and be very strong about what you want? What if she starts to get angry? _____

Are you likely to say:

B1. "Hey, this was *your* idea? What's going on? Do you want to work it out or not"? _____

B2. "Calm down. We're each concerned about this. Let's work it out." _____

B3. You ignore it and say nothing. _____

2. It's time for the office party and Marie is in charge of arrangements. Some people want an expensive dinner, but most want a simple inexpensive place where the gang can get together. You've been chosen to represent your work group. When you meet with Marie, who favors the expensive place, how do you start?

A1. You mention all the items you agree on, then bring up the place. _____

A2. Get to basics—begin with *where* it will be held and at what cost. _____

If Marie gets upset and threatens to leave it all for you to work out or if she gets personal and questions *your* taste, are you likely to:

B1. Respond in kind? Bring her up short in order to get some cooperation? _____

B2. Remind her of her responsibilities and ignore the personal attack? _____

B3. Ignore her frustration entirely? Just speak to the concerns of your group? _____

3. You want a raise, a title, and an office to go with all the work you've already been doing. How do you handle it?

A1. Start with one request and work up? _____

A2. Demand all three and see what you can get? _____

Your boss would rather not give any of the three items and points out that lots of people would love to have your job. You:

B1. Tell him about the new affirmative action laws and threaten him in return? _____

B2. Tell him no one would want your job unless the proper title, salary, and space come with it? _____

B3. Ignore his outburst? _____

4. Joan and you just don't get along. Everything you do seems to be wrong! She's just an entirely different personality altogether. But both of you need to work together. You:

A1. Be yourself? Act natural? _____

A2. Try to "settle in" gradually and slowly and pay attention to how quickly she can accept your style? _____

The route to acceptance hits a snag. She accuses you of being sloppy, lazy, and incompetent. In fact, you're just less neat. You:

B1. Tell her she's narrow-minded and her overorganization takes up so much time it is slowing down the work. She'd better get used to some different ways? _____

B2. Tell her performance counts, not neatness, and point to your record. _____

B3. Ignore it. Time will show her what's happening. _____

5. Your new superior just gave you a performance rating of average in production. You think you deserve better on that item. You:

A1. Tell her you deserve "excellent" and that other superiors would agree?

A2. Start talking about the ratings you agree with and then present a strong case for a better rating in production? _____

She gets angry about the disagreement and tells you to "Sign—or else!" You:

B1. Challenge her? Tell her you'll sign, but only under protest and put that right next to your signature? _____

B2. Say, "Or else what? Let's try to settle this more calmly!" _____

B3. Leave. Let her calm down and bring it up later? _____

Overview

Perhaps your answers indicate the style you prefer to use most often. Take a look at the number of times you checked each kind of response. How often did you check:

A1. _____   B1. _____   B3. _____

A2. _____   B2. _____

Understanding the Negotiating Style Inventory

How do you begin negotiations?   The questions marked A present some ideas of how you might begin a negotiation. If you picked A1 three or more times, you probably start out gently and build to a stronger case as the negotiation continues. Checking A2 most of the time means you start strong and give in as necessary. Think about it: does that seem to describe your style? Or do you use different approaches with different people and situations?

How do you react?   The questions marked B indicate how you might react to a show of force. In general, 1s are a counterattack that let the other person know you can't be "pushed around": you'll push back! The 2s stop the attack and provide a form of self-defense. The 3s ignore the outburst of the other person. What tactic did you choose most of the time? Counterattack? Self-defense? Pacifist (give in, peacemaker)? Or did your style change with the situation and your assumptions about the people involved and their possible response to your style (situational)? What kind of style do you seem to have right now?

Beginnings:

- Gentle start
- Strong start
- Situational

Style when attacked:

- Counterattack
- Self-defense
- Pacifist
- Situational

Adjusting Your Style

Your negotiating style reflects the way you approach the give and take of discussions over career and work issues. Styles can adjust to fit the personalities involved and the importance of a problem. You might use a different approach to discuss an idea with a shy co-worker from the one you would use to present an emergency request to a tough superior. Negotiating style —the way you present your concerns and ideas—often determines how attractive you or your ideas seem to others.

Your negotiating style should fit the situation

In the final analysis, good negotiations need from you all of these:

- Spirit of cooperation
- Time to think over the concerns of all involved
- Knowledge of what you want and can offer in return
- Information about the other's concerns
- Willingness to find a way of involving give and take.

ACTION CHECKLIST FOR CHAPTER 15

Checklist	*My Ideas and Action Steps*	*Date*
√ Negotiation reflects your values and career style.		
√ Skill in negotiation requires a willingness to exchange and the ability to influence others.		
√ Influencing others is based on trust generated by past and present behavior. What you do now and the appropriateness of your behavior affects future negotiations.		
√ Your negotiating style includes your initial orientation as well as your approach when your position is challenged by others.		
√ Negotiations with others require cooperation, time, information about what you and others want and can exchange, and a willingness to give and take.		

16

Exchanging—A Key to Good Negotiations

Nice guys just don't make it where I work. I've had the same job for four years straight. It's getting so I day-dream just to get through the day. Maybe I should write down the daydreams. It'd be less boring than doing what I'm doing! Maybe I should be more pushy, like Jennifer, but I don't know how. Besides, it's not my style. I want a change. How come the managers never notice us nice types who do our jobs, keep our mouths shut, and don't make all those big waves they're afraid of? What do I do to get something differ-ent going?

BARBARA

I need help—another worker on the line, Al, is the boss and he knows it. So does everyone else. But every-one supervising high-priority batch jobs needs help. That's my biggest problem. Even the marketing de-partment agrees that demand for service is increasing. For sure, my work and my workers are suffering. But it's going to upset the apple cart if Al gives me more help instead of all the others who say they need it, too—and it's expensive. I know all this. And besides, what if our sales projections are wrong? It's all one big hassle for Al, and none of the solutions are easy. But that's what he's paid for—to consider and decide and manage. My job right now is to present my problem before it gets bigger and ruins his job. And I say we'd better add on people. How can I convince him of that?

MICHELLE

We closed the last chapter emphasizing that good negotiations need give and take—and, perhaps most of all, a spirit of cooperation. But cooperation,

Three kinds of exchanges

exchanging help in work situations, isn't always simple to come by—no matter how willing you are. Often there are people, career moves, work activities, and important career goals at stake. Let's look at what exchanging *help* can mean in three different ways:

1. When it is *routine* and simple

2. When it is *not routine* and needs some thought

3. When exchanging requires *working it out*

EXCHANGING HELP: THE ROUTINE APPROACH

Exchanging help provides us with whatever we need for our work while giving others something of equal value in return. Sometimes the exchanges are simple and obvious even when the "agreement" isn't discussed, such as:

- Lunches where it is expected that advice or information will be fully shared

- Work trade-offs where, with permission, people master different procedures and equipment

- "Borrowing" in situations when the favor given is returned with a sign of special gratitude

Routine sharing is common and well understood

Lots of routine sharing occurs among work associates in any kind of organization—a hospital, a law firm, an insurance company, or a school system. What is given by one person and what is expected in return are usually well understood by everyone involved. Exchanges meet the emergencies of the day and often help prepare others for new or different work activities. The exchange, the "something for something," is also taken for granted. However, the exchange of help isn't always immediate and one may store obligations for future redemption, keeping the personal ledgers balanced out over the weeks and months ahead—even years.

Of course, exchanges often include items that aren't covered by the general rules of give and take. Perhaps you want to develop a specific skill or working arrangement. Or maybe you're at a new career stage and want some informal advice from an old timer. In some exchanges, one party's payoff may be simply a sense of satisfaction in helping another.

Always consider the other person's point of view

Start with the realization that your career needs often require assistance; getting that help depends on others. Correspondingly, the question exists, "How can I help them?" Look at it from their point of view as well as your own; and since you've done some real self-searching by now, you should have genuine insight into that important area labeled "How others see me." Give it careful thought as you consider the following sketch and the examples that follow.

THE GIVE-AND-TAKE MODEL OF EXCHANGE
RELATIONSHIPS AT WORK

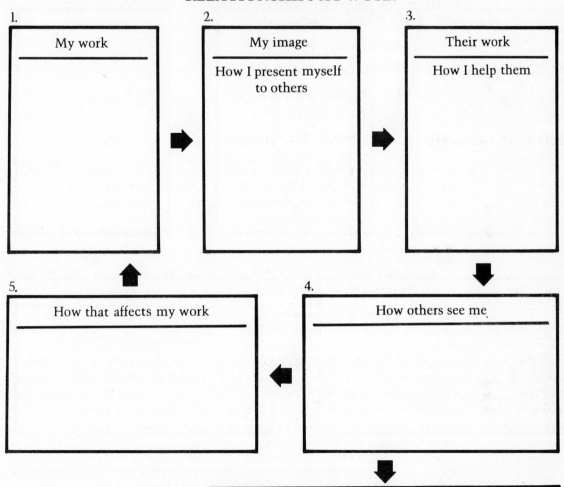

1.
My work

2.
My image

How I present myself
to others

3.
Their work

How I help them

5.
How that affects my work

4.
How others see me

Helping? Cooperative? Neutral? Unthinking? Competitive?

An Example of the Routine Approach: Barb

Let's consider the problem of Barbara, who likes to be called "Barb." You met her at the beginning of the chapter. Barbara wanted a job change, but she wasn't sure how to go about it. She certainly knew her request wouldn't get an automatic seal of approval, so she started to think about the relationship she and her supervisor, Al, had developed over the years. Using the Give-and-Take Model, Barb spelled it all out for herself.

The routine approach: Barb's example

Pretty obvious. From Al's point of view, Barb was just one of the girls. Capable, of course, but no real reason to notice her—or treat her differently

BARB'S GIVE-AND-TAKE MODEL

1

My work
_____

Fairly routine — I need a change.

2

My image:
_____

How I present myself
to others

not much contact — I avoid him and am pretty quiet when I do see him. I keep my place

3

Their work:
_____

How I help them

Do my job!

5

How that affects my work
_____

No changes — I fit into the woodwork —

4

How others see me
_____

Probably as a "typical" female

Neutral —!

Helping? Cooperative? Neutral? Unthinking? Competitive?

*Barb's
strategies:
Plans A, B,
and C*

from the others. Besides, what had she done to deserve any special treatment? With that insight, Barb worked out some strategies:

Plan A: Pout. Look miserable. Be unhappy until he notices it, and then make some plans for change. Tears would help.
Plan B: Be threatening. Make a scene. Yell. Demand some changes or else.

But neither of these plans was her style and she knew it. Barb valued peace, harmony, and responsibility. And these values had formed her style. Furthermore, even if she could pull it off, she didn't want the reputation that would come with plan A or B.

"Self," she said, "no one sees you as a winner. In fact, no one sees you!"
Time for a new plan.

Plan C:

1. Present an image that fits my career plans: capable, cooperative. Look for more challenging tasks.

2. Keep an eye open for ways my work can help meet the concerns of my superiors.

3. Keep an eye on future events.

A Model for "Exchanging Help: Routine"

Barb went ahead with Plan C. She laid a foundation for her career plans, earning herself a reputation both as a late bloomer and a cooperative and concerned worker. When an opportunity for a different position became available, she was able to recognize the quid pro quo (trade-offs) that matched her to the newer shift in work activities. It wasn't just that she *wanted* to work on the new line. She could do the job her superiors wanted done—and by now they could see that, too. She thought of the exchange of career concerns—her, Al's, her organization's—and wrote those out, too. As with the THINK Model, we've included a blank of this Exchanging Help Model for you, along with Barb's completed work.

An exchange model that works

Laying the foundation and speaking to the obvious concerns of all involved paid off for Barb in more than just job variety. The office crew, including Beth and Peggy, recognized the fairness of the job change. Barb, Al, and Peggy each had a good understanding of the kinds of performance and skills needed for their part of the production. Providing whatever help was needed to get the job done became a routine part of the working day.

How the exchange paid off

EXCHANGING HELP: NOT SO ROUTINE

Sometimes exchanges aren't routine or evenhanded. You want the difficult, and the quid pro quo doesn't look too promising. What, you wonder, would persuade this person, perhaps a stranger, to bring her/his help, advice, or influence to solve your current problem? "Not so routine" exchanges often take place when we:

Kinds of exchanges; not so routine

- need help

- from someone who doesn't need to help

- and doesn't need our help in return

- but we can't do without it

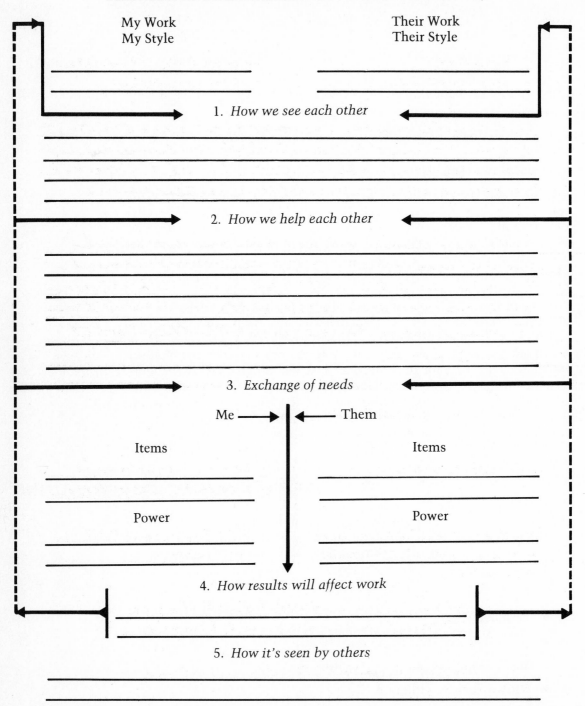

THE MODEL FOR EXCHANGING HELP: ROUTINE

My Work
My Style

Their Work
Their Style

1. *How we see each other*

2. *How we help each other*

3. *Exchange of needs*

Me → ← Them

Items

Power

Items

Power

4. *How results will affect work*

5. *How it's seen by others*

BARB'S MODEL FOR EXCHANGING HELP: ROUTINE

My Work
My Style

Their Work
Their Style

"Helpful"
"Productive"

"Responsible" "Productive"
"Tough guy"

1. *How we see each other*

I see Al as someone out to get ahead but not at our expense. He wants high volume and is usually fair about getting it. Al sees me as a cooperative person who can offer practical advice.

2. *How we help each other*

Al is helping me see how our work and schedules fit into all the other work around here. I help Al but making sure his concerns get a fair hearing with the crew and I try to make sure he hears what they want him to hear.

3. *Exchange of needs*

Me ⟶   ⟵ Them

Items	Items
Different work	Needs someone to handle the new line.
Power	**Power**
My bills and style fit in! I can give him the volume he wants.	Al names that person.

4. *How results will affect work*

Should help us both and not change too much; more work with Peggy.

5. *How it's seen by others*

Fair; helpful to all involved

Of course, there are lots of people who offer a helping hand whenever needed and often free of charge, too. The growing skills of others may advance their own careers, boost morale around the work place, or make them feel better about themselves. But their cooperative reputation and goodwill are well known and usually returned in routine fashion.

Jennifer's problem

The difficult problems take a little more time and thought. Jennifer (who works in the same organization as Barb) found that out after she "earned" her new position with tears and threats. Now she's wailing:

> I just can't handle it. It's too much too soon. I don't know how to get supplies, organize the work, run the equipment, or even make out the work orders. And Al can only do so much. Ted put me in here, and he's really in charge of this operation. But every time Ted straightens out a problem of mine, he dumps more work on me. Right now, he wants me to supervise a new worker who seems to have two left hands and is absolutely lazy. "Jennifer, you owe me one," he says. Sure, I owe him; but I also owe that new kid *and* myself a better deal. So how do I convince Ted? How do I get out of this mess? What I need is help!

Jennifer tries exchanging

Al wasn't free to help and Ted asked too much in return. But Jennifer discovered that some of the other workers knew the routine reasonably well. The secretary started her off. "Ask Beth and Joe," she suggested. A few luncheon sessions convinced Jennifer that Beth knew the work, but little else. Beth was fresh from school and hadn't found her niche; she needed a sounding board for her career plans and work ideas. Because Jennifer had learned to think about things in terms of exchange, she realized she and Beth could easily assist each other in terms of career help. It wasn't discussed, but lunches and some early morning meetings soon found them both talking about ways to improve their work. The advice they exchanged often extended to tips on hobbies and friends. In fact, they soon became friends and continued to meet long after immediate work problems were resolved.

But that still left Jennifer with her problems—and Ted's: not enough time, space, money, and people. In this kind of situation, negotiating and exchanging requires more thought and planning. That's when "not so routine" negotiations become a problem in "working it out."

EXCHANGING HELP: WORKING IT OUT

Why solutions can be difficult

Even when concerns are shared and problems clearly identified, solutions can be difficult. Questions of "Can I trust the other guy?" "How will the idea affect my work?" and "Is it fair?" are often the "hidden agenda" that guide a discussion. Many of our problems require solutions that are costly, in resources of time, money, rearrangement of work procedures, or emotional investments. Sometimes reputations or other people's egos get involved.

For example, take Michelle's "simple" request for another worker in her line—her fervent plea at the beginning of this chapter. Michelle supervised two technicians, but she was still swamped with work.

A Model for "Exchanging Help: Working It Out"

The following model shows some ways to consider all the issues and assumptions and strategies of more difficult exchanges. Use the blank model when you need it, and check Michelle's for good tips.

A model for working it out

Michelle thought her problem through—all the spoken concerns and hidden agendas. She then gave a lot of thought to her "bottom line—not negotiable" item, as well as to what *was* negotiable. On her part, she needed help, but she was willing to settle for a part-time worker or any other reasonable solution that anyone could come up with. She wasn't sure, though, that saying so was a good way to begin. By the time she thought about it carefully, she had a lot of ideas. Her working model, filled out, looked like this:

With facts, figures, and lots of discussion—and certainly using her own style—Michelle laid a foundation of trust and spoke to shared concerns about the future. Her exchange worked; the negotiations paid off. Michelle was told that production "better go up" and was given some part-time help. Nobody protested too much. There were some good-natured complaints about "What's *she* got? There must be a magic way to reach the boss." But after all the griping, the employees figured Michelle's "luck" was a victory because it became one basis for the firm's new hiring plans.

How an exchange succeeded

That's the secret of good exchanges and negotiations: solving issues in ways that are appropriate and fair for everyone. It doesn't always work. But the routine exchanges, those that are "not so routine," and those that take a lot of effort to "work it out" can help solve big and small career matters.

The secret: fair for everyone

Whenever you're ready to think about a negotiation or exchange, start using the models we've placed in this chapter for you. You'll find they can help you see all of the different concerns that are factors in negotiations, just as they did for Barb and Michelle. And if your problem isn't "how to" but "who," we know that people can create new opportunities in a career; and they can create problems, too. That's the topic of the next chapter.

THE MODEL FOR EXCHANGING HELP: WORKING IT OUT

My Work
My Style

Their Work
Their Style

_____   _____
_____   _____

1. *How we see and help each other*

_____
_____
_____
_____

2. *Issues/concerns*

Me   Them

Items:_____   Items:_____
_____   _____
_____   _____
Power:_____   Power:_____
_____   _____

3. *Assumptions*

My negotiable   Their negotiable

Items:_____   Items:_____
_____   _____
Bottom line:_____   Bottom line:_____
_____   _____

4. *How to begin and end*

_____
_____
_____
_____

5. *How results will affect work, how it will be seen*

_____
_____

MICHELLE'S NEGOTIATING MODEL—EXCHANGING
HELP: NOT SO ROUTINE

My Work - *Michelle*　　　　　　　　Their Work - *Mr. Hayes*
My Style　　　　　　　　　　　　　　Their Style

Active, problem　　　　　　　　Thoughtful,
solving, impatient　　　　　　　reflective

1. *How we see and help each other*

I see him as taking no chances but fair.
He probably sees me as young, impatient,
and concerned. My work is important for
the firm.

2. *Issues/concerns*

Me	Them
Items:	Items: 1) Dollars
1) new worker	2) others who need help
2) concerns about future	3) saving face 4) productivity
Power: The organization needs	Power: He calls the shots and
higher volume & he knows	he's usually right.
my reputation.	

3. *Assumptions*

My negotiable	Their negotiable
Items: 1) Kind of worker	Items: Dollars,
2) More volume.	hiring plans.
Bottom line: Help for the future	Bottom line: Morale of the others
and proof I will have it	and reputation for planning

4. *How to begin and end*

Present the problem. Demonstrate a strong need.
Have several meetings so he can think over the
problem. Provide a rationale for new
hiring plan.

5. *How results will affect work, how it will be seen*

Another worker will definitely help my work
and the work of those under me. I need to make
sure the other supervisors see its fair and
will help overall production.

ACTION CHECKLIST FOR CHAPTER 16

Checklist	*My Ideas and Action Steps*	*Date*
√ Exchanges provide you and others with opportunities for sharing information, advice, and resources.		
√ Progress in a career requires the cooperation and assistance of others.		
√ How you present yourself to others and how they see you provide a basis for the "give and take" of exchange relationships.		
√ Understanding the concerns of others, their assumptions, and the ways in which different results will be seen by others are important for effective negotiations.		

17

Reaching Out to Others

The courage to take new steps allows us to let go of each stage [of life] . . . and to find the fresh responses that will release the richness of the next. The power to animate life's seasons is a power that resides within us.

GAIL SHEEHY, *PASSAGES*

Work is a part of that passage through life, a part of experiencing, doing, and relating that expresses ourselves to others, conveys and uses our skills, and mirrors back some satisfaction, rewards, and a sense of self. Our work does all of that all of the time. But at times, we want to find ways to redirect that experience, to reach within and without for more satisfying ways of working and relating to others.

Finding these ways is what this chapter is about. We want you to understand how your career style can be used to establish good working relationships with others, creating those relationships as you reach out takes thought, planning, and effort.

You can improve relationships using your style

While these materials help guide you through various work encounters, the basic techniques apply also to scenarios acted out in personal lives. A thoughtful consideration of the human side of work can help you better understand yourself, your reactions to the world of people around you, and the ways you can create "good" working relationships.

Careers and people blossom in a nourishing environment rich with people who provide ideas, opportunities, and encouragement. But careers can also flourish and grow strong in relatively barren environments that test determination and skill. For most, daily work provides contact with a variety of equally helpful or helpless, cooperative or uncooperative folks—all of whom see a job from slightly different perspectives.

Working smoothly with these differing personalities sometimes transforms simple jobs into marathon events affecting health, careers, and personal decisions. Finding new ways of presenting yourself, working well with others, and straightening out any tangles in the work place jungle are priori-

Working well with others has payoffs

183

ties that can provide immediate payoffs. They also strengthen personal skills and thus result in possible career payoffs.

CAREER STYLES AND WORKING RELATIONSHIPS

Many different kinds of people

People pop in and out of your work reality so often that it is easy to forget the human dramas surrounding the work event. More often than you realize, you are engaged in reassuring those who depend on your skills, cooling down the temperamental and sensitive, holding hands with newcomers fearful of their new responsibilities, and congratulating people for jobs well done. In truth, most of us also seek shoulders to cry on. The very fact that people are human means they (may) misunderstand each other or come through to meet each other's needs in kind, thoughtful ways.

Hothouse or greenhouse?

The office landscape, then, is dotted with different kinds of people, including you, who bring both an ideal, picture-perfect self as well as the real self to the work place each day. The actions and reactions of people to each other can create a *hothouse* that stifles creativity and learning or a *greenhouse* that promotes productivity, keeps people healthy and active, and helps them to grow and be more of what they want to be.

How do you and others see each other? How do you bridge any gaps in career styles and career goals to create a good working relationship? Let's look at how this can be done:

- The first time around

- The second, third—the one more time around

- The times when the mischief makers and troublemakers are met along the way

RELATING TO OTHERS: THE FIRST TIME AROUND

How people see each other matters

Working well with others *the first time around* depends a lot on how people see each other and how they express a concern for each other's careers in helpful and appropriate ways. Often, people in a particular work place already know a bit about each other, either via the grapevine or via an already emerging sound work relationship. Even more often, we need to create bridges between ourselves and others in order to strengthen that mutual knowledge and further the work relationship.

A FOCUS Model

Just focus your career compass to the opportunities, the responsibilities, at hand. Our FOCUS Model, which you can use for yourself when you need it, works something like this:

THE FOCUS MODEL

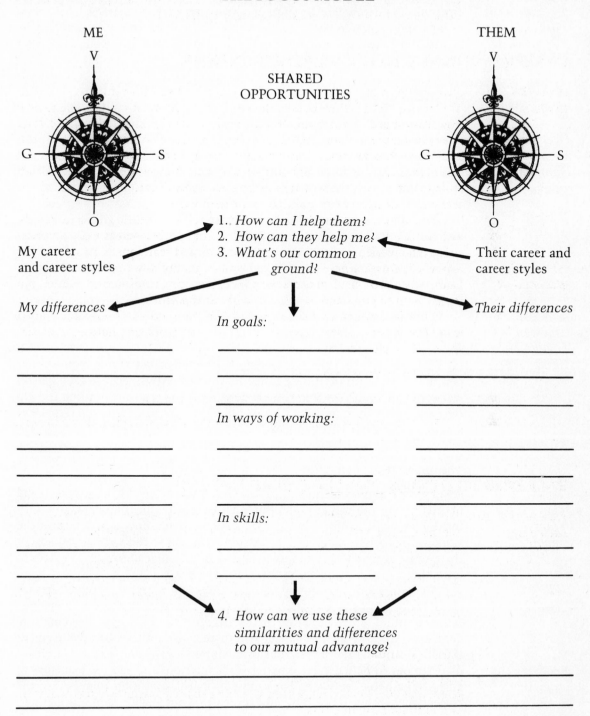

ME

THEM

SHARED
OPPORTUNITIES

1. *How can I help them?*
2. *How can they help me?*
3. *What's our common
    ground?*

My career
and career styles

Their career and
career styles

My differences

Their differences

In goals:

_____
_____
_____

In ways of working:

_____
_____
_____

In skills:

_____
_____

4. *How can we use these
    similarities and differences
    to our mutual advantage?*

_____
_____

*Your career
compass used
to focus*

Goals, values, style, and skills brought to the work place can make a big difference in how people see their opportunities to work with each other and in how they react to those opportunities. Consider how two individuals, Laurie and John, see and react to each other in the filled-out form that follows.

How Focusing Works

*Focusing
surfaces
common
ground*

How Laurie and John react to each other and what they learn from each other depend on their willingness to see a common ground and relate to each other in appropriate ways. At first they reacted with mutual dismay at the idea of working together. But they worked out some simple exchanges that provided each with the work she or he preferred and the opportunities to use each person's own work methods on the individual parts: they agreed, for instance, that Laurie would make any presentations, while giving full credit to John for his effort and ideas. And they tried to support each other by giving encouragement and praise when each came through to create a better report, even if each one thought the other's methods were a little unusual.

*Laurie and
John were
supportive*

Laurie seemed to be always on the phone, checking information, while John buried himself in reports. Each wondered if the other's way would work. It worked well. Over time, Laurie learned to be more orderly, and John learned to handle other people a little better; yet each retained her/his essential style.

Focusing on the career responsibilities and career styles of the other person as well as on their own concerns worked. Why? Because each person was concerned with getting the job done well and was also willing to help the other contribute in ways that would be satisfying and productive. Here are some hints that will help you.

The Importance of Empathy

*Good
relationships
require
empathy*

Good working relationships imply an ability to accept the other person and her/his career and career style. But each person requires empathy—a willingness to walk in the other person's shoes to see how she/he views the work world; a willingness to understand and share their concerns, accept their skills and values, and create opportunities that allow each person to bring their concerns and strengths to the work you share.

*Reaching out
strengthens
work*

We do this almost automatically at times when we parcel out chores for community organizations when everyone is expected to share responsibilities, or at times when we sympathize with those having a hard day. On these occasions, we take all the concerns into account and create ways to meet those concerns while turning out the required work. The very fact that we do reach out to help creates a better work relationship, and the exchange of help strengthens the work. For example, Laurie and John understand and respect each other more now and often seek out advice from each other.

LAURIE AND JOHN'S FOCUS MODEL

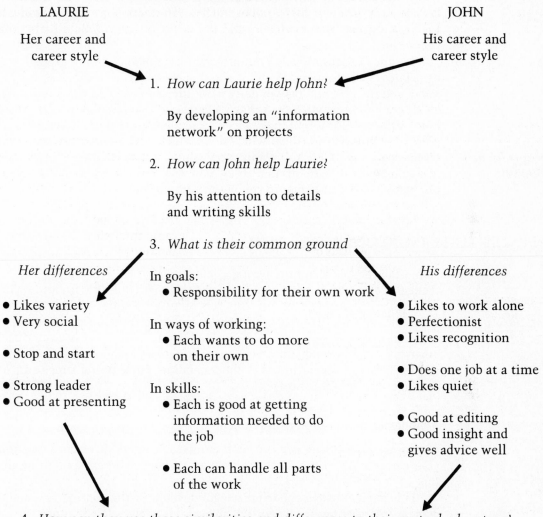

LAURIE

Her career and
career style

JOHN

His career and
career style

1. *How can Laurie help John?*

By developing an "information
network" on projects

2. *How can John help Laurie?*

By his attention to details
and writing skills

3. *What is their common ground*

Her differences

In goals:
- Responsibility for their own work

His differences

- Likes variety
- Very social

In ways of working:
- Each wants to do more
  on their own

- Likes to work alone
- Perfectionist
- Likes recognition

- Stop and start

- Strong leader
- Good at presenting

In skills:
- Each is good at getting
  information needed to do
  the job

- Does one job at a time
- Likes quiet

- Good at editing
- Good insight and
  gives advice well

- Each can handle all parts
  of the work

4. *How can they use these similarities and differences to their mutual advantage?*

- Laurie sees John as a strong individualist who would probably rather not work
  with her and doesn't seem to approve of her free-flowing work style.

- John sees Laurie as a disorganized "social butterfly" who doesn't seem to care
  about his needs for establishing procedures, ordering the work, and covering all
  the details.

- If they can work together, each has skills that would add to the work and help
  the other learn new ways of working on different parts of a project.

Their careers are enhanced by their ability to work with each other. In fact, many organizations fit the idea and the practice of empathy into the working day and encourage their staff to reach out to customers and others so that the organization, the employee, and the customer can all be a little more successful.

Work requires cooperation: your role

Try the FOCUS Model. Your ability to establish common ground with associates is what much of work is about. This means sharing ideas, cooperation, and the give and take of daily work life. You can't be expected to like all those you work with or to have a good social relationship with everybody, although this might make work more pleasant. Yet the nature of work propels us into relationships with others which require cooperation if your objectives, as well as the organization's, are to be accomplished. If others don't understand these ground rules, you may have to assume the role of teacher or peacemaker just to get on with responsibilities.

PERSON-TO-PERSON: ONE MORE TIME

When relationships get off to a bad start

Sometimes people bring the wrong assumptions to the work place, express themselves poorly, or have some selfish goals that conflict with job responsibilities you share. The relationship gets off to a bad start. Tension builds to its predictable result—strain, isolation, lower performance, and unhappiness that makes the experience of working together, even being around each other, an uncomfortable one. Yet the work plan and your own feelings may call for greater cooperation and understanding. Such trying times call for patience and "building bridges."

A Model for Person-to-Person Problems

The bridge symbolizes any common ground you share. It reaches out from your career style to the career and career style of another, something like this:

Debbie's problems on her first job

This model creates opportunities for developing the common ground to pass on information or recognition that builds bridges to the other person. You can use the Person-to-Person Model when you need it, and the example of Debbie and her boss should prove helpful when you come to your own bridge building.

Debbie was a high school graduate who went on to take some additional training in data processing. As the only female and only black in advanced math courses and in computer programming courses, she felt as if she were constantly on stage. In fact, some males in the class even sabotaged her computer runs and let her know more than once that women just weren't logical enough for the field.

Debbie's problems didn't stop when her first job came along. An assistant to the top senior systems analyst, she heard lots of rumors she was

THE PERSON-TO-PERSON MODEL: "ONE MORE TIME"

ME   OTHERS

1. *Establishing our common ground—*
   things to build on

	Work-related	Social
Goals		
Skills		
Values		
Opportunities		

Career and career style

2a. *Assumptions about others*   2b. *What I believe to be their*
                                           assumptions about me

_____   _____

_____   _____

3. *Points of tension, conflict*

_____

_____

_____

4. *Areas of common ground—bridges*

_____

_____

_____

5. *How to work it out*

_____

_____

_____

given the job to be the token black and token female. The charge seemed to her as if it might be true. Her work assignments were not at all challenging and carried no responsibility. Worse, her boss kept referring to her race and sex. Comments like "Our talented young *woman* programmer" or "Debbie really understands the black employee" sounded like a way to keep her in her place and isolate her from "the boys" and their more challenging and lucrative accounts. With some other guys commenting on how she added a "touch of black beauty" to the office, Debbie started thinking about quitting the job and maybe the field. Finally, the whole thing got to be too much, and she told her boss a thing or two about what was happening and what she thought of his part in it all.

Her boss meant to be accepting

Off to a bad start before the work relationship had hardly begun! *Naturally*, they apologized; and *naturally*, they tried again; and *naturally*, they each felt miserable. In fact, Debbie's boss thought he was giving her time to settle in, trying to show he accepted and valued her as an individual rather than treating her as one of the boys. That was his intention. But he wished he had made those career plans of "settle in, then stretch" a little clearer to Debbie. Also, he wished he had talked to her openly instead of having to straighten her out after their heated discussion. Now that the relationship was strained, he tried to speak to her real concerns and build on a common ground. His Person-to-Person Model looked like the figure opposite.

They found shared concerns

Debbie responded to that shared concern. Within time, a good working relationship was established and both career styles became acceptable to each of them. Patience, planning, and building a common ground don't always advance careers; skills and performance advance a career fastest. But a common ground does create the environment in which skills can be used, shared, and exchanged to produce the better work and generate more opportunities.

"Seeing" Others

Past experience can shape opinions

As the scenario illustrated, some problems of understanding, of "seeing" others, may come with each shift of job responsibilities or change in work personnel. Many times past experiences encourage people to act on appearances and not see the person behind the clothes, face, figure, or title. The people involved, like Debbie, may shape a first meeting, or a second or third, with assumptions from the past. The issue really goes beyond the chauvinistic remark that's heard (but may not be meant) or the implications of that remark when the time comes for work. The point is: *Learn to see and respond to the person.* The empathy you develop allows you to understand other people, their needs, and their problems so that you can extend yourself for the sake of your career and theirs and the work environment you share.

The stability of work relationships generates a bond among you, your co-workers, and your shared work responsibilities. Sometimes, however, those bonds never have a chance to develop. Doors are closed because people

DEBBIE'S BOSS'S PERSON-TO-PERSON MODEL WITH HER: "ONE MORE TIME"

ME   DEBBIE

1. *Establishing our common ground—things to build on*

	Work-related	Social
Career and career style	Debbie and I both enjoy our work-the challenges, the reports—and we both want to get ahead and be cooperative. In addition, we both like settling in on one account at a time.	I'm not sure we have any social interests in common.

2a. *Assumptions about her*

She wants to stay and succeed and wants more challenging work.

2b. *What I believe to be her assumptions about me*

She thinks I am the male chauvinist pig of the year.

3. *Points of tension, conflict*

My pointing out her sex and race when I talk about her work.

4. *Areas of common ground—bridges*

Our respect for each other's goals and abilities. Accounts that are challenging. Ways we prefer to work.

5. *How to work it out*

- Don't say anything that makes her think I only see her as a black female with limited abilities for that reason.

- Give her opportunities to work on more of the kinds of accounts that she enjoys.

- Praise her abilities and treat her with respect, especially around the rest of the staff. Show them she is a valuable addition.

"Seeing" others: Often, the worker who wants more respect may need to look no further than the mirror.

fail to speak up when they really want to express a preference or an opinion or because they pretend to be what they are not. It is not surprising to find that people are treated consistently with the image they convey through their conversations, dress, ways of working, or ways of talking about their work. Often, the worker who wants more respect may need to look no further than the mirror when she shows up in jeans, tight sweaters, unkempt hair, and untidy look. So, too, the worker who never expresses a

We may convey a misleading image

preference or never demonstrates a concern for others may wonder why she feels a little left out. Bridges are easier to build when your ways of presenting yourself to others genuinely reflect your own career style and build from that style to an acceptance of the preferences of others.

PEOPLE PROBLEMS: REACHING OUT

People problems are really outreach problems. You need, for the sake of your own feelings and responsibilities, to stop the fun and games and get on to the responsibilities at hand. It's your problem when you have a responsibility for the work of a mischief maker or when your feelings and reactions reach the breaking point. Most of the games used by mischief makers have some common elements:

The games of mischief makers

- People get you upset

- On a regular basis

- To get out of work, create a stir, or sometimes because they enjoy your frustration

And sometimes they do it for all three reasons.
Here are some examples, some snapshot looks at mischief makers.

How they work: two examples

Snapshot: Every time the young supervisor approached the established and almost retired "general" of the office with a high-priority but low-level job, she was reduced to tears by his comments. His caustic comments had a grain of truth in them as he pointed out her inability to plan, her lack of understanding about the job, or her inability to recognize how busy the general was already. As a result, the general never did do such high-priority work; and it didn't help the office morale or get out the rush orders.

Snapshot: The nurse's aide, overworked and underpaid, found herself assigned to too many patients; and her resentment was fed by streams of seeming ingratitude. No recognition, bonuses, or thanks marked the path of her career effort. Her anger over her own helplessness and the way she was treated bubbled over every time Sam delivered the mail to her. "I wish I had all the time you had just to sort the mail," he quipped. Or, "Guess your work isn't very important if you're stuck with this." When she tried to ignore him, he said, "Oh, you do have things to do once in a while. Glad to hear you're working for a change!" She exploded, and he seemed to enjoy it.

The snapshots portray a reality that repeats itself routinely. Doors are closed over and over, almost battered down with the extra force of frustration and anger. Usually that kind of anger spills over to work and causes a lot of unnecessary wear and tear on emotions.

Ways to Cope with People Problems

People problems take their toll on all involved. They usually leave a few scars or bruises if they are damaging enough. But there are two good ways to reach out more carefully—both to stop the bruising and to meet any responsibilities you may feel for the real concerns of work or people:

1. Stop the games

2. Move the relationship forward

Breaking up the games

How? Stopping a people problem (breaking up the game) means trying something different—like ignoring what someone else says or does. Or it may mean acting in a different way—doing the unexpected. It definitely means trying not to give the usual responses that keep the game going. If you have a people problem, do you usually react in either of these ways?

Check your response to people problems

- Do nothing because you're having trouble finding solutions, then feel occasionally frustrated—and often have outbursts of temper or tears?

- Try to shape up everyone by venting lots of criticisms and demands? Do you find out later you're making some people miserable and didn't even know it?

Neither of these responses is useful or appropriate as a routine way of working out problems. If you answered yes to either or both, do some thinking. Are you being non-assertive or overly aggressive? Keep in touch with your own feelings. You can sense if you should have taken the initiative and didn't, or if you were too aggressive and overreacted to a problem. Try using the Person-to-Person Model. Perhaps some of the ideas below will also help.

GETTING THROUGH TO OTHERS: MORE WAYS TO COPE

Don't assign fault

Of course, everyone has people-to-people problems. But you can make these problems easier to handle if you don't think of them as being *their* fault or *your* fault. Your problems and the way you handle them are facts of life. Some people may provoke you to anger without realizing it. Just like bored children, they get excitement by stirring up trouble. Here's one way to solve that people problem. Ask yourself:

Ask good questions

- *What happened?* What did you do? What did they do?

- *What happened as a result?*

- *What could you do that would stop your problem?* Would ignoring their behavior or changing your reaction help?

If your first plan doesn't work, try another. See how you feel about that particular problem. Maybe you'd rather not change it right now. Maybe solving the problem would lead to more problems than finding a way to live with it. The THINK Model helps you think through whatever is holding you back. Use it. But do make a decision about what, if anything, you want to do about your people problem. Here are two helpful guidelines:

Use these guidelines

1. *Remember that people are only human.* Think about the fact that mistakes happen. Don't be afraid to admit your mistakes, and don't make it too hard for others to admit theirs. Try not to place blame on yourself or others for each problem.

2. *Let others solve their own problems.* When mistakes occur, ask the other person involved to help you look at the facts and find out what she/he thinks can be done to solve the problem. Then ask how you can help. Don't solve the problem for them and don't lose your temper.

If you are afraid to handle the problem, or if you're either non-assertive or overly aggressive and fear you're not reaching others effectively, try our "Getting Through to Others" exercise. It helps to meet your people problem in realistic ways and helps you to reach out more effectively to the other person.

Try a realistic exercise

"GETTING THROUGH TO OTHERS"

1. Name one specific instance where people seem to be "walking all over you." What can you do that seems reasonable and will work? _____

_____

2. What stops you from doing what is reasonable? What are you afraid of?_____

_____

What is the worst thing that could happen to you as a result of trying a different approach?__

_____

Is that likely to happen? Is it so terrible? _____ yes _____ no. If it's terrible, can you think of something else that will work? _____

_____

If it's not so bad . . .

3. *Try it!* If you are not sure about how to act, rehearse it beforehand with someone else, or by yourself, or talk over your plan with a friend.

4. After you've tried it, see how you feel about it. Evaluate how you handled that situation and learned from it. If your first attempt didn't work, why? Try again.

And use your compass

Then what? React to the people you've found. Build a bridge. Speak to their real concerns. Establish a better working relationship. Let that part of your career compass marked "Style and Skills" and a genuine concern for yourself and others act as your strong guide as you reach out to others. You won't flounder.

ACTION CHECKLIST FOR CHAPTER 17

Checklist	*My Ideas and Action Steps*	*Date*
√ Good working relationships require a desire on your part to reach out to the concerns of others.		
√ Finding a "common ground" helps you build a bridge from your career and preferences to the concerns of others.		
√ Differences with others are often based on faulty assumptions and need empathy, patience, and a thoughtful concern to work out problems.		
√ Solving "people problems" may require a change of attitude or behavior on your part. Learn to modify behavior that you find overly aggressive or unassertive on your part.		
√ Be realistic in meeting your concern for other people and the needs of the job at hand.		

PROFILES FOR PART THREE

Alice Rossi, Florence Berg, Marian Chandler

Alice Rossi—The Story

Last night, Alice Rossi received the annual achievement award from the local chapter of the American Institute of Architects. The award was given for her interior designs in a new commercial building. She was still glowing this morning when Duncan White, managing partner of the firm, dropped by her office.

"Congratulations, Alice. They had an article in this morning's paper about your award—thought you'd like a copy."

"Thanks, Duncan. Frankly, my head is still spinning, and not just from the excitement either—there were an awful lot of toasts! Somehow, it seems a little unreal. Ten years ago, when I started with this firm, I really hoped for this kind of recognition. Five years ago, I never thought it could happen—things were so mixed up here that I didn't think anything could be salvaged."

"Yes, I know, Alice. Don't forget you were working for me at the time. You sure had a lot of ideas about wanting to 'express' yourself —the 'artistic' you."

"I know, Duncan. The funny thing is that my desire to create hasn't changed, but I've learned a lot about how one has to be 'creative.' We had that small O'Brien Electric project—showroom, executive offices—not really much to it; but I thought that I would really make something out of it despite the size."

"Yes, Tom O'Brien, Sr., is probably still in a state of shock. It wasn't so bad when you told him about the 'design, balance, and coordination' to rule out some of his ideas; but when you practically said he couldn't have the layout he sketched because it lacked 'integrity'—I thought it was all over. The man turned different colors. So did I! I wasn't only worried about losing his account, but O'Brien was an old pal of a lot of our other clients. It could have been really rough."

"I remember. Your suggestion that we talk it over came just in time. When we got back to the office and sorted things out, I realized that I had to change a good deal. Somehow, what I wanted to do, to create, was more important to me than what the client wanted for *his* office. That was immature, and I finally saw it."

Questions for You

1. What was the nature of the goal conflict described in this case? What were Alice's goals and those of the organization?

2. To what extent did Alice's personal goals lie outside those of the organization and in what areas did there appear to be much common ground?

3. What was the potential cost of this goal conflict?

4. How was the potential goal conflict resolved?

5. How might organizations anticipate these activities? Are there some ways in which situations like these can be resolved in routine fashion?

Our Comments

1. This profile illustrates some of the problems that emerged due to goal conflict between Alice's and the organization's goals. There were two levels of goal conflict described in this situation: (a) Alice's personal goals and style and the economic welfare of her employer, and (b) Alice's personal goals and those of the firm's client (O'Brien). Alice is seeking a sense of personal achievement and accomplishment—the organization seeks profitable jobs through the satisfaction of its clients.

2. Her goals were outside those of the organization to the extent that they could cause her to take actions destructive of its interests. On the other hand, if Alice can do a good job of satisfying clients and this results in her achieving her goals, recognition for her work and talent, and possible promotion, much common ground may exist.

3. Another important point is the cost of goal conflict—loss of immediate client (O'Brien) and the possible impact of that loss and the O'Brien rationale on other clients of the firm.

4. Resolution of goal conflict: It's important to notice that the basis of conflict resolution was achieved by Alice's supervisor —a promise to sleep on things, let O'Brien cool off, and give Alice a chance to think things through. In addition, Alice developed some flexibility in dealing with the client's wishes, an important factor that would respond directly to dealing with the conflict.

5. Finally, one can take a more productive approach by anticipating goal conflict: It's possible that more detailed discussions between Alice and her supervisor at the start of the job could have unearthed some of her more deeply seated feelings and how she proposed to deal with some of the design problems.

Florence Berg—The Story

Florence Berg had been with Family Shoe Stores for almost five years. It was her third job since graduating from college with a degree in psychology. When Florence first started college, she had planned to go into graduate school and then work in counseling. She was two years into her college program when she started to realize that her occupational goal of counseling and the availability of jobs were simply not matching up. More and more she heard stories from her friends about people graduating in the social sciences and not being able to find work in their field.

By her junior year, Florence realized that she was at an important decision juncture in her college program. She talked to a great many people that summer. After sorting things out, she decided to remain in psychology. She reasoned that all of her basic courses were completed and that she was just starting to enjoy her program. Second, although the availability of counseling jobs was likely to decrease, chances were that she'd be able to find work in another area where her talents and knowledge could be used.

The worsening job situation did encourage Florence to think about other job fields. By the time she graduated, she had identified several different occupations that she thought might prove interesting. One of these was the personnel field, and a second possibility was the social work field.

Florence started following up on want ads in the newspaper and leads from friends to secure a job. She was soon hired as a Personnel Trainee at a large commercial bank. She received general on-the-job training in the personnel department for three months and was then assigned to the training department. At first she found the work interesting and challenging, but then work became a routine. Florence thought about asking for a change in job assignments, particularly when some of the women in the bank began urging her to seek out new opportunities, saying, "You're entitled to a better job; they've kept women in these 'clerical' jobs long enough."

Florence felt some confusion and uncertainty. True, she felt her job was becoming boring, and some of her friends were urging her to push for a more responsible position. But she wondered to herself if going in the direction urged by her friends was the only alternative. Finally, she asked for a transfer and was accepted as a supervisory trainee in the savings department—a logical job choice because of her skills in personnel and training and her ability to learn quickly. She became a savings supervisor and found some aspects of her work interesting and challenging. But the size and pressure of a large organization eventually seemed too much to cope with. After four years with the bank, Florence resigned.

She took a job with a smaller savings and loan company where her prior experiences were most useful. Before long, she was asked to apply for an assistant manager's job. Much of what she read in the newspaper and heard on TV regarding women in the business world indicated that she was being given a deserved right and opportunity. It seemed foolish not to try the job of assistant manager. As might be expected, Florence was successful in her performance; but inwardly, she felt pressured and restricted by many of the company's conservative fiscal policies, as well as by the job itself. With some surprise to her supervisor, Florence announced her intention to leave the savings and loan organization. She looked around for something that might provide her an opportunity to use more of her abilities but wasn't quite sure what she was seeking.

Family Shoe Stores, Inc. (FSS) differed substantially from the bank and the savings and loan company. It was a successful nationwide chain of small stores featuring modern styles and medium-priced shoes for the entire family. Florence had handled some of their accounts at the bank, noticed their ads, and inquired about their openings in management.

Florence joined FSS as a management trainee in one of their Florida stores. After six months, she was transferred to a larger store in Texas, which carried a slightly different line of merchandise. After a year and a half, she was assigned to a midwestern store, first as assistant manager and then as manager. Florence liked the store, the customers, and the company a great deal—and the town itself. As manager, she had a full range of problems; but she felt considerably less pressure than she had felt in her earlier jobs. She enjoyed training new employees and developing management trainees assigned to her store. For variety, she waited on trade and was an effective salesperson in her own right.

After nine years of experience in the job world, Florence felt career confident but wanted some additional assurance that she was pointed in the right direction. She wondered why her earlier jobs had not worked out for her personally even though she was rated as a good performer by the companies. Florence started talking to some of her friends, and she read several interesting career-development books. As she discussed her job with others and continued her reading, her understanding of her own skills, likes and dislikes, where she wanted to go, and what she wanted to do became more clear.

Now, after four years with Family Shoe Stores, Florence has been asked to consider a managerial position at the home office in Boston. She says she wants to think it over for a few weeks before responding.

Questions for You

1. How do Florence's job experiences compare with those of women you know? What events or circumstances have shaped her career?

2. Do you think a newer concern for women's rights has played a part in her career? In what way?

3. How is it that a given organization could see Florence as a good or even superior worker, yet she herself appeared to be uncertain or unhappy?

4. To what extent were the objectives of the bank, savings and loan, and shoe organizations compatible with her apparent objectives? To what extent did they differ, perhaps being in conflict?

5. What do you think Florence will do about the offer for the managerial position at the home offices of Family Shoe Stores, Inc.?

Our Comments

1. It's likely that you have known someone who has had at least some of the types of work experiences which Florence encountered. Her educational preparation started in psychology; and right in the middle of plans, the "bottom fell out," jobs became hard to find, and there were many more specially trained people than available jobs. This trend actually started years *before* Florence even entered her program. Poor communication of vital job information has led to many disappointments and has kept people from making realistic choices regarding careers, even when they knew what they wanted to do.

    Florence started to learn the importance of information before graduation so that her choices for her initial jobs were probably logical ones. Moving into the personnel field and the sub-specialty of training seemed to provide an outlet for some of her major strengths and represented a good opportunity to gain experience and test out alternatives in her career.

    Many different considerations shaped her career. Opportunity, opinions of friends, and general excitement about the status of women in the work place all played a part in her initial job choices and moves. Interestingly, her personal self did not surface in her earlier work experiences, but became of increasing importance as she broadened her work experience and gained more self-knowledge.

2. The women's movement seems to have had an influence in Florence's earlier career. Friends caught up in the spirit of the

movement, and an enhancement of her own sense of freedom and independence, supported and led Florence to a high sense of personal enthusiasm and willingness to explore various career possibilities. The decreasing opportunities for some jobs related to her psychology degree and the strength and momentum of equal opportunity movements may have been an important force in her earlier work-related decisions, but it appears that Florence's experience provided a foundation in which more personal factors assumed increasing importance later. Some of these personal preferences included using a broad range of skills in a managerial position that provided some job variety and opportunities to use a flexible approach in meeting employee needs.

3. The case involving Florence Berg is a good illustration of why work performance and personal satisfaction must be considered as two separate issues. Florence had the intelligence, ability, and continued spirit to be successful in her work assignments at the bank and the savings and loan firm. Yet, though performing well, she wasn't that pleased with the impact of these work performances on her inner sense of what she wanted to derive from her career. Until she could get a better match between work opportunity requirements and her inner needs and style, she was bound to feel tense, frustrated, or unfulfilled in her career.

4. The organizations in which Florence acquired experience had profit making as a major objective. This is understandable and necessary for survival. In this context, people are a necessary part of meeting the organization's end objectives and are paid for the services and abilities they provide. To this extent, the goals of the organization and individual can be harmonious.

    Also, it's well known that economic organizations have a social dimension; Florence developed some good friendships and satisfying social experiences. However, organizations also represent particular combinations of work activities, clients, and associated events. The right combination differs, depending on individual needs. For Florence, the work demands at the two financial institutions involved activities that became unattractive to her as she gained additional experience.

5. Florence didn't accept the transfer to Boston. She remained as manager of the midwestern store. Her sense of career confidence meant that she knew what she wanted from her career at this particular point. The combination of responsibilities and activities at FSS and the knowledge from previous work experiences

had satisfied her curiosity regarding other career alternatives. True, in a few years she might once more examine career alternatives, but for now she felt comfortable with her work situation at FSS and with her personal life in the midwestern town.

Marian Chandler—The Story

Marian Chandler was the most unproductive real estate salesperson ever employed by Homehunters, Inc. But no one, least of all Marian or her boss, could figure out why. Can you?

After real estate training, Marian was delighted to land a job at Homehunters. She was 37 years old, divorced, with four children. She was mature, attractive, and eager for work. Marian loved to meet, understand, and help others. She was well organized and a hard worker. She spent a lot of time helping clients, screening choices for them, and taking them out to look at suitable properties. She was honest and diligent in pointing out the good and bad points of each home, but Marian did not make sales. Her income from child support was quite low, and she had been counting on making commissions to help her support her family. That's why she had so happily taken the job with Homehunters.

Marian's boss, Kay, could not understand Marian's lack of sales. Marian was on a commission-only status, and she had earned almost nothing after a full year of working close to 50-hour weeks. Kay herself had helped with Marian's training, encouraged her, and given her good leads to follow up. She gave Marian every opportunity, every bit of knowledge and encouragement that a boss could possibly provide.

Questions for You

1. Marian had a tremendous wish to succeed but did not. What went wrong? To determine the problem, think through what Marian's stated goals are and describe her style as you see it:

   _____

   _____

   Now think through what goals and subgoals are necessary to make a sale: _____

   _____

   _____

2. Can you see a conflict between Marian's basic desire to understand and help others and the need of a real estate agency to get people into homes?

3. Do you see any way(s) in which Marian could both use and/or adapt her style so that it would be in harmony with the goals of the real estate firm where she has spent the past year?

4. Or must she change her occupation? If she does, what might be suitable? How will her problems in the work place be different from those she has now? Remember that she has invested time, money, and effort in training herself to sell real estate. What do you think you would advise Marian?

Our Comments

1. Marian did not "sell" people into buying houses at all. She ended up entertaining and helping them, showing interesting and desirable homes; but she never *persuaded* them that they personally must, should, or would want to own those desirable homes. Her goal was not the goal of a salesperson—to get someone to purchase the firm's product.

2. Marian's goal came from her basic style and her values. It conflicted with the goal of her firm because she could not expand her idea of being helpful to others to the idea of being helpful to the firm by persuading people to buy appropriate homes.

    On the surface, Marian's style—her need to help others as a goal—did conflict with the needs of the firm she worked for. Can you see, however, that this very need might well suit a real estate company? A good realty firm, after all, is genuinely helping others, not just selling a product. Kay understood this and that is why she had been eager to have Marian work for her and willing to spend time training her. Nevertheless, she was puzzled by Marian's lack of sales; and although Marian did not know it, Kay was close to letting her go. The decision as to whether she would stay in real estate had almost been taken out of Marian's hands.

3. Kay was a practical woman—and also a warm one. She liked Marian. She herself liked to help people, in fact; and she well understood Marian's special problems as a divorced woman with four children. Kay and Marian went to work on her problem: Marian entered a workshop in career counseling at her local junior college. She regularly went over what she discovered with Kay—and Kay even went through some of the inventories and exercises with Marian.

    For Marian, the values scales were particularly helpful. She saw the terminal values of "family security" and "world at peace" as numbers 1 and 2 on her list; and she saw her instrumental values listed out in a clear message: "helpful," "loving," "cheerful," "polite," and "honest." She laughed to Kay, "I sound like some dumb Pollyanna type—or a Boy Scout!"

But Kay said, "No. Those are just the qualities that should make you able to sell houses like hotcakes. That's your style. And it should work. I'll bet the key is simple. You just have to decide that for you to sell Mr. and Mrs. Randall that ranch house on Ivy Circle is just the most helpful thing you can do for them! How about it?"

Kay was right. It worked. Marian hit the million-dollar club before the next year was out.

4. Marian, of course, had intuitively selected an occupation she was well suited for. And it fit her family circumstances, too, for she could be home in the afternoons when school was out if she needed to be and she could take a child to a ballet lesson or the dentist when she needed to—and the other children, in turn, could help out with cooking or cleanup on evenings or weekend days when Marian had to show houses.

The point is that whatever work Marian chose, she would remain essentially the person she was—and thus take her special problems *and* her special skills with her. She needed to gain insight about her own needs, values, and style and then adapt to meet the realistic requirements of her job. And she did it.

ADDITIONAL RESOURCES

Part Three: Moving On—with Your Style

CLARK, ANN. *New Ways to Work: A Gestalt Perspective.* Vitalia, P.O. Box 27253, San Francisco, Calif. 94127, 1975. An informative discussion of the newer working styles and arrangements that permit women to arrange for other demands for or uses of their time.

FENSTERHEIM, HERBERT, and JEAN BAER. *Don't Say Yes When You Want to Say No.* New York: Dell, 1975. An assertiveness training guide that helps to target personal problems, choices, and responses.

LE SAN, EDA J. *The Wonderful Crisis of Middle Age: Some Personal Reflections.* New York: David McKay, 1973. Provides helpful information and perspectives for viewing the "middle" years.

Publications of the Women's Bureau. Washington, D.C.: U.S. Department of Labor Workplace Standards Administration, Women's Bureau, 1971. A useful guide to the variety of pamphlets published by the Women's Bureau and the information, guidance, resources, and support they provide.

WEINBERG, GEORGE. *Self Creation.* New York: Avon, 1978. Breaking habits that limit your effectiveness in work or personal life.

ZANGWILL, WILLARD I. *Success with People: The Theory Z Approach to Mutual Achievement.* New York: Bantam, 1979. Using creativity and insight to help yourself and work associates handle job stress.

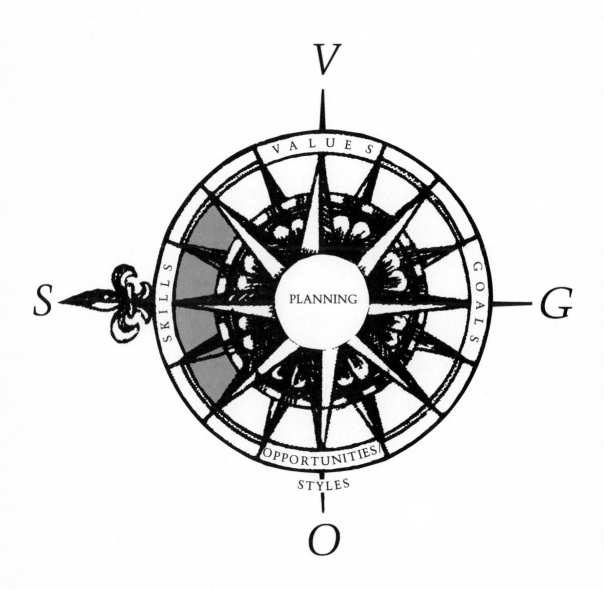

Part Four

MOVING ON—WITH YOUR SKILLS

In this final section of *Growing*, you will find information, models, and exercises designed to strengthen your career potentials as they relate to your career skills. Your skills—both general and specific —link you to your basic career goals as well as to your personal values and your career style, thus bringing all four points of your career compass into balance.

Part Four shows you how to:

- Identify both your general and specific career skills

- Analyze your career skills in terms of work responsibilities and possible jobs where these can be used

- Use six occupational categories to help increase flexibility in thinking about career activities

- Assess the transferability of your skills—and loosen up your thinking regarding similarities between specific jobs in different organizations, industries, or professions

- Start recognizing and working with organization networks

- Start developing practical career strategies

As you work through the following chapters, it's important for you to keep in mind that skills are but one point on the career compass. Thus, skills *and* goals, opportunities, and values must all work together for you. Important goals often suggest developing certain skills, and your current skills or strengths may suggest important career goals that tap these abilities. There is no fixed way these things work—at times the thrust is from goals or values; the next time may be opportunity or skill. But in the end, you need a comfortable balance between all the elements of your career compass for personal satisfaction and a sense of growth.

All the information you gain in other parts of *Growing* are the skill potentials, perhaps glimpsed by friends or others that you may be only partially aware of or perhaps unaware of totally. Thus, this section has a very important mission in helping you to become better acquainted with skills representing past, current, and future time periods.

18

Gaining a Perspective on Career Skills

I like to work by myself and I like to work with my hands. My dad's a master carpenter and he taught me most of what he knew by the time I was 14. Sure, he didn't have a son, but I like to think he'd have taught me anyway—even if he'd had five boys. Because I'm just naturally good with a hammer and saw, and he could see that. I'm not out to build any big shopping centers, though—or even houses in the suburbs. I want to do something a little more creative—something individual. . . .

KAREN

Job counselors are always saying everyone they talk to claims, "Oh, I just love to work with people!" Well, I guess a lot of women think they're expected to say that. But with me, it's for real. I had to figure that out the hard way. Until I sat down, did some thinking about my job, and got my head straight, I was ready to quit. Pay, vacations, fringe benefits—I didn't care! I was bored stiff. "I'm dead-ended," I kept telling my friends. I was ready to move on, that's for sure. . . .

JANICE

In Chapter 3, we defined skills as abilities you put to use, for example, the kind we've emphasized as part of your career style. These can be the kind of abilities you put to use in working with people, or they can be technical abilities having to do with office equipment, science areas, or the computer.

Technical abilities and the related skills are not always that obvious. Consider the following (additional) examples of technical abilities and their use: the ability to type, write shorthand, or use a transcribing machine

Skills are abilities put to use

(secretarial skills); the ability to program a computer (data-processing skills); the ability to persuade people to buy a product or service (sales skills); the ability to operate specific kinds of adding and calculating machines (book-keeping skills); the ability to monitor certain medical treatments and dispensing of medicines (nursing skills). Each of these different abilities depends upon various skills, skills that come together to get a job done. For example, typing involves many skills, including interpreting instructions, copying, and operating different types of communication equipment. Much of what we think of as abilities or skills can be broken down into more fundamental or elemental skills concerning *data* (information), *people,* and *things.* Your work—any work—requires that you function successfully in relation to each of these components (data, people, and things).

THE CAREER-PLANNING TRIANGLE

Three phases of a career

One of the most useful ways we've found to understand your skills in relation to your job is to think through your situation using the three-phase concept we call the "Career-Planning Triangle." It looks like this:

THE CAREER-PLANNING TRIANGLE

Career
skills

Job responsibilities
and behaviors

Function Areas

Think of this triangular figure from its tip to its base. Think of it as a way to broaden your perspective on career growth.

Skills

At the tip of the triangle are something you now have some knowledge of: skills. We just discussed these in the preceding section. But what about job responsibilities and behaviors, where the triangle begins to broaden?

Responsibilities and Behaviors

In most work environments, responsibilities are the tasks and projects—the job behaviors—to which you apply your skills. For example, job descriptions and job specifications usually define the ways in which skills are connected to the responsibilities and behaviors of a particular job position. The secretary might be responsible for compiling lengthy reports, writing up minutes, or doing general correspondence. The computer programmer might be responsible for testing or "debugging" pilot computer programs. The salesperson might be responsible for opening new accounts only, for maintaining established accounts, or for both. She might carry out job behaviors of writing up sales calls, making customer contact on the phone, and so on. The bookkeeper might be responsible for payroll, accounts receivable, or month-end statements. The nurse might be responsible for direct patient care or for developing a general nursing plan. The teacher might be responsible for classroom teaching and parent conferences. In each case, however, the individual is applying skills *to* responsibilities and these result in various work-related behaviors for successful job results. In short, the discharge of a responsibility (behavior) requires that various skills be put to work. When a group of related responsibilities is brought together, it makes up a function area of a job.

Responsibilities are tasks and projects

Function Areas

At the base of the triangle, and providing the broadest perspective for your thinking about work activities, are function areas. These are jobs or groups of jobs with similar tasks or orientations. Most people use a job title or an occupational category to define their function area, such as actuary, teacher, or chemist. Also, many use terms like "creative" or "artistic" to emphasize further the fit between their personal orientation and their vocational choice.

Function areas: where responsibilities are carried out

One of the problems with most terms used to describe function area is that they are usually very imprecise because many different responsibilities (and their skills) may be involved in a specific job. For example, a chemist in the research department of a petroleum firm has much different responsibilities (and needed skills) than a chemist assigned to a quality-control laboratory. In fact, as we think about it, it becomes clear that most all of us start out our career or thinking about careers in very general functional area terms (doctor, lawyer, engineer, secretary). It's only after we gain some experience that it becomes clear that widely different responsibilities are involved in particular jobs and they thus require quite different skills to be performed successfully. In this chapter, we are taking a grass roots approach that calls for starting with elemental skills—and then building on these in terms of responsibilities you could undertake—and determining how the responsibilities could be packaged so as to lead to the widest possible career choices for you.

Many start a career by thinking about a function area

Let's try to come at these points in a slightly different way because they represent critical conditions related to skills. People start careers with ideas about a specific occupation they might enjoy and choose a job that seems to fit their preferences. In time, you realize that the job title or description of a job provides only a limited picture of all that a person does and the greatly differing skills needed to be considered successful. For example, a given secretary might copy reports having to do with the board meetings of an industrial firm, supervise part-time typists at a research lab, or compile sales data for quarterly reports at an advertising firm. Although the general title is the same ("secretary") and many of the work activities use similar skills as other secretaries, each work assignment or job involves a rather unique set of skills relating to information (data), people, or things.

Skills often are the secret to career responsibilities

Each position also places the secretary in contact with different types of information and people. So the secretary who spends a great deal of time copying figures and supervising other staff may actually have a lot more in common with assistants in the quality-control division of her organization than with some other secretaries. Similar skills, responsibilities, and job behaviors may be found in many different jobs, though the titles might suggest otherwise to you. This means you should stay open to possibilities or opportunities even if at first they sound unfamiliar or appear to be in the "I've never done anything like that before" category. With careful examination, it may turn out that very similar things are involved. Or it may be that even a slight job change, like movement from "secretary" to "secretary-receptionist," provides the right use of your skill package. You want to consider in a creative way the skills you have and the ways in which those skills may indicate to you activities (responsibilities and behaviors) you find rewarding.

As you think about this triangular relationship between *skills, responsibilities,* and *career function areas,* remind yourself that skills are used to carry out responsibilities in specific career function areas of one organization or industry. This means that you must not only consider the skills you wish to develop but also the kinds of responsibilities you wish to fulfill in utilizing those skills and the career function areas within the organization or industry where you wish to pursue your responsibilities.

PEOPLE, DATA, AND THINGS: THE D.O.T. CLASSIFICATION

It's not always easy to think about the world of work in terms of this triangular pattern of skills, responsibilities, and career function areas—especially if you have not been working long enough or in a wide enough range of jobs to know exactly what your full spectrum of skills might be, what responsibilities and job behaviors your skills might apply to, and what career function areas combine your skills with responsibilities in that area.

We'd like to make the process easier by reminding you that skill sets can be analyzed according to those three classifications we mentioned earlier: data, people, and things. As we explained in Chapter 3, these are the three components set forth by the *Dictionary of Occupational Titles* (D.O.T.). When you think of skills in these terms, you can relate them more easily to job behaviors and the sets of responsibilities used at work.

Analyzing your skills: information, people, things

These D.O.T. classifications tell us, first of all, that jobs are much more than just the skills utilized in them—and haven't we been saying that right along? In other words, jobs combine skills into job behaviors. Those behaviors put the jobholder into different relationships with data, with people, and with things.

Jobs are more than skills

Think about that for a moment. In your own job, or in any job you know about, what is involved on that job with regard to information? To people? To things? We are going to discuss each of these three factors, data-people-things, more fully because they can be quite helpful in broadening your thinking.

Data (Information) and the Job

Does the person in that job compare pieces of data? Copy data? Compute, compile, analyze, coordinate, synthesize, or develop data (quite advanced skills) regarding skills?

Working with data can use a full range of skills

You can see from looking at this brief list of the things people do with data in jobs that a very full range of skills could be involved—from the fairly simple skill sets needed to compare and copy data to the fairly complex skill sets needed to synthesize or develop data. This is a typical way to view skills—from the simple, routine type of skill application to activities requiring complex or technical skills.

People and the Job

The same holds true for the relationships of jobs to people. Working with people can mean so many different things, as you've discovered exploring your career style in Part Three. The D.O.T. classification system gives us a further base for thinking about the "people factor" in jobs. According to the D.O.T., jobs relate to people in every way from simply taking instructions, helping and serving others, to exchanging information, to coaching, persuading, consulting, instructing, treating, to supervising and negotiating with people, all the way up to mentoring people. Notice how this list suggests a sequence of more complex or difficult activities.

The "people" factor involves skills

Again, these job relationships to people involve a full range of skills from the fairly simple skill of following instructions to the fairly complex skill of mentoring or guiding another's career.

Things and the Jobs

Things require skills, too

Things—that is, machines, tools, materials, equipment, and so on—also have a range of job relationships. In their work with things, people do everything from precision work and setting up (quite advanced skills), manipulating, operating, controlling, driving, handling and feeding, to simply "tending" to things (basic and simple skills).

Let's now summarize this D.O.T. approach as it relates to thinking about your skills. First, consider your skills as these relate to *data, people,* and *things.* Second, consider the level of skill or complexity involved in each of the three categories. The preceding discussion suggests a sequence of gradually increasing complexity for each of these skill areas:

- *Data/information:* Compiling, analyzing, coordinating, synthesizing, developing

- *People:* taking instructions, helping/reviewing others, exchanging information, coaching, persuading, instructing, treating, supervising, negotiating

D.O.T. APPROACH FOR CLASSIFYING JOB SKILLS

DATA	PEOPLE	THINGS
(Higher-level, complex)		(Higher-level, complex)
Synthesizing (develop data)	Mentoring*	Precision working, setting up
Coordinating, innovating	Negotiating	Manipulating, operating-controlling, driving-controlling
Analyzing	Supervising	
Computing, compiling	Consulting, instructing, treating	
Copying	Coaching, persuading, diverting	Handling, feeding—offbearing, tending
Comparing	Exchanging information, helping, serving	
(Lower-level, simple)		(Lower-level, simple)

* Act as counselor, guide, and sounding board for person

- *Things:* tending (to things), handling and feeding, driving, controlling, operating, manipulating

People who work with these skills usually prefer to think of them in ranks or columns of descending complexity or skill requirements.

Higher-level skills build on lower-level skills and abilities; and, as you've seen, different kinds of skills combine to create the occupations of a nurse, accountant, or data processor. Knowing how you want to relate to data, people, or things helps you select a career area and think about the responsibilities and work behavior that come with a job. In a later chapter, we'll indicate some of the ways to make connections between these factors and jobs. For now, it's important to begin thinking in terms of skills and the ways in which skills combine to create different ways of relating to data, people, and things.

YOUR CURRENT D.O.T. PROFILE

In thinking about skills, it's important to know where you are and what the skill demands may be in exploring your career possibilities. Think about your current job and in general fashion see if you can check off the levels of skills you are currently using in each of the three—data/information, people, things—categories. (Application examples follow in the next discussion.)

Find your D.O.T. profile

YOUR D.O.T. CHECKOFF FOR SKILLS

DATA/INFORMATION			PEOPLE			THINGS		
	Current Job	Other Job(s)		Current Job	Other Job(s)		Current Job	Other Job(s)
Synthesizing	___	___	Mentoring	___	___	Precision working, setting up	___	___
Coordinating, innovating	___	___	Negotiating	___	___	Manipulating, operating, controlling	___	___
Analyzing	___	___	Supervising	___	___	Driving, controlling	___	___

Computing, compiling	___ ___	Consulting, instructing, treating	___ ___		___ ___
Copying	___ ___	Coaching, persuading, diverting	___ ___	Handling, feeding	___ ___
Company	___ ___	Exchanging information	___ ___	Tending	___ ___
		Taking instructions, helping, serving	___ ___		

A "reality check" provides useful clues

Most work doesn't fully require all of the skills that we may possess. Friends or work associates or past activities can often give you clues as to other types or levels of skills that you have.

Why not recheck your D.O.T. Checkoff for Skills list with a friend or work associate and then check off in the second column other skills, capabilities, or possibilities? Also, you may wish to recheck some of the items in the first column as well to see if others share your estimates. As a matter of information, the government has published *The Dictionary of Occupational Titles* that contains over 20,000 descriptions of jobs using the types of words and terms described in this section. The government (U.S. Department of Labor) has also developed helpful estimates of skills required in these occupations. The interested reader may wish to look at a copy of this resource material. It is available in most larger libraries and depositories for the federal government. Examples of some of these work function or occupational areas are presented at the end of Chapter 19.

THE HOLLAND SYSTEM: CONNECTING SKILLS, ABILITIES, PREFERENCES

Another way to look at skills

Different types of schemes have been developed to assist in joining up skills with responsibilities and function areas as described in the career-planning triangle heading off this chapter. Work done by John Holland is an outstanding example of this and can prove useful to you in making assessments of your skills and their use or transferability to various jobs or occupational areas.

It helps to think about the work you do or you'd like to do and analyze it according to the ways skills relate to *data* (information), *people*, and *things*.

We've found, for instance, that many people are talking about the kind of person they are. If you really think about these phrases, you can get some incredibly useful career information. For example, if you say, I want to work "for myself," or "in management," or "with people," ask yourself, "What do I really mean by that? What kind of work would I genuinely enjoy? What's my orientation in terms of skills and personality?"

John Holland, one of the great minds in career development theory, has developed a system to help you answer that question for yourself. Holland's system classifies skills such as manual skills or numerical skills according to the personal characteristics and/or traits of people who are successful in different types of work activities. Chances are you'll find yourself in one or more of Holland's categories, described below.*

Jobs classified by the types who succeed in them

The Six Categories: Preferences and Skills

- *Realistic:* "People who have athletic or mechanical ability, prefer to work with objects, machines, tools, plants or animals or to be outdoors."

- *Investigative:* "People who like to observe, learn, investigate, analyze, evaluate or solve problems."

- *Artistic:* "People who have artistic, innovating or intuitional abilities, and like to work in unstructured situations, using their imagination or creativity."

- *Social:* "People who like to work with people—to inform, enlighten, help, train, develop, or cure them, or are skilled with words."

- *Enterprising:* "People who like to work with people—influencing, persuading or leading or managing for organizational goals or for economic gain."

- *Conventional:* "People who like to work with data, have clerical or numerical ability, carry things out in detail or follow through on other's instructions."

Six types described

These six classifications of personal characteristics are important. When you study the D.O.T. classification systems, you'll see many of the same words used. That should help you to gain some further insights as to the kinds of jobs and their relationships to data (information), people, and things that you prefer. These six categories represent the ones used on the Strong-Campbell interests inventory. You can also apply them to many of the occupational categories defined in the D.O.T. We'll show you how.

*Richard Bolles, *The Three Boxes of Life* (Berkeley, Calif.: Ten Speed Press, 1978). Adapted from copyrighted material by John L. Holland, Ph.D. By permission of Consulting Psychologists Press, Inc., Palo Alto, Calif.

Short Recap

Before proceeding with a discussion of the "career wheel," let's pause a moment and pull things together. A number of different terms, schemes, and ideas that could easily result in losing sight of the thread that connects all of these points was set out in the skill discussions.

A short recap: points to remember

First, the world of work contains all kinds of occupations or work functions. Particular work functions bring together various sets or collections of responsibilities and behaviors needed for successful performance. Any given work-related responsibility or need work behavior requires that various types of skills be applied. The D.O.T. scheme represents a simple and practical way to think about the skills you currently have and those that should be considered in exploring career possibilities. The D.O.T. scheme of data (information), people, and things should help to give you some ideas about types of skills and the fact that these exist at many different levels of complexity or technical know-how. A job will require some skills in each of the three D.O.T. categories; a *specific* job in a given organization will require some skills in each category *and* various levels of technical, professional, or managerial accomplishment.

Second, people often have a natural style or a sense of preference for general types of work. Although this may not be that easy to specify, certain types of work feel "right" for you. Further, when you refer to your interests or friends describe your abilities, the terms often used are those that Holland selected for his classification scheme of six items. However, each Holland classification is associated with various occupations and work functions based on much research done in this area.

Third, if you can relate to one of the Holland classifications, you may be able to identify broad classes of work activities in which you are currently engaged or perhaps areas that you could start thinking about.

Fourth, the job you're in and the work function or occupation whose possibilities you are considering require various combinations of data, people, and things (and, of course, various levels of skills in each of the three categories).

Fifth, the challenge from a skill viewpoint is to see if the skills you currently use in your work activity can be successfully transformed to the work function or occupation you are considering.

The Career Wheel

The career wheel relates people to occupations

Reproduced next is a career wheel with some specific occupational fields identified within each spoke. Each compartment of the wheel corresponds to one of the Holland classifications just described. Not all occupations are mentioned, but the examples can help to get you started relating "types of people" to occupational fields. That should help to get you started thinking about the skills (data/information, people, things) and career function areas that relate to occupations and jobs.

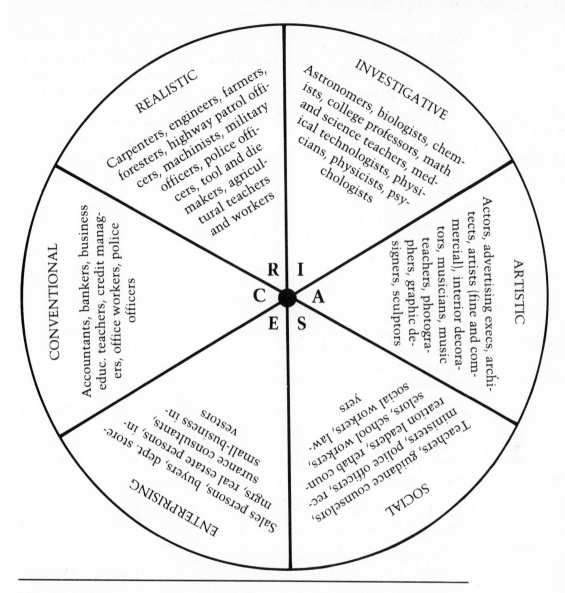

REALISTIC

Carpenters, engineers, farmers, foresters, highway patrol officers, machinists, military officers, police officers, tool and die makers, agricultural teachers and workers

INVESTIGATIVE

Astronomers, biologists, chemists, college professors, math and science teachers, medical technologists, physicians, physicists, psychologists

ARTISTIC

Actors, advertising execs, architects, artists (fine and commercial), interior decorators, musicians, music teachers, photographers, graphic designers, sculptors

CONVENTIONAL

Accountants, bankers, business educ. teachers, credit managers, office workers, police officers

ENTERPRISING

Sales persons, buyers, dept. store mgrs, real estate persons, insurance consultants, in-vestors

SOCIAL

Teachers, guidance counselors, ministers, police officers, recreation leaders, rehab counselors, school workers, social workers, law-yers

R I E S C A

HOW THE SYSTEM WORKS: TWO EXAMPLES

Now you can begin to think about career skills in the ways that really give depth of meaning to your personal goals and values. You can think about the kind of person you are, the type of work that kind of person often does well, the skills used in that work, how those skills relate to information and things, and how those skills are used to meet responsibilities within given career function areas. Two examples will help put this together.

One Type of Person: Karen

Karen's skills and preferences

Karen often described herself as a very "basic, down-to-earth" individual. As she said at the beginning of the chapter, she liked working with her hands; she liked putting things together, crafting them, and seeing a finished product at the end of the labors. She talked about herself as a loner, and she enjoyed working with other people only to the extent that they were all involved in "doing their own thing" in order to get a job done.

If you look over the Holland classification, you'll see that Karen would probably find herself within the Realistic spoke of our career wheel, with some features of her character in the Artistic spoke, like this:

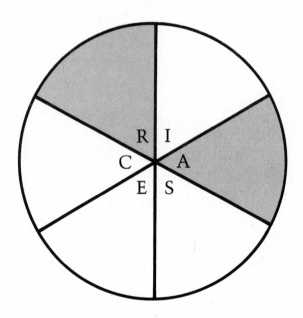

Karen's career triangle

Karen also used the D.O.T. classifications to help choose her career. As a young woman, Karen had learned carpentry from her father. Considering carpentry as a basic *skill* she enjoyed, Karen found out about all the different *responsibilities* and activities of carpenters: roughing-in work, basic construction, finished carpentry, cabinetmaking, and many more. She could then think about the different positions and environments in which a carpenter might work: in a large office building on the crew of a construction company, teaching woodshop classes, or any of the other environments in which carpenters would be called upon to use different combinations of skills to carry out responsibilities. Thus, Karen could construct her own career-planning triangle, like this:

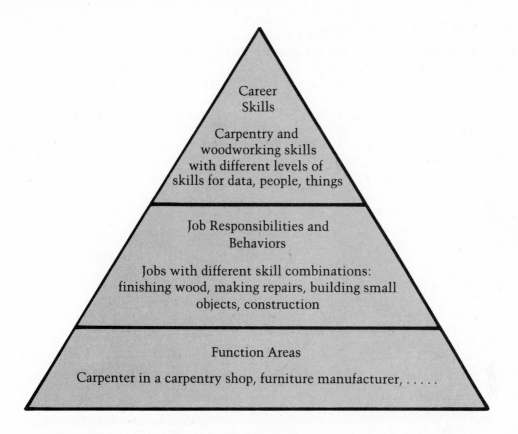

With so many possibilities, it might be useful for Karen to consider investigating her potentials further by analyzing her desired job in relation to the three D.O.T. classifications. Thinking of carpentry as a basic work category, Karen might consider how her interests and skills in carpentry relate to information, to people, and to things. Her D.O.T. analysis is summarized in the next table.

Looking at her D.O.T. analysis model, Karen could quickly note that *her* strongest interest in carpentry had to do with the *things* dimensions of that model, particularly with the highly skilled craftsperson elements of working with things. With this information in mind, Karen could begin to look for the kinds of carpentry jobs that would give her the greatest potential for working alone in a highly skilled, fairly individualized area of the broad field of carpentry.

She did this by applying for an apprentice's position in a fine custom-cabinet shop. That position related her skills to her own "Realistic/Artistic"

Karen's analysis pays off

type of person. She structured the best of the world of work for her talents and interests. In her job, she'll have the right balance in that relationship between information, people, and things for her to feel comfortable and probably be more successful throughout her working life. If it turns out that her interests start to shift and/or she gains additional skills through her work, Karen will want to reexamine her career possibilities in terms of these ideas—and she'll have the tools to do so.

KAREN'S D.O.T. ANALYSIS

| Work Category | Relates to | | |
	Data/ Information	People	Things
Carpentry	Analyzing, interpreting	Taking instructions, exchanging information	Precision work, including manipulating and operating
(As Karen would like to do it)	(Going from plans to a finished product)	(Working with others)	(The craft part of the work)

A Second Type: Janice

Janice began her career as a clerk in the accounts receivable department of a very large sales and manufacturing organization. She came into the position with a basic understanding of and liking for the detail attached to bookkeeping work. She was quickly trained to utilize her high school math skills in operating the special billing equipment used in her department.

Janice: using some skills was not enough

For the most part, Janice enjoyed her work. She supplemented her on-the-job training by taking accounting courses at the local community college. But within time, Janice discovered that, for her, the process of operating the bookkeeping/billing equipment was too far removed from transactions with customers, sales representatives, and others to provide her with the human contact and working-with-people feeling that was so important to her. She began to feel vaguely disgruntled, as she said at the beginning of the chapter. She felt dead-ended but didn't quite know why. To help think her way through her situation, Janice developed models much like the ones Karen did. Janice began with a D.O.T. analysis of her current job.

As she studied this model, it became clear to Janice why she felt the negative way she did about her job. Although it was in a career function area

JANICE'S D.O.T. ANALYSIS OF CURRENT JOB

	Relates to		
Work Category	*Data/ Information*	*People*	*Things*
Bookkeeping/ accounting	Comparing, copying	Taking instruction	Operating (business equipment)

she liked (accounting), the mix between people, information, and things and what she did with them in her job was all wrong for her general career goals and her personal value system. Janice did another D.O.T. analysis of a job in the same area (accounting); but this time "the job" was the way she would like it to be in terms of different levels of her skills with data (information), people, and things:

JANICE'S D.O.T. ANALYSIS OF TYPE OF JOB DESIRED

	Relates to		
Work Category	*Data/ Information*	*People*	*Things*
Bookkeeping/ accounting	Compiling, computing, analyzing	Exchanging information, persuading, consulting	Operating

Looking at the two analyses, Janice realized that her current job was no longer meeting her needs in the ways she wanted to work. Janice wanted to use her skills not just to compare and copy accounting information but to compile and analyze it—make some decisions about it. She wanted to do more with people than just take instructions from them on an infrequent basis. She wanted to interact on a lively and challenging basis for herself —exchanging information, persuading others, acting in a consulting role regarding accounting and finance. She did feel good about the *things* aspect of her work, for she enjoyed working with math computing and calculating equipment.

Janice also thought about the type of person she was and where she might find herself on the career wheel. She decided she was "Conventional"

What her job lacked

The type of person Janice was

herself but that she liked many different types of people, particularly the outgoing persuasive types and the helpful types. Thus, she thought of herself as having "Enterprising" and "Social" dimensions as well. She knew herself quite well in this regard but decided to do some commonsense reality checking with some close friends at work—they confirmed Janice's own analyses and thus gave her more confidence in her career exploration.

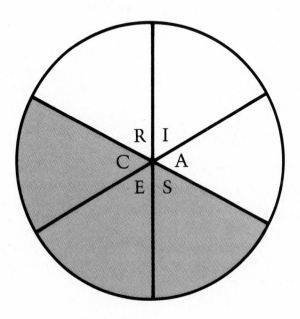

Her career triangle

With that information in mind and more confidence in her approach, Janice was able to move from the D.O.T. analysis to the triangular career-planning model. She looked around her organization and asked herself, "Where can I use my skills in bookkeeping and accounting? Where can I carry out responsibilities related to my skills but involving more people contact? What areas of bookkeeping and accounting are used by my company to carry out responsibilities that will use more of the skills I have and enjoy and put me in touch with more people?"

Janice found the answer

Janice asked others, too, beginning with her own departmental supervisor. She recognized the importance and value of keeping others, especially her own supervisor, aware of what she was interested in for her future development. Based on her analysis, Janice determined that she should stay in the functional area of accounting but move to a different department within the function. When an opening became available, Janice transferred from billing to credit and collection, where certainly there was much more contact with people. Here she found the best ladder for her success—both immediate and with good long-range possibilities.

Janice made successful career plans in terms of her skills—both present skills and those she wanted to develop as well as the kinds of responsibilities to which she wanted to apply those skills (numbers and people-related projects). She's found the overall function area in which she wants to work —accounting and finance. Her career planning included immediate training and a transfer and a combination of future jobs and education that will create a career in financial management.

And success

Of course, Janice could have found some other ways to use her unique talents for data, people, and things. It's important to remember that skills are only a part of the career compass. Janice's mix of values, goals, and opportunities (from the career compass) helped direct her skills to a specific combination of responsibilities and behaviors (accounting) and a specific use of her functional area (the credit and collection end of bookkeeping). She's found a way to create her career in financial management and her present and future jobs will (increasingly) provide the training and right skills by way of information, people, and things for her—and fit the type of person she is.

She could have chosen a different way to use her skills

Another important point to recognize and evaluate for yourself is the idea of "transferability"—movement of skills to different responsibilities or the movement of skills and responsibilities to new function areas and sub-areas. Work function titles often confuse what is in reality a common foundation of similar or identical skills. Knowledgeable people in your organization and informed people outside of work can help you get down to the bedrock of skills underlying responsibilities and work function areas.

A UNIQUE TYPE: YOU

As you worked through the problems Karen and Janice had with career skills, we assume you found that you were beginning to think about yourself —and not just about your skills. The perspective you've been gaining will surely take you back to your personal values, to your career style, and to the goals and path-steps you designed for yourself earlier in *Growing*.

"Just what type of a person am I?" you are ready to ask again—and to bring even better, more satisfying answers to that question. That's why we conclude this chapter with three models for you to fill out for yourself before you use the chapter checklist. You'll find the career-planning triangle first; then the career wheel, with its six classifications or themes represented as spokes; and finally, the job analysis based on the D.O.T. classifications of *information, people,* and *things* (your checkoff sheet discussed earlier in the chapter will help you with this). And we've given you space for both a present and a future job analysis.

What type of person are you?

Save all of these to use after reading the next chapters on skills if you wish. But we think you'll find you have beginning ideas to put down right now. Put your mind and your imagination to work—like this:

You have the answers

- *About that triangle:* What are my skills—what words might best describe skills I use with data, people, or things? What responsibilities, what tasks, do I fulfill or perform? How can I best describe what I do (function area) and the environment in which I work?

- *About that wheel:* Which spokes describe me and what I like to do?

- *About that D.O.T. analysis:* Why not do the one for now and then make the future one out for my "ideal" use of my skills? Are the levels and combinations of skills alike or different?

MY CAREER TRIANGLE

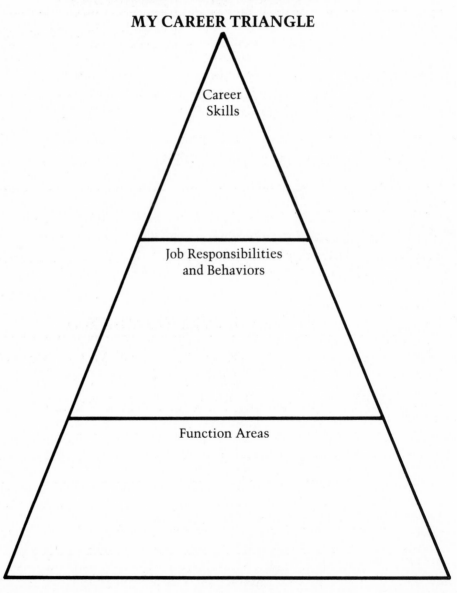

Career
Skills

Job Responsibilities
and Behaviors

Function Areas

Go back in this chapter and take another look at your D.O.T. checkoff to see if you have any new or additional ideas beyond those you have already recorded.

MY CURRENT JOB ANALYSIS

	Ways I Now Usually Relate to		
Work Category	Data/ Information	People	Things

MY FUTURE JOB ANALYSIS

	I Wish to Use These Skills More Often to Relate to		
Work Category	Data/ Information	People	Things

MY CAREER WHEEL

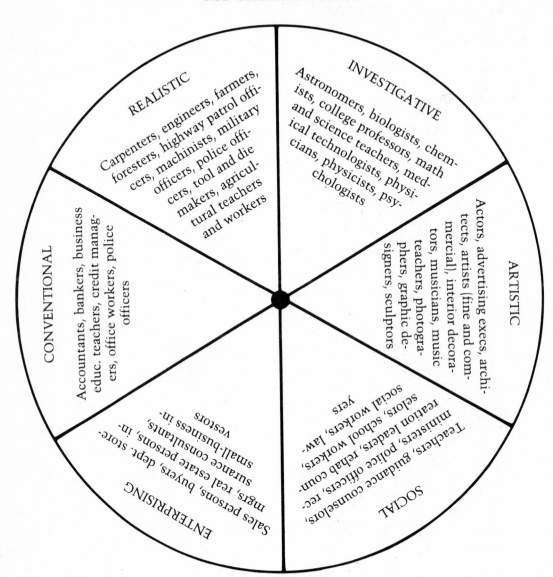

ACTION CHECKLIST FOR CHAPTER 18

Checklist	*My Ideas and Action Steps*	*Date*
√ The career-planning triangle peaks with career skills because these are	_____	_____

the bases for getting down through work responsibilities and behavior to function areas representing career possibilities.

√ The D.O.T. classification of data/information, people, and things gives you a way of thinking about skills that can represent what you have been doing and what you want to do.

√ Holland's six categories (realistic, investigative, artistic, social, enterprising, conventional) provide an opportunity to consider work functions that you prefer or that really describe you or your sense of yourself.

√ The career wheel adds work function areas to preferred work function so that you can start considering occupational possibilities.

√ The work function occupation areas on the career wheel each contain combinations of skills involved with data/information, people, things.

√ The work function you are in must be considered "alongside of" the ones you are viewing as future possibilities for dealing with needs for skill building and skill transference.

√ Career goals, values, and opportunities combine with your current work to suggest preferred work functions for the future.

√ Preferred work function for the future must deal with what is likely to be available, let alone time and cost matters.

19

Identifying and Directing Your Own Skills

If I didn't have my schedule worked out down to the minute, I'd be a wreck within a week. I like doing copy at the ad agency where I work, and I'm good at it. But it's a business where the pressure is always on. I keep that pressure down by controlling my schedule and really being a considerate, work-organized supervisor. If I don't hit the office by 8:30, I'm not collected for that daily 9 A.M. staff meeting and the time I need for my people. And if I don't clear my desk and shut myself into my cubicle every day from 11 to 1, along with my typewriter and a bag lunch—well, I won't get my creative stint for the day done at all.

MARY LOU

I get cross, I know, when friends sort of pat me on the head and say, "Oh, yes, dear Leslie free-lances because she couldn't get to an office at the same time every day even if you paid her double time—or made the time 12 noon!" Very funny! It's true; I hate watching clocks and I don't have one anywhere except for the wristwatch I keep in my purse—in case I have to catch a plane or meet an editor. But I'm free-lancing because I love to write and work alone, and there's a big plus: I can learn more about writing and the field, and I buy time to work on my own novels. If I want to hit the typewriter at 4 in the morning and stay right there until 3 in the afternoon if it's going well—then, thank God, I can do it. And it means I have the same flexibility in terms of finishing an assignment. I like it this way . . . for now.

LESLIE

Mary Lou and Leslie are both writers. Each one has identified her skills in relation to information, people, and things. But more important, each also understands those skills in relation to her own values and style, and each has learned to direct her skills in ways that are appropriate and satisfying to her.

Defining career skills

It's time now for you to reflect on your experience with *your* skills—to look at supervisory skills as well as some of the functional skills you identified in Chapter 3—and to learn how to direct them. First things first—don't get excited, don't panic. When we speak of career skills, keep in mind that the words are not assigned outrageous importance. What we mean is this: Career skills are essentially varying degrees of ability that come with experience and training. They also reflect what you enjoy doing.

Technical and general skills

Some of these skills are quite general and describe your overall activity or important parts of it. Other skills are highly technical and relate to job responsibilities and behaviors. Some of these require formal preparation in school; others are learned in training programs or on the job. For example, Cindy, who works as a supervisor in the assembly room of a bicycle company, and Eileen, who is a supervisor in a knitting shop, have learned different technical skills because of their own positions and work environments. On a more fundamental level, however, each is using supervisory skills to direct tasks and organize things. Of course, being good at what you do makes it more enjoyable—we are often challenged to find ways of doing more of what we find rewarding.

Most women have had an exposure to different kinds of skills but haven't had the opportunity to reflect on their experiences, abilities, or functional skills. Many are considering changes that will place them in positions of newer responsibility, such as supervisors or managers; others want to advance the skills currently used or find a better fit between skills, preferences, and current opportunities. Chapter 3 in Part One and Chapter 6 in Part Two provided you with opportunities to explore your utilization and preferences in terms of some functional skills and basic skills that you might use in your career; later chapters in this section help you consider those responses. In the same spirit of self-inquiry, the following inventory focuses on the set of skills useful for careers that have supervisory or management features. It's an area being explored by many women. Based on your life and work experiences, you'll have time to reflect on the degree of your experience and mastery of skills and possible fits with opportunities in this area.

It is also reassuring to keep in mind that many different career skills can be developed—to the limit of your capabilities—but only if you are willing to invest the energy, time, and money in building that skill. So, when you think of skills, please consider not only those you already have but also those you've tried with some success or are interested in and might consider developing.

HOW TO IDENTIFY YOUR SUPERVISORY AND MANAGERIAL CAREER SKILLS

An inventory of general skills

The questionnaire that follows provides an inventory for you of supervisory-related abilities that are beneficial to women in careers of all kinds—even if you don't wish to become a supervisor. They are especially helpful if your career goals include supervising or managing. You'll find the generalized career skills that are listed include such areas as time management, planning, investigating, evaluating, decision making, negotiating, representing, thinking creatively, and so on. These are aspects of "commonsense management" that exist in just about every job but are emphasized for those in administrative positions.

How to take the inventory

What we ask you to do on this inventory is to evaluate your experience levels on a six-point scale. No experience will be indicated by zero, varying degrees of experience will rank from one (a minimum of experience) to five (maximum amounts of experience).

For example, if you have never seen or had the need to interpret any financial statements, such as a corporation's statement of consolidated net earnings in its annual report, then you have no career skill in analyzing financial statements and you would assess your ability at zero. If you've seen a consolidated statement but couldn't figure out what all those numbers were supposed to mean, then your skills would be assessed at one—and so on up the rating scale to a score of five. If you have actually worked on gathering the data that comprises a consolidated net earnings statement, understand the process, and feel competent in the area. There's also a place where you can note whether, in terms of your skills development, you'd like to think about exploring or strengthening a skill area.

Skills: not the same as expertise

Skills are not the same as expertise. If you know something about a subject, you have the beginning of a "skills development" program in that subject. Your preferences, goals, and opportunities will help you decide which skills to emphasize or develop.

One last note: The general career skills categories listed on the following self-assessment questionnaire are broadly based responsibilities that almost all working people are called upon to exercise to one degree or another, especially those whose career goals include supervising or managing. Planning, for example, involves the same functional career skills of organizing and prioritizing, regardless of whether that planning is being applied to a marketing strategy, a districtwide classroom schedule, or a cocktail party for the moguls from the coast. So relax. This is going to be an enlightening and helpful experience.

All working people use basic skills

SKILLS FOR CAREERS

Listed on the following pages are 13 general skills. These skills are most often used by supervisors or managers. The inventory allows you to tap into your experience in these areas and evaluate the current level of your skills, regardless of the jobs or positions you've held. You'll assess your current abilities in each of these skill areas, using the following scale:

0   Terrible (I hardly know what that means)

1   Doubtful (I know what it is, but I've never really done it)

2   Fair (I can do it, but not easily)

3   Good (I can handle it)

4   Fine (I do it and do it well)

5   Great (Not only do I do it well, I really enjoy it)

Circle the appropriate number for each subcategory listed below. Then average those rankings to get your overall rank for that category. Do this by taking your total score and dividing by the number of items—in this case, five.

1. Managing Time

	T D F G F G
• Setting priorities	0 1 2 3 4 5
• Understanding the relationships between my priorities and those of others	0 1 2 3 4 5
• Being able to assign appropriate time values to various tasks	0 1 2 3 4 5
• Delegating when appropriate	0 1 2 3 4 5
• Not doing everything myself	0 1 2 3 4 5

Total: _____ ÷ 5 = _____ (average)

I would like to explore or strengthen these skills (yes or no): _____

2. Planning

	T D F G F G
• Determining goals and objectives	0 1 2 3 4 5
• Establishing policies and procedures for getting things done	0 1 2 3 4 5
• Being able to consider dollar budgets, human resources, and such in making plans	0 1 2 3 4 5
• Forecasting future needs based on current information	0 1 2 3 4 5
• Setting standards of performance	0 1 2 3 4 5

	T D F G F G
● Preparing agendas	0 1 2 3 4 5
● Programming a total project	0 1 2 3 4 5

Total: _____ ÷ 7 = _____ (average)

I would like to explore or strengthen these skills: _____

3. Investigating

	T D F G F G
● Being logical	0 1 2 3 4 5
● Collecting appropriate information	0 1 2 3 4 5
● Being able to present information in records, reports, or accountings	0 1 2 3 4 5
● Knowing how to inventory	0 1 2 3 4 5
● Being able to measure output	0 1 2 3 4 5
● Analyzing financial statements	0 1 2 3 4 5

Total: _____ ÷ 6 = _____ (average)

I would like to explore or strengthen these skills: _____

4. Problem Solving

	T D F G F G
● Being able to pinpoint problems; not thinking in terms of "that big mess"	0 1 2 3 4 5
● Willing to risk changing the status quo	0 1 2 3 4 5
● Thinking in terms of goals rather than problems	0 1 2 3 4 5
● Being able to think creatively	0 1 2 3 4 5
● Identifying alternative solutions	0 1 2 3 4 5
● Brainstorming	0 1 2 3 4 5

Total: _____ ÷ 6 = _____ (average)

I would like to explore or strengthen these skills: _____

Coordinating

	T D F G F G
● Exchanging information across organizational lines to adjust and improve programs and activities	0 1 2 3 4 5

	T D F G F G
• Expediting	0 1 2 3 4 5
• Advising other people or departments	0 1 2 3 4 5
• Acting as a liaison	0 1 2 3 4 5
• Getting cooperation	0 1 2 3 4 5
• Arranging meetings	0 1 2 3 4 5
• Providing information to supervisors	0 1 2 3 4 5
• Giving and getting feedback	0 1 2 3 4 5

Total: _____ ÷ 8 = _____ (average)

I would like to explore or strengthen these skills: _____

6. Evaluating

	T D F G F G
• Assessing proposals, reports, or suggestions	0 1 2 3 4 5
• Judging output	0 1 2 3 4 5
• Making financial judgments	0 1 2 3 4 5
• Approving requests	0 1 2 3 4 5
• Conducting appraisals of other employees	0 1 2 3 4 5
• Inspecting products or assessing services	0 1 2 3 4 5

Total: _____ ÷ 6 = _____ (average)

I would like to explore or strengthen these skills: _____

7. Decision Making

	T D F G F G
• Willing to take time, not rush	0 1 2 3 4 5
• Knowing what information to gather before trying to reach a decision	0 1 2 3 4 5
• Involving others, getting expert assistance	0 1 2 3 4 5
• Being responsible about carrying out a decision once it has been made	0 1 2 3 4 5
• Being willing to admit a mistake and reverse a bad decision	0 1 2 3 4 5

Total: _____ ÷ 5 = _____ (average)

I would like to explore or strengthen these skills: _____

8. Supervising

	T D F G F G
• Directing, leading, and developing others	0 1 2 3 4 5
• Counseling others	0 1 2 3 4 5
• Training people	0 1 2 3 4 5
• Explaining work rules	0 1 2 3 4 5
• Making work assignments	0 1 2 3 4 5
• Disciplining others	0 1 2 3 4 5
• Dealing with conflicts	0 1 2 3 4 5
• Communicating and listening	0 1 2 3 4 5

Total: _____ ÷ 8 = _____ (average)

I would like to explore or strengthen these skills: _____

9. Staffing

	T D F G F G
• Being able to determine the appropriate size of a work team	0 1 2 3 4 5
• Recruiting people	0 1 2 3 4 5
• Interviewing	0 1 2 3 4 5
• Selecting employees	0 1 2 3 4 5
• Placing employees in specific jobs	0 1 2 3 4 5
• Recommending promotions and transfers	0 1 2 3 4 5

Total: _____ ÷ 6 = _____ (average)

I would like to explore or strengthen these skills: _____

10. Negotiating

	T D F G F G
• Dealing with colleagues, clients, or representatives of other organizations	0 1 2 3 4 5
• Contacting suppliers	0 1 2 3 4 5

- Purchasing or selling goods
  or services

  T D F G F G
  0 1 2 3 4 5

- Contracting for advertising
  or other professional services

  0 1 2 3 4 5

- Finding workable compromises

  0 1 2 3 4 5

  Total: _____ ÷ 5 = _____ (average)

I would like to explore or strengthen these skills: _____

11. Representing

- Being a spokesperson for your
  group or company

  T D F G F G
  0 1 2 3 4 5

- Attending conventions on
  behalf of your company

  0 1 2 3 4 5

- Participating in professional
  groups, activities

  0 1 2 3 4 5

  Total: _____ ÷ 3 = _____ (average)

I would like to explore or strengthen these skills: _____

12. Communicating

- Writing with the reader in mind,
  selecting words and phrases
  appropriate to that reader

  T D F G F G
  0 1 2 3 4 5

- Being brief, direct, and accurate
  in written communication

  0 1 2 3 4 5

- Speaking and writing with
  expression of feeling as well
  as information

  0 1 2 3 4 5

- Saying what I mean

  0 1 2 3 4 5

- Being aware of voice tone and
  body language

  0 1 2 3 4 5

- Giving and asking for feedback

  0 1 2 3 4 5

- Listening with patience,
  openness, and concern

  0 1 2 3 4 5

  Total: _____ ÷ 7 = _____ (average)

I would like to explore or strengthen these skills: _____

13. Thinking Creatively

	T D F G F G
• Taking the time to develop and practice strong reading habits in a variety of subject areas	0 1 2 3 4 5
• Finding challenge rather than threat in ideas, books, and such which may be contrary to my present perceptions	0 1 2 3 4 5
• Looking for similarities between what I read, hear, and such, and what I already know	0 1 2 3 4 5
• Seeing and working with new relationships between people, ideas, and things	0 1 2 3 4 5
• Giving myself an opportunity to daydream or free associate	0 1 2 3 4 5
• Asking questions	0 1 2 3 4 5
• Approaching situations with a positive point of view	0 1 2 3 4 5

Total: _____ ÷ 7 = _____ (average)

I would like to explore or strengthen these skills: _____

COMMENTS AND INTERPRETATIONS

First of all, don't be surprised if your scores contain many highs or lows or look like a roller coaster with lots of highs and lows. The point of this inventory of skills is simply to take stock of where you are today. You're just exploring some of the general skills needed to keep things organized for yourself, what you are interested in, your current abilities and preferences in terms of managing work activities.

Skill strengths and preferences

Now, let's review: what are your strongest administrative career skills? Are there some where you have strong preferences? Look over your answers and put a check next to those where you have both particular strengths and desires. Make a note of areas where you're weak in experience but want to learn more about that skill, whether it's to get more experience so you can make future career decisions, to strengthen skills needed for your current career activities, or to reach for career goals requiring supervisory or management skills.

SKILL STRENGTHS AND PREFERENCES

	STRENGTH	PREFERENCE	WANT TO EXPLORE OR STRENGTHEN
1. Managing time	_____	_____	_____
2. Planning	_____	_____	_____
3. Investigating	_____	_____	_____
4. Problem solving	_____	_____	_____
5. Coordinating	_____	_____	_____
6. Evaluating	_____	_____	_____
7. Decision making	_____	_____	_____
8. Supervising	_____	_____	_____
9. Staffing	_____	_____	_____
10. Negotiating	_____	_____	_____
11. Representing	_____	_____	_____
12. Communicating	_____	_____	_____
13. Thinking creatively	_____	_____	_____

You now have an overview of yourself in relationship to general supervisory and management career skills. If you once thought of these as magical or mysterious qualities, you can see now that they are often made up of many skills which you may enjoy using and use well. Identifying such skills, whether they are basic skills (Chapter 6) or administrative skills or functional skills (Chapters 3, 19), allows you to plan for the advice, experiences, and understanding that keep the skills portion of your career compass in perspective. That way your skills become abilities you master, enrich, and direct in terms of your career plan rather than factors that control your choice of jobs and career experiences.

That's important, because your skills are one of your most specific points of access to your own career planning. It's important for you to know what skills you possess as you start off toward that goal.

Remember, only a few things can stand in the way of the career advancement you are interested in. Among them are:

- *Failing to assess your skills and abilities* . . . and therefore
- *Setting the wrong goals* . . . which leads you to
- *Build on weaknesses rather than on strengths* . . . or to
- *Make a tactical error*

Understanding your current levels of career skills, how well you do the kinds of things that you will be called upon to do each day, can help you to:

- *Set appropriate goals*—goals that are realistic and obtainable given the person (Part One) and the circumstances (Part Two) you have to work with; goals that have been thought through and cannot only be obtained but will have built into them the payoffs you want . . . not some hollow victory that forces you to ask, "What did I ever want to do this for?" And goals that are of your own choosing, not hand-me-down goals from some more-or-less well intended other.

- *Identify building blocks of solid strength*—the things that are right with you, not the things that are wrong . . . those aspects of your skills in which it pays to invest development time and effort . . . skills that fit your career plans.

- *Avoid tactical errors*—understand that it's what you can *do*, what you can accomplish, the results you obtain, that will count most. Personality changes and "dressing for success" may be useful, but ultimately good career tactics require that you recognize what is needed in the organization and that you provide the skills and abilities to do what is needed.

Remember, career skills are built from your strengths and preferences. Let's look at how that's done.

HOW TO IDENTIFY YOUR SPECIFIC CAREER SKILLS

Reviewing specific job skills

Sound career growth calls not only for the general career skills on which you have already assessed your abilities but also for specific job skills based on organizational requirements. In Chapter 3, on pages 24–27, we asked you to inventory your potential for gaining specific job skills. These skills also covered your whole life experience—not just your work activities—and included your hobbies and recreational activities and your outside intellectual interests.

Look back through this skills inventory now and note particularly page 28, where you identified five skills that you like, or would like, to do most. Let's analyze these skills now by answering three questions:

1. How do these preferred skills relate to the D.O.T. classifications —information (data), people, and things?   *A D.O.T. analysis*

2. How do these preferred skills fit into the career wheel of occupational themes?

3. How do these preferred skills fit with the administrative skills you just finished analyzing on the previous pages?

Let's look at your answers, one at a time.

Your Functional Skills and a D.O.T. Analysis

For convenience, list the five preferred skills from your inventory in Chapter 3, page 28:

1. _____

2. _____

3. _____

4. _____

5. _____

It will be helpful to keep these in mind as you relate them to data/information—people—things items.   *A D.O.T. analysis*

The skills inventory in Chapter 3 analyzed some of your abilities in terms of eight general classifications of skills: physical skills, four different uses of mental skills, creative skills, leadership skills, and helping skills. The following outline shows how those skills relate in general fashion to data/information, people, and things. You may wish to check off an area in which you have particularly high preferences or note the number or name of a particular skill within a broader skill category.

MY SKILL PREFERENCES AND DATA/INFORMATION, PEOPLE, AND THINGS

DATA/ INFORMATION	PEOPLE	THINGS
____ Mental skills: Using numbers (Nos. 16–21)	____ Mental skills: Using words (Nos. 12–15)	____ Physical skills (Nos. 1–11)

_____ Mental skills: Using ana- lytical logic (Nos. 22–28)

_____ Leadership skills (Nos. 41–48)

_____ Mental skills: Using intuition (Nos. 29–33)

_____ Helping skills (Nos. 49–54)

_____ Creative skills (Nos. 34–40)

The profile and the indication of your preferences indicate which skills you'd like to use in relation to data/information, people, or things. Quite naturally, it's not the number of skills that is important but the overall picture. It helps clarify your strengths and the way you might prefer to use these skills in your work. That information can be helpful in a variety of ways:

1. To upgrade a particular skill found useful for your career.

2. To improve performance. (For example, a saleswoman using her pre-ferred and strong skills, *except creative ones*, might want to consid-er ways of incorporating this desired skill set into her regular job activities. She might consider shifting into positions dealing with display that would require creative ability and thus make a current job more satisfying.)

3. To provide information useful for planning career goals. (Long-term goals will prove more satisfying when they spring from skills you enjoy using. Knowing what skills you prefer to use, even when addi-tional training might be needed, helps you visualize some "natural-ly" enjoyable ways of working. Your values will help you position those skills in terms of goals and continuing opportunities to reach out for those goals.)

Using the Career Wheel

You can also get some additional information about skills and work possibil-ities by relating skills to the career wheel. As previously noted, the career wheel describes six categories of work functions or work styles. The follow-ing diagram shows generally how the eight categories of skills from Chapter 3 relate to each of the six "spokes" of the career wheel; you may wish to check off areas important to you. As a reminder, the definition of each

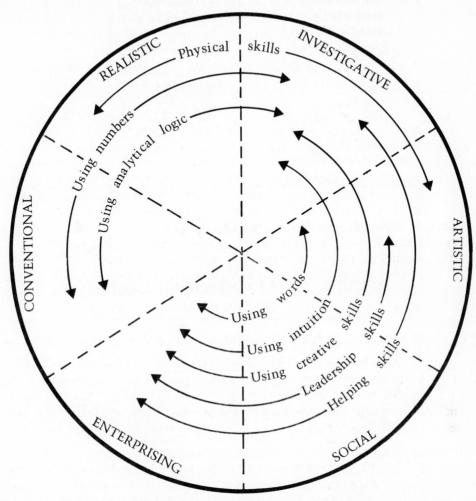

- *Realistic:* People who have athletic or mechanical ability, prefer to work with objects, machines, tools, plants or animals or to be outdoors.
- *Investigative:* People who like to observe, learn, investigate, analyze, evaluate or solve problems.
- *Artistic:* People who have artistic, innovating or intuitional abilities, and like to work in unstructured situations, using their imagination or creativity.
- *Social:* People who like to work with people—to inform, enlighten, help, train, develop, or cure them, or are skilled with words.
- *Enterprising:* People who like to work with people—influencing, persuading or leading or managing for organizational goals or for economic gain.
- *Conventional:* People who like to work with data, have clerical or numerical ability, carry things out in detail or following through on other's instructions.

orientation or career wheel theme is also on the diagram. That will help you locate a section where you might place a unique skill.

How do those skills seem to line up in terms of your skill preferences and orientations to work? That information may help you see a little more clearly the kinds of specific functional skills you may wish to use as you search for a better fit between your personal orientation to work and the responsibilities and activities stressed in different jobs.

You can add occupations to the wheel

With this information, notice which of the spokes of the career wheel contains more of your preferred activities than the others. Then begin to think about other specific career orientations that are closest to that spoke. And we have also included as a resource here the D.O.T. descriptions of nine occupational categories. The D.O.T. lists thousands of occupations. Here 97 broad occupations and categories are listed. See if you can find "yourself" in that list, or some possibilities. Add any occupation that is interesting to you on the career wheel you've been filling out.

OCCUPATIONAL CATEGORIES, DIVISIONS, AND GROUPS

OCCUPATIONAL CATEGORIES

Professional, technical, and managerial
Clerical and sales
Service
Farming, fishery, forestry, and related occupations
Processing
Machines trades
Bench work
Structural work
Miscellaneous

Professional, Technical, and Managerial Occupations

Architecture and engineering
Mathematics and physical sciences
Life sciences
Social sciences
Medicine and health
Education
Museum, library, and archival sciences
Law and jurisprudence
Religion and theology
Writing

Art
Entertainment and recreation
Administrative specializations
Managers and officials, n.e.c.
Miscellaneous professional, technical, and managerial occupations

Clerical and Sales Occupations

Stenography, typing, filing, and related occupations
Computing and account-recording occupations
Material and production recording occupations
Information and message distribution occupations
Miscellaneous clerical occupations
Sales representatives, services
Sales representatives and salespersons, commodities
Merchandising occupations, except sales representatives

Service Occupations

Domestic service occupations
Food and beverage preparation and service occupations
Lodging and related service occupations
Barbering, cosmetology, and related service occupations
Amusement and recreation service occupations
Miscellaneous personal service occupations
Apparel and furnishings service occupations
Protective service occupations
Building and related service occupations

Farming, Fishery, Forestry, and Related Occupations

Plant farming occupations
Animal farming occupations
Miscellaneous farming and related occupations
Fishery and related occupations
Forestry occupations
Hunting, trapping, and related occupations
Agricultural service occupations

Processing Occupations

Processing of metal
Foundry occupations
Processing of food, tobacco, and related products
Processing of paper and related materials
Processing of petroleum, coal, natural and manufactured gas, and related
   products
Processing of chemicals, plastics, synthetics, rubber, paint, and related
   products

Processing of wood and wood products
Processing of stone, clay, glass, and related products
Processing of leather, textiles, and related products
Processing occupations, n.e.c.

Machine Trades Occupations

Metal machining occupations
Metalworking occupations, n.e.c.
Mechanics and machinery repair persons
Paperworking occupations
Printing occupations
Wood machining occupations
Occupations in machining stone, clay, glass, and related materials
Textile occupations
Machine trades occupations, n.e.c.

Bench Work Occupations

Fabrication, assembly, and repair of metal products, n.e.c.
Fabrication and repair of scientific and medical apparatus, photographic and
    optical goods, watches and clocks, and related products
Assembly and repair of electrical equipment
Fabrication and repair of products made from assorted materials
Painting, decorating, and related occupations
Fabrication and repair of plastics, synthetics, rubber, and related products
Fabrication and repair of wood products
Fabrication and repair of sand, stone, clay, and glass products
Fabrication and repair of textile, leather, and related products
Bench work occupations, n.e.c.

Structural Work Occupations

Metal fabricating, n.e.c.
Welders, flame cutters, and related occupations
Electrical assembling, installing, and repairing occupations
Painting, plastering, waterproofing, cementing, and related occupations
Excavating, grading, paving, and related occupations
Construction occupations, n.e.c.
Structural work occupations, n.e.c.

Miscellaneous Occupations

Motor freight occupations
Transportation occupations, n.e.c.
Packaging and materials handling occupations
Extraction of minerals
Logging

Production and distribution of utilities
Amusement, recreation, and motion picture occupations, n.e.c.
Graphic art work

Pulling Together Career Skills

Let's draw together the information you have about skills and the ways in which that information helps you identify function areas and positions. The following career-planning triangle provides some space for your ideas and reminders concerning the inventories and exercises you've just completed. We can show you how Debbie used those reflections in her career planning.

Putting it all together

Debbie used her skills inventory to consider a career change. As one of the few history teachers specializing in minority groups and their cultural history, she was a popular member of the local staff. Quite naturally, the school board asked if she would direct educational policies and programs and assume a board position. It sounded tempting. But she knew very little about the new job. Analyzing her skills relative to data/information, people, and things, she realized she was doing a lot of coordinating, supervising, and machine tending (visual aids). The new job would require a lot of synthesizing of current ideas and programs, negotiating skills (with other teachers or learning specialists or administrators), and handling of visual aids. She'd need to upgrade her skills in terms of data/information, people, and things.

Other self-assessments of skills convinced her she had some but not all of the skills and preferred skill applications needed for administration. Her planning skills were weakest and she had little experience in or desire to learn skills in the area of staffing. Still, she found some of her strengths seemed to fit as she considered her functional skills and career wheel. She was a whiz at all the intuitive mental skills (but low on logic and words and numbers); and quite naturally, she scored moderately high in leadership and strong on helping and creative skills. Her physical skills and preferences were very low.

Basically, she felt she fit in the "social" spoke of the career wheel with some lesser interests in the "investigative" spoke. How did all that stack up against the job of an administrative board member? Not too well. The more she found out about that job, the more she realized her qualms were justified. The newer position required strong verbal skills, logic, and leadership ability and would provide her with fewer outlets for creative ideas. It wasn't the job she thought it was. Debbie thought through the reasons why she was attracted to this job in the first place and the reasons for her discontent with the current job. Basically, she wanted more opportunities to use her creative and intuitive skills and to find ways of coaching more young people and monitoring other youths as they started on their careers. Bringing those

Career
Skills

Job
Responsibilities
and
Behaviors

Function Areas

My preferences concerning:

___ Data ___ People ___ Things

Fill in any descriptive terms or ideas
you have about the level of your skills
preferences in terms of the D.O.T.
(D., P., or T.). What are my preferences
and skill in supervision or
management? Jot down these skills.

_____

_____

_____

Do I have any ideas about changes in
my current positions that would
provide me with opportunities to use
more of the skills I enjoy?

_____

_____

_____

Using Holland's classification, what
is my orientation to work? What
strong skills might support those
orientations?

_____

_____

_____

What occupations seem to fit that
orientation and are of interest to me?

_____

_____

_____

ideas back to her career compass and checking them against her terminal values for wisdom, freedom, and security and her instrumental values for independence, she began to explore some other opportunities and to see that what made sense for her was staying put.

Her analysis indicated searching out a position which would combine several preferred skills and activities: as an area resource counselor in minority programs and a teacher in the area of black history (if that were possible). These types of assignments seemed to fit her best, her personal circumstances and preferences as a career goal. She also had lots of ideas to bring to her career compass and lots of ideas to check out in terms of planning (and training). Her "almost" leap into administration turned into an exploration of (real) skills and preferences and the beginnings of a rewarding career.

SOME FINAL NOTES

Now that you've had the opportunity to think about skills in relation to responsibilities and work, why not bring these together again for yourself. For this purpose, we have provided the following diagram to help you review your skills, responsibilities, and the functional areas to which they apply. Remember, *skills* are used to meet *responsibilities* that are carried out in a given function area.

As you can see, information about skills is just one factor in identifying and planning a career. All points of the career compass are important to target a meaningful use of skills. But information about skills and their use plus skill possibilities are important. If you are not certain what skills are used to meet specific responsibilities in a given function area of your company, for instance, make it a point to speak to someone—secretary, supervisor, or manager—in that area to learn about those skills (and activities). Go to the library and browse through the *Dictionary of Occupational Titles* to learn more about the skills required in a given job; how they relate to data/information, people, and things; and what attributes are helpful in that job. Write to professional organizations, trade associations, unions, schools, or governmental groups. Do whatever is necessary for you to collect all the information you'll need to make meaningful career decisions. And most of all, take risks. Ask that one last bold question. Check out an off-beat source. Be creative about your own working life.

What skills for which jobs

As you finish this chapter, then, you should have a basic idea of the skills you can bring to your work, as well as the skills you'll want to develop for work. Always evaluate your skills specifically and realistically. Take advantage of opportunities to develop your strengths in those skills necessary for increased success in your current job assignment. And take advantage, too, of opportunities to develop your strengths in those skills and responsibilities that will lead you into career function areas where you will have the highest level of success potential.

Now you know your preferences

MY RECAP: SKILLS, RESPONSIBILITIES, AND FUNCTION AREA

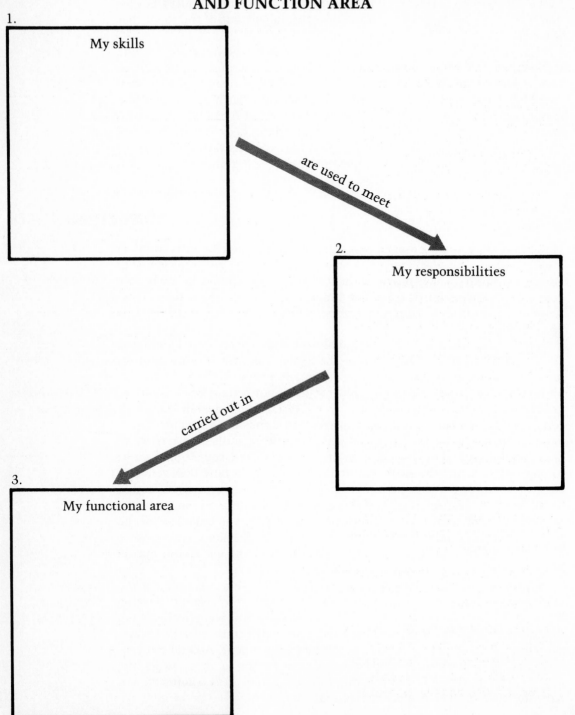

ACTION CHECKLIST FOR CHAPTER 19

Checklist	*My Ideas and Action Steps*	*Date*

√ Skills underlie responsibilities that are combined in a function area.

√ "Supervisory" skills areas (as developed in this chapter) contain important and needed skills that are widely used regardless of supervisory responsibilities.

√ People register great differences among areas of "supervisory" skills and preferences.

√ Skill strengths quite naturally affect preferences, but other career compass points (goals, values, and opportunities must be considered.

√ Many areas of low skill ability can be strengthened — desire, time, and cost are critical considerations.

√ D.O.T. categories of data/ information, people, and things can help you profile your current skill accomplishments — and also act as a planning tool for building future skills strengths for your function area.

√ Holland's classification scheme of six categories helps you to identify in a general way your overall work styles and preferences.

√ Each Holland category represents a number of function areas to help you tie these together.

√ Each function area combines various responsibilities; and these are supported by skills so that you are able to achieve closure on skill, responsibility, and function area.

√ Your career compass acts as a check
to make sure you are thinking
through together skill — goal —
value — opportunity.

_____

_____

_____   _____

20

Finding Your Niche: How to Transfer Career Skills

I sold cosmetics door-to-door while my kids were young, because I could pick my own hours. Now I'm still selling cosmetics at the big department store downtown. The salary isn't much, but the benefits are great and I do all right with my commission. Well, the point is, I'm not really doing what I like. Oh, I like selling—I love it! I'm the one they meant when they said, "She could sell a refrigerator to an Eskimo." Except, of course, they said "He." And that's my point. Selling cosmetics is too restricting for me—a sort of hothouse atmosphere. I want to get out into the world of machines. Quite frankly, I'd like to sell automobiles or trucks or farm vehicles. But talk about a man's world! My résumé shows solid experience for 11 years, sure, but all of it selling lipstick and eyeshadow. I just get stonewalled—even at my own local dealer's. How do I break out of this bind?

MARGE

I'm the director of safety for a pretty big outfit and I'm really sold on my job. It's funny, though, a guy I went to college with was in for an interview last week. And the first thing he said was, "Hey, Esther, I thought you went into nursing!" And I said right back, "I did." Then I saw the puzzled look on his face. It's happened before. If you're a nurse, everyone expects to see you in a white uniform with a little starched cap carrying a tray full of needles and pills. I had to go through the whole trip with him—how I got from my job as nursing supervisor in the emergency room at Memorial Hospital to teaching safety at the junior college—and finally to the plant here, with not too many steps in between. It seems a pretty logical path to me. But you'd be surprised how many people just can't seem to figure out how or why I got where I am. . . .

ESTHER

Transferring can mean mobility

Without realizing it, Marge and Esther are talking about the transfer of their career skills. Along with building your skills, being able to transfer them is one of the most important concepts in career development. It can make the crucial difference between mobility and stagnation.

Thus far we have spoken about transferability with regard to applying skills in different functional areas of your organization. You remember how Janice, the clerk/bookkeeper, found a more people-oriented job by transferring within her company from billing to credit and collection. However, transferability applies not only to functional areas *in* an organization, but to other types of organizations as well. You may have skills that are necessary to carry out the responsibilities of a function area that is common to a number of different industries or professions.

Skills can transfer across industries

The secretarial skills we mentioned in Chapter 18 might have been used to meet reporting and correspondence responsibilities in a sales function. But sales itself is a function, or operational activity, that crosses many industrial, professional, and business lines. The secretary in our example might have worked in the heavy equipment industry or in a service-related industry—health, education, social, or business services—or in virtually thousands of consumer product industries. Similarly, a saleswoman like Marge could well use her persuasive skills in the sales efforts of any number of different product types—literally in products as seemingly diverse as industrial real estate and dresses.

How it works

Our friend, the computer programmer, could write programs in work scheduling for everything from a small manufacturing plant to a giant airline. Bookkeeping is a basic work in almost every business, whether profit or nonprofit; thus, those skills are transferable across the entire spectrum of the world of work. We will see that Janice could move to another industry. And Esther proved that nursing skills have transferability; nurses work not just in hospitals—or in plant safety departments—but also in banks, schools, research labs, and any number of other places. Teachers, who have specific skills in subject areas, have some built-in ability to transfer with success, as our profile of Liz Hoyt at the end of this part will illustrate.

A SCHEMATIC OF TRANSFERABILITY

Use a schematic

Using this schematic, you can see that your present level of skills and responsibilities gives you mobility into different function areas of a company and that work in a given function area can take you into many different industries or even many different locations in the same company.

Skill Transfer Across Companies, Industries, or Professions

We can adapt a wheel model to help you get a clearer picture of your inter-industry mobility. By this we mean simply your ability to move between companies in different industries. Place your functional preference (set of skills, job, or occupation) in the center circle. The first outer ring of circles should be the skills and responsibilities you would like to utilize in that function area. The outer rim of the large circle represents the boundaries of the industries using those skills and responsibilities in that functional area:

The Transferability Model

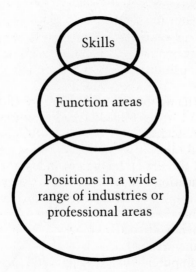

Skills

Function areas

Positions in a wide range of industries or professional areas

An Example: Janice, the Bookkeeper

Janice, as we have suggested, might eventually have wished to expand the scope of her investigation beyond the company in which she worked. She can use a Transferability Model to develop that broader perspective.

Using the Transferability Model

Thinking her way through the Transferability Model enabled Janice to identify a great number of possibilities for her career future. Take some time now to think your way through the Transferability Model. Identify your functional preference, the skills and responsibilities you'd like to handle, and the different kinds of industries, organizations, or professions to which those apply. You may fill in all of the circles provided, you may find that you need to draw a larger circle on a separate sheet, or you may not be able to use

Thinking your way through the model

THE TRANSFERABILITY MODEL

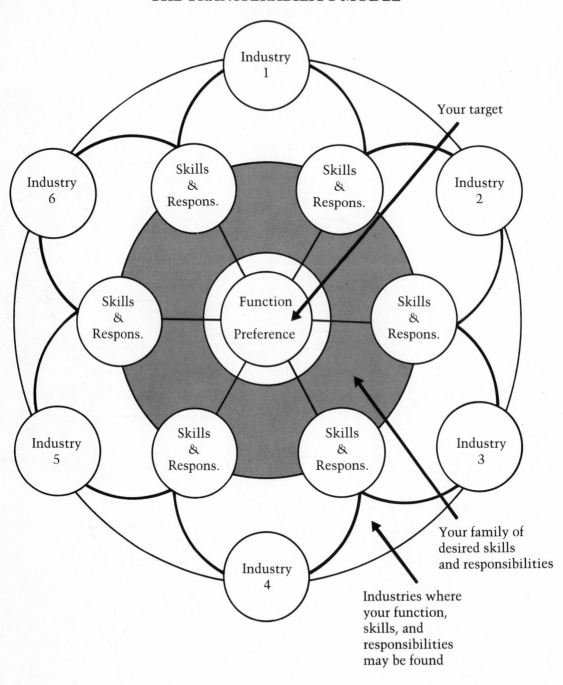

THE TRANSFERABILITY MODEL: JANICE'S EXAMPLE

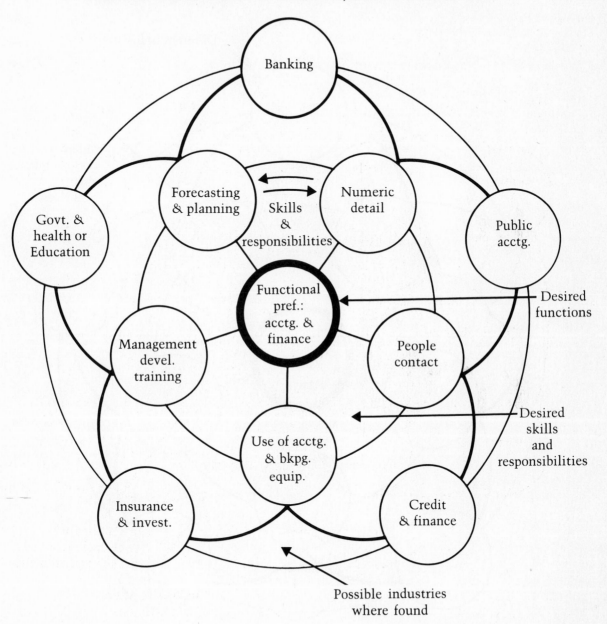

MY TRANSFERABILITY MODEL

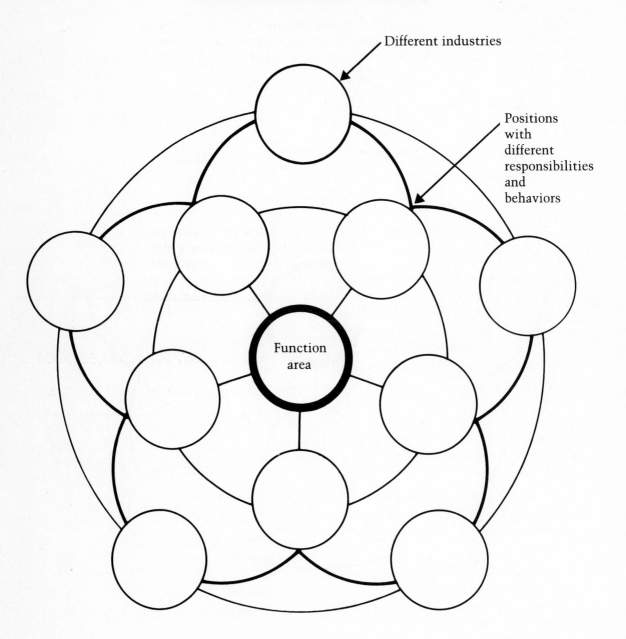

Different industries

Positions
with
different
responsibilities
and
behaviors

Function
area

all the circles provided. The important point is to give free rein to your creative thinking.

Obviously, each new opportunity you have identified will require you to take on the responsibility for investigating requirements and potentials. Within each new industry "circle," you must explore and evaluate opportunities such as:

Evaluate each opportunity

- Education/experience requirements

- Hiring practices

- Number of available jobs/employment trends

- Pay levels/benefits

- Advancement, growth, and transferability potentials

This is the kind of evaluation you learned to make in Part Three when you studied your work environment as an important part of your career style —and it's a good example of the way in which you can use all four points of your career compass to consider possibilities and preferences. Putting it all together as a whole and planning for the future are what will bring about your most important goal—career satisfaction.

ACTION CHECKLIST FOR CHAPTER 20

Checklist	*My Ideas and Action Steps*	*Date*
√ Skills can become a part of carrying out many different responsibilities that in turn make up a variety of function areas.		
√ Skill transferability means that you can look at function areas in many different industries, companies, and locations.		
√ A given function area represents sets of skills and responsibilities that will differ (somewhat), depending on organizational and industrial circumstances.		
√ A given company can represent a wide range of possibilities and		

opportunities for applying preferred skills to desired function areas.

√ Increasing your possibilities means pursuing widely different and available sources of information and also cultivating these in a creative way.

√ The career compass is needed as a check to make sure that skills, goals, values, and opportunities are working together.

21

Developing Tactical Career Strategies

Talk about complicated: I thought all my problems would be solved once I had a job. Now I'm thinking of moving ahead—or is it around? The golden pathway to my future looks like a chess set, what with transfers, promotions, and all the job changes possible. I get tangled up thinking about all these lines of advancement. Which way is up?

CYNTHIA

I just don't feel like a member of the "in" group. Oh, part of it's me; I imagine I'm treated differently at times just because I'm not really "one of the boys." But it's more than that. There's a way of treating me that tells me I've much to learn and do before I'm really accepted. Is it time, or attitude, or experience, or a way of acting? Or is it them? What can I do to break into that magic circle of insiders?

BETTY JO

In this part, we have asked you to fill in a number of schematics and complete a number of different models—all to help you do the self-assessment so necessary for establishing realistic and obtainable goals that you can fulfill by building on your strengths.

Adding these materials to those you worked with earlier in the book, you have now gained skills in:

- Building your career compass
- Planning to meet those goals
- Creating positive interpersonal and behavioral skills

*After two and a half years, Cynthia began to see how
promotions worked on paper and how they really
worked.*

- Assessing your general and technical skills in the context of their
potentials in the world of work

*You are ready
for tactics*

You have also learned how to expand the horizons of your career path
potentials by using the Transferability Model. Now you are ready for a
tactical plan that will move you ahead in your career—ahead, that is, in the
sense of going where *you* wish to go (which may include stabilizing or
enriching your current position).

A TACTICAL PLAN FOR GROWING IN YOUR CAREER

Edgar H. Schein, an outstanding organizational psychologist, thinks about organizations in a way that provides a unique perspective for planning your growth in an organization. He conceives of organizations in three ways:

The Schein Model

THE ORGANIZATION MODEL

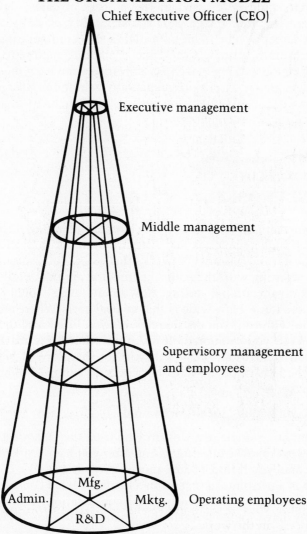

Chief Executive Officer (CEO)

Executive management

Middle management

Supervisory management and employees

Mfg.

Admin.   Mktg.   Operating employees

R&D

Adapted from Edgar H. Schein, "The Individual, the Organization and the Career," *Journal of Applied Behavioral Science* 7(1971), no. 4, by permission of the author.

Within this organization model are a number of different boundaries and filtering systems that affect people's career progress and development with-

*Three ways
to grow*

*Hierarchical
growth*

in that organization structure. For example, in our organizational cone above, there are three hierarchies (or levels) between the chief executive officer (CEO) and the operating employees. Each of these levels represents a *hierarchical boundary* that must be passed through if someone aspires to move upward ("upward mobility").

But not all career growth is upward. Our conelike company has a number of different function areas, and each of these areas represents another boundary that could be crossed in the process of career development—

*Functional
growth*

functional growth. Remember your transferability of skills. And there is even a third career-development potential of this configuration. Notice the central core running through the cone. That line represents the core of power and decision making that exists at every level within the organization —the "insiders group." A person can actually gain much additional prestige

*Inclusionary
growth*

and pay by focusing career development in movement toward that central core—termed *inclusionary growth*.

UNDERSTANDING BOUNDARIES, FILTERS, AND NETWORKS

*Boundaries,
filters,
networks*

An important tactic in your career-development planning is understanding the organizational boundaries and filtering systems that will affect your plan—the formal and informal networks that exist. You can gain that understanding by working with the conical configuration that would depict your own current organizational setting. How many levels would it have? How many function areas? How wide is that central core? Where are you on that configuration? How did you get there? Were you hired into the company at that spot? Were you promoted? If so, from where else in the company? Where do you want to go? How will you get there? What boundaries and filters will you pass through? What networks do you need to be aware of?

Using the Organization Model: An Example

Let's consider an example of a woman who used the Organization Model to provide answers to these questions. And after you have worked through her completed cone, you'll find a blank model for your use.

*How Cynthia
used the
Organization
Model*

Cynthia is a personnel assistant in a medium-sized consulting firm specializing in management recruiting and consultation. Cynthia's areas of responsibility have included updating personnel records, tracking consultant assignments, and taking care of benefits. She feels that things are at a standstill and has started to investigate her career possibilities. She came to the firm shortly after graduating from college with a business degree and has been there two and one-half years. Strangely, they had told her very little about the firm when she was hired; or at least it didn't register—she was so happy with getting a job and getting started on her career and being self-supporting. She started to talk to the consultants, members of home office departments, and her supervisor, too, as to how the firm was organized—and she started to learn how things worked on paper and how they really worked: where people started in when recruited from colleges, departments where they started, how long it took to make moves, and where they moved to. For a relatively simple firm, there were many possible moves involving the transferring of her skills into other staff departments or into their "line operations," which were consulting.

She learned that the firm, which had two branch offices, was planning a third and that the main organization functions involved administration (office, personnel, reports processing), marketing (mostly by senior staff members), client research, and consulting. Promotions and transfers (represented by arrows on the diagram) had been between administration and research and/or consulting, research and administration, and research and consulting. When an assignment was secured, a team representing the needed specialists for dealing with the client's problems was assembled. The information Cynthia gathered is represented on the following sketch and helped to clarify possible career moves and what it might take to actually make them.

Passing Through Filters

Once you have a good visual perspective on your organization, think not just of the boundaries—hierarchical, functional, and inclusionary—but even more important, think of the filtering systems that surround these different organizational boundaries. Filtering systems are made up of *formal policy statements*, like educational or experience requirements for certain jobs, and *informal practices*, like promoting only people who fit the "old buddy" network pattern.

What are your organization's *hierarchical boundaries?* What kinds of knowledge, experience, or credentials are necessary for a person to move upward? How much seniority? If you wanted to move from a secretarial-clerical position to a supervisory position in your department, what filters would you have to pass through? Would experience count as much or more than educational background? What about age, gender, and ethnic or racial background? Would they make it easier or more difficult to move into certain positions and pass through the filters that exist in every organizational setting? If it is difficult, what can you do to reduce those concerns by using your skills?

Identify hierarchical boundaries

Keep in mind that, while most companies *do* want to practice positive affirmative action, companies are made up of people, many of whom have blind spots to their own biases pro and con the different characteristics of different people. Many of these same people control the informal power structure in an organization. That suggests that good tactics in career plan-

CYNTHIA'S ORGANIZATION MODEL

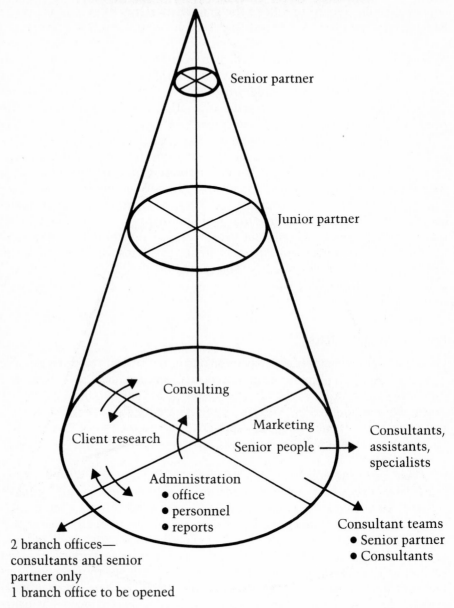

Senior partner

Junior partner

Consulting

Client research

Marketing
Senior people → Consultants, assistants, specialists

Administration
- office
- personnel
- reports

2 branch offices—
consultants and senior
partner only
1 branch office to be opened

Consultant teams
- Senior partner
- Consultants

ning require that you assess such potential opportunities and barriers. Often that means helping others see you as a talented individual and learning to work in ways that reduce their "blind spots" in terms of your work. Part Three of *Growing* has many ideas about creating a realistic, workable relationship with others.

MY ORGANIZATION MODEL

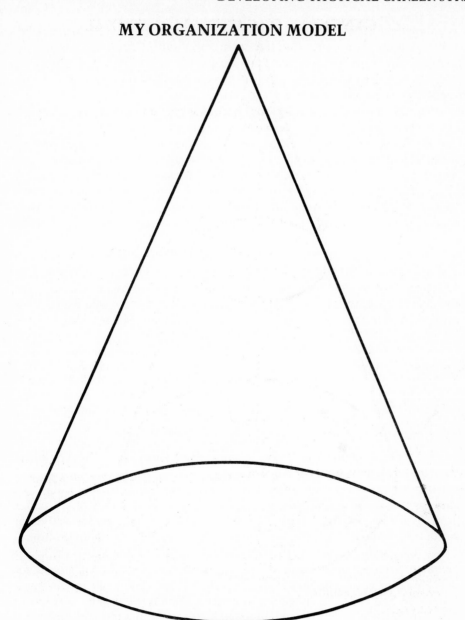

What about *functional boundaries?* How does a person move across departmental or unit lines in your organizational configuration? Functional movement is often based on technical skills. You must find out what skills are valued and gain them, as we pointed out in Chapter 19. Even more often, functional movement can be based on creative approaches to demonstrating

Identify functional boundaries

the transferability of your skills from one function area to another. Credentials again can figure into functional career growth. Check this out in your own organization. What credentials do people in the jobs and functional areas to which you aspire possess? Can you get similar credentials? Would night classes or community college courses help?

"Out and up": often the best way

Another issue to consider when thinking about functional growth is this: often the fastest way up is out and up. It may be easier to achieve passage through a hierarchical boundary by simultaneously passing through a functional boundary, even in the same organization. For example, one executive secretary we know was promoted to supervisor of her company's financial public relations department from her former position as secretary to the corporate treasurer—an upward move to the level of supervisory management and a functional move from administrative finance to public relations.

The organization's responsibility

Of course, the organization itself should accept a major responsibility for functional growth by making opportunities available, as Rosabeth Kantor, the author of *Men and Women of the Corporation,* has pointed out. In an October 1979 interview with *Ms.* Magazine, Dr. Kantor was asked what structural changes might "humanize" the work place. She responded:

> Extending the options for movement within the organization and more lateral transfers across functional areas. . . . Structural change doesn't necessarily mean completely revising the organization. It does mean systematically making available to the many the opportunities that have always been available to the few. "Opportunity" has ordinarily meant moving up, but promotion is not the only way to grow.

Identify inclusionary boundaries

Inclusionary boundaries can be the most difficult to cross. The filters surrounding inclusionary boundaries tend to be those expressing your personality and your acceptability—which make you a part of "the gang." But this does not mean that women are excluded from inclusionary career growth. It does mean that you must assess the characteristics valued by insiders in your organization or learn to create a niche in your environment.

If that is the growth path you wish to pursue and if those skills and characteristics are acceptable in your personal values system, go ahead and develop them yourself. Frequently, they are not as vague as we might think. Study the habits of the people who control the informal power structure. What are those people like? What do they seem to value most in each other and in their working relationships? What helps them work more effectively?

Dealing with "old buddy" networks

One friend of ours was startled to discover that in her organization a sense of humor was valued far more than many high levels of competency because it made leadership skills more effective at a time of pressure. In the many crisis situations that seemed to take place in her company, the highly competent, deadly serious folks were frequently ignored while their competent but jocular peers were given great accord. At first this seemed incongruous to her; but the more she observed that organizational reality, the more she realized that, for the people around her, humor broke the tension of the many problem situations that had to be faced. It really was a valuable attribute, influencing the decisions and performance of an entire group when it was used to direct attention to real issues.

Quite naturally, there are times when no fit is possible or desirable. The value systems you hold may conflict with expected work behavior; or it may not be possible to adapt quickly and meaningfully to the needs of a group, for example, a "high-pressure, extremely competitive group." You may need to plan for a transfer or seek a more compatible organization if you find the fit you strongly value isn't attainable. On the other hand, your skills and style may be different and become a valuable resource for an organization. Look around!

What characteristics are highly valued in your organization's "in" group —its inclusionary network? Can you cultivate these characteristics in yourself without compromising your personal value system? Is it even possible that you already have these characteristics without realizing it—that they are really just "undeveloped skills," like being organized or thoughtful?

Working Out a "Picture" of Your Organization

Use the worksheet to work out your organization's boundaries and filtering systems so you can develop the best tactical career plan possible. You may find it helpful to refer to the cone schematic, the Organizational Model, that you just completed.

Your organization a structural analysis

WORKSHEET: ORGANIZATION STRUCTURAL ANALYSIS

The number of hierarchies (levels between the CEO and operating employees) is _____ . The filters for moving from level to level in my organization are the following skills and characteristics:

_____

_____

_____

_____

_____

My organization has _____ functional areas (such as Production, Accounting, Administration, Personnel, Marketing, or Research). These different divisions are:

_____   _____   _____

_____   _____   _____

_____   _____   _____

(If there are subunits within a functional department, be sure to consider those.)

In order to move across functional boundaries, one must _____

_____

_____ .

In my organization (division or group), getting close to the core of decision making (inclusionary growth) requires the following kinds of characteristics and attributes:

_____

_____

_____

_____

_____

_____

_____

Completing Your Tactical Career Plans

Tactical plans: five important steps

Tactical career planning requires just this kind of critical assessment of yourself, the organization in which you are currently working, and your potentials in other organizational settings. In order to complete your tactical career plans, be certain that you are taking each of the five steps detailed below.

Who you are

1. *Know who you are.* What are your values? What are your goals, skills, and opportunities? What is your career style? What is your personal situation in terms of health, responsibilities, references, and lifestyle? Good self-knowledge is the basis of adequate career-development planning. Your career planning is more effective when you think more about yourself—who you are and where you are right now—before considering any shifts to implement plans.

Your opportunities

2. *Investigate opportunities.* Knowing who and where you are now forms the basis for your looking into the kinds of jobs and career opportunities that fit someone like you. To learn about these opportunities, take advantage of all the resources that are available to you: your own company's personnel department or human resources staff; peers in other departments of the company (ask them what

they do all day long, how well they like it, what they don't like); people you meet in social situations, like church groups, PTA, sports and hobby groups (get them talking about their jobs; they may never stop, and you'll learn a lot about the kinds of work opportunities that surround you).

In addition to talking, you can use a library's reference facilities that can provide you with a wealth of information; their reference shelves contain professional journals, business magazines, and the D.O.T. (the two-volume *Dictionary of Occupational Titles* we introduced in Chapter 20). The D.O.T. contains a list of approximately 35,000 jobs that are available in our American economy and further provides information about the levels of different skills, aptitudes, worker traits, and conditions related to those jobs. Other sources of information are government agencies, private agencies, private career and occupational counseling services, public lectures, and local "job fairs," all of which can provide you with a veritable gold mine of career insights. Look for them.

3. *Establish career goals and objectives.* Having analyzed yourself and investigated the kinds of opportunities that fit the person you are, practice all of the goal setting and alternatives building you have gained from this book. Make your goals realistic, obtainable, and manageable. Determine where you wish to be in your career one year from now, three years from now, five years from now. Decide to be there. Make reality checks along the way. Use the career compass to develop plans that are YOU and fit YOU.   *Your goals*

4. *Identify skill-development needs and fill them.* With your goals firmly in mind, ask yourself what skill supports you'll need to gain in order to meet these goals. Use reality checking to maintain accuracy and think of development needs on a three-part basis: *Your development needs*

   a. My goals require: (then list the skills called for to reach the career goals you have established)

   b. I possess: (then list the skills and degree of skill you already have)

   c. I need: (then list the skills and proficiency levels you'll have to gain)

   With your three-part listing completed, you can map out your career staircase design—the path-steps—with an accurate and realistic picture of the skills and attributes your goal plans call for.

5. *Promote yourself.* All of the preceding steps will be meaningless if you fail to actively market your skills, abilities, and growth aspirations. Nothing is more disheartening than going through all the steps and then silently waiting for rewards or opportunities that never come. If you want to move ahead, *you* must help those people   *Your image: be visible and valuable*

who can help you become aware of your growth aspirations. Tell them how you are preparing yourself for additional responsibilities and job potentials. Ask to be trained on the job. Seek out challenging projects and compliment yourself (and others) when you successfully complete those projects. Document your achievements and ask for feedback on your performance. Do what is realistic and appropriate to remain visible and valuable to your organization and its growth and success.

CAREER GROWTH: YOUR RESPONSIBILITY

Remember, it begins with you—and your value system, your needs and wants, your abilities, and the realities of your life. Make your own decisions about your career development. Keep in mind that career development can mean you stay at the same job, or it can mean you shift your job activities or responsibility to fit your career, or that you change jobs or seek promotions. You can drift, or you can take charge of your own work life by planning.

Sometimes one step of your career path, like an educational course, can become very difficult to find and fulfill. Often it means rearranging other life habits. Don't be afraid to try. But keep your balance and all your life priorities in perspective. You may need to slow down or accelerate your own plans as events and people around you change your life situation. Keep your goal in mind, review your alternatives, and use your career compass to keep steadily aimed forward. The goal is your focus; the means to achieve this goal are the alternatives that you periodically review.

Career satisfaction is a goal you can meet. Plan for your career growth on a forward thinking basis—a proactive, not reactive, basis. Build for it by moving from one success to another in small, easy steps that encourage you to keep going. Challenge yourself and GROW!

GOOD LUCK AND GOOD SUCCESS IN YOUR CAREER!

ACTION CHECKLIST FOR CHAPTER 21

Checklist	*My Ideas and Action Steps*	*Date*
√ Implementing your career possibilities requires a "tactical plan" reflecting an awareness of how things work—like organizational politics *and* job activities and relationships.		

√ Organizations have boundaries, filtering systems, and formal and informal networks that affect your career plans.

√ Filtering systems include formal/informal policies, "old buddy" networks, and the like.

√ Affirmative action practices are facilitative, but significant personal effort is still required.

√ All functional areas (and heads) are not equally receptive to transfers — it pays to know how the system works and to map out practical tactical plans.

√ Tactical career plans mean knowing who you are, investigating opportunities, establishing goals/objectives, identifying development need, and promoting *yourself* — career growth is self-directed.

PROFILES FOR PART FOUR

Sheila Wyzinski, Liz Hoyt, and Wendy Tanaka

Sheila Wyzinski—The Story

Sheila Wyzinski, second vice-president of the operations department, had been with Marina Bank for 15 years. Sheila had interviewed with Marina Bank as a liberal arts major finishing up her last year of school. She had been invited to visit with bank officials at the headquarters in a large midwestern city and had even been taken around to a few of the bank's 20 branches.

The job didn't pay well to start, but Sheila was invited to become part of a management training program that extended over a five-year time frame and involved starting with one of the small branches, moving to various jobs in larger branches, and then receiving a "permanent" department assignment at the end of the five-year period. It was the bank's policy that the supervisory staff be thoroughly prepared and technically competent when a regular department assignment was made. In addition, the bank's management did not wish to make any commitments until the individual had more or less "proven" herself.

After Sheila had been employed for some years, she learned more about the bank's promotion policies, especially as they pertained to officerships. The bank's tradition was not to make any major investment in individual development beyond the initial training period until it seemed clear that the individual had made a career choice. Thus, most first rungs on the office ladder (second vice-president) were not offered until a person was with the bank at least 10 years. After a number of years of experience, she decided to work for a vice-president's position and maybe even seek the top job somewhere.

Sheila worked hard and for long hours; gradually, her efforts were recognized. Several years after completing her training, she became a department supervisor in one of the large branches. Shortly after her tenth anniversary with the bank, she was made a second vice-president and placed in charge of a whole branch operation. After almost 13 years, she was transferred to the headquarters operation as a second vice-president in its largest department, bank operations.

276

After 15 years at Marina Bank, Sheila started to feel a bit uneasy about her career. It had been her idea that "If I work hard, I'll be rewarded," and to an important degree things had worked that way. On the other hand, she realized that there were just so many *first* vice-presidencies at the bank; the competition was tough, and many of the incumbents were comparatively young people. Also, the bank was deeply involved in affirmative action programming, which meant more competition looming up for the limited number of senior officer jobs from capable minority and other female members of the bank's staff. If she had ever thought her sex would be an asset, she now had second thoughts about that "advantage."

Recently, Sheila worked through a career-planning book that offered good career advice, a structure for self-planning, and some exercises to assist in the planning process. One item that Sheila spent much time with was "What are my alternatives? Stick with the bank job? Try a different bank? Consider a different field in the banking-finance industry?"

Questions for You

1. What features of the bank's promotion process made it increasingly difficult for Sheila to seek alternate careers?

2. All of Sheila's experience has been in the banking industry. What set of strengths has this provided to her? What limitations?

3. What additional considerations in Sheila's bank employment may provide other possibilities in identifying career alternatives?

4. What considerations will affect Sheila's transference of knowledge to other financial fields? Other occupational fields?

Our Comments

1. The bank pursued a promotion policy that led to a relatively good position at the end of the initial training period. Further major promotions required that the individual make a substantial commitment of personal time and energy to rise to the next major stages. Thus, having achieved a higher-level position, plus pay and prestige, a decision to leave was a difficult one for Sheila and for most officers who had learned a great deal about the organization and often helped to build it and develop it.

2. *Strengths:* Sheila had experience in various sizes of banking units, contacts with many different customers throughout the

state, experience in a variety of banking operations, an important position in the bank requiring technical and managerial skills, and an understanding of many other business fields. *Weaknesses:* Quite understandably, Sheila realized that her experience may be quite specific to Marina Bank. In addition, there are the possible peculiarities of banking in one state and a limited access to other types of financial institutions. Her experience is limited to one organization.

3. Sheila can expand her ideas and possibilities for career alternatives through contacts at other banks, businesses, and financial institutions. She'll need to consider whether her general management skills will fit into a variety of other institutions and facilities and how well she has and can maintain flexibility—through training programs and other personal development experiences (not expressly noted in the case) and the community positions she's held over the years.

4. Sheila also needs to consider the transfer of her knowledge to other fields. She'll think about her own sense of adaptability, her willingness to learn, and her distance from the very specific experiences that fit the needs of other banks while keeping in mind the similarities of work skills and knowledge, irrespective of job title. Working in other financial fields would probably not pose great problems so long as these were not highly technical or specific; but a transfer to seemingly unrelated occupations will probably pose a great challenge, no small part of which will be the biases of people that a bank officer just isn't qualified for a job in a different field.

Postscript on Sheila

Sheila stayed with the bank job. Her many years of experience there weighed heavily in this decision. Additionally, the bank assumed an aggressive equal employment program that indicated good future possibilities for her in a field once dominated by males.

Liz Hoyt—The Story

Liz Hoyt was a 34-year-old high school English teacher in a university town in the West. She was a divorcee and the sole support of herself and her two children, 11 and 13. She had the good salary she valued and as a tenured teacher; she had job security, too. And she liked her work—enough so that she'd taken on the high school newspaper as an extra assignment. She liked her students, her fellow faculty members, and the work hours that allowed her to be with her children after school and on holidays, even if she had to stay up correcting papers at night. In short, Liz was a satisfied career woman.

When the late '70s tax revolt in her state hit her school district, Liz was the last to take it seriously—even when she heard that tenure was not to be honored and that teachers with 10 years or less experience would be fired. She had nine years. When her department head and good friend, Barney, called her in and said grimly, "You'd better start writing your résumé. You're on the list," she didn't believe him. "Oh, come on, Barney," she laughed. "They couldn't do without me around here. Who'd help the kids get the paper out!"

But Barney was serious. "*I'll* get the paper out, Liz! Can't you see this is real? It'll be the paper for me this year—and next, a load of counselees from fired counselors. And after that, coaching basketball, I guess. Damn it, Liz! Start looking for a job!"

Liz looked. But she was thinking all the time, "What can a high school English teacher do?" Barney said she should be an editor—or try technical writing. He suggested she check out the local prestigious "think tank," one or two of the electronic firms in the area, and the university itself. She made the rounds—with no luck. Her self-confidence sank. They didn't want her—even at the university. And that hurt, because it was *her* university. "No specific experience and not the right credentials, they all said. Oh yes, they were sure she'd been a good high school teacher, and they were sure seeing a lot of those these days; but an M.A. or Ph.D. degree was required for university teaching.

Liz began to panic. It was already June and beginning in September she wouldn't have a paycheck. What was she to do? She couldn't move out of state; she couldn't afford to. And if she found a nine-to-five job here, what would happen to the two kids? She'd always been home after school. Liz didn't even feel rescued when the teachers union negotiated a compromise with the district: The 100 fired teachers could work half time for the next year—and then resign. "Big deal," she said to Barney bitterly. "I can't live on half pay."

Barney did his Dutch uncle act then. "Look, Liz, what's happened to you is happening to a lot of bright people all over. Now get yourself together. Use the half time. Take courses, for heavens sakes! Try freelancing to make a little money. There are two or three good smaller publishing firms around here and a branch of at least one big one. Call some of your old college friends; you must know an editor or two. Say, come to think of it, I know someone who heads up the production end of one of those companies. Let's see—what was his name?"

Questions for You

1. Liz's story illustrates that society's "hard times" can affect even people in a good profession, with high skills and longevity. Liz

had to face the fact that she must leave her profession and find another occupation. Barney suggested editing or technical writing. Does this seem a good transfer of skills to you? What skills do you think of a high school English teacher as having? What other possibilities might Liz consider?

2. What models presented in Part Four on skills might have been useful in helping Liz to solve her problem?

3. Did Liz have realistic reasons to panic? What were some of the ingredients that made up her emotional response? How do you think she views change, for instance? What reasons does she have *not* to panic?

Our Comments

1. English teachers have skills that may be hard for them to identify, but in fact their career skills can transfer well. Preparing lesson plans, teaching classes, giving grades, and supervising the school paper all mean that Liz has skills in organizing work, presenting programs, appearing and speaking before groups, writing, and analytical reading. From our inventory of general skills, the likelihood is that Liz has some good skills in managing time, planning, evaluating, supervising, negotiating, communicating, and thinking creatively. That's 7 of the 13 we listed and it's a conservative estimate.

   Barney, who knows her work and her, is right that either editing or technical writing could be good fields for Liz. Other fields she'd do well in include personnel, especially training, and development. She'd make someone a good executive assistant, too.

2. The career-planning triangle in Chapter 18 would have helped Liz see how wide her skills base was when she got down to "Career Function Areas." She would have benefited from the general skills inventory in Chapter 19 and from working on transferring skills in Chapter 20. Just filling out the Transferability Model might have led her to consider editing and writing, without considering all her skills. And she'll need to consider all that information about herself in the context of the career compass. Her values and opportunities will help her decide on some short- and long-term goals and plan for the essentials of her career. Some of the confusion cleared up when she put skills in the context of the career compass. As it has turned out, Barney, a kind of mentor, and her old college friends, an informal network, have helped here, too.

3. It's never helpful to panic. But sometimes we do. And Liz did have some realistic reasons and values that would lead to her being at least discouraged, if not panicked.

The hard facts: Liz, at age 34, must transfer to a new occupation. She is a single woman, alone, with responsibilities for two children. She has some savings but no family to stake her in taking time out to retrain. And because other teachers are in the same fix, the job push in other fields is tough—very competitive. She can't afford, however, to move geographically—at least she thinks so, and she prefers to stay in the city of her choice.

The hopeful facts: Note first that Liz just did not see many of these facts and her strengths, or only began to see them after spending a lot of energy in panic and some depression. But in fact Liz has good health, a good education, is still fairly young, and has skills that can be identified, are valuable—and most important, definitely transferable. With her education and experience, it's likely that what seems to her like years of "retraining" will be just a matter of picking up some technical knowledge in evening classes and getting some small amount of actual experience under her belt. Barney's mention of freelancing was right up her alley.

As for her personal life, values, and circumstances, Liz had not really recognized that her children were no longer three and five, as they were when she was first divorced and greatly concerned about being with them. They have a strong relationship with her and want to help; and they can certainly be left alone after school. This is change that Liz has not internalized—though it was right before her eyes.

The outcome: Fortunately, Liz did not have to move. She realized her house could be second-mortgaged through the teachers credit union, and this way she could finance some classes and tide herself through a year on half pay. She began to freelance—and here her college friends and Barney helped her make the contacts that brought her first assignments. The pay was hourly and it was low, but she learned editing skills fast. In spring, with her freelancing and a course in technical writing and another in copyediting all behind her, she made up a second résumé, which she took directly to the "think tank" where she had been interviewed and rejected by personnel the year before, solely on the basis of credentials and with advice to "keep in touch." She did as she created her plan, knowing the plan was a solid one. This time, her confidence high, she had managed an appointment with the director of technical writing. He hired her as a reports editor but assured her (verbally and with written confirmation) that he'd have her writing the reports as soon as she had the "in-house" lingo down cold. Her starting salary almost equaled her teaching pay—and today, a year later, Liz makes more than she did teaching. She expects to be the associate director within two years. She likes the continuing direction of her career and is branching out into educational writing that will help train young researchers and scientists for growth into an editorial or writing position in many similar organizations in her city.

Liz Hoyt has made a successful transfer of her professional skills.

Wendy Tanaka—The Story

It was almost 10 years ago that Wendy Tanaka graduated with a bachelor of science degree in mechanical engineering. She had done well academically and placed in the upper 5 percent of the graduating class from a large, well-known university. Wendy was one of 50 female engineers graduating that year out of a total of 500 engineers. Despite her fine grades, she, like others, had found it difficult to find a job without any experience in a specialty. She took a number of job interviews while still in school, but none of these led to employment. Finally, after four months of job hunting, she found work with a small air-conditioning contractor as a design engineer. Her work consisted of cost estimating, developing system designs for new installations, assistance in preparing bids, and even some troubleshooting on installations that involved technical problems.

Wendy worked for the air-conditioning contractor for almost four years, and in that time received several wage increases. She was often complimented on her performance. The experience was great because it gave her an opportunity to get into most of the phases of the business and try out her schooling at a practical level. She liked the informality of the small company and, after a while, came to be well accepted by the other engineers and many of the installation crews. Some of the customers were not as accepting as most of her associates; but she had started to develop a tough skin and a warm competent style that charmed even the incredulous males who, at first, thought a woman "couldn't know *anything* about engineering problems."

Wendy decided to leave the company, primarily because she felt that (1) she wasn't learning that much new and her experience had started to "peak out"; (2) she wasn't going to be promoted, even though she had worked hard and had received positive signals of accomplishment from the company, such as compliments and raises; and (3) she suspected that she wasn't receiving as much money as the other engineers, who were all men. Company people were secretive about pay. Once, when she had raised the subject, she had been told that "everybody's" pay was an individual matter and that the value of each person's contribution was the key consideration; this involved past experience, performance, and potential for the future. She was also told her pay was "in line" with others with her performance record, and she didn't believe it. She quit.

Wendy's next job was as assistant to the chief design engineer of Frostline Furniture Manufacturing Company, which provided a large line of modern office furniture, clothes lockers, and various metal and plastic products to the office furnishings field. Wendy found this job search much easier than the first, and she was able to attain the job before leaving her first employer. As assistant, she found that once more she was "learning on the job." In fact, there were times when she wondered (to herself) if she had really taken on too much. She was unfamiliar with manufacturing and had a great deal of new terminology, techniques, and "Frostline's way of doing things" to get used to.

At Frostline, Wendy worked closely with various department heads. One in particular turned out to be a "super guy" as an informal mentor, and her career blossomed. So did her personal life. Her network of friends developed with lots of dating possibilities. A romance developed, and within a year Wendy was married. A year later she took a maternity leave to await the birth of her first child, with advice from Mr. Chaffee to "hurry back."

Wendy had intended to return to work as soon as the new routine of motherhood had been settled, but that took almost two years—much longer than she had anticipated. After the first year's absence, she found that she was getting anxious about her work because she realized that things were changing, not only at Frostline but in the entire engineering field as well.

Through friends at work, she was able to stay up on the policies and major company changes in lines and procedures. On the other hand, changes in the engineering field and mechanical and electronic advances in new product design were technical matters she knew she had to learn. While still on leave to take care of her young child, Wendy found it possible to attend a two-course program on new design advances offered by a local university.

When Wendy was ready to return to work, she found Mr. Chaffee had been able to keep her position still open to her, as he'd hoped to do when she asked for more leave. "No promises," he said, "a year is a long time and one more year is almost impossible; but I'll try. You try, too, to figure out what you want and how you can work out your career and family life." She had worked it out, firmed up her skills and commitment, and the chief design engineer was glad to have her back. Still, returning to her work routine, Wendy felt some anxieties about her ability to meet fully the responsibilities of her job.

Questions for You

1. In what general ways had conditions affected Wendy's career area and job over the years since her graduation?

2. At the time of Wendy's leaving her first employer, did her decision reflect career planning or was it largely an emotional decision?

3. Could she have brought about a situation more favorable to her career interests with her first employer? How?

4. What were the differences in career challenge faced by Wendy at the time of her employment with Frostline and her return to Frostline after her maternity leave?

5. What career challenges are presented to professionals such as Wendy by various kinds of environmental and technical changes?

Our Comments

1. Wendy's search for employment, both immediately and after graduation, as well as work with the Frostline Company, shows the changing receptivity of employers toward females and minorities, even in professional jobs, as well as the sensitivities they bring to a field "new" for them. This professional field was largely a male-dominated occupation; and although it appears that important changes are taking place, the understandings and activities that smooth the path of these changes will be highly uneven among employers and clients and even more so among employees who hold onto biases long after the times have changed.

2. It appears that a variety of considerations led to Wendy's departure from her first employer. Both career "logic" and emotionalism governed her reaction. It seems clear that she knew at this point what she didn't like or want, but it was *not* clear that she had a positive idea of her career objectives or had even thoroughly investigated areas of concern to her, especially her advancement and salary.

3. This profile also poses some of the problems faced by one returning to work after a leave of absence of some duration. Wendy's situation was eased because her job was still available with her employer, but she still faced the fact that relentless change made her anxious about job relevance. In Wendy's situation, it appears that reestablishing her confidence in the job relatedness of her skills would be of immediate importance and was a realistic concern; her course work helped considerably.

4. Everybody is challenged by changes in her/his jobs, companies, or environment. This challenge is increased to the extent that a

person depends on technical or management skills which are subject to varying degrees of change. The more refined the change or the longer a person is out of the work force, the greater the problems posed for professionals and managers in staying relevant in their fields.

ADDITIONAL RESOURCES

Part Four: Moving On—with Your Skills

BARTLETT, LAILE E. *New Work/New Life.* New York: Harper & Row, 1926.

BOLLES, RICHARD N. *The Three Boxes of Life, and How to Get Out of Them.* Berkeley, Calif.: Ten Speed Press, 1978.

FINE, SIDNEY A. *Guidelines for the Design of New Careers.* Kalamazoo, Mich.: W. E. Upjohn Institute for Employment Research, 1967.

——— . *Nature of Skill: Implications for Education and Training.* Kalamazoo, Mich.: W. E. Upjohn Institute for Employment Research, 1970.

Personal Strengths Assessment Service. *The Strength Deployment Inventory.* 571 Muskingum Ave., Pacific Palisades, Calif. 90272.

U.S. Department of Labor, Wage, and Labor Standards Administration, Women's Bureau. *Jobfinding Techniques for Mature Women.* Washington, D.C.: U.S. Government Printing Office, 1970. A listing of techniques and women's associations which can help provide assistance in locating jobs.

WELCH, MARY SCOTT. *Networking: The Great New Way for Women to Get Ahead.* New York: Harcourt Brace Jovanovich, 1980.

List of Headings

Part Three. Moving On—with Your Style   133

FEEDBACK

MAIL TO:

Elmer Burack, Maryann Albrecht, and Helene Seitler
P.O. Box 4348
Chicago, Illinois 60680

The parts of *Growing* I found most helpful were:

☐ End-of-chapter checklists   ☐ Career compass

☐ Profiles   ☐ Inventories

☐ Other: _____

_____

_____

_____

In future editions I would like to see you expand or add the following features:

_____

_____

_____

_____

_____

_____

_____

_____

(Optional) Name _____

Address _____

City _____ State _____ Zip _____

DISCHARGED

DISCHARGED

MAR 21 1989

DISCHARGED

DISCHARGED

DISCHARGED

JUL 23 1985

MAY 11 1985

DISCHARGED

AUG 15 1985

DISCHARGED

JUL 26 1985

DISCHARGED

OCT 22 1985

DISCHARGED

MAY 2 1985

MAR 30 1990

DISCHARGED

DISCHARGED

DISCHARGED

DISCHARGED

DISCHARGED

MAR 30 1989

DISCHARGED

DISCHARGED

DISCHARGED

DISCHARGED

MAY 10 1986

DISCHARGED

FEB 18 1987

SEP 19 1989

NOV 25 1986

DISCHARGED

DEC 16 1987

DISCHARGED

DISCHARGED

MAR 18 1996

DISCHARGED

DISCHARGED

DISCHARGED

NOV 4 1993